Imagining Gay Paradise
Bali, Bangkok, and Cyber-Singapore

For my parents, my son, my grandsons, my amicus usque ad aras, my friends,
All those people, spaces and places that make my own paradoxical home

Imagining Gay Paradise
Bali, Bangkok, and Cyber-Singapore

Gary L. Atkins

香港大學出版社
HONG KONG UNIVERSITY PRESS

SILKWORM BOOKS

Hong Kong University Press
14/F Hing Wai Centre
7 Tin Wan Praya Road
Aberdeen
Hong Kong

www.hkupress.org

© Hong Kong University Press 2012

ISBN 978-988-8083-24-4 (*Paperback*)

British Library Cataloguing-in-Publication Data
A catalogue copy for this book is available from the British Library

Silkworm Books

ISBN 978-616-215-036-4 (*Paperback*)

The Southeast Asia edition published in 2012 by
Silkworm Books
6 Sukkasem Road, T. Suthep, Chiang Mai 50200, Thailand

www.silkwormbooks.com

info@silkwormbooks.com

10   9   8   7   6   5   4   3   2   1

Printed and bound by Liang Yu Printing Factory Ltd., Hong Kong, China

Contents

Prelude

This is a story about hunting for home and founding paradise instead.

In July 1939, halfway through his jail time in the Dutch East Indies on charges against him inspired by Nazi sympathizers, the gay German painter Walter Spies sat in his cell writing his most remarkable letter.

He addressed it to his friend, Jane Belo, an anthropologist who had worked with Walter in that part of the Indies he had creatively turned into his own homeland – the island and, more importantly, the aesthetic paradise, of Bali.

Walter wrote in careful strokes. He made sure the salutation was twice as big as the rest of the text and followed it with an exclamation point, as if the text itself could be a shout across a room, the kind you give when you have not seen an old friend for a long time.

Sometimes with Jane it was "My dearest of all!" or "Dear Pachong!" – his nickname for her – or, one time, "Dear Tutti-frutti or any other ice cream!" Walter seemed to find magic in almost everything – even severe topics.

> Dear Jane!
>
> It is a rather chilly evening, it's windy and rainy and so I come to you to warm myself. Something dreadful happened darling. I began to paint again! I don't really know why! I was so nicely translating Balinese stories and suddenly I thought: what about that special light distribution that was haunting me one day long ago, taking form in a rather boring landscape (with lots of hills and trees, which I am so sick of) and then later it was transformed into a possibility of a kris dance and barong.[1]

Light drove Walter. Light could change from one object into another, a hill into tree. Light could roll into the sounds of dance or form the rhythmic undulating dagger that the Balinese called a *kris*. Light could transform into the fantastic lion-like barong that led forces of good against evil in constant tension.

Walter wrote past the first page to Jane, then halfway down a second. He apologized for a photograph he was enclosing of his latest painting. He had finished it inside the jail and had titled it *Scherzo für Blechinstrumente,* which in English meant *Scherzo for Brass.*[2] Unlike most paintings meant to be seen all at once, Walter wanted this one also to be heard like a concert – moment after moment, the visual images on the painted canvas passing through time like miniature chords.

A painting that was meant to be like a rhythm in a symphony. Walter knew that could not make much sense to most people. Painting claimed space. Music defined time. It was like holding opposite ways of thinking and of communicating in hand at the same time: a painting that was simultaneously music, music that was simultaneously a painting.

He told Jane he was sorry because the flattened two dimensions of the photograph did not fairly represent all the "nuances of accelerandos" that he assured her did exist within the layers of paint on the more textured canvas itself.

He had finished a page-and-a-half. That was good enough for any lazy Dutch censors who might open the letter and read the first few words.

Walter had long been careful to code his letters in metaphors. Sixteen years earlier when he had left Germany, he had warned his mother he would have to do so.[3] He worried the letters would be opened as they moved from one colonial empire to another, in the present case traveling from Surabaya to the Dutch colonial capital in Batavia and then onward to Holland and across the border into Germany. The Spies family had already had its share of bad luck with imperial boundaries. During the Great War, the Russians had arrested Walter's father despite his status as a German consul. Walter himself, although born in Moscow, had been considered a potential hostile and, at age twenty, had been exiled to the Ural Mountains to live among Tatar nomads.

Empires tended to sweep individuals into a monumental identity to be feared even when the miniature details of their lives carried other truths. Walter, a German now locked in a Dutch jail, was not so much a man without a homeland as a man of many spaces and times solidified – by others – into their own constant tension. Unfortunately, at that moment in 1939 all the colonial empires seemed to mistrust one another, most especially the Dutch and the Germans.

And that was the reason Walter was sitting in a jail, writing the letter.

After that first page-and-a-half, Walter abruptly changed topics and started underlining phrases for emphasis. He had arrived at the real subject of the letter: a coded commentary on the odd people who had put him where he was and on the story of the world they wanted to impose:

> Dear, you know, I am always so astonished at how different people are! A man who is here and who is *not at all* conventional in all his ideas and actions – has suddenly a complex of neatness and orderliness and a rather agonizing cleanliness. His room looks *always* as an "operation room" or a modern kitchen, all white and shiny, and one imagines white tiles, aprons and chrome-nickel

polished instruments everywhere! . . . All his pencils, pens or
whatever are lying in rows like soldiers. Cups and pots with an
even distance between each other, and arranged by their height.
In the whole room there is not a single thing which is not forced
to behave . . . I can't imagine how one can have so little respect
for nature! He must be absolutely blind and deaf to any harmony
of the universe![4]

For Walter, pleasure lay in a life surprising and infinitely divided into miniature
objects and, of course, both uncertain and magical:

For me it is one of the most exciting and fascinating experiences
to watch all the things in the world of my little home here move
and live their own life in accordance with each other. How books
and cigarettes, or a piece of bread pile on each other and then
suddenly fall into a lovely pose on the ground, finding there some
torn envelope from Berlin; what a joy that must be for them!
From there they can see quite different things . . . Sometimes a
bottle of tomato catsup after having performed all kind of stunts
up and down the table finishes this table life and with a large leap
flies into the paper basket, where it finds herself bedded softly
between a torn manuscript or some sketches to a painting.

Don't you think that the *letters* on the bottles are happy to
find their brothers and sisters there?[5]

It was a rather queered way of looking at things, emphasizing not the vast
difference that might seem to exist between certain large categories − mundane
catsup bottle and discarded drafts of art − but the sibling relationship between the
small letters on the bottle and the tiny marks on the manuscripts and sketches.

Walter then turned to the role of those − like himself − who were considered
either disposable or dangerous:

One of the most lovely lives has the role of toilet paper. It stands
up and lies down and unrolls, and pieces of it fly off and crumble,
and they clean cups and spoons and rub themselves on the table,
get all wet and dirty and jump one by one into the waste basket . . .

Sometimes is the way a box of matches is moving on, during
a few days or hour, even a most interesting one. From the table
to the bed, then into a pocket, out of the room, into the room
again . . . sending off some of its children, igniting them, seeing
them lighting a cigarette higher up, and then being thrown away
without [a] head! O, o, o!

I always seemed to have had a special attraction for them.
Sometimes, coming home, I find a whole gathering of them in my
pockets! What is it, I wonder, what they like in me?[6]

Walter conceded that often the relentless effort to secure order triumphed: "There are days where something has to be done to the things! Everything is replaced somewhere, where one thinks they have to be!" But the "objects" would always challenge order and seek their own fluid companionship:

> Already a few hours later, every object can be seen moving again! They don't like to be commanded like that I am sure! They don't feel happy where one puts them – they want companionship with other objects and they know better than we do in what distance and what relation, what equilibry they have to be with the other things and with the world they are in and live for.[7]

He reflected again upon the other male who supposedly occupied the same "jail" – the same world – with him:

> The wretched orderly neat man, of whom I spoke, is afraid to come into my room! He says that he would die if he had to live in such a mess. Isn't that funny? . . . I am sure he must be a tyrannei kind of person who has to order round, and everyone has to follow all his wishes.[8]

Walter finished the main section of his letter:

> "0, o, o! What funny people there are in the world."

He signed with another shout: "Many, many kisses."[9]

The pages that follow recount the saga of a king, an artist, a mastermind, and an entrepreneur. All lived during the past century in those islands and peninsulas we call Southeast Asia, and all created small geographies – their own islands – where orderly, neat stabilizations that are supposed to tell us about the male body, male desires, and male gendering were instead disturbed and set free into miniature "mismatches," rather like Walter's catsup bottles and discarded drafts.

Mostly the story centers on their search for a homeland to call their own, but it also considers the contest between two metaphoric constructions of body, desire, and gender in the times in which these men created. One such construction, which I refer to as the "triple supremacy," came to be considered a marker of the civilization that colonial empires insisted upon in Southeast Asia. The other, which I call the "triple taboo," formed its flip side of evil.

What unites the four men is that each sought a home that could not be contained within the triple supremacy, and so each had to create something new, something that those around them would consider quite queered – a different definition of manhood.

The story unfolds over an entire century for it can take a long time for new homelands to be imagined.

Part One

At the End of Empires

1

The Triple Supremacy

The death had come quite unexpectedly.

Stomach trouble had begun a week earlier. Then the coma.

But forty-eight hours before the end, the First Queen — there were many queens — had been reporting that the king was fine, that "His Majesty has improved in all respects." The king was not especially old, only fifty-seven. He was the only king most of his subjects had known, having ascended the throne four decades earlier when he was still a teenager.[1]

It was October 23, 1910. The son who was about to become king was still asleep in his own palace about two miles away. As was tradition, once royal sons came of sexual age — about eleven or twelve — they left their father's palace so as to be away from the presumed temptation of the king's expansive Inner City of women. It was this protected Inner City that had provided one of the most important means of male royal control of the Siamese empire, and so the women's sexuality needed close regulation. Even non-royal minor wives swore an oath to report not only any sexual liaisons they or others had with men but any they had with each other too.[2] So far, with the help of the women of the Inner City, the first five kings of the Chakri Dynasty had fathered 324 children by 176 wives. That was an average of sixty-five children and thirty-five childbearing wives per king, sufficient to solidify the bonds among powerful families as well as supply enough royal males to run the imperial bureaucracy.[3]

Reproductive sex, not romance and certainly not monogamy, was key to any Siamese king's power, and young princes were expected to immediately acquire their own women.

Chulalongkorn, the king who lay dying, had come to be known as one of Siam's greatest rulers: They called him *Phra Phuttha Chao Luang*, which means something like "The Royal Buddha," an important indication not only of his secular but his spiritual status, something European kings had long foregone and, at any century, had always had to share with the Roman pope. Over the course of Chulalongkorn's reign, from age fifteen to age fifty-seven, more than 150 women had been given to him as minor wives, double the average and triple the number that had been acquired by his own father.[4] As a vigorous teen, he had fathered children with two concubines even before he had reached the age of fifteen.[5] Inside the royal palace, the Inner City was populated and fully administered by women – and protected by three walls. At its height under Chulalongkorn, it held about 3,000 women, counting all the queens, princesses, their servants, and slaves. Of those, thirty-five had borne Chulalongkorn seventy-seven children, which included thirty-three sons.[6]

In 1881, when the king was twenty-eight years old, child number thirty-nine – son number twelve – had been born. He had been named Vajiravudh.

He was still in his bed at his own Saranrom Palace when the notification came that Sunday morning. It's not certain what he had been doing the Saturday night before, but if it was a typical Saturday night, he would have been awake as late as 3:00 a.m. or 4:00 a.m. or even 5:00 a.m., engaging in nighttime games and storytelling with the courtiers who surrounded him – all males, all young, most of them commoners rather than the usual royal cousins and brothers.

Although Vajiravudh was already twenty-nine years old – a year older than Chulalongkorn was when Vajiravudh was born – the crown prince had proven quite unlike his father when it came to sex. He had not yet taken any concubines or wives and had had no children whatsoever. He had not even tried, at least as far as was known publicly. Instead, Saranrom with its splendid Chinese-style pagodas and Victorian buildings, its forests and meticulous gardens, had become a male island in the Chakri capital of Bangkok.[7]

To the Siamese, Vajiravudh was a puzzle of manhood, almost like someone come from another land to set up a different home in the center of a traditionally ordered village. Maybe that was not surprising, since he had been sent at age twelve not just across the city of Bangkok for his formative adolescence but all the way to London. At the time, no one had any idea he would become king. A half-brother had been designated for that role and was being kept safe for his own education in Bangkok.[8] Like the dozens of other sons, Vajiravudh initially had more freedom to discover what else he might be interested in doing rather than ruling.

That, as it turned out in London, had been theater. He loved the London plays. Siam itself had traditional *khon*, which were stylized dance and music performances with narratives told by a chorus. But London had spoken drama and comedies organized around strong characters played by individual actors and actresses. Vajiravudh enjoyed the Western approach so much that he would eventually translate some of Shakespeare into Siamese, including one romantic tragedy, *Romeo and Juliet,* that argued against family interference in personal relationships, and one romantic comedy, *As You Like It,* in which Shakespeare had planted the famous monologue, "All the world's a stage." Writing and theater became Vajiravudh's passions, and he lived in Ascot, known for its famous royal racecourse.

Circumstances had altered his fate. A few years after Vajiravudh had been sent to London, the half-brother who was supposed to become king had died, and

Chulalongkorn had then picked Vajiravudh as his heir. At age fourteen, Vajiravudh went to the Siamese legation in London for a ceremony and then acquired a three-man bodyguard. The new title of Crown Prince enabled him to meet Queen Victoria herself. In a laudatory article about him on April 25, 1895, *Vanity Fair* noted:

> He came to England a year-and-a-half back; and being then nearly thirteen and knowing more of Pali and Sanskrit than of English, he was not sent to school, but confided to the care of a private tutor, who was to coach him for the House at Oxford. But his new Dignity has altered the outlook, and Greek and Latin have been discarded for International Law and Political Economy, subjects whose knowledge is more needed in a coming King. He now talks English with much fluency and a foreign accent; he is fond of mathematics, history, and walking; and he believes in the English gentleman. He is not an athlete, but he takes life very seriously; and he was very kindly received by the Queen in private audience . . . The honours that have been thrust upon him have not at all spoiled him. He is a dignified, polite, very amiable boy of some promise. He is so nice a Prince that no one is jealous of him.[9]

Not all the comments would be so kind. Once Vajiravudh had enrolled in school, his British class chums sometimes subjected him to taunts, nicknaming him "Siam" and teasing him about his father's well-known lack of monogamy.

"Siam," a typical salutation would go, "how many brothers and sisters have you?"

The young Vajiravudh had taken the teases good-naturedly but also unapologetically.

"Can't say," he had responded. "Haven't opened my morning's mail yet!"[10]

Coincidentally, the day after the *Vanity Fair* story appeared, the British press focused on another type of sexual desire that the Victorians also frowned on: the April 26 start of the gross indecency trial for homosexuality against the noted writer Oscar Wilde. The trial would seal in the popular mind a sense that homosexuality could be explained by adopting what was known as "degeneracy theory" — a sort of reverse evolution that supposedly explained various sorts of sexual immorality and crimes, such as the notion that insanity could be caused by too much masturbation. A German psychiatrist, Richard Krafft-Ebing, had promoted the theory in *Psychopathia Sexualis* in the late 1880s, using European bourgeois ideals as the norm against which sexual behaviors could be put into various categories such as pedophilia, masochism, and sadism and then explained by hereditary and environmental degradations.[11] Krafft-Ebing would eventually change his mind about homosexuality being caused by degeneration, but at the time of the Wilde trial, his initial theory had been popularized in Europe and the United States by Max Nordau, who had published his summation, *Degeneration*, in

Germany in 1894. Nordau had then seen his book translated into English just in time for the trial. Nordau linked degenerate criminals and anarchists with artists and authors. He wrote in his preface, "Degenerates are not always criminals, prostitutes, anarchists and pronounced lunatics; they are often authors and artists . . . [who have] come into extraordinary prominence and are revered by numerous admirers as creators of a new art and heralds of the coming century." Nordau considered himself on a crusade against such degenerates. Editors quickly picked up the theme.[12]

It is not clear how much of the London press a teenage Siamese prince would have been reading, but certainly the headlines about Oscar Wilde had been everywhere.[13]

The drive from his own palace at Saranrom to his father's probably did not take long on a Sunday morning. Fortunately, because of Chulalongkorn's designation of him as crown prince fifteen years earlier, there would be none of the messiness that sometimes accompanied exchanges of power within an absolute monarchy – and there was no doubt that the empire had just acquired a new absolute monarch. Within the structure of Siam, Vajiravudh now held more power than Queen Victoria had within her empire. He had no Parliament to persuade. He had no Magna Carta of rights to observe, nor any philosophical traditions of free speech from the likes of John Milton or John Stuart Mill. He had no separation of state and religion to contend with; he was ruler of both military and monk. He had no sensationalistic press likely to challenge him – not unless he allowed one. As one observer at the time put it, "When the foreign missionary desires to convey to the Siamese mind the idea of God, he is compelled to use the words 'pra chow,' which are already used for 'King.' Omniscience, omnipotence, and absolute rightness are the inherent attributes of the King."[14]

According to a *New York Times* report, the ceremony of allegiance would be held quickly that same Sunday morning of October 23 in the temple attached to the royal palace. The oath included phrases intended to discourage any sort of dissent or disobedience. All the other princes would pray that "the powers of the deities to plague with poisonous boils and with all manner of horrible diseases" would descend upon "the dishonorable, the disobedient, and the treacherous."[15]

The prince who had not yet taken a woman had ascended.

The ideals of Saranrom would now be offered as a new center for his empire.

From a practical point, any king establishing a dynasty is often first a warrior who commands the strongest military, but once his family is in power and once successive generations achieve the throne, other justifications have to be performed. On October 23, 1910, Vajiravudh became the sixth king in the Chakri Dynasty, begun in the 1780s. By the early twentieth century, the demands on him from the dance of manhood ideals that had accumulated from traditions in Siam and from its contact with colonial powers had turned to nothing short of crushing.

First, there were local animist expectations, the oldest of the traditions in the lands that had been incorporated into Siam. The king, among other things, was supposed to be the symbol of reproductive fertility, attending plowing rites to bring the rain and ensure abundant rice. Taking wives and concubines was not just a matter of male lust or even just politics to align with powerful families. It was a magical signal of the king's own potency, so powerful it could fill the well-protected female Inner City of the royal palace and still extend to making the land itself fertile.[16]

Parallel to those animist ideas for almost two millennia was a Hindu ideal. As with the Khmers who had ruled Angkor Wat, the Siamese king was to personally embody a spark of divinity from Shiva and be a man capable of perceiving the rules that created harmony in the cosmos and on earth. His capital in Bangkok was more than just a political center; it was, as one political scientist wrote, "the magic center of the universe."[17] In the Siamese language, Bangkok actually had one of the longest city names on record, its various phrases translating as: "Grand Capital of the World Endowed with Nine Precious Gems," "Divine Shelter and Living Place of Reincarnated Spirits," "Highest Royal Dwelling," "Great Land Unconquerable," "A City Given by Indra," and so forth.[18]

Another step in defining ideals of Siamese manhood had come a comparatively recent seven centuries earlier when, in the twelfth century, the Sukothai state had aligned itself with Theravada Buddhism. The king had then come to represent the ideal male who best pursued the principles of Buddhist dharma: who shaved his head to become a monk in a tonsure ceremony, who gave alms, who accepted impermanence and selflessness, who practiced mercy and meditation, and who built and patronized temples, and encouraged schools of Buddhist thought. The emphasis was more on action and practice than on divine spark. The Buddhist king did not have divinity as a matter of Hindu male virtuous essence; rather, he earned and conveyed it through rituals of merit making that all men, in turn, were expected to follow or through which they could participate, indirectly, by supporting the king.

Eventually had come the European colonial powers with their expectations. Kings who were to survive also had to become performers in the European male arenas: mastering new steps of military command and control, new understandings from European science, and new uses of European technology, whether that meant building railroads or comprehending the exotic international economic systems demanded by imperialism.

Numerous Southeast Asian royals had failed at the military role in the face of superior European weaponry and had either been removed or left to command puppet auxiliaries. Some had tried to understand European science, promoting new health or agricultural practices in their lands. But how did one conduct a magical fertility rite one day and then be taken seriously by European empiricists the next? As a partial solution, some kings and sultans had turned to promoting European arts and letters.

Siam itself had never been directly colonized. Instead, the British in Burma and Malaya and the French in Indochina nibbled at Siam's land edges and joined the Americans and Germans in extracting trade and legal concessions as well as money. One of the most galling concessions had been agreements prohibiting Siam from applying its own laws to prosecute the increasing numbers of British, French, American, and German citizens working in Bangkok. The monarchy Vajiravudh now ruled had even had to agree that other Southeast Asians — workers or traders from the British colonies of Malaya and Singapore — had to be treated with the same special care. Whatever crimes the foreigners committed in Siam, they could only be handed to the Western consuls for whatever punishment was to be laid, if any.[19]

In 1893, when Vajiravudh was a child, a French gunboat had entered the Chao Phraya River and anchored astride the royal palace in Bangkok. The French had not fired, but the point was clear. They wanted concessions of land and money for their Indochinese empire. While Chulalongkorn had an army that could have fought in the lands that would become French Laos and Cambodia, he had no navy capable of stopping the destruction of his own palace by a single European gunboat.[20]

The British had one. So did the Americans. But to Chulalongkorn's disappointment, neither came to his aid. Siam lingered for decades in pincers. The Chao Phraya River, its northern tributaries leading toward China, was a rich prize, but no imperial power could afford to seize Siam as a colony and risk direct war with the other Western empires. The Chakri kings who preceded Vajiravudh had been left somewhat to themselves to learn from the more powerful colonial empires how to operate their own smaller empire, as well as how to script-switch among the various rhythms of ideal manhood.

The same year the French gunboat parked astride Bangkok, Chulalongkorn had called Vajiravudh aside. Until that point, the twelve-year-old had lived only in the palace and was privately tutored. Now, his father told him, he was to begin a mission. He would go to Britain with three tasks. He was to learn how Britain's monarchy controlled a global empire through its bureaucratic network of non-royal males rather than through intermarriages with powerful families. He was to study military science so that as Siam's army "modernized" the monarchy could continue to lead it. Finally, he was to transform his own male body into a symbol of Siam's "civilization," what was coming to be called in the Siamese language *siwilai*. It was a hybrid notion describing the way the elite could adopt certain behaviors and techniques of the powerful colonizers, not as victims but rather with twists heavily colored by local meanings and traditions. The concept embraced everything from mastering new European technologies and laws to dressing properly and encouraging white teeth instead of betel-nut stained ones.[21] Vajiravudh would learn to look like, talk like, and, to some degree, act like a British man. He was to familiarize himself with Western understandings of the male body and its desires and its gender performances and how those fitted to building so-called "civilized" nations.

But, at the same time, he would also learn how to hybridize and script-switch when necessary, which meant making sure that he continued enough local tradition to maintain royal legitimacy within his own empire. Thus, when he would leave London after a decade away from Siam, he would assert to those gathered to say goodbye that "I shall return to Siam more Siamese than when I left it."[22]

Vajiravudh would become an aspiring mass media writer who could wield the mightiest pen in the empire and create his own favored ideal of manhood. *Siwilai* gave him the fused hybrid character he would use for the story.

All he needed was a plotline.

The British governess who had taught Vajiravudh's father, Chulalongkorn, when he himself was a child had helped staple an image of Siam's males into the European mind in the nineteenth century. Anna Leonowens had arrived at the court of Vajiravudh's grandfather, King Mongkut, and had then written about her experiences in an 1870 book, *The English Governess at the Siamese Court*, later to be converted into the American Broadway musical *The King and I*. Although Mongkut was highly educated – a Buddhist monk for more than a quarter-century and skilled in Sanskrit, Latin, and English, as well as Western science – for her American and British audiences Anna had portrayed him as something of a baffled, if kindly, male despot, and, exaggeratedly, as a profligate polygamist. Mongkut had invited Anna to teach his many children, including Chulalongkorn, but in her writings published after she left Siam, she had referred to his prime minister as a half-naked barbarian, and she had then constructed an image of women suffering in the Inner City that was right out of *Uncle Tom's Cabin*.

Imperial representatives, such as Anna, insisted that the Siamese needed to correct three "problems" related to sex and gender in order to be considered "civilized."

First, the Westerners could not always tell who was a Siamese man and who was a Siamese woman – at least when it came to certain kinds of male or female behavior that the Westerners expected, the kinds of clothing that "civilized" male and female bodies were supposed to don, the kinds of names that males and females were supposed to have, and the types of beauty their bodies were expected to portray.

An American who visited Bangkok in 1832, for example, wrote that he had attended a royal dinner and:

> . . . as I cannot tell a Siamese man from a woman when numbers are seated together, so it is out of my power to say whether any females were present . . . The hair of the Siamese women is cut like that of the men; their countenances are, in fact, more masculine than those of the males.[23]

Sometimes it was the hairstyles that confused Westerners, and sometimes it was the clothing, since all Siamese tended to wear a loose-fitting unisex *jong-kraben* that to Western eyes looked like a skirt. When Anna Leonowens wrote her comments three decades after the American diplomat had described his confusion, she adopted a moral judgment about this androgynous clothing. Anna described "women disguised as men and men in the attire of women, hiding vice of every vileness and crime of every enormity." Anna had hidden her own background as a lower-class, mixed race child raised in the barracks of the British East India Company, instead presenting herself as a fully British-born, white, upper-class woman. She knew how to re-invent identities by changing costumes, changing gestures, and altering accents. She knew how to "perform British."[24]

Siamese clothing influenced Western accounts of Siamese beauty, which also did not conform to "civilized" standards. Many nineteenth-century Western observers described the Siamese as ugly or comical. Of the men, one observer wrote, "The flat nose, wide nostrils, large mouth, thick lips, and black bristly hair form an ensemble of which it is difficult to give an idea by means of the pen only. The natural plainness is even more marked in the women, among whom a pretty face is very rarely to be seen." Another referred to one of the queens as wearing puffy knee breeches, having "hair cut short like a boy's" and being "not handsome in face" in her "comical, yet piquant costume." Another pitied the children: "I was charmed with them from the first moment, but it grieves me to think that some day they will become as ugly as their fathers and mothers."[25]

The Siamese body, it seemed, was incapable of attaining the beauty to be found in a Greek statue of the sort then popular in Europe.

Siamese names also contributed to gender confusion. Although Europeans had a few proper names that could refer to either man or woman – "Leslie," for example – they had long ago broken the world into "Robert" and "Roberta," or "Louis" and "Louise." No one asked whether King George had a male or female body because European bodies had been already been gendered by their names, as well as their titles.

The Siamese had not followed that tradition. Proper names could refer to either sex, and for the Europeans the strange names indicated nothing. Mongkut – male or female? Chulalongkorn? Vajiravudh? Saowapha, Vajiravudh's mother?

In short, then, to be more "civilized" like Europeans, the Siamese needed to become more differentiated.

The second concern Westerners had about Siamese bodies and gender was that, when those bodies were not being clothed androgynously, they seemed practically naked most of the time. An early account from the seventeenth century noted that the Siamese "went about almost naked except for a cotton cloth length they wore from the waist to the calf."[26] In Anna's first view of the king's prime minister, she wrote that he had "his audacious chest and shoulders" covered only by "his own brown polished skin." She added that neither men nor women in Siam wore hats to protect their heads or shoes to protect their feet. Instead, they often bathed lightly clothed in a sarong or nude in rivers. At the other end of Southeast Asia, in Bali, the Dutch and Germans were reacting to similar nudity by romanticizing it in countless voyeuristic photographs, courtesy of the new communication technology of easily portable cameras. But in Siam, the more puritanical British and Americans saw only sin. One American wrote, "As a nation they do not know what shame is . . . their usual dress consists of a simple waist-cloth adjusted in a very loose and slovenly manner, while many children until they are ten or twelve years old wear no clothing whatever. When foreigners first arrive in Siam they are shocked almost beyond endurance at the nudity of the people." Going beyond even Anna Leonowens, the American added not only a moral judgment but also a moral command: "Not until Siam is clothed need she expect a place among respectable, civilized nations."[27]

As early as 1851, when Vajiravudh's grandfather, Mongkut, ascended the throne, he had become concerned about the impressions being left among Europeans, saying that the "upper torso looks unclean, especially if the person has a skin disease or if he is sweating." As part of *siwilai*, he mandated that those coming to a royal audience would henceforth have to wear some sort of upper garment, but he did not try to change other clothing in public.[28]

A third European concern related directly to the male body and its desires and behaviors. Often in colonial writings about Southeast Asia, Europeans and Americans portrayed the slender, less haired Asian male body as being feminine and less sexually potent than that of a Caucasian male. Whites were assumed to be more rugged, larger, more muscular, and more penetrative. As the French colonized Vietnam, for example, French essayists noted that the Southeast Asian male seemed frail and, as one wrote, "prepubescent with his naked mouth, hairless chest, smooth armpits, ambiguous voice, and female hairstyle." One French medical expert had even argued that beardlessness among Vietnamese men suggested they could not achieve satisfactory erections. "*Natura glabrum infecundum*," he solemnly pronounced: By nature, what is hairless is unfruitful.[29] As historian Ann Stoler would later write, this way of demasculinizing colonized men was a key element in asserting white supremacy.[30]

But colonial images treated the Siamese male quite differently. His "problem" was that he was *too* potent and *too* promiscuous — and nothing reflected the supposedly insatiable sex drive of the Siamese male more than the longstanding custom of polygyny in the Siamese empire.[31] Portraying male desire as hyper-driven was also to be a way of discrediting colonized men.

Throughout the nineteenth-century trade negotiations, the British emissary had constantly lectured Vajiravudh's grandfather, Mongkut, about male practices the British found to be "exotic, self-indulgent, and uncivilized."[32] An American missionary close to the king complained in a public newspaper that neither virtue nor prosperity could come to Thailand until non-monogamy was made into a crime.[33] Such Western thoughts quickly linked it with notions about the right to rule. Just as with Nordau's theory about homosexual degeneracy, so non-monogamy was thought to bring about moral degeneracy as well as physical exhaustion, undercutting any moral right to rule – and thus justifying European intervention. An American diplomat in Mongkut's time exaggeratedly reported to Washington that "the present King of Siam is a sensualist having no less than a thousand women in his harem."[34] Mongkut probably had only about fifty wives, and if there were a thousand in the palace's Inner City, most were servants and royal relatives learning court rituals, not wives betrothed to the king.[35]

The virulent propaganda had not stopped when Chulalongkorn assumed the throne in 1868. One British envoy, concerned about the French pressure on Siam, wrote that "the King, who is honest . . . is quite incapable mentally, exhausted by women, anxiety and opiates."[36]

The Anna-educated Chulalongkorn would gradually become known for his adoption of *siwilai* into Siam. He would displace the powerful families who had previously selected kings and name his own heir. In the provinces, more neutral administrative structures would begin to appear, resembling the male imperial bureaucracy of Britain. He replaced the lunar calendar resembling the Chinese and Vietnamese ones, adopting in its place the Gregorian solar calendar. He introduced banknotes and even opened the traditionally Buddhist kingdom to religious freedom, guaranteeing safety to Christians and Muslims, the latter of whom he was incorporating into his empire by posting warships off the coast of three Muslim provinces just north of Malaya. In 1899, he issued a decree that extended Mongkut's concern about clothing in royal audiences to the streets of the country, specifying the kind of dress that should be worn in public and beginning to adopt the *siwilai* idea that nakedness and lack of gender difference in fashion reflected not just practical choices but a poor moral upbringing. When he traveled in Europe – the first king of Siam to do so – he carefully dressed and posed for cameras in the costumes of his imperial hosts. He also accumulated treasures from Florence, from Tiffany in London, and from Fabergé in St. Petersburg.[37]

Yet, for all his adoption of certain expressions of *siwilai*, Chulalongkorn had held fast in one area: His Inner City of women actually expanded beyond that of his father's. He grew exasperated with the European demands to cement their views of marriage and women's roles into Siam. Although Vajiravudh's mother, Queen Saowapha, tried to establish girls' schools in Bangkok, the king himself was reluctant, one day clearly expressing his annoyance at the likes of his own tutor, Anna, who had been strongly critical of polygyny. "I cannot bring myself to think about my daughters' education," Chulalongkorn wrote in 1898, just a few years after sending Vajiravudh to London. "I have never endorsed it . . . because it reminds me of my own teacher who authored a book which many believe. So whenever the suggestion is made that a girls' school be founded, I am quite annoyed."[38]

Europeans responded by constructing dual images of Siam. The Siamese man was oversexed and out of control and needed to be rescued by the disciplined manhood of Europe. Siamese women were imprisoned and lacking sexual choice. A European drumbeat emerged: Until Siamese men "civilized" and eliminated their multiple sexual relationships, white men and white women would need to protect Siamese women from those men.[39]

In Vajiravudh's Siam, the ideal male, the king, lived in relationships with wives of varying ages and varying local races. But Western literature celebrated monogamy and spoke of romance of two types. Early tragic romantic lovers such as Romeo and Juliet, or Lancelot and Guinevere, or Abelard and Heloise, or Tristan and Isolde existed outside arranged marriages and coped with the subsequent obstacles only through secrecy and, eventually, death. But a second style of romantic love being popularized in the new mass media of the nineteenth century instead simply treated any obstacles – such as family objections – as hurdles that enhanced the romance, made it more exciting, and then were eventually overcome so that the couple could marry and "live happily ever after."[40] The English queen that Vajiravudh had met, Victoria, had served Britain not simply as a powerful ruler but also as a romantic, married, monogamous model with her husband, Prince Albert. Hers was an imperial plotline of supposedly "civilized" love that, as far as Europeans were concerned, had not been followed by Mongkut or Chulalongkorn.

The Western stories also used characters with strong gender distinctions between the male body and its costumes, behaviors, desires, and mannerisms and the female body and its. By the beginning of the twentieth century in Europe and the United States, this character construction was beginning to be called a "heterosexual."[41]

"Civilized" romance also assumed those involved had similar ages and were of similar races. Cross-age or cross-race relationships were not nearly as acceptable in these Western plots as in Siam's polygynous culture. Europeans had given cross-race relationships an ominous sounding label – "miscegenation" – and then had frowned upon them, considering them a form of Nordau-like degeneracy and sometimes even criminalizing them.[42]

This was the "civilized" plotline then: The mating of two similarly aged, similarly raced and distinctly gendered heterosexuals through an obstacle-strewn ritual called "romance" that then ended in either artful tragedy or a monogamous "happily ever after" marriage resembling Victoria and Albert's.

That was a narrative about manhood and family structure quite exotic to the royal narratives that Vajiravudh knew back in Bangkok and that defined Siamese manhood.

To be "civilized" was to embrace the new triple supremacy: romantic, monogamous heterosexuality. Other forms of intimate relationships and of family organization would have to be considered "degenerate" and "uncivilized."[43]

A year before he left for Europe in 1893, Vajiravudh had passed through his tonsure ceremony, donning heavily gilded robes and a towering, pagoda-like crown. The ritual lasted a week. His head had been shaved, the traditional first step in becoming a Buddhist monk earning merit. That reflected one pillar of Siamese manhood. Then, Chulalongkorn had built a forty-foot-high mountain. On top of it, in an elaborate Hindu-influenced ritual, the king himself had appeared as the god Siva and had deified his young son as the god Ganesa.[44]

In London, though, a painting showed the changed expectations of Vajiravudh as a young teenage male. He had a long thin body dressed in a British gray suit with a five-button vest, gold watch chain, and stiffened ascot collar. He wore toed and heeled black shoes that had been shined but that seemed disproportionately small for his height, foot size sometimes being used as a coded visual reference for male phallic power.[45]

Lines, thinness, and motionlessness defined Vajiravudh, in contrast to the dynamic, muscular, in-motion statues of Greece that were part of the European ideal of manhood.

When his father, Chulalongkorn, passed through England on his Grand Tour of Europe in 1897, Vajiravudh's body had filled out and he had a more rounded face. But even at age seventeen, he still looked very much the boy as he gathered with other princes for a photograph and stood behind his father's left shoulder. All had dressed in British suits. Vajiravudh smiled slightly, contrasting with the somber expressions on both the lips of the king and of the other princes.[46]

To him would fall the task of writing the story of the new Siamese man, the *siwilai* romantic, monogamous, heterosexual male. That morning of October 23, 1910, Vajiravudh's call to Chulalongkorn's bedside would be a drive into an anxious moment of personal and cultural paradox.[47]

Figure 1.1   Emblems of Siamese Manhood, 1897: King Chulalongkorn seated, Prince Vajiravudh over his left shoulder
Public domain, Wikicommons

2

The Problem with Home (1)

By summer 1923, the news in Germany had turned grim. Along the Ruhr River, French and Belgian troops occupied the factories. Industrial production had stalled, and that, combined with the flight of German gold, had pushed the price of a loaf of bread in Berlin to trillions of marks. Just four years earlier the Weimar Republic had been launched hopefully in the city of Johann Wolfgang von Goethe, that nineteenth-century polymath of poetry and philosophy, drama and literature. The city of Weimar had been chosen as a deliberate symbol for the new Republic, intended as a counterpoint to the German militarism that had provoked World War I. The Weimar, as one historian would write, was "an idea seeking to become reality," the notion that a Germany of poetry and art and philosophy could overcome the contest-based masculinity of empire.[1]

But the Weimar had faced a line of unending crises and so, in the port city of Hamburg, on Thursday, August 23, a young German male readied his good-bye to the Europe he had known since birth.

Walter Spies was only twenty-eight. He was young and had almost stereotypical Caucasian beauty: blonde hair, pensive blue eyes, a prominent nose that looked as if it had been cut from marble. What he lacked in muscularity he made up for in slender proportions. At first glance, he looked as if he could have been cast from the Aryan model of manhood that the National Socialist Party would be promoting once it controlled the German imagination. But Walter was homosexual, and he had different ideas from those of the Nazis.

For months, he had been exceedingly restless. He had written to a friend:

> It's only when you're outside Germany that you notice how horrible it is to live in Germany — what a terrible country it is and what appalling people are there, how dry and unfeeling they are, and how being among them one becomes like them. I can't stand it anymore![2]

It was as if he were in exile in his own supposed homeland:

> I will never find myself in alignment with European people and I
> don't want to. My whole thought and feeling has grown in such a
> different direction that it makes no sense to wear myself out here
> and let time evaporate doing nothing, or to contest about things
> that don't concern me. Here, in order to buy a feeling that this is
> my homeland, I would have to relinquish everything that makes
> up my entire Being, somehow sell myself. I can't do that.
>
> I prefer to leave all these people and try to find myself a new
> homeland.[3]

In Berlin, his sister, Daisy, had gone to the train station to see him off for what she would later call "a farewell to last forever."[4] Walter had not yet told his mother that he had no plans to return. His brother Leo would later recall that Walter seemed acutely detached whenever he said farewells. "In every goodbye that you give," Leo would write, "you avoid people around you and depart. Any emotional outburst would be a strong sentimentality."[5]

Walter had reason to maintain his guard. He had already learned that, if he was to be happy, he could allow no claims by others to dictate his life. Family, nation, church – none could hold sovereignty over his emotions. The well-ordered imperial societies in which he lived were collapsing, and even by his still young age, he had already suffered their whims, having been interned during World War I in a Russian camp simply because he had been born a German in Moscow.

Walter had a few days alone to wander the riverside docks at Hamburg. He had confided in his letter:

> I will try different ways of getting myself on board a steamer as
> a sailor or worker and wherever I feel like it, I'll disembark and
> remain – preferably Australia, maybe an island in the South Seas
> or East Asia, India or South Africa; if that doesn't work then even
> America.
>
> I'm not running away from work. I'm still young and know
> that I can do any kind of work, and that with zeal and joy![6]

Fortunately for Walter, a man by the name of Schlüter, the captain of a new ocean steamer operated by a British-Australian line, had been persuaded to take him on as a sailor. Walter planned to board the *Hamburg,* make a quick run across the Channel to England, sail down the French coast to Spain, pass through the Suez Canal, and then cross the Indian Ocean to the Dutch East Indies. The *Hamburg* was scheduled to stop in the Dutch colonial capital of Batavia on Java before continuing to Australia and then return to Europe. Although the captain did not know it, Walter had no intention of being aboard beyond Batavia. He was already carrying letters of introduction for Java.

Figure 2.1   Walter Spies.
Courtesy of Tropenmuseum of the Royal Tropical Institute, Wikicommons

He had carefully hidden that fact in the notes he wrote to his mother. He would be back in "three months or four" he cheerily said at the top of one. When she chided him for not saying good-bye in person, he wrote that "it is certainly better that didn't happen, since leaving would be much more terrible when we are crying over each other face-to-face, not wanting to let go, and all that."[7]

He cautioned his mother that he would be sending letters to her in broken German to lessen the chance of anyone understanding what he was telling her. It would become part of his style, communicating in an occasionally cryptic code or through metaphors and anecdotes that censors would overlook.

"I have to write that way, "he explained, "since the letters may be opened somewhere!"[8]

Walter also warned his mother to be careful of what she wrote on the outside of her envelopes. Most especially, she should not include any reference to his father's previous title, "German Consul to the Russian Tsar Nicholas II," lest it give him away to the crew. In the last letter he wrote before the *Hamburg* sailed, Walter scribbled: "Everything is settled, and I am as happy as a spider monkey!"[9]

A second letter mailed just a week later hinted at one reason for his joy. While waiting in Hamburg that August week, he had found a surprisingly pleasant and simple preoccupation, walking from place to place along the docks and sketching.

One of his favorite spots had become a café run by Asians. In a small indication of a desire of which he seemed to be becoming more aware, Walter confided to his mother, "I have already made some sketches of unbelievable Chinese."[10]

As the center of the imperial world he knew descended toward chaos, Walter prepared to sail to its colonial margin to imagine a new homeland.

Walter did not go alone on the *Hamburg*. A friend named Heinrich Hauser accompanied him, and as they approached Batavia in early October 1923, the two young men schemed about how to sneak Walter off the ship. They thought they might hire a small boat to transport him at night, dodging Dutch customs agents. When none of the local boatmen wanted to try, the two created another plan. Walter would pose as a sailor transferring ships. Hauser later described their ploy, using the typical colonial term for a low-paid Asian male: "I fetched a coolie and stuck Walter's trunk in a bag."[11] With his duffel, Walter headed to the customs agent, acting "very elegant," Hauser noted. Walter calmly declared that he was transferring to the freighter *Cassel* in Surabaya, about 450 miles away in eastern Java. In reality, Walter planned to go to Bandung, south of Batavia. There, he knew, the uncle of one of his Dutch friends would help.

The customs agent scribbled a number on Walter's duffel and then waved him on. But then trouble: A man who had overheard the conversation offered to buy Walter a train ticket directly to Surabaya. The last thing Walter needed was a witness to see him buying a ticket to Bandung. "I was about to die," he wrote to Hauser.[12]

Walter dallied, trying to figure an escape. Fortunately the man eventually lost interest and walked away. Bandung ticket quickly in hand, Walter boarded the train. Finally, he wrote, "The horn had sounded and the bell had rung, and I became ridiculously lighthearted":

> Mountains, mountains, mountains, right and left, and of such fantastic shapes, like in Chinese pictures, you know, with banana groves and forests of coconut palms, and it became more unbelievable, I soon forgot Mr. Schlüter – the *Hamburg's* captain – and was catching Atlas butterflies and silkworms in the gorges we were flying over.[13]

At the station, he met the uncle and his wife and, once again, felt safe. But at their house, the conversation turned dangerous. The uncle had been a ship's captain and once, he told Walter, he had taken German naval officers from England to Holland. One had become a close friend, a man by the name of Schlüter, who was now working for a shipping company in Hamburg. Did Walter happen to know him, the uncle asked?

"How's a person not supposed to go crazy?" Walter wrote to Hauser.

Walter spotted a piano in the house, and "that," he wrote, "was the salvation."

> I pounded the keys with all my heart . . . and after I had played everyone limp, they were melted . . . They determined that it was a shame for such an artist to travel as a sailor . . . I couldn't rightly confess that I had skipped out, but said instead that I was only taken on as a sailor by the shipping company as a favor, not signed on and not assigned to any definite ship, and that I could go back with any ship of the Australian Line when I wanted. Isn't that really believable?
> And almost the truth![14]

At age twenty-eight, Walter had stolen his freedom. He signed the letter to Hauser gleefully: "Dein Walter Spies, spielt er was, Spalt er was, wilder Spaß!" which means "Your Walter Spies, if he plays it, then he cracks it, wild fun!"

In Bandung, Walter soon found work playing accompaniment to the silent movies showing inside a theater that catered to Chinese workers. Finding a bright, large room with a veranda and a view of the mountains, he rented it, started making payments on a bicycle, and that November, wrote to his mother that he had adopted a confident if self-deprecating slogan: "Motto: Unkraut vergeht nicht!" meaning "Weeds never die!"

He added, "I am happy and alive, more than ever!" Not only did he have a paying job, but he was practicing hard for a concert with a music professor and he was optimistic he could earn money by painting. As for Bandung, it had "fairytale forests of fir high above" and a "thousand secrets and tigers" in the forests. Walter had begun accumulating pets. "I have a dear, dear monkey, a bird Anne – who speaks better than even a parrot can." And geckos: "four lizards that run tamely along the walls and eat up the mosquitoes."

"So tell me," he wrote to his mother, "isn't this paradise?"

Then there were the men. Walter wrote excitedly about them too, although not as directly. He was still cautious about mail inspectors. But the letter to his mother hinted at his desires. He had especially noticed the Asian men's long slender limbs. "The people," he wrote to his mother, carefully framing his compliment as genderless, "are so unbelievably beautiful, their members so delicate, brown and aristocratic, that everybody should be ashamed not to be like them!"[15]

That autumn, he would begin sketching not only Bandung's mountains but also Bandung's men. In particular, he chose for one study a man who might have been his housekeeper. Walter would title the sketch *Hamid*.[16] The man appeared to be in his late teens or early twenties, a few years younger than Walter himself. Walter asked him to pose shirtless. Then he had Hamid turn his head to look over his right shoulder, slightly away from the artist.

Walter would draw only half of Hamid's chest. He shadowed it as a vast smooth plane, without any markings of pectoral lines or muscles or suggestions of nipples, or even a sternum. Hamid's chest instead seemed to form a tranquil pedestal from which the rest of the sculpted male could emerge.

At the top of the chest, Walter drew Hamid's clavicles as sharp horizontal edges, powerfully squared and slightly more darkened. They filled the sketch left to right, but Hamid's shoulders vanished beyond the frame, creating the illusion that his chest extended infinitely beyond the boundaries of the picture. For Hamid's neck, Walter penciled triangles out of the muscles.

Next came Hamid's face.

Walter drew a long, curved and prominent jawbone that, mirroring the chest below, dissolved upward into a high-planed cheek and fulsome lips. Hamid's nostrils pitched upward and, where they met his wide black eyebrows, formed a striking T-shape. His eyes gazed downward. Then his bushy black hair spiked from beneath a rounded cap.

All of this contrasted severely with the earlier paintings of the European men that Walter had been making. Those had been cartoonish figures, bounded by harsh edges, tilted at odd Expressionist angles, always fully clothed. Men in his European portraits had stood outside of his landscapes rather than extended into them.

Walter had begun to draw his new ideal of the male body – of the Asian male body – and it looked nothing like the ideal of the male body he had left behind in Europe.

What had struck those who had known the young Walter best was that he had always seemed to live his boyhood in a world squeezed between magic and reality. An older sibling, Ira, once recalled that when "Walja" was four years old, one moment he would be lying on a bearskin rug sketching animals, and then, in a surprising flash, would be running, laughing and dancing akimbo so wildly that the family's maid would collapse on the floor, rolling and crimping with laughter. "He was a funny boy," Ira wrote, "always in a good mood."[17] His younger sister Daisy once said that, even as a teenager and World War I was approaching, Walter was just "a half-grown child." He stuffed frogs and snakes in his pockets and then displayed them to others. He teased her terribly, hanging her dolls out the windows of the family home in Moscow.[18]

His family had enjoyed the trappings of imperial life. Both his grandfather and his father had been appointed German consuls, his father serving during the time of the Kremlin court of Nicholas II, the tsar who had ascended to the throne one year before Walter was born in Moscow on September 15, 1895. As Walter grew, his father treated him to the best of aesthetic boyhoods at the height of tsarist culture: ballet performances starring Anna Pavlova and concerts at which the young Walter met the two greatest Russian composers of the time, Sergei Rachmaninoff and Alexander Scriabin. Rachmaninoff and Scriabin could not have been more different. The dour Rachmaninoff was precise and logical. By comparison, Scriabin was unpredictable – sensual, colorful, tending toward sudden shifts in his style as he matured – so much so that a later music historian described him as "a flaming, mercurial, probably insane (toward the end) man" who had begun his career with "charming little piano pieces" but had "ended up a mystic who wrote near incomprehensible music that was going to pull together all the arts and religion."[19]

The story about Scriabin goes this way: When he listened to operas or symphonies, he heard musical notes like everyone else, but he also saw flashes of light moving and choreographed to particular vibrations. For him, sound, light, and rhythm fused. Musical notes were brushes. The medical doctors called it a genetic difference in his brain, something they would name "synesthesia." It gave him an awareness of a kind of magical reality in which dimensions often perceived as separate instead penetrated one another and had to be held in some sort of dialectic. He subscribed to his own brand of the degeneracy theory: that the present was "a degeneration of what was *before*, the cult of real magic." "That's the magic I want to reestablish," he is supposed to have said, where "there was real transfiguration, real secrets and sanctities."[20] He thought: If the real world is made of something as fluid as the pulses of energy that create sound and light, could not the world itself be changed by a deft manipulation of such intangibles? Nature was not a solid *object* built of essences but a fluid *performance*. As Scriabin had neared the age of seven, the aunt who was raising him worried that he was not following the rules of music properly and, in particular, that he was not learning to read the traditional patterns of scripted music as fast as he should. She had taken him to see one of the most talented piano virtuosos in history, Anton Rubenstein. Impressed with the child's talent, Rubenstein had told her not to be concerned. "Don't worry the child," Rubenstein had supposedly said. "Let him develop in freedom."[21]

It was Scriabin who most fascinated Walter, even as young as he was. Scriabin's Third Symphony, *The Divine Poem*, had been produced when Walter was only eight, and Scriabin had written of it that, for the first time, he had found "light in music," producing "intoxication, flight, the *breathlessness* of happiness." He began to mark his scores not only with the usual musical notes but also with optical references such as "luminously and more and more flashing," trying to fuse musical theory with optical description.[22]

Pieces of his idea were not altogether new. For centuries, the Christian church had suggested that certain harmonies or chords could be considered sacred, while others evoked the diabolical. Certain colors associated with particular religious rites. Scriabin would eventually develop his own "mystic chord" constructed from C, F sharp, B flat, E, A, and D.[23]

Walter spent his high school years in Dresden at a boarding school, the Vitzthum Gymnasium,[24] but during summers he would return to Russia for vacations outside Moscow at a family manor called Nekljudovo. Walter and his brother Leo would sometimes lie about playing Richard Strauss's newest compositions on the family piano. But when Walter dabbled at his own composing, he instead tried to imitate Scriabin. By then, the composer had just released his Fifth Symphony, *Prometheus: The Poem of Fire*. The score had been written with an extravagant and not yet technically possible light show in mind. Scriabin intended to invent a special instrument for it, a *clavier à lumières* – an organ that produced colors that matched notes. The note "G," for example, vibrating at 405 waves per second, was supposed to generate a flash of rosy orange, which to Scriabin's mind would stimulate human creative play. The note "C," at 256 vibrations per second, triggered a red lightning spark. That, Scriabin felt, catalyzed the human will to change the world. Violet was the most sacred of colors, representing the incarnation of spirit into matter. Its note was a C sharp vibrating at 277 waves per second. The most intense note, B, at 490 waves per second, dissolved into a pearly blue.[25]

Scriabin believed he was not so much inventing connections as discovering those that already mysteriously existed in different, albeit juxtaposed, planes of reality. He began to dump triadic harmonies and base instead on fourths.[26] He started to believe he could use his discernments in art to transform the cosmos itself through a combination of sound, light, and rhythm. Eventually, he developed a plan for his magnum opus: a multi-day performance combining light, music, and rhythmic dance – to be held somewhere in Asia.[27]

It was all heady stuff. Maybe crazy stuff. No wonder Rachmaninoff was more popular. But it was Scriabin who fired Walter's imagination.

If Scriabin influenced his thinking about music, then Marc Chagall had played the mentor's role for art, at least initially. At the Vitzthum, Walter's drawings of animals paled against the other students' rages of cubism and expressionism, so he began to adjust his style and wonder more about the rules of painting as well as the rules of music. His brother Leo, four years younger, noticed the change. Walter, he would later write, seemed to be becoming "an enemy of the normal convention and prevailing culture."[28]

Canvas, musical score, and life: How did they merge, one changing the other? Could music be heard in painting and colors be seen in concerts? What if all art was not to be guided by the conventions that had evolved in Europe; what if it were to be fused in special rituals or in special geographies? What if not only art but nature itself was not so bounded by the monumental categories and labels that Europeans seemed to keep manufacturing?

Was paradise not to be attained, as religion seemed to suggest, but enacted?

Of his summers with Leo, Walter wrote: "We whistle symphonies for two voices. Splendid practice in holding a part or a tune. The weirdest of ideas keeps popping up."[29]

Leo preferred the orderly classics, Bach and Beethoven. Walter instead kept insisting his brother pay attention to Scriabin. Leo would write of his brother: "You gather together these different spirits." To Leo, it was all "an unreachable, shimmering world" that Walter had to explain repeatedly. Walter instructed Leo simply: "In your compositions, you must combine Beethoven with Scriabin."[30]

A classical form with a mystical ideal.

Walter also began to absorb ideas from the group that would become known as *die Brücke*, "the Bridge," who during those years were disputing the academic art world being offered in Dresden, declaring instead that they would create "freedom opposed to the values of the comfortably established older generation." The *Brücke* artists had expanded Wagner's idea that opera should unify all art forms: music, visual art, and theatrical acting. For them, the unification had to be even more holistic, drawing together all forms of creativity: jewelry, furniture, material crafts, architecture, interior design.[31]

In the summer of 1914, when he was nineteen, Walter returned as usual from Dresden to Nekljudovo. He sat for a formal portrait, and the photographer posed him against a dark backdrop. He appears as a solitary, thoughtful young man, detached from both background and foreground, floating as a free-form, timeless figure in space. His darkening blond hair is neatly parted on the left, and his legs and arms cross in a package of self-containment and assurance. He wears a dark, broad-lapelled jacket and a black bowtie. His eyes gaze sharply out of the left side of the frame. His head is turned slightly downward, looking across his right shoulder – just as years later he would pose Hamid.

Indeed, it is easy to see in Walter's later *Hamid* the twin to the photograph taken almost a decade earlier at Nekljudovo: the young, handsome Caucasian male at the center of empires about to crumble and the equally young but unbounded Asian male about to expand at the colonial periphery.

Much of the responsibility for setting the standard of nineteenth- and twentieth-century male beauty has been ascribed to a thin, monkish, German scholar of the previous century – although, of course, Johann Joachim Winckelmann had help from many others who promoted his ideas once he published them.

Winckelmann was born in 1717, when the import-based, agricultural empires of Europe were at a zenith. It was an era when images of ideal manhood celebrated landed aristocrats such as George Washington for the Americans, or adventurers like Captain James Cook for the British, or the stolid burghers overseeing the finances of domination for the Dutch. An image of a noble male peasant or craftsman could also be romanticized, although those male bodies could sometimes be a bit too untamed, the exception being America, where such roguish males cleared wildernesses for agricultural settlement.[32]

But economies were about to change decisively. By the end of the 1700s, steam engines would arrive, and with them the need for new ideals of European manhood.

By the time Winckelmann was thirty, he had settled near the city that had become one of Europe's cultural centers, Walter's German home, Dresden. Employed by the city's art-collecting cardinal, Winckelmann combined his two interests in art and history and laid the foundation for what would be his eventual reputation as one of the creators of the academic discipline of art history. Winckelmann passionately loved Greek male sculpture, and eventually he was dispatched to the Vatican to catalogue its large collection. His own interest in male bodies was more than academic, though. Soon after moving to Rome, he wrote to his friends that he had discovered "someone with whom I can speak of love: a good-looking, blond young Roman of sixteen." He could see his lover once a week, "when he dines with me on Sunday evening."

"All else is nothing," he wrote. "You don't know the half of it."[33]

In 1755, Winckelmann published his *Reflections on the Painting and Sculpture of the Greeks*, the first of two influential books. His argument was that the paradigm of male beauty could be found in Greek sculptures and that the medium of sculpture conveyed not only the visible aesthetic of the male body but also its internal morality. Sculptors as early as Polykleitos in the fourth century BCE had said similar things, and Renaissance artists such as Michelangelo had spoken of what they called *disegno*, the idea that studying the male form was like studying God. So Winckelmann's ideas were not new. But none of his predecessors had had steam engines attached to printing presses that could put the images and demands of this male beauty on bookshelves across Europe, as well as spread the sound bite that Winckelmann would become known for: "The only way for us to become great is to imitate the Greeks." The sculpted male body found in Greek art, he argued, reflected "noble simplicity and calm greatness."[34]

Although Winckelmann seemed to be proposing an old standard of male beauty, by the beginning of the nineteenth century it had a new appeal. "Winckelmann," historian George Mosse would later write, "defined an aesthetic ideal of manliness that corresponded to one of the deepest needs of modernizing society. The new speed with which Europe was being transformed into an industrialized modern society frightened many people at the beginning of the nineteenth century just as it seemed to threaten chaos at the century's end. Modern society needed order, but it needed a certain dynamic as well . . . The 'noble simplicity and quiet greatness' of Winckelmann's figures allowed for virility – a certain dynamic – as well as for the harnessing of any untoward movement through bodily harmony and proportion."[35]

It was a male ideal that empires needed for industrialization: a symbol that was neither aristocratic landholder nor adventurer, neither peasant nor craftsman. And since Winckelmann's standard of male beauty conveniently looked backward to a culture that no longer existed, the image could safely belong to everyone in Europe, whatever the empire. Mosse would add: "A messianic element was introduced in the formation of the male body, never to leave it entirely. The notion that a true man must serve a higher ideal became in the end an integral part of what could be called the militarization of masculinity."[36]

For Winckelmann, the most important representation of the ideal male rested in the Belvedere Garden at the Vatican: the monumental marble called *Laocoön and His Sons*. According to the Roman commentator Pliny, it had been created by three Greek sculptors to honor the death of the priest who warned against taking the wooden horse hiding Greek soldiers into the city of Troy. Supposedly, a goddess supporting the Greeks had sent sea serpents to strangle Laocoön and his two sons. In the center of the sculpture was the helpless Laocoön himself, held in place by the snake curling past his groin and then pulling his torso and arms backward, twisting him into an agonized S. Next to him were his nude sons, also entwined. Supposedly,

Nero had owned the sculpture, but it had been lost for more than a thousand years until it was unearthed in 1506 – just in time to inspire Michelangelo, whom Pope Julius II dispatched to witness its excavation. By then, the statue had pieces missing, especially the right arms of all three male bodies, and so the pope commissioned sculptors to replace the parts. Michelangelo thought Laocoön's original forearm was bent behind his head, a position that would emphasize his vulnerability and agony. The pope, however, ordered a heaven-reaching forearm, and it was this sky-grabbing Laocoön that Winckelmann, 200 years later, would see and then envision as the ideal male body.

Even in the midst of being strangled, Winckelmann argued, Laocoön had balanced his pain with the greatness of his soul, showing neither anger nor rage but only harmonious, proportionate strength, "noble simplicity and calm greatness."

The original forearm would be found five centuries later, in 1906, when Walter was eleven, and it was bent vulnerably backward as Michelangelo had suggested. But that was too late to change either the impression solidified by the new printing presses or the eventual German sculptures that would be based on Winckelmann's interpretation of manhood and on Julius's interpretation of the *Laocoön* – the ones that the Nazi Party would soon be commissioning.

One key to this representation of the male body was the medium used to express its beauty: marble. Of the possible media for sculpture – soapstone, sandstone, limestone, wood, bronze – it was white Italian marble that would become synonymous with European concepts of male beauty. One could hardly imagine a bronze-toned *David* or a sandstone-colored *Laocoön*. Male physical beauty came from the combination of the marble's hardness, its blanched simplicity, and the curves of the male body that could be extracted from the stone. That the marble was white communicated the necessary racial message.

Two emphases carved from the marble would dominate and become part of performing gender. First, *contrapposto*. The weight of the male marble figure shifted to one foot rather than being borne equally by both. That meant the pelvis no longer formed a straight axis with the rest of the body. Instead, the shoulders and arms twisted, giving the male body dynamism and enabling it to seem constantly poised at that moment between choice and action, as with Michelangelo's *David* or with *Laocoön and His Sons*.

The second focus was on what a scholar of Winckelmann's ideas called "an endless shifting set of dynamically elliptical curves": pectoral muscles, half-moon biceps and triceps, stretched and tiered abdominal muscles, a V-shaped pelvis aimed triangularly downward to the groin, long elliptical quadriceps and calves.[37] Male beauty did not arise from vertical or horizontal lines on a smoothed chest, or from softness at the stomach.

Marble-sculpting language would become the words by which the male body could be evaluated. Chiseled. Roughed. Riffled. Pointed. Cut. The medium condensed to a single message: Be hard.

By the nineteenth century, writers had melded Winckelmann's ideas further into European popular culture, especially in Germany. Winckelmann's admirers included many men much better known than he was: Friedrich Schiller, the German poet and philosopher; Jacques-Louis David, the French Revolution's most significant painter; and most important of all, that German that no educated European or American interested in aesthetics could avoid, Johann Wolfgang von Goethe. Drawing on Winckelmann, Goethe would write that an autonomous man would rise to greater humanity through an education in art, aesthetics, and physical training. With Winckelmann's thoughts as one of their most important texts, Schiller and Goethe were to introduce the powerful cultural and literary movement known as Weimar Classicism, which would influence a wide range of thinking both about politics and poetics. Each European nation-state would modify the ideas a bit: a "German man" grown from idealism and romanticism would not be quite the same as a team-playing "British man" formed at Eton, or an "Italian man" constructed from a nationalist revolution against the Catholic Church, but the template of each would be recognizable as having grown from Winckelmann's ideas.

By the early part of the twentieth century, Winckelmann's definition of male physical and moral beauty had become the dominant representation of imperial manhood. Some German universities even celebrated his birthday.[38]

That summer of 1914, when Walter returned from Dresden to the summer home at Nekljudovo, his father, Leon made a significant mistake that would reshape Walter's life. Likely, the family had already arrived at Nekljudovo outside Moscow for their summer holiday when the news came in June that the archduke of Austria had been gunned down in Sarajevo by Serbs. By July, allies of each offended nation had fallen into step like dominos, putting the Spies family in a dangerous position. Their national homeland of Germany had formed the Triple Alliance with the Austrians and Italians, but Russia, Walter's actual birthplace and the family's home, had become part of the Triple Entente with the French and the British. Still, Leon let his family enjoy the summer at Nekljudovo, apparently believing that they might be able to stay in Russia or be given safe transport out. They returned to Moscow in August, after Germany had declared war against Russia. The tsar's secret police soon arrived, searching for documents that might provide clues about Germany's military. Then Leon was sent to Siberia.[39]

It was a harsh lesson about empires and their rules of loyalty. Walter's mother immediately tried to prove her own loyalty by converting the Moscow home into a Red Cross center for Russian war casualties. That winter of 1915, Walter tended to injured Russians, teaching some of them how to paint and turning stairs in the garden into a snowy toboggan run.[40] The following spring, his musical god Scriabin died, and in September, Walter turned twenty – old enough to be a soldier, a German one as far as the tsar's police were concerned. So they came again, this time to take him a thousand miles southeast of Moscow to an internment camp along the steppes near the Ural Mountains.

That would be Walter's first exposure to the periphery of the empires he had called home. Catherine the Great had secured the land only a century earlier, driving the Islamic Ottoman Empire steadily southward. The local population still consisted mostly of Bashkirs and Tatars. They remained mostly Muslim, and they resisted speaking Russian.

That first spring of 1916, Walter lived in what he described through postcards to his family as "old quarters, alone with my piano" along the banks of the thaw-fed, overflowing Volga River. He started trying to learn the Tatar language. He sketched a cabbage and sold it for five rubles. Mostly, he reported, "I paint different fantasies. Many call them futuristic, but I don't see it." He was organizing a private concert at which he planned to play pieces from Chopin and, "naturally my god Scriabin."[41] In the summer, he described a hike in the mountains with an aunt who had come to visit along with her two younger sons:

> We amused ourselves, laughed until we tired, climbed the highest heights . . . The war is a second-rate thing for us. It is better that way. When all this muck ends, then we will come back to consciousness.[42]

In another letter, he added that he had played piano to raise money for poor schoolchildren, in one case accompanying "a very uneducated, naïve Bashkir who had a gorgeous voice." Walter described the experience the way he would later describe the Indies: "With one word, beautiful, heavenly paradise!"[43]

A year passed. He reported: "I don't work for the future anymore, just enjoy the present. One must always wonder if there will not be another morning."[44]

Walter appears to have led a life of not hiding his attraction to other men, but neither did he disclose much in his writing. As he grew up in tsarist Russia, homosexuality had seemed to be little of the "problem" it was being defined as in Western Europe. The law prohibited sodomy between soldiers, but gay subcultures existed in Moscow and St. Petersburg, particularly in the arts world. In 1903, just eight years after Walter was born, the influential Vladimir Nabokov, the father of the later well-known Russian novelist, had argued that the state held no power to interfere in private sexual relationships. Homosexual intellectuals and artists, such as Scriabin's own piano teacher, Nikolai Zverev, lived openly, as did members of the Imperial Court. Sergei Diaghilev and the most gifted of Russian dancers, Vaslav Nijinsky, had become the best-known male couple in the tsar's empire.[45]

In the Ural Mountains, Walter was not at all dismayed, according to Hans Rhodius, one of his later biographers. Instead, he "felt utterly happy . . . nominally in chains, but inwardly liberated . . . Among the simple country folk of the Urals,

Spies discovered his own identity."[46] Jane Belo, his later friend in Bali, suggested that it was while Walter was in Russian internment in his early twenties that he likely discovered and first acted upon his desire to be with other men.[47]

After the war, Walter struggled across the thousand miles that had separated him from his family, but by the time he arrived in Moscow, they had made their escape to Germany. He turned to friends for help, surviving by working on sets for the Grand Opera. For the first time, he also saw Henri Rousseau's paintings in a gallery. One was *The Sleeping Gypsy*, an eerie canvas that shows a strongly outlined woman lying amid desert hills, a full moon shining in a dark sky above, and an inexplicable lion standing behind her. The painting seemed to defy all academic rules about what should be the content, or the forms of coloring, or the perspective to be used in a landscape.

Walter wrote: "It was like a revelation and a confirmation!"[48]

He stole rides on trains and in 1919 reunited with his family in Dresden. Despite the contortions of empire occurring all around them, there seemed hope for normalcy. A friend named Gela Archipenko visited one day and around the Spies's tea table found "that wonderful person" Walter, who "radiated warmth and friendliness, a shyness mixed with curiosity and wonder." Walter moved toward the piano "and with inimitable grace and a twist of the hips" sat on the piano stool and began to play.

He still had the childlike innocence she remembered.

Suddenly he stopped playing.

"Quick, Leo, tell me what that was," he said to his younger brother.

Leo was not to be fooled. He knew Walter's musical god as well as anyone else. "Scriabin, of course," Leo responded.

"Rubbish! Nothing of the sort!" Walter laughed. It was a Tatar folk tune.[49]

On May 5, 1919, two days before the Allies presented what was left of the imperial German government with their version of a peace treaty, Walter announced in a letter to his father: "I have arrived at the conviction that I draw too technically and childishly . . . All the pictures I have made before are simply reminders of childhood prejudices . . . I believe that I now endure a crisis."[50]

He wrote that he had to escape the restrictions of the past, the rules about which colors harmonized and the techniques that were nothing but "grooves and riverbeds" holding the imagination "in barriers" and forcing it only in one direction. "The concept of beauty for each individual," he declared, "is subjective."[51]

He wanted to learn from nature directly "how many possibilities there are that one can take!" If he could do that, he exclaimed, that would be "fireworks!"[52]

Walter stayed in Bandung for only two months, before leaving for Yogyakarta two hundred miles east and the seat of one of the most important pre-colonial Islamic kingdoms. The Dutch had strategically left its Islamic Sultan, Hamengkubuwono

VIII, in charge of the religious and cultural life of the millions of Javanese Muslims.

For the move, Walter carried yet another letter of introduction, this one to a European singer, Maria Sitsen-Russer. He would teach her children piano, and he would try something new: to defy rules of music and make the percussion of the Western piano sound like the gongs and timing of the Javanese gamelan. Sitsen-Russer's Javanese servants seemed amused by his efforts.

As he had in Bandung, Walter turned his music-making into employment, this time playing piano at a local club, "DeVereeniging," which means "The Union" or "The Association." Each afternoon the men of the ruling merchant and political hierarchy gathered there for Dutch gin, which would be served, as one of Walter's biographers later noted, by usually silent, barefoot Javanese males.[53] Walter tried to amuse everyone by playing light renditions of Brahms, Beethoven, and Mozart.

Across a grassy plain from the club lay the sultan's palace, known as the Kraton. One night, Walter was invited to play at a dance there for the visiting president of the Philippines. Once again, he was amazed. "Is it possible," he would write afterwards, "for such a fairyland still to exist on the Earth!" The palace seemed "something outrageous" with a giant doorway of sculpted wood festooned by multicolored "gigantic dragons and snakes." Beyond the doors were "endless passageways and paths through the garden," and, finally, open verandahs beneath banyan trees that seemed to rear on their hind legs and have their "roots hanging from heaven."

But the sultan himself impressed Walter even more than did the huge doors and the gravity-defying banyan trees. "He sits," Walter wrote, "on the golden throne fanning himself, with all his wives along the walls: simple, beautiful, barefoot girls – everyone is always barefoot! – peaceful, quiet, as if made from the most delicate wax."[54]

But it was the males closest to his age that riveted him. "In every corner crouch princes waiting to receive you: delicate, slim, beautiful as the gods in the most unimaginable costumes," he wrote. They were mannered and deferential. "When entering and leaving they crouch down once again and give a quiet, respectful salute to the Sultan by holding both their hands as if in prayer and lifting them to their mouth."[55]

When Walter finally sat at the piano to play that night, choosing a European foxtrot, the sultan was so struck by the young German's skill that he asked the Sitsens who the new blond piano player was. Then he strolled over to meet him. Walter's heart skipped to a boyish triple time. "The aristocracy of a genuine Javan streams from the tip of every finger," he enthusiastically wrote later. "There is nothing more civilized, nothing more true in the world."

"God, what people."[56]

The next day, the unbelievable happened. Carriages approached Walter's small guesthouse carrying what he would describe as "princes with an entourage of a dozen attendants, with all the trimmings, gold pajungs [umbrellas] expanded and golden implements carried high on golden trays, and the princes wanted to speak to me on business from the Sultan. And what was it? The Sultan had them ask if I wouldn't take over directing his court dance orchestra!!!!!"

The sultan had thirty or forty Javanese men in his European orchestra. He wanted Walter to teach them how to play European rhythms.

> For God's sake, is there anything more wonderful than working with these dear people, almost all of whom have perfect pitch and feel everything through and through! Think of being in the palace every day, among all the demigods.[57]

On New Year's Day 1924, Walter moved in with the men he considered demigods. Sometimes the local expressions of male gender would confuse him. In a letter to a friend he referred to one male as "das Liesel," feminine in German for a "maid," but then added "my nice young boy or servant – whatever you want to call it."[58]

Soon, he was writing to his mother from the palace: "My dinner has just been brought in by my delicate, lotus-eyed, barefoot boy, whom I have as good as adopted."[59]

In the first letter Walter wrote to his mother from Bandung, that previous November when he had arrived, Walter included two premonitions. The first served as a rationale for not returning to Europe: "Think of traveling through the Bay of Biscay in the winter during a storm. Many accidents have happened there. And as I said, I had a really odd feeling that I shouldn't travel back now." The second was about the fate of Europe: "Oh, I could go crazy, thinking how magnificent it is here, and how dreadful it is that all of you are there in Germany and smothering in mud and nastiness."[60]

The attempt to create order at the center of the empires was failing. In the face of inflation, German farmers had begun to refuse to ship their produce, and food riots had started. Workers were starving and members of the bourgeois class, like Walter's family, were losing their savings. The contest over the type of man needed for salvation was sharpening.

Walter had written that letter to his mother on November 1, 1923. A week later, on November 8, 600 young German men surrounded a beer hall in Bavaria. They pointed a machine gun at the door and demanded the cooperation of the three Bavarian leaders who were inside. It was supposed to be the start of an uprising to topple the Weimar government, but the "Beer Hall Putsch" failed. Sixteen members of the National Socialist Party were shot when soldiers finally confronted them. Their leader was sentenced to five years for treason, but a judge who was convinced that the leader had acted honorably left him eligible for parole in six months. The judge also agreed he would be exempt from hard labor and he could have his own writing desk in his cell.

As Walter settled into the Kraton that winter of 1924, in Germany at the Fortress Landsberg prison near Munich, Adolf Hitler began writing *Mein Kampf.* The new Germany, Hitler argued, had to be built upon a particular configuration of the Winckelmann fusion of male body and male desire. The new Laocoön would not be a voice warning against evil or bearing his suffering with "noble simplicity and calm greatness."

He would be an Aryan warrior of pure blood, out to slay imagined serpents.[61]

3

Men of the Feast: Saranrom

As Walter Spies eventually would, Prince Vajiravudh had said his own "farewell to last forever" to Europe – as Daisy Spies would put it – years earlier. He was twenty-one at the time and had seen the century turn, leaving England at the end of 1902 to return to Siam. Although the young prince was supposedly going home, he had fused values from London, much as Walter would later absorb rhythms from the Tatars when he was the prince's age. And as Walter would find when he went back to Germany, "going home" to the place of one's nationality and family was not the same as "coming home" to the place where one's own imagination and desires could be made real.

Vajiravudh's return to Siam included a month-long tour of the United States. "Oh," Vajiravudh had told a reporter for the *New York Times*, "I could not go home without visiting your great country." Pressed about his itinerary, he boyishly admitted he did not have "the slightest idea" what it was.

"It's so much more fun not knowing exactly where you are going," the future king had joked.[1]

His entrance into New York was not what Americans might have been expecting of a Siamese crown prince. For the journey, he had chosen the relatively modest *Furst Bismarck*, an ocean liner from Hamburg with an intermediate stop in Southampton. It was one-sixth the size of the *Imperator* that the same Hamburg-American Line would be launching in just a few years to rival the *Titanic*.[2] The *Times* reported that if Americans expected Vajiravudh to arrive in "a glory of multi-colored silks" and "greet his official hosts with strange Asian kow-tows and salaams" – as if a prince would have kowtowed to anyone other than the king of Siam – they would be disappointed because Vajiravudh "has been away from Siam for nine years and he has been educated out of many of his oriental ideas." The newspaper continued: "The education that he received in England at Sandhurst and Oxford was trimmed in Germany and ornamented in France and now, according to one of his friends, he has come to America for the finishing touches."[3] It was a tacit nod to the *siwilai* or "civilized" concepts of the male body that Vajiravudh now quite literally *embodied* in the way he thought, dressed, moved, spoke.

At Oxford, the *Times* added, the young prince had taken "a prominent part in everything that was going on," except for one thing, "athletics in which he never took an interest."[4] The coming years would prove the *Times* wrong about that, for Vajiravudh had acquired a keen intellectual understanding of the British emphasis on team sports as a way to develop the male body and establish its role in empire-building.

In America, Vajiravudh visited shipyards and the stock exchange and publicly exuded enthusiasm. He never seemed to tire, even on a six-hour visit to shipyard and locomotive factories in Philadelphia. "It is all so big, so wonderful," he said – although he tended to be more interested in history and culture than in mechanical details. Shown the new *Maine* warship under construction, he skipped interest in the technology and chatted instead about the history of the Spanish-American war. The *Times* noted that that was in stark contrast to a previous visit by the prince of Prussia. "He didn't ask anything like the number of questions the German did," the reporter wrote.[5]

By early 1903, after crossing the United States and exiting via Seattle and Vancouver, Vajiravudh was back in Siam, and, as was the custom, he no longer lived in the king's palace but moved out to one his father assigned him, called Saranrom. Almost as soon as he returned, Vajiravudh's mother, Queen Saowapha would begin complaining about her son's sexual behavior – or apparent lack thereof. By his age, princes had sometimes fathered children or at least taken concubines.[6]

Malcolm Smith, one of the Western physicians allowed to visit Saowapha in the Inner City, would write that Vajiravudh's refusal to pursue relationships with women would become "a source of continual distress and irritation" to the queen who had borne him. She repeatedly tried to play matchmaker, making sure that attractive female cousins and other princesses always encountered him whenever he came to her palace to visit.

"It was of no avail," Smith wrote. "She protested loudly. Celibacy was for the priests, she said, and no man outside a monastery ought to remain celibate." Wives – with an emphasis on the plural – were essential. When Vajiravudh became king, she argued, he would need the political alliances the women provided, as well as an heir.

"Her lamentations," the doctor wrote, "were in vain." Vajiravudh "obstinately refused to marry." Dr. Smith added, "Finally, she accepted defeat and gave up the attempt. But it was the beginning of the rift between them – a breach that steadily widened as time went on."[7]

One male desiring another or one female desiring another was not a problem in Siam. What the Europeans had begun to call "homosexual" eroticism was a difficulty only for the palace women who were supposed to swear allegiance to the king. What was considered a problem was that males also needed to desire women and then marry in order to be considered virile and complete – especially if that male body belonged to the next king.[8] Vajiravudh was resisting the practice that had served the Chakri Dynasty through five kings and that was expected by the people who were to be his subjects.

Instead, Vajiravudh set about building his relationships with the young men his own age who were his pages and his courtiers. That broke another extremely important Siamese taboo: economic and social class separation. In Siam, body, desire, and gender were intrinsically wrapped with a fourth category, social class status. Princes usually socialized and formed friendships only with those close to their own social rank, which generally meant those who were brothers, half-brothers, cousins, or members of similarly important families. Marrying outside class status had been explicitly criminalized for aristocratic women, for example, and remained so until just two years before Vajiravudh ascended the throne.[9]

At Saranrom for the seven years between the day he returned from London and that October day in 1923 when he received call to come to the king's palace, Vajiravudh would imagine and create his own island home populated by young men who were not from the royal family.

At Saranrom, he would begin to deploy the strategy he would use to link the oppositional narratives he now needed both to write and to live.

Saranrom had been built by Vajiravudh's grandfather, Mongkut, who had located it just to the east of the Grand Palace on the Chao Phraya River. Mongkut had planned to live in it once he turned power over to his son, Chulalongkorn, but he had died before living there and Chulalongkorn had then assigned the palace first to his brother and eventually to the Crown Prince. As with the other palaces built in the late nineteenth century in Bangkok, Saranrom fused European and Siamese themes, imperial European elements dominating the structure – heavy stone columns and arches, elaborate triangular pediments above interior doorways – while Siamese touches occurred as accents, for example in intricately carved teakwood portals.[10] The royal gardens at Saranrom covered almost four hectares (about nine acres) and had been decorated with a pond, ornamental fountains, birdcages, orchids, and Chulalongkorn's favorite, red roses. Henry Alabaster, a British Foreign Service officer and botanist who had become a personal adviser to the king, had designed the gardens, making them an example of the *siwilai* the royal family was promoting.[11]

Biographers writing about Vajiravudh would later say that at Saranrom he would try to recreate the male camaraderie and bonding he had learned in Britain, where he had moved mostly within an all-male world constructed quite differently from the one he would have experienced inside Siam had he remained in Bangkok. In Siam, his male companions would have been royal brothers or cousins suitable to his own rank and who were also being privately tutored for roles in government. In Britain, he still moved among such young aristocratic men, but he also encountered male groups based more on shared intellectual interests and hobbies than just vocational fates. Experiences at Sandhurst and the Royal Durham Light Infantry as well as at the all-boys Christ Church College at Oxford appeared to have given him a different perspective on male bonding. He joined prestigious gentlemen's clubs in London: the United Service Club founded in 1815 for senior military officers; the Army and Navy Club, no females permitted; the Travelers' Club for men who had traveled more than five hundred miles from London; and the Bachelors' Club, for those who were enjoyably single.[12]

Of course, British upper-class males belonged to such clubs and still quite comfortably slid into the expected romantic, monogamous, heterosexual relationships. But it seemed as if the disturbances in the categories about whom and why he should be marrying had caused Vajiravudh to come full stop and to question the role he could take.

The model of the fraternal male club would offer a way for Vajiravudh to create both a personal homeland and promote a new nation-state.

At Saranrom, the young prince initiated a male association called Thawipanya Samoson, the Enhancement of Knowledge Club, inviting not only those of princely rank but commoners to join, including of course his male pages and courtiers. Sometimes they held European-style debates. The topics could be lightweight. Did ghosts exist? Did electric lights work better than lanterns? Behind the princely initiatives was a serious purpose: constructing a new if somewhat magical circle of male bonding and discourse within the small world he controlled at Saranrom.[13]

He turned to theater too, almost as if he were playing with the possibilities of fluidity that were available in that particular kind of public discourse rather than in others, such as palace governance or religious duty. He assembled some of his men into an amateur troupe to stage both classical Siamese plays emphasizing dancing and music as well as London-style plays with spoken drama. He began to write more. In a move that drew more ire from the Queen Mother, he even started acting in the plays. She argued that the prince should not mingle with lower-ranking males on stage and that future Buddhist dharmic kings should not be seen as actors taking on multiple personalities and, quite literally, donning different masks.

Again, Vajiravudh ignored her. In effect he set aside his expected script in one piece of the dance of Siamese manhood in order to pursue a different step. He enjoyed experimenting with roles other than the one dictated for him. It was a way to try on different personalities, to adopt and reject different masks. Eventually, the symbol of the theatrical mask would become associated with him in political cartoons in a way not at all complimentary.[14]

Drama and storytelling also went beyond the stage at Saranrom. The young prince often called together his male courtiers and pages so that he could dim the lights in the palace and tell them ghost stories before they went to bed. He also organized outdoor male contests with storylines that imitated war or police actions against this or that opponent. It was the idea of chivalry and combat, and usually these male contests were held late at night, after 10:00 p.m., the fireworks used to imitate gunfire resounding all around the palace grounds. The year of his father's death, the plot of the games had grown quite serious after a general strike by Chinese merchants in Bangkok had inspired Vajiravudh to organize one team as police and the other as the Chinese strikers. Whenever a "Chinese" was caught, Vajiravudh served as the magistrate for issuing a sentence.[15]

At age twenty-four, after he toured northern Siam, Vajiravudh returned to Saranrom and added something new to the gaming: a life-sized village of rooms for the young male pages to live in and practice self-governance, with a meeting house, a police station, and even a bank that collected taxes from the pages. The pages voted for a governor who then appointed a secretary-general to direct the police and the bank. Some thought Vajiravudh might be experimenting with ways the Siamese might eventually govern themselves.[16] At the very least, he seemed to be reimagining the architecture of his palace. At Saranrom, there would be a city run by the young males.

It was a kind of Homeric Phaeacian palace presided over by a benevolent king. Like King Alcinous in *The Odyssey*, Vajiravudh added one other element: a daytime schedule of sporting games. Not Siamese ones, but British ones: cricket, tennis, billiards, croquet and, eventually, soccer. Britain had become distinguished by its emphasis on training males in team sports, while Germany focused on individual gymnastics.[17] Siam had long had contests, such as *muay thai* kickboxing, that tested individual males against one another as well as sculpted their bodies in particular ways, but the male team sports taken from the British preparatory schools and universities were new introductions.

Ever absorbing and adjusting his own male body to British standards, at Oxford Vajiravudh had learned that such team sports might serve as the foundations of the kind of male bonding that would be needed in a new nation-state that did not rely on the polygynous marital connections used to operate a huge bureaucracy. Siam did not yet have structures for governing as understood in the British Empire so much as it had men who needed to either be linked by family interests or be somehow otherwise motivated in certain ways to accomplish certain tasks. "Politics" was mostly about mobilizing those men, and an effective way to do it was by shaping their ideas of the kinds of activities male bodies should be engaged in.[18]

One of Vajiravudh's later biographers, Stephen Greene, noted that, at Saranrom, the prince "seemed determined to make up for all the intimacy, merrymaking and camaraderie he had missed while pursuing his long, lonely education in Britain." Greene noted: "Vajiravudh's pages were more than just his personal servants; they were his family."[19]

Vajiravudh seems to have especially enjoyed his friendship with a young man just one year older than he was. The man's mother had been one of Vajiravudh's wet nurses, and he had thus been able to make his way into the Royal Pages regiment serving the crown prince. Vajiravudh eventually gave him the name Ram Rakhop. Greene wrote: "Vajiravudh's affection for Ram Rakhop increased year by year; what in 1904 had been a close relationship had by the 1920s become a consanguineous one." The name "Ram" had been taken from "Rama" in the famous Hindu play the *Ramayana* and "Rakhop" from the name of another character in the Thai version of the play. "Rama" is also the name Vajiravudh eventually assigned to each of the kings in his own Chakri lineage, so that in European fashion they would become known as Rama I, Rama II, and onward. Vajiravudh was Rama VI. That gave both him and Ram Rakhop the same initials for signing government correspondence: "Rama R [ex]" for the king, "Ram. R." for Ram Rakhop.[20] By the time Ram Rakhop was twenty-five, Vajiravudh (at twenty-four) had named him Director of the Department of Royal Pages, the Commander of Royal Entertainment, and Lord-Chamberlain of the Ministry of the Palace. He would eventually become Vajiravudh's chief military aide and, by virtue of that position become a brigadier-general, and then a major general, in the army.

Ram's younger brother, eventually named Aniruttha, would also be highly favored, being appointed Lord Steward of the Palace even while in his mid-twenties.

Once Vajiravudh had become king, a British diplomat would write of the three young men that:

> Ram Rakhop is . . . the King's prime favorite . . . He has no pretensions to birth, but by reason of the King's favoritism has been granted the highest titles and decorations and is the subject of the greatest hostility to the nobility. His mentality is neither striking nor able . . . He's nowadays the only channel of approach to the King. [His brother Aniruttha] is . . . youthful, effeminate. He usually plays the female parts in the King's theatricals. He is pleasantly mannered . . . and is mentally neutral.[21]

Once he had succeeded Chulalongkorn, Vajiravudh quickly set about founding additional new male clubs: a paramilitary Wild Tiger Corps, a Siamese version of the Boy Scouts, a Chitralada Association of thirty male friends who dressed in long, flowing robes like Freemasons to dine with him once a week and who, at other times, placed triangular emblems with secret letters on their lapels.[22] One of his first acts as king, coming only two months after his accession, was to establish a Royal Pages College for the young men he had surrounded himself with at Saranrom. Normally a new king would have built a Buddhist temple, but Vajiravudh instead declared there were already enough of those. By August 1911, he was saying that, if anyone wished to earn Buddhist merit, that person should build schools for boys. "To build temples is not to my liking." He went so far as to tell one noble who had built such a boys school that the "meritorious act will yield better results than the building of a temple for the shelter of sham monks who don yellow robes in order to escape their obligations."[23] It was virtually a direct assault on that notion of the dharmic male, replaced with a new Saranrom male who learned in more European-style schools and who savored in chivalrous, Edwardian games.

His Royal Pages College was organized like an English boarding school, students and faculty living together and the king himself appointing its masters. Vajiravudh also visited several times a year and lectured at least twice each year. His royal policy on the school was clear: He wanted it to create men of "pure heart and pure body," linking the moral and emotional components of manhood to the body, much as Winckelmann had done.

"I don't want them to be walking textbooks," he said. "What I want are manly young men, honest, truthful, clean in habits and thoughts."[24]

Noting the new male-oriented circles Vajiravudh was creating, historian Tamara Loos would later write, "The king's daily activities and intimate associations shifted from the Inner Palace to these new locations of desire."[25]

On that Sunday, October 23, 1910, when Vajiravudh succeeded to the throne, the Inner City of women was a complete town in itself, but within five years, he would practically abolish it. The number of Chulalongkorn's wives and princesses left in the city would be reduced to twenty-five, the administrative structure and all official positions occupied by the women abolished, the amount of land it occupied slashed.[26]

Promotions would no longer come via the status that women held as queens or consorts, or via the polygynous marital alliances they offered. Instead, promotions would come through the positions and the alliances that men made through the Saranrom male circles: through the feast of male games, male salons, male storytelling, and male banqueting that surrounded the king.

It is an open question, however, whether Vajiravudh could actually be fitted into the monumental labels for male bodies, desires, and genders that were then being solidified in Europe, those categories of "heterosexuality," "homosexuality," or "bisexuality." Some popular writers take his interest in an "inner city" of male courtiers and pages as confirmation of homosexuality;[27] others are more cautious, especially since both Siamese and subsequent Thai laws strictly govern what can be said about either living or deceased royalty. Still others, such as historian Tamara Loos, think the question beside the point, since it would assume that the European category of "heterosexuality" had been an appropriate definition of previous Siamese kings against which Vajiravudh's supposed "homosexuality" might be contrasted. What is more important, she argues, is that, regardless of European sexual labels, Vajiravudh was indisputably refusing to continue certain key elements of the Siamese political culture: the marriage alliances that had maintained the official political body through the reproduction of children, the oaths and laws that regulated women's sexuality, the usual demonstration of the male body's virility through sex with multiple women.[28]

Whether or not he personally fitted into any particular medical or legal labels the Europeans were inventing, he was changing the discourse the Siamese had inherited about male bodies, male desires, and male gender performances, and he was coming home into a paradox. He would create a world of miniature choices that fit his own identity as well promote what he thought was needed for a *siwilai* makeover of Siam. Vajiravudh would not choose to be an adjective or a noun — a European label for a particular category of male body and desire — so much as a verb. At Saranrom, he would perform and feast with the men of his choosing.

In his early plays, some of which were written at Saranrom, Vajiravudh focused on two sorts of plotlines: those that would promote a sense of Siamese nationhood based not so much on family lineages as on a commonly held history and those that would promote romantic, monogamous heterosexuality. The two fit together as ways to modernize Siam according to British standards, but certainly the latter choice seemed strange, given Vajiravudh's own refusal to court women or to marry. That second plot, however, also provided him with a public rationale for his refusal: In true romantic fashion, he was simply waiting for the right woman, rather than marrying any female gifted to him by some important father.

Vajiravudh's plays most forcefully promoted the idea that romantic love, rather than family or cultural demands for reproduction, must be followed — wherever such love might lead. That "follow your heart" command could provide an underpinning for same-sex love as much as opposite-sex love, because it shifted the locus of power over the male body and its desires from the family and the cultural tradition to the individual. Therein lay a seed for those trying to understand the masked identities of Vajiravudh himself. This king would perform his own passion. If necessary, he would defy a definition of manhood that required him to participate in arranged polygynous marriages. But he would also defy culturally coerced sex with any woman, even that required by the triple supremacy of romance, monogamy, and heterosexuality that his plays were now promoting as part of that concept of *siwilai*.

Typical was of his early plays was one called *Lord Vermont V.C.*

Vajiravudh opened the script with a British soldier, Lord Valentine Vermont, in love with his cousin Mildred. That type of cousin relationship was slowly being defined as an incest taboo in the "modernizing" West, but Vajiravudh ignored that particular element as a point of tension for his plot. Siamese audiences likely would not have understood it as a potential obstacle anyway, since polygynous kings and princes regularly intermarried with their relatives. Instead, Vajiravudh adopted a customary "love triangle" as the play's source of tension: Vermont mistakenly thinks Mildred has snubbed him for another man. Hurt, he departs to fight for the British Empire in India.

One of his male companions then offers a lesson about emotion and masculinity: "Love is not a small thing, Val," he tells the heartbroken suitor, "but still you mustn't let it unman you. Fight against it and be a man."[29] Men do not surrender to love; they adhere to social roles.

But Vajiravudh then wrote Vermont's answer in words that encapsulated his new ideal: that the heart must count above all else, *whatever* its desires. "I'd rather fight a whole lot of tribesmen," Vermont replies, "than my own heart."[30]

It was a clever dual thrust. Vajiravudh would help undermine the ideals of polygynous manhood by promoting the modern triple supremacy of romantic heterosexual monogamy, but he would also argue that the heart should be allowed to pursue its own course, including – it seemed – fraternal associations with men.

In Vajiravudh's script, Vermont attempts to get himself killed in battle to relieve his aching heart, but instead he becomes an accidental hero, sufficiently wounded to be sent home and awarded the Victoria Cross for valor in the face of the enemy. For the predictable happy ending, he learns that Mildred still loves him.

Vajiravudh published the play under one of many pseudonyms that he would adopt so that he could more freely engage in public debates and in the popular media of newspapers and magazines beginning to emerge in Bangkok. For *Lord Vermont V.C.*, he referred to himself by what seemed an especially pertinent name given his own anti-marriage interests at the time: Marcus Virginius.[31]

In a second play titled *A Turn of Fortune's Wheel*, Vajiravudh strongly countered the Siamese tradition of family arranged marriages within particular economic classes, declaring forthrightly that the new ideal of romantic love should transcend all other considerations. In *Fortune's Wheel*, he imagined two former playmates that had grown up together, Toby Vincent and Clare Phillimore.[32] They meet again at Clare's nineteenth birthday. Like Vermont, Toby is preparing to leave to fight for the British Empire. In the opening scene, Vajiravudh sets the two characters to awkwardly talking about the games they used to play as children when they pretended to be "king" and "queen," possibly a not-so-veiled reference to his own childhood of preparing for royal power. Toby is twenty-three, four years older than Clare, and about the same age as Vajiravudh when he was writing the script. Clare laughs that Toby's idea of being king is to take his queen out in the fields and try to kiss her without any romantic preludes – much as a Siamese king might have simply taken a wife as a matter of polygynous necessity rather than out of love.

At the end of the scene, Toby tells Clare, "I should like to hear you say that you cared for me. Will you?" Vajiravudh wrote into the stage instructions what was to happen next: "Clare makes no answer, but [Toby's] arms are, all of a sudden, filled with silk and lace, and a little golden-haired head is laid on his shoulder. The rest is left to the reader's imagination."

Later, Clare confronts her father, who is planning to marry her off to the Earl of Ostenthorp, Toby's wealthy commanding officer. Clare angrily refuses, even though Toby is a pauper.

"Are you my daughter or not?" the father demands.

"I am, but I am not a puppet," Clare responds, in words that Vajiravudh himself might have targeted at his own family. Clare adds, "I am not going to be forced into marriage just to convenience my father."

"If I marry at all, I mean to marry to please myself."

When her father threatens to disown her, she tosses power and money in his face: "Father, cut me off with or without the proverbial shilling, but I am going to obey my heart . . . What is money compared to love? There is nothing in the world to be compared to love."

After pleas from her mother to be "practical" and realize that "one can't live on love alone," Clare gives in. But instead of getting angry, Toby as a man proves he is even more worthy of the new ideal than Clare. He swears that out of his truly monogamous love for her, he will remain a bachelor.

Vajiravudh had tackled the question of which counted most: class and economic status as a determinate of marriage or the new Western ideal of romantic heterosexual monogamy, complete with its gender costuming and swooning feminine behaviors. His answer had come down firmly on the side of romantic love.

In much the same way as Vermont had, Toby ends up an accidental hero in battle. Wounded, he too returns home to receive the Victoria Cross. By then, Clare's father has gone bankrupt, while one of Toby's uncles has died and left him a fortune, hence the title of the play, *A Turn of Fortune's Wheel*. Toby now has the higher-class economic status, but he refuses to gloat or to now refuse to marry lower-class Clare. Instead, he tells "my own darling little sweetheart" that "it's the work of Heaven . . . and those whose hearts God has joined can never be put asunder." As at the end of the first scene, Clare rests her head on Toby's shoulder, and the play closes with the reading of their marriage announcement.[33]

In both plays, nationalistic fervor provided Vajiravudh with the *deux ex machina* that he needed to transform the situation of his two male characters, Vermont and Toby. They both leave to fight wars for the British Empire. Importantly though, Vajiravudh used nationalism as a theatrical device more so than as the definer of a militaristic style of manhood. Neither Vermont nor Toby achieves manhood through war or through imperial conquest; they are not fully Winckelmann-style males. Vajiravudh avoided scripting either character as a real hero who shows actual valor in the face of the enemy and thereby overcomes the obstacles to his romance at home. Instead, the men receive medals only through accidents while they are behaving less than courageously. The true victory of manhood lies in the ache for love. Romance is what makes them men.

Vajiravudh had simultaneously satirized Western concepts of militarized masculinity while promoting Western ideals of romance. His plays encouraged a shift in the way men formed emotional relationships – away from the stage of extended family arrangements and into what one gender-studies scholar refers to as "the arena of individual competition in a gender market."[34] Male sexuality in

Siam was now to become regulated via its competition in romantic heterosexual monogamy rather than through family arrangements. Eventually Siamese men, as well as women, would have to compete as individuals in that gender market – with all of the resulting implications for changes in their fashion, their language, their bodies, and in what was considered masculine performance.

During the early 1900s, when he was writing, Vajiravudh was not the only promoter of these new images of heterosexual, romantic, and monogamous love in Siam. Two years after Vajiravudh became king, Bangkok hosted its first locally made commercial motion picture. The movie, *A Siamese Elopement*, portrayed what the *Bangkok Times* called "a loving couple" running away from an infuriated father. In the final chase scene, the father's boat capsizes. The young male lover then rescues him so that, in the plot, the family is saved – not through the actions of the older male adhering to tradition but through the younger male who challenged it. Romance and monogamy triumph over family demands.

The message was the same as that in Vajiravudh's plays: That which was oppressive and dangerous was the old cultural emphasis on arranged marriages. What was powerful and saving – and what now had the blessing of the most important playwright in the kingdom – was the new Siamese man, the one who feasted in male groups and fraternal contests and who followed his heart in matters of love.[35]

4

The Escape from Nosferatu

Walter had had at least one romance while in Europe – enough, it seemed, to keep a distance. After World War I ended, he arrived in Dresden in June 1919, rejoining family members. On June 17, still acting like the mischievous boy who hung his sister's dolls out the window, Walter walked into a room at the family home. Another young man was visiting and still asleep. Walter perched next to the bed and stared at him until the man awoke with a jolt.

"I'm Walja," Walter laughed.

"Really?" the other man mumbled. Blinking awake, he flirted.

"Haven't we known each other for a thousand years?" he coyly asked Walter.[1]

Hans Jürgen von der Wense was twenty-four, just a year older than Walter, but he had already built a reputation in Berlin as a star pianist. Critics compared his playing to Sergei Prokofiev's and Igor Stravinsky's; one even termed Hans "the most individual, most expressive" and "most future-looking" among all young pianists in the emergent Weimar Republic.[2] It helped that Hans was handsome, with a masculine cliff of high cheeks, long etched nose, and thrusting chin.

Hans chronicled the next few months in his diary. From the first long gaze, the two men seemed bonded. First, they escaped to Hellerau, which had begun a decade earlier as a planned community. Hellerau's ideal was to fuse work, life, and the arts into a single zone of space, place, and time rather than dividing them into certain urban locations or specialties – an art gallery here, an opera house there, a craftsman here, a painter there. The idea appealed to Walter from his stay among the Tatars, and it fit with his own rebellion against the strictures of his old Dresden boarding school, the Vitzthum.[3] Hans and Walter moved into the home of a sculptress named Hedwig Jaenichen-Woermann, a student of Rodin and a woman who one writer later described as having a penchant for holding "open house for 'birds of the most varied plumage.'"[4]

During the day, Walter and Hans wandered the bucolic fields around Hellerau.

"Walked with Walter through the grain," Hans wrote. "Fantasized. Spoke in poems that make no sense, only sentiment."[5] They were two males pursuing the Weimar ideal of aesthetic German masculinity rather than of militaristic male contests. The political Republic was still two months from formation, but the cultural one had already started to emerge.[6]

Walter, Hans thought, seemed "a wild child like Rimbaud," that restless nineteenth-century poet of the decadent movement. Rimbaud had had a torrid homosexual affair and – notably, given Walter's later plans – had joined the Dutch colonial army to flee to Java. One day Hans and Walter were sitting in a garden with Walter's mother when suddenly, Hans wrote, "He stood up and toppled the whole table over. Then he threw water on his mother's neck. Oh, he tore laundry from the line and [threw it] in the dirt. Then he climbed up a tree!"[7]

Hans was absolutely enchanted.

By July, Walter hung paintings in his first exhibition in Hellarau. Hans wrote, "We acted like strangers and listened to how to the visitors were talking. But most of them were just speechless. This painting, bolder even than Kandinsky, offends even the snob."[8] Walter made the first sale of his new career. Both men were exuberant.

Hans: "I'm always with Walter now. Equilibrium."[9]

Later, he added: "His soul moves around in me like a ghost . . . We're solving each other. Like two puzzles."[10]

October 1: "Very, very happy! Unfettered! No more thinking, only being! Every day is our eon!"

October 2: "We are like summer clouds that trail along far in the distance . . . or stars."

October 3: "It is as if the bonds of life are dissolved. There are no laws, no rulers. We pierce the night with the day . . . We are afraid of nothing, for everything is ours."[11]

Walter had turned twenty-four by then, and the two constructed a manhood based on delight. "People always look as if they have just gotten out of school," Hans wrote. "You have to liven them up. We talk to them, in the middle of the street, give them flowers and fruit . . . We wander through the shops; they throw brocades over the tables in front of us, silk fabric that we feel and admire, and then go and jump on the streetcar already standing there, to anywhere, roam farther and compose poetry and deliver it, sealed, to an inn."[12]

They walked together in the hills around Hellerau: "We looked down on the city from the heath; her lights bounced, came apart, fidgeted, as the tranquil stars looked on."[13]

They created together: "We selected more bold chords on the piano, composed them together. And then: We even dreamed the same. When we awaken, the sun is setting. We squander ourselves."[14]

But then, the romance between the two men stumbled, as if it had hit both a public and a private limit beyond which it dared not move.

On October 5, Hans walked alone in the fields: "Doubt. Today I was in him too much without boundary. When I dive, I don't hit bottom. I'm caught up in him like a storm in a beautiful cloud. How do I dissolve it?"[15]

October 9: "Swallowed up in him. Drank the air like a spring."[16]

October 13: "Unsettled. Have I worn him out? Today still: I want to improve things . . . But the evening didn't succeed. Mrs. Woermann returned. The conversations were lively. But the separation rose up in me."[17]

It is not clear whether Walter reined or Hans.

October 14: Hans and Jaenichen-Woermann held an enigmatic conversation:

> I have breakfast with her. I was grumpy, because it seems
> to be broken for me here.
>> She asked: "Do you have a goal?"
>> "No, just a road."
>> "A road?"
>> "Yes, one that all other roads cross. It can't have a goal,
> because it's a circle."
>> "A circle. . . so it's. . ."
>> "Yes, it is."

"If other people also have this road?" she asked. Hans replied, resigned, "They travel it with me."

Unlike heterosexual romance, which had its outcomes of either tragedy or marriage, the romance between two men could not be a line leading anywhere – only a circle. The three friends joined once more. Hans wrote: "For us, it was like before a big break-up. . . . We all walked hand in hand."[18]

The attempt at a romance had ended.

A year after Hans and Walter parted from Hellerau, Walter chose Europe's two most famous tragic romantics, Shakespeare's *Romeo and Juliet*, as the subject for one of his paintings. He dressed Romeo in a modern dark suit and Juliet in a long bridal gown, and then set them at a log home in the countryside at the moment of their balcony scene. In the dominant plane of the painting, the modern Romeo – looking a bit like a Charlie Chaplinesque version of Walter – stands on the ground doffing his hat to the longhaired Juliet, who in turn dangles her handkerchief from the skewed balcony. Other planes jumble at different angles, the land's horizon pointing in one direction, the log cabin and balcony in others. Walter stitched the images together with curving roads and fences. In the night sky, a full moon scatters its light through minutely drawn leaves. In front of the house, a dog barks at Romeo as he limps with a cane toward a carriage harnessed to a child's hobbyhorse.

The sentimentality of the lover's parting had been evoked but also caricaturized. Its style seemed influenced by Marc Chagall, who was using vivid colors almost like a prism. The colors communicated optimism and hope even if the fragmented planes created tension and reduced humans to cartoon-like renderings. Walter seemed to be showing that quality his brother Leo would later comment upon: Good-byes had to be kept short and unsentimental. Walter called the painting *Der Abschied,* or *The Farewell.*[19]

One scholar later wrote that *The Farewell* recalled Walter's good-bye to a woman friend in Hellerau.[20] Possibly. But Walter's romance in Hellerau had not been heterosexual. The long walks, the gazing on moons, the nonsensical poems – those were all experiences with Hans.

Forty years later, Hans would slip Walter's biographer Hans Rhodius a photograph. It showed the two in profile side-by-side, "modeled," Rhodius wrote, "as if from a Roman coin."[21] Hans had dressed in a dark suit that matched his dark hair. Walter had worn a light field jacket that matched his sandier hair. They were planned male complements, dark and light.

"Full of strength and confidence," Rhodius wrote. "One wonders how both these nearly same-aged friends ignited each other; how together they were strong enough to defy an entire world of conventionality."[22]

In winter 1920, Walter returned to Dresden and Berlin. World War I had left Expressionists focused on art with knifelike edges and displaced bodies. Asked to design the stage for the first German presentation of Knut Hamsun's play, *The Game of Life*, Walter adopted sharply lined rocks that contrasted light and dark. He objected when the director softened the edge with a water landscape. Theater critics noted that Walter's design had added a kind of imaginative spiritual essence to what had become Hamsun's customary aversion to civilization – an aversion that would win him the Nobel Prize for Literature later that year for his epic, *Growth of the Soil.*[23]

The Weimar Republic had officially begun, and that winter posters were warning citizens, "You will become Caligari," referring to the movie *The Cabinet of Dr. Caligari,* which had premiered in Berlin the month Walter arrived. It offered a thinly disguised allegory ascribing Germany's defeat to distorted male values. In the movie, a carnival magician, Dr. Caligari, creates a sleepwalking murderer, Cesare, who terrorizes the unsuspecting citizens of a German village. One of Cesare's targets is a young woman named Jane, but captivated by her feminine beauty he carries her away rather than kills her. During a pursuit by townsfolk, he falls to his death, but his act of recognizing true beauty has saved Jane from Dr. Caligari. She returns to the village to expose the actual power-obsessed male behind the murders.[24]

The film would best be remembered as a visual trademark of the German silent movies of the new Weimar Republic. Standard three-dimensional sets had been replaced with strangely painted flat boards that portrayed chairs, windows, and rooftops twisted at distorted angles in a world of dim lighting and heavy shadows. The human actors moved not with the confidence born from the German giants of the classics like Goethe and Schiller but as thin shadows passing in front of a contorted landscape that they barely perceived.[25]

The movie also contained a coded message about homosexuality that those in the know in Berlin could easily read. In *Caligari,* the sleepwalking Cesare had been portrayed by a twenty-six-year-old actor, Conrad Veidt, gaunt and shadow-eyed with extraordinarily long fingers that seemed capable of wrapping around any neck. The year before *Caligari* was released, Veidt had also starred in the German film *Different from the Others*, partly funded by Magnus Hirschfeld, the sexologist and founder of Berlin's Institute for Sexual Science. The film had been one of the new movie industry's first sympathetic portrayals of homosexual men, and in it, Hirschfeld had included a plea to abolish the section of the German penal code criminalizing homosexual behavior, Paragraph 175. Veidt had played a violinist blackmailed because of his love for a male student, and Hirschfeld himself had appeared in the film as a doctor who urges the violinist's parents to "not condemn your son because he is a homosexual." In the film, he explains to Veidt's character that "love for one of the same sex is no less pure or noble than for one of the opposite."

One scene shows Hirschfeld lecturing that "nature is boundless in its creations."

None of that saves Veidt's character from committing suicide – pointedly collapsing in front of a Winckelmann-style statue of a nude male warrior. Hirschfeld appears at the bedside of the dead violinist and urges his distraught lover to "keep living to change the prejudices whose victim – one of countless many – this man has become."

"May justice soon prevail," Hirschfeld says.[26]

In *Caligari*, Conrad Veidt had returned to star with yet another message about manhood. The Veidt who only months before had appeared as a homosexual victimized by German law would now help save the German village from the German father's distorted manhood.

Veidt had come to these near-simultaneous movie portrayals after a previous short stint running his own studio with another young German, Friedrich Murnau. Through the connections that Hans Jürgen von der Wense had, Walter and Murnau would soon meet, and Walter would find himself incorporated among the men who, through movie texts and Expressionist images, were creating questions about contest, empire, and definitions of manhood.

Murnau and Walter were similar types – smart, imaginative, and perceptive – and they appear to have been immediately attracted to one another. The war had left Murnau scarred emotionally. He had lost his young lover, a poet named Hans Ehrenbaum-Degele; the two had been so close that after the war Hans's mother invited Murnau to live at the family estate in Grunewald, just outside Berlin. Soon after he and Murnau met, Walter moved in to live with him.[27]

At thirty-one, Murnau was seven years older than Walter, not a full generation ahead but more established in his career in Berlin than Walter, and so Murnau would not be another Hans offering a sentimental romance. Instead, the relationship would assume the characteristic of a more experienced mentor passing along his artistic insights to, as well as showing his love for, a younger man. After Walter moved in,

Murnau immediately gave him a piano. In return, Walter painted Murnau's office with frescos of miniaturized details, like the tiny leaves that had created shimmers of light and shadow in *The Farewell*.

Then Murnau offered a special invitation: The filmmaker had decided to create his own version of *Caligari*. Walter could become an apprentice in a medium that seemed quite suited to ideals of Scriabin. In darkened movie houses, the multiple arts of sound, light, and rhythm could be fused to transform audiences.[28]

The film Murnau would call *Nosferatu: A Symphony of Horror* had a simple story line, a repeat of Bram Stoker's tale of Dracula.[29] He planned it so that a young romantic heterosexual couple find themselves linked to what can only be described as a different plane of realities controlled by competing ideas of manhood. The first scene of the movie would portray newly married romance and happiness, the promise of the triple supremacy. But then the scenes would darken. The young husband, Hutter, would be sent by his older male employer into the mountains to conclude a real estate deal with the aristocratic Count Orlock. After traveling miles through bucolic farmlands, Hutter arrives at Orlock's castle and then encounters a strange male body equipped with a huge bald head and protruding long ears that turn his entire face into a single, hollowed, hungry eye – almost as if Murnau intended to update the Homeric myth of the Cyclops. Count Orlock, having tired of his life at the margins of civilization, wants to buy a home in town – the heart of the German nation and of heterosexual manhood. He selects one directly across from Hutter's own.

At a dinner with the count, Hutter mishandles a simple symbol of male virility, cutting himself with a bread knife. Later as Hutter rests, Orlock materializes from the deepest part of the camera focus to penetrate Hutter and suck blood, throwing Hutter's male identity into chaos. The young heterosexual male spends the rest of the story vulnerable and useless. Orlock now becomes the *nosferatu* – a name that means "plague-carrier" – and sails to the city to claim his new home in the village. Recalling Veidt's sleepwalking Cesare, Orlock sleeps in a coffin along the way. Once in the heart of civilization, he unleashes a rat plague of disease and then stalks Hutter's wife, Ellen, much as Cesare stalked Jane in *Caligari*. In *Nosferatu*, however, Orlock does not steal the woman and save the village, but he does pause before Ellen's beauty, long enough that his departure is delayed until sunrise. The light then destroys him.

As with *Caligari*, audiences could watch *Nosferatu* just for its scare – or it could be dissected for the fears upon which it had been built. First among those had been the Spanish flu pandemic that had hit Germany along with the rest of the world from 1918 to 1920 and had killed more people than even World War I had. The penetration of the imperial center by a "plague-carrier" was a real event in the minds of the audience-goers. Too, racial fears had been aroused by war-forced migrations.

Surges of Jewish and Slavic refugees had moved from Eastern Europe, much as Orlock was moving from his castle to the German village. German audiences felt the fear of an empire now under assault from what had been its racial margins. As one film scholar wrote, Murnau had zeroed in on "the imperial colonizer's bad dreams of a reverse colonization of the mother country by the colonized subjects."[30]

For those who knew how to look, *Nosferatu* also commented on fears of sexual difference. The danger to the romantic, monogamous heterosexual couple comes from the sexual borderlands of the empire, where odd creatures with strangely figured male bodies, odd erotic desires, and peculiar genderings – like Orlock – live and where not fully understood sexual bonds between men first lead the older male agent to send Hutter to Orlock and then lead to the penetration and disruption of Hutter's own male identity. Murnau was among the first of the new gay directors to use the symbol of the vampire to focus fears about a creature living on the margins of society, ostensibly heterosexual by day but homosexual by night.[31] As a symbol, *nosferatu* embodied – and horrified – the degeneracy theory about homosexuality that the German Max Nordau had written about thirty years earlier.

As Murnau's new assistant, Walter watched and learned. He seems to have been intrigued by Murnau's ability to use powerful lighting and shadowing as well as distorted angles and surprising camera perspectives. The fusion of the grammars was fascinating: words telling one story through the captions on the silent film; camera angles and lighting telling another; musical accompaniment by a live orchestra enhancing what was on the screen. Murnau, after all, wanted more than a movie; he wanted a *symphony*. That fusion of artistic grammars was a reminder of Scriabin.

Ultimately, though, Walter seemed to grow uncomfortable with the content of Murnau's story. His experience among the peoples in the Urals had given him a different view of those living on the periphery. Even if there was some artistic benefit to be had from evoking certain geographies as liminal and scary through lighting and unexpected distortions of perspective, for Walter the people themselves were not Orlocks. Nor did his understanding of his own sexual desires seem to be as darkly cast.

From the time Walter had moved in at Grunewald, he had continued his own painting. In 1921, he had completed *The Farewell*. In 1922, as Murnau began filming *Nosferatu*, Walter finished an exuberant testimonial to a peasant street fair called *The Carousel*.[32] Fluid dancers packed the canvas, some small-bodied and painted in a primitive, childlike style, others with oversized heads – an Expressionist distortion. In the background Walter decorated trees with tiny leaves reflecting mesmerizing dots of light, as if, like Scriabin, he were trying to render each particle of light as decipherable as a single musical note. In other works, he colored exuberant landscapes that included Tatar horse races and rural folks cheerfully pulled in horse-drawn carts. Walter was busily affirming life and innocence on the borderlands, while Murnau was drawing on a racist horror of it. Walter was painting in flamboyant colors, while Murnau was creating erotic worlds edged in black and white shadows. If nature was indeed "boundless in its creations," as Magnus Hirschfeld had explained in *Different from the Others*, the question seemed to be what type of lens to use to see it.

In the year of *Nosferatu*'s release, Walter painted *The Skaters*. One of its elements was the same as in *The Carousel*: the happy peasants arranged in a circle. This time they skated on or danced away from a frozen pond. Conifers bordered the pond, each miniaturized needle glowing from the snow. Walter placed several elements into the landscape that suggested a development in his sexuality. Prominently in the foreground, he painted a male observer with a sharp nose like Walter's own and with wondering eyes like those that had been in the photograph taken at the summer estate at Nekljudovo. Walter isolated the man behind a fence above the skaters. His head angled to link his gaze to the other largest figure, also solitary although surrounded by a circle of skaters all coupled, man and woman. That other solitary figure was neither Russian nor German but an Asian dancer dressed in a loincloth. Just below the male observer, Walter painted a thin shadow wearing a bowler hat, a Charlie Chaplin accessory reminiscent of the movie world Walter had entered via Murnau. The shadow danced happily away from the pond.

Walter seemed to be more conscious of a new desire – one that celebrated rather than feared racial differences.

His moody companion, Murnau, was employing lights and sounds and movements to prick the idea of the triple supremacy: innocent heterosexual romantic monogamy. He was also exploiting the triple taboo, and in this case Orlock was not only a man penetrating another man, but he was also of a different race as well as of a different age. That made him the scariest, most dreaded *nosferatu*.

For Murnau, the *nosferatu* would find no home in the center of the village. Coming out of the shadows, he would instead be destroyed by his desires.

Inside the same Grunewald house as the movie director, Walter instead was using light and rhythm on a canvas to gaze curiously upon another possibility of manhood latent within the musical notes of a folk dance.

Nosferatu opened in Berlin on March 4, 1922. Two weeks later, Magnus Hirschfeld and the Scientific Humanitarian Committee he had organized officially asked the Weimar Reichstag to repeal Paragraph 175 of the Imperial Code. More than 6,000 people signed Hirschfeld's petition. They included Sigmund Freud, Albert Einstein, and Leo Tolstoy. But the petition failed. On June 24, young right-wing militants assassinated the Weimar Republic's foreign minister, Walther Rathenau, a Jew who had been widely excoriated as a homosexual because he was unmarried and had a liking for blond Nordics. Those who had begun extolling blond Nordics as the superior race had slain him.[33]

In July, exhausted by the production of *Nosferatu*, Murnau rested at a sanatorium in the Black Forest outside Berlin, taking Walter with him. There, the two met a Dutch couple, Georgette and Johan Schoonderbeek, the husband an orchestra conductor. While Johan and Murnau relaxed, Georgette Schoonderbeek and the twenty-six-year-old Walter walked for hours through the surrounding forest, Walter regaling her with stories about his life with the Tatars.[34] He also invited her to see his paintings at Grunewald. Noting the piano Murnau had given Walter, as well as the room the filmmaker had converted into a painting studio for his young protégé, Georgette wrote that Murnau seemed to have done "whatever he could to make Walter's life easier." She added that she thought the film director "needed Walter's sunny cheerfulness and indomitable joy of life around him."[35]

The following spring, Georgette arranged for exhibitions of *The Farewell, The Carousel,* and *The Skaters* at Amsterdam's prestigious Stedelijk Museum as well as at a gallery in The Hague. Even more blessedly for Walter, she invited him to stay in Holland while his paintings were being shown. Berlin had begun to feel like an extension of Murnau's movie, a shadowy life lived at a skewed perspective. In Amsterdam, Walter could be free. He made regular trips to what was then called the Koloniaal Institute, where the Dutch had placed their collection of relics from their trading empire, including the East Indies.[36] Georgette later wrote: "What began to possess him more and more was an addiction, a yearning, for the Indies . . . It became an obsession . . . He wanted away, away from Europe, where he felt crowded, un-free and unhappy . . . The big difficulty for him was that Murnau, his friend and benefactor, did not want to let him go."[37]

In July 1923, Walter wrote to his old friend Hedwig Jaenichen-Woermann in Hellerau:

> You no doubt know from Hans Jürgen that I bummed around in Dalmatia for two months. Filming, unfortunately − that was less pleasant. You see, dear Mrs. Jaenichen, it's only when you're outside Germany like that that you notice how terrible it is to live in Germany − what a terrible country it is and what appalling people there are there, how dry and unfeeling they are, and how being among them one becomes like them. I can't stand it anymore! For me, who saw, learned and felt real life during my three years of internment with the Bashkirs, it will never again be possible for me to feel comfortable here in Europe. I cheat myself when I lie to myself about everything here. Why should I struggle along with it any longer! Everything that was simple and obvious there is wedged into theories and laws here . . . There, nobody asks if something is beautiful or ugly, good or evil; it's just there and is obvious, and people are happy amongst each other and in nature, and no one needs to worry himself over anyone, because everybody is somehow concerned for each other . . .

> I will never find myself in alignment with European people, and I
> don't want to . . . I prefer to leave all these people and try to find
> myself a new homeland.[38]

He sent a far shorter cry to Georgette Schoonderbeek.

"You must help," he wrote.[39]

Georgette later remembered:

> I traveled to Berlin and had a long discussion alone with Murnau
> until deep in the night. I tried to make clear to him that whatever
> one gives up freely and lets go remains ours forever, while that
> which we hold on to we unavoidably lose. He who releases, keeps;
> he who holds on tightly, loses forever. And immediately this truth
> became clear to Murnau so that he was able to say with complete
> assurance: Walter must be free to go; I cannot try to hold him.
> And the next day he said this himself to Spies.[40]

Walter had begun his escape from the notions of the male body and its desires
that he had found in Berlin. Getting ready to board the *Hamburg* and depart for
Southeast Asia, Walter pleaded in a letter to his mother.

"Mom, Mom, please do everything you can to get out of Germany!"[41]

5

A New Man for Siam

Even the newspaper images of Vajiravudh and his father, Chulalongkorn, presented different masculinities. Chulalongkorn cut a mustachioed, debonair man-about-town image, wearing smartly tailored Western suits and military uniforms. He could have passed for a Siamese version of Errol Flynn. Vajiravudh took after his more circular-faced mother, Queen Saowapha. As he aged, he would keep his roundness and what was once a lean figure would turn squatter.[1]

Chulalongkorn presented a picture of male potency. He had been able to centralize power in the throne even while pursuing Western-style reforms. Key to that had been his steadfast refusal of Western pressure to change the foundation of the male body and its desires: the polygynous relations through which his power could be asserted. He might have favored certain queens or consorts, but he never succumbed to trying to be a model of romantic heterosexual monogamy such as was being promoted by the popular representations of Queen Victoria and Prince Albert.

Figure 5.1   King Chulalongkorn
Public domain, Wikicommons

In a famous speech on unity that Chulalongkorn presented in 1903, shortly after Vajiravudh had returned to Siam, the king had made it clear that reforms designed to modernize his empire would go only so far. "The use of Western ideas as a basis of reform in Siam is mistaken," he said. "The prevailing conditions are completely different. It is as if one could take the European methods for growing wheat and apply them to rice growing in this country. There would be absolutely no benefit in this whatsoever."[2] *Siwilai*, the adoption of Western symbols of "civilization," had to be a project carefully managed by the royal elite. It could reinforce the elite's power, but it also had to be carefully controlled lest it subvert that power.[3]

Vajiravudh faced many of the same challenges his father did of creating an elite-sanctioned style of official nationalism that would preserve the monarchy's power rather than result in the royalist system being overthrown from within by popular nationalists or conquered from without by colonialists.[4] But his own preference for not marrying put him at odds with the very system he was trying to maintain. He was simultaneously an insider and an outsider, a man from the margins of his own empire who was still entitled to the most exquisite of homes in that empire. He was a Western man in a Siamese skin as well as a Siamese man in an Edwardian ascot. He was refusing to perform the politics of male bodies and desires as expected.[5]

Figure 5.2   King Vajiravudh, 1925
Public domain, Wikicommons

Chulalongkorn may have taken note of the young prince's dilemma shortly before his own death. He certainly must have been aware of Queen Saowapha's concerns that the young prince sequestered in his own male island at Saranrom, dressing in masks and costumes and acting in plays, was not showing any signs of wanting to maintain the polygynous system. Shortly before Chulalongkorn's death in 1910, he told the ministers who had assembled that he had changed his mind, at least about parliaments.

"I entrust onto my son Vajiravudh," he told them, "a gift for the people, that upon his accession to the throne he will give to them a parliament and constitution."[6]

It could have been a way out. While the two political institutions of parliament and constitution would not have automatically precluded the continuance of royal polygyny, it was hard to escape the empirical observation that constitutional monarchs in other nations no longer tended to marry many wives and reproduce prodigiously in order to staff bureaucracies and run empires.

But, for all the Western values Vajiravudh had absorbed in England, he still doubted parliaments. Even as a prince he had denounced them as "marked by interminable and pointless speeches."[7] Instead, he preferred male leadership built upon the metaphor of a ship:

> On a ship, power is in the hands of the captain. All others on board must follow his orders to the letter. If this is not done, the ship will be at risk . . . and the lives of the passengers thrown into jeopardy . . . The nation may be compared to such a ship; the king is the captain and the people are the passengers.[8]

During the years between his accession in 1910 and the start of World War I in 1914, Vajiravudh did continue the efforts to modernize – or Europeanize – male and female bodies in Siam. He discouraged women from the traditional practice of chewing betel nuts, because it blackened their teeth and made them unattractive to Europeans. He encouraged women in the royal family to start wearing their hair long, instead of short like men, noting that "every book I have read by a Western writer has commented on the great oddity that, for whatever reason, women cut their hair short. And they state that Thai women would be very pretty except for their short hair which makes them ugly."[9] He asked Siamese women in the court to give up the unisex *jong-kraben*, a kind of sarong, and instead wear more stylish, tightly cut skirts. He dropped his father's reluctance to see women educated and instead signed Siam's first compulsory elementary education act, making no distinction between the sexes. He even challenged the Siamese tradition that women should not accompany their husbands to public social functions and should not dance with them. Instead, he regularly took women friends out in public, even to the modern dances that were beginning to arrive in Bangkok.[10]

He also decreed that all Siamese needed surnames. Traditionally, they had had single names, often changing them as their status or jobs in life altered or even when they simply worked in the same place as another Siamese with the same name. That practice de-emphasized the relationship between their names and any individual and family connections. The year Vajiravudh ascended the throne, a newspaper correspondent suggested that surnames were "one of the signs by which one may judge of the progress of civilization in a people." Vajiravudh agreed. After he had issued his decree in 1913, he wrote: "Now we have surnames and it can be said that we have caught up with people who are regarded as civilized." For himself, he had implemented the Western numbering of kings within dynasties, Rama VI. The decree was easier to issue than implement, though. Most Siamese would still not have surnames by the time Vajiravudh's reign ended.[11]

Perhaps surprisingly, given the previous *New York Times* observation that Vajiravudh had had no interest in athletics while studying in England,[12] one of his major means of remodeling the male body, its fraternal relationships, and its masculinity came to be based on the introduction of English sports, most especially British football, soccer. In contrast to the Germans, who were emphasizing individual gymnastics to build Winckelmann-style male bodies, the British had decided that chivalrous team sports provided the best training for manliness. The famous saying that the Battle of Waterloo had been won on the playing fields of Eton had not actually been uttered during the Napoleonic years. It had become popular after 1889, while Vajiravudh was in school in England.[13] And so he cultivated soccer in schools and colleges, even pitting those young male favorites attending his Royal Pages College against military cadets. He did not hesitate to choose sides when he attended games, something that produced the unusual effect of Siamese crowds sometimes cheering for teams the king disfavored.[14] The *New York Times* would eventually change its observation about Vajiravudh's interest in sports and celebrate him for using games and scouting to make Siam a "new nation," even helping its young men escape the twin vices of gambling and opium. Notably, the reporter described the accomplishment in combating male degeneration and of increasing male potency, implied within the wording, since males were the only ones playing the games. The reporter even threw in an image of Vajiravudh as a *puer aeternus,* an eternal boy.

> Making over a nation by the introduction of the modern game of football and the Boy Scouts movement, changing the youth from a life of enervation and luxury to one of vigorous athletic competition — this is the accomplishment accredited to Rama VI, the 31-year-old king of Siam . . . In the days before football, Young Siam lacked patriotic impulse and a sense of national obligation.
> . . . The new King saw the importance of vigorous outdoor sport. Thirty-one years of age, he was still a boy at heart. As a monarch, he had the wisdom to realize that legislation could not change the moral tone of a nation; as a recent college student he saw that the hope of the kingdom lay in the awakening of youth.[15]

When World War I came, Vajiravudh pondered whether to take a unique step for Siam: Join the Allied powers by declaring war against Germany. Because he had close relations with both the British and the Germans, Vajiravudh remained neutral for three years. Woodrow Wilson's decision to add the United States to the conflict in April 1917 made the choice a bit easier. On July 22, 1917, Vajiravudh joined the Allies and began preparations for a first: the sending of Siamese troops overseas to a French training camp. He personally designed a new flag to represent the idea of a new nation-state. Before, the flag had been the king's only; a white elephant on a red background symbolized an animist token of good luck. Instead, Vajiravudh copied the usual red, white, and blue patterns of his Western allies. Always given to literature, he wrote a poem to explain the combined Buddhist, national, and kingly symbolism to his subjects:

> White is for purity and betokens the three gems
> And the laws that guard the heart.
>
> Red is for our blood, which we willingly give up
> To protect our nation and faith.
>
> Blue is the beautiful hue of the people's leader
> And is liked because of him.[16]

Nation, religion, and king. That would become Vajiravudh's new national slogan, an echo of the British "god, king, and country," except that in Britain those were conceived of as three separate categories, whereas in Siam the three tended to be seen as one male body, the king also giving body to god and country. Siam would not just be an extended family based on the intermarriages of its king and its princes but a geographic and bureaucratic nation-state founded on the triple prongs of Buddhism, monarchy, and geography. Vajiravudh introduced a new national holiday into the calendar to reinforce the idea: April 6, Chakri Day, named after the dynasty. He even coined a new national cheer that Siamese crowds could use when they greeted him: "chai-yo!" which means "victory." Kings had not been cheered before, just held in Buddhist silent reverence.[17]

It was all quite theatrical – the flag, the cheers, the all-male fraternal clubs, the king at the sporting matches. Some credit him as the father of a new national identity, but at the time others criticized Vajiravudh for installing his own male comrades in undue positions of power as he broke with the older expression of manhood through polygynous relations.

Critics also accused him of grossly mismanaging the state funds he used to support his new fraternal alliances and males clubs, castigating them as personal indulgences – although compared to Chulalongkorn's budgets, the percentage that Vajiravudh spent in comparison to the rest of the government budget seemed to stay about the same or even decline. Scholars such as historian Tamara Loos have observed that it was *how* Vajiravudh spent the palace's money, rather than the total amount, that was likely the real source of the complaints. Chulalongkorn had used vast amounts to support the female Inner Palace without any criticism except from

Europeans. But the fraternal male desires Vajiravudh brought forth from Saranrom defied the past images of Siamese masculinity.[18]

Just thirteen months into his reign, Vajiravudh's opponents attempted a coup, allegedly trying to install one of his brothers or half-brothers as president of what would be a new Siamese republic. They complained that the king had been spending too much time writing plays; they were especially angered because he was installing his own male companions in top roles.

They failed, but it was a warning that the monarchy's absolute control was beginning to falter.

For all of Vajiravudh's apparent embrace of romantic heterosexual love in his popular plays, when it came to writing those ideas into law, he stopped short, avoiding what might have been too deep a confrontation with other members of the nobility and with the traditional understandings of manhood. In 1913, two years after the attempted coup, he received a memorandum from one of his royal relatives promoting the idea that monogamy should be the central principle in drafting new family laws, primarily to please the Europeans. But, the relative argued, the laws would not have to be enforced – just adopted.

Vajiravudh steadfastly refused. He wrote a detailed response, beginning with what at least one historian would later note was possibly a "thinly veiled allusion to his own homosexuality."[19] He wrote: "I shall neither gain nor lose by the adoption of either the system of monogamy or polygamy, so I feel that I am competent to state a disinterested opinion on the subject."[20]

One of the relative's arguments had been that outsiders would continue to frown on Siam as long as Siamese men seemed promiscuous and engaged in polygyny. It was a claim based on the notion of what "civilized" men should and should not do. But Vajiravudh, still trying to create a hybrid notion of gender, rejected it as a legitimate reason to change: "Our moral plane and that of the Europeans [cannot] . . . be compared with fairness, because they are so different, and it is most difficult to judge who is on the higher plane and who on the lower."[21]

Replacing polygyny with monogamy through a stroke of law, he argued, would result in all minor wives losing their legal standing and thereby declining into being nothing more in the eyes of the law than prostitutes. Similarly, their children would suddenly have no legal rights. They would become "illegitimate," an idea the Europeans subscribed to but that the Siamese did not. To his ethical credit, Vajiravudh also rejected the suggestion that a law requiring monogamy should be adopted but then simply not enforced. "If we are going to practice polygamy then there is no need to hide it, but if it is thought best to hide it, then do not practice it at all . . . Let us not be hypocrites."[22]

Vajiravudh, then, would use his imaginative power to promote the triple supremacy of romantic heterosexual monogamy in his plays so as to transform Siamese constructions of manhood, but he would not use his political power to impose it into supremacy over the Siamese male.

What he did do, however, was to issue a new law in that fateful year of 1914, when the archduke of Austria was assassinated. In a major shift of royal attention away from regulating female sexuality in the Inner Palace, Vajiravudh declared that all men working in the Ministry of the Royal Household, the Royal Secretariat, the Fine Arts Department and the Education Department, as well as all royal pages and all palace police, soldiers, and men of the royal cavalry would have to declare the names of their family members. They had to register marriages as well as names of all wives and children, the names of their parents and their wives' parents, and everyone's home addresses. Prostitutes, harlots, and mistresses whom they frequented only occasionally were to be excluded from the lists. Single men had to register too, and if they chose to stay overnight anywhere outside their usual home, they had to secure permission from their immediate superiors.

Men living in or near the palace, in other words, were to be called to account for their relationships and their ongoing sexual encounters. "For the first time in Siam's history," scholar Tamara Loos noted, "a moral discourse about the constitution of a proper family regulated the sexuality of its male governmental officials."[23]

The effect of the plays and the legal discussion was to push questions about polygyny into public discourse and to make it part of a complex tug-of-war about manhood, nationhood, and *siwilai*. Polygyny was not abolished by Vajiravudh's new approach; rather, its tangled networks became a matter of written rather than oral record. "Modernists," influenced by Europeans, smeared the royalty for its allegiance to polygyny and began to criticize Vajiravudh personally for his fraternal alliances and for his spending on male friendships.

Disapproval of his sexuality and performance of gender grew into a barely disguised subtext for disapproval of all his policies. The British Foreign Office was becoming especially critical. As early as March 1912, only seventeen months into his reign, a Foreign Office dispatch equated him to his mother, complaining that Vajiravudh had inherited "all the worse feminine nature of his mother."[24]

Ram Rakhop and his brother also became favorite targets of gossip. In the 1920s, for example, British diplomats reported that Ram Rakhop was being referred to by the pseudonym of "Rasputin" on the streets of Bangkok, while his brother was being called "the Angel." One especially vicious rumor the British Foreign Office reported to London had it that Vajiravudh had lavishly prepared suites for the brothers at one of his palaces, ordering that each be painted in the men's favorite colors. After only a week, the rumor went, the brothers decided they wanted to swap the suites, so each room then had to be lavishly redecorated – all at public expense.[25]

By the 1920s, Bangkok had developed a raucous popular press — an indication that classes other than the royal elites were beginning to make use of the ideas of *siwilai*. Historian Scot Barmé noted that cartoonists quickly shifted into modes of mocking the king that seemed right out of British magazines like *Punch*.[26] One cartoon, which may have referred either to Vajiravudh himself or to Ram Rakhop's brother, the "Angel," made use of the well-known interest Vajiravudh had in theater and masking. It showed a man wearing a feminine mask that had a look of innocence and that sported a crown. The caption read, "Outwardly I'm an angel." To the right, though, the mask had been pulled back to reveal a bug-eyed demon grasping bags of money, the captions on them referring to him as a "criminal," a "thug," and a "swindler." Another cartoon referenced Vajiravudh's interest in theater by showing one of the characters from the *Ramayana*, a dancing ten-headed demon king. Each head bore Vajiravudh's image. One face laughed while the caption below read "philanderer." Another face winked while a hand descended onto the shoulder of a woman, the caption reading "prostitution." A third cartoon portrayed an emaciated rickshaw puller representing morality trying to haul an obese and balding king up a steep hill toward heaven, the clear implication being that the king — rather than being the dharmic model of Buddhist manhood — was a heavy weight on Siamese morality.

In what seems to have been an even more explicit criticism of the king's sexuality, another cartoon showed a set of scales with a bag of money marked "treasury funds" hovering in the air, while a young man dressed like a Westerner and smoking a cigarette weighed it down to the ground.

"In effect," Barmé wrote, "what the cartoon suggested was that the king carried out his homosexual lifestyle (patronizing and supporting male friends) at the expense of the nation."[27]

As he became subject to more criticism and as the tensions over his refusal to marry grew, Vajiravudh sometimes retreated to his own islands of imagination, almost as if he were trying to re-create the feasts and games he had held at Saranrom. In 1918, after vacationing with a group of thirty male companions at the beach and building sandcastles together, he returned to Bangkok and decided to convert four acres of his palace grounds into a miniature city of two- and three-foot tall private homes, Buddhist temples, commercial buildings, and government offices. He called it Dusit Thani, or "Heavenly City." Instead of fast-disappearing sandcastles, he had built a more solid, miniature Phaeacia.[28]

It was another male game and club, meant to pass the time with male friends but also engaging a possibly serious purpose for the nation itself. In Dusit Thani, Vajiravudh's male friends bought "real estate." He drafted a constitution, its preamble declaring that its intent was to promote self-governance in the new city. All citizens could elect Dusit Thani's chief administrator, who would then appoint financial and public works directors. A council of people's representatives was also to be elected and two political parties created. Two newspapers and a weekly magazine began publication in Dusit Thani, Vajiravudh arguing that if the constitutional government were going to succeed, the standards and ethics of journalism would have to be raised.

Within this world of Dusit Thani, Vajiravudh pretended he was an ordinary citizen and adopted the private profession of architect – an indication of how he saw himself. His friends knew better. They instead elected him the first chief administrator, while Ram Rakhop headed up the other political party and became the second chief administrator.

Word leaked out that perhaps the king was considering converting Siam to democracy because he had granted a constitution in Dusit Thani. The conservative royal nobles among his relatives went apoplectic, even though the constitution, as one of Vajiravudh's biographers, Stephen Greene, would later note, was only "a playtime one for a doll's house city."[29] Anarchy, one royal uncle complained, would be the only result of a constitution.

What seems to have been equally at issue, though, was Vajiravudh's continuing insistence on performing different theatrical roles, testing fluid definitions of his own masculinity rather than conforming to expectations for his gender role of king: that he would be "serious" as a Buddhist king who did not engage in such experimentation.

Confronted with the opposition, Vajiravudh continued his creative play at his own "Heavenly City."[30] But he never insisted on bringing either a constitution or a parliament into Siam's real life.

While he steadfastly refused to impose the monogamy in family law that his theatrical plays were promoting, eventually Vajiravudh himself had to accept a reality. The brothers he had hoped would inherit his throne were dying one by one. He could continue to refuse the cultural coercion to have sex with women and thereby be the last king of the Chakri Dynasty, or he could marry.

There could be no "nation, religion, and king" if there was no king.

And so, after ten years of bachelorhood on the throne, in 1920 the palace announced that Vajiravudh, then 39, would engage a 28-year-old princess, Vallabha, the daughter of one of the sons of Mongkut. The two had met, the palace said, at a public exhibition and had fallen immediately, romantically, in love. For four months during the winter of 1920–21 – while in Berlin a young Walter Spies had begun to live with Friedrich Murnau – Vajiravudh and Vallabha swirled through a mesmerizing romantic engagement. She accompanied him to no less than twenty-seven public functions, including dance exhibitions of the foxtrot and tango.[31] That had not been the form of courtship Siamese kings had followed during the days of polygyny. It was as if Vajiravudh was living one of his plays. At the public gatherings, Ram Rakhop and his brother no longer sat next to Vajiravudh, "a fact that some observers felt . . . was significant," according to Greene.[32]

Vajiravudh and Vallabha had become the modern, romantic, heterosexual monogamous couple the king had written about. But this play did not end as happily.

After four months, Vajiravudh annulled the betrothal. The palace announcement said that the princess, supposedly, had a "nervous system [that] leaves much to be desired, so much that His Majesty is under the impression that, in the event of the Royal Marriage being permitted to take place as formerly arranged, undesirable consequences may follow in the future in regard to the throne."[33] But, the announcement also made clear that the engagement had been a matter of policy, not romantic passion. The king, it said, had "had no other desire than firmly and definitely to ensure the succession to the Throne."[34]

The romantic plotline had vanished.

Eventually, Vajiravudh began to pursue a connection with Vallabha's half-sister, another princess, but then switched to one of his cousins. He elevated her to royal consort, and in 1922 the palace announced that, instead of trying to stage any elaborate public marriage that seemed based on a romantic courtship and a promise of monogamy, Vajiravudh had decided to instead "follow the old and trusted custom of Siam."[35]

In other words, he would be polygynous.

Quickly, he added the cousin's sister as a consort, and then elevated her to queen, Indrasakdi Sachi. For a while, it looked as if she might give birth. Instead, she miscarried.

The final performance in Vajiravudh's own attempt to personally balance the oppositional narratives of manhood in which he had found himself entrapped began on June 20, 1924.

He and the queen had gone to a new palace he had had constructed near Cha'am alongside a beach about 90 miles southeast of Bangkok. It was a whimsical new home rambling through sixteen buildings and sixty-four rooms and a maze of open-air corridors, all covered in Victorian gingerbread, painted yellow and baby blue, perched ten feet in the air atop more than a thousand columns, all built out of teakwood, all fitted together without nails. Vajiravudh had designed this palace in the air himself. Carved around each of the 1,000 columns was a tiny moat for keeping the ants away. Fittingly, given the romantic plotlines he had been promoting in his writings, Vajiravudh had named it Mrigadayavan, the Palace of Love and Hope. Among the buildings was one that opened to the sea breezes on all four sides. It was to be used as a royal theater for the staging of plays — some of them Vajiravudh's own.[36]

On that Tuesday night of June 20, the scheduled play was one Vajiravudh had written in 1917, *Phra Ruang*, about a legendary king in the village of Lavo in central Siam who had supposedly helped unite the Siamese to throw off the control of a Khmer despot from the land that had become Cambodia. It was one of his nationalistic, more so than romantic, plots, but it held his favorite themes: that the

Siamese were clever enough to outwit superior military forces, that their supposed passivity did not mean they were fallen or defeated, that they could unite around a compassionate leader.

The play's poignant opening lines seemed to speak of Vajiravudh's perception of his own accession to throne after his father died:

> I should be gay and happy in my heart
> To be the far-famed father of Lavo
> Since my sire's death, I have ruled this city
> With the people's free favor and good will,
> But alas, joy is not mine, with sad sighs
> I pity the woe-burdened populace
> Lacking sustenance through much prolonged drought.[37]

Vajiravudh was acting in the play himself, taking the role of one of the minor actors, as he had done since the days of Saranrom. But a maid had to touch his face in one of the scenes. The character was played by Tew Abhaiwongse, a descendent of the traditional rulers of an eastern province, schooled in classical music by her grandmother. Such a touch of a king's face was an outrage, perhaps especially since Abhaiwongse was only nineteen. When the moment arrived in the play, Queen Indrasakdi supposedly called on the courtiers and other members of the royal family to stamp their feet and make loud noises of disapproval.

The tactic backfired. Outraged, Vajiravudh fumed back at the queen, "Your behavior is shameful!" and not long afterward, Indrasakdi was demoted. By August, Abhaiwongse bore the title of royal consort.[38]

It was a curious fusion of romantic plot and polygynous practicality.

Even American students at Harvard University, where Vajiravudh had visited years before while still crown prince, noted the strangeness and insisted that the triple supremacy identified with Western progress and civilization – romance, monogamy, heterosexuality – had to be followed to its logical end, even if it meant no heir. In an editorial in *The Crimson*, they praised Vajiravudh for being a "king who translates Shakespeare" and who, "after the Oxford manner," had gotten rid of "one of the most fundamental traditions, the harem."

But, the students added, "King Rama's admiration of the West could not reconcile him to the absence of an heir. As a result, the 'Siamese Official Gazette' of last week announced the royal decree demoting the Queen for failing to carry out her high duties." The students added caustically, and stereotypically, "The motive and method were Oriental, but the idea was as Western as soap or bathrooms. Reno, Paris, the divorce mills of the Occident are but crude counterparts of the Eastern system of demotion. Many men would appreciate the opportunity of getting rid of their wives by the smooth working machinery used by His Highness of Siam. With judicious advertising, Bangkok could become the demotion capital of the world."[39]

By October 1925, Abhaiwongse – renamed Suvadhana by Vajiravudh – was pregnant and clearly on her way to delivering. Vajiravudh wrote a lullaby for the unborn baby, whom he seems to have considered male, and ceremonially honored Suvadhana for her "loyalty to the throne, and to uphold the prince soon to be born."[40]

Within a month, he lay fatally ill – a sudden death approaching, just as had been the case with his father. The British Foreign Office reported to London that "in his occasional intervals of consciousness, the King spoke English not Siamese."[41]

On November 22, 1925, a particularly bitter cartoon appeared on the cover of the Bangkok newspaper *Kr'o lek*, drawn by an artist who had been chronicling what he referred to as the six kinds of *hia* to be found in Siam. As opposed to a white elephant that symbolized good luck, the *hia* was a monitor lizard that brought misfortune. In Siam, the word was one of the strongest pejoratives that could be applied to an individual. In the cartoon, a skinny-legged, fat-bellied Vajiravudh was presented as the sixth *hia* in the series, a reference to his Europeanized title of Rama VI.[42]

Two days later, Suvadhana gave birth to a girl. Vajiravudh's own palace law of succession adopted in 1924 dictated that only a male heir could take the throne. It was the final ironic twist in the plot he had been creating. Vajiravudh died thirty-six hours later, on November 25, 1925. He was only forty-four.

King George V of Great Britain seemed astounded when he heard the news. His response showed little understanding of the kind of pincers and multiple narratives that imperialism and *siwilai* had created for manhood and masculinity in Siam.

The British king wrote into the minutes of a Foreign Office report:

"What an extraordinary state of affairs, and after being educated at Oxford."[43]

Into his own body, Vajiravudh had fused the contradictions: the monumental notion of the triple supremacy of romance, monogamy, and heterosexuality for the modern Siamese man to be created, contrasted with the fluidity of the multiple miniature variations of body and desire and gender that he himself also lived.

Decades later, at another male-dominated island in Bangkok, this one only about a half-mile from a statue of Vajiravudh standing in a park the king had designed as one of his last acts, a young Thai man named Toc hung a portrait of Vajiravudh at the entryway to his own re-conception of a place for male feasting. The photograph was a standard one of Vajiravudh in a marble white military uniform, meant to convey noble simplicity and calm greatness.[44] What was different was the frame. It was of wood but had hundreds of nails driven into it, as if a reminder of suffering.

It was the only photograph of a real man in Toc's version of Phaeacia. Asked why, he simply answered with a question:

"Don't you know the story?"[45]

6
Magical Reality, Running Amok

In April 1925, a few months before King Vajiravudh's death, Walter traveled to Bali for the first time. Through Yogyakarta's sultan, he had been introduced to the head of the village district of Ubud, Tjokorde Gde Rake Sukawati, who, like the sultan, was interested in Western art and music. The decisive moment came one night in mid-April when Walter and Sukawati entered a temple courtyard about 7:00. There, Walter saw what he described in a letter to a friend the next day as "the most important and essential of all that I have seen in Bali so far."[1]

It was already dark, and the courtyard was full of villagers, but in the middle a circle had been kept open for a dance called the *Sanghyang*. The purpose of the dance was to protect people from the evil that could be stirred by practitioners of dark magic. It was said that, in the case of epidemics being brought from the outside, the dance could produce a counter-charm.[2] It was the local way of dealing with *nosferatus* of a sort, although the villagers did not call them that, of course. Practitioners of black magic could be anyone already inside a village; the idea of a spreader of evil had not been racially or sexually projected onto any marginalized group as it had been in Europe. The local name for the evil spirits was *leyak*, ordinary human by day but by nighttime an animal, a ball of fire, or a hungry head with only a stomach for consuming human embryos.[3]

Walter was taken to a corner where there was only a flickering oil lamp. Two girls kneeled in front of a fire into which white-robed priests tossed herbs while chanting formulas Walter did not understand. A large, brown, partly nude woman sang long, single tones. Walter thought the sounds surprising, a different scale that he had not heard anywhere else. The girls slowly fell into a trance. When one began speaking other sounds Walter found confusing, she was dressed quickly in golden anklets and a golden flower headdress, and then led away from the dark corner and into the circle surrounded by the crowd.

"Then began a strange thing," Walter would write the next day:

> Fantastically dressed men sat in small, closed circles — large, low energetic circles tightly nestled together, almost touching. Each group was a choir. The dancer stepped into the circle and entered a dead silence.

A distant, abstract voice began to sing a high and glassy indefinable melody, something so abstract I've never heard. It was not a person who was singing, but something deep from the underworld, and high out of the sky or from where I do not know, came the voice of a man of flesh and blood. The disembodied dancer walked around the circle, bent, twisted, rattled with the anklets scarcely audible.[4]

Suddenly, one of the male choirs started to sing, "a loud, unanimous, robust melody, a rising crescendo, then everything suddenly stopped. A stunning silence."

Then the song began very softly and, in-between, unexpected, unprepared, insane screams (all in the choir), then the melody increasing until it is somehow at one point trapping itself, remaining stuck. The last phrase is repeated again and again, slowly and forcefully. It reminded me of a Grammophone with the needle stuck at the same place. But it was getting faster and faster, louder and louder, until suddenly, after an infinite crescendo and accelerando, everything ended again with a high cry and the whole choir of thirty to forty men fell again with a fortissimo and then a rattle, a rhythmic *tsik-take, take-tsik* . . . Then everything broke again, again the indescribable, absent, distant grave voice began, pianissimo, accompanied by the rhythmic murmur of the chorus, again endless crescendos, again accelerandos, like a crackling shot.[5]

Walter was intrigued by how the men were swaying their bodies, "sitting so close together, persistently moving rhythmically."

They either swing, depending on the melody, to the right and left, shake as they would on a big tremor, or then throw themselves all together suddenly with a loud outcry to the left, then come back to the right, or after particularly intense increases of the song, often all the way back, so that as they sit so close together, they lie on each other, as a wide-open giant flower, or finally with an uncanny shout of "Hu," which sounds like a long, subterranean gong that slowly fades away in the distance, they closely lump all their heads together! Never in life have I seen or heard anything so suggestive.[6]

"Dear friend," he finished his letter the next day, "it was something strange I can never forget. They were bewitched, spellbound, and I would have liked to have screamed and danced with them!"

Walter would later write that in Bali he had climbed mountains, heard gamelans, "saw celebrations and church services," and walked away with the impression that "there is only God on this island."[7]

In that year of Vajiravudh's death, 1925, another event occurred that would help clarify intellectually and artistically the themes that were beginning to evolve between those who controlled the centers of the empires – along with their solidified definitions of body, desire, and gender – and those who lived on the colonized peripheries. Franz Roh, an art historian in Munich with clout in the appropriate imperial circles, published a book in which he explained aspects of art that he was beginning to track as well as to champion. Expressionism had arrived in Germany even prior to World War I. Its distortions of perspective and color evoked emotional *angst,* Edward Munch's *The Scream* of the 1890s being the model. By the 1920s, Expressionism had moved into popular embrace – Murnau's *Nosferatu* was a good example of that – but Roh believed he saw new approaches being developed by the postwar Weimar-era artists.

They had begun to focus, he suggested, on portraying objects realistically but also presented via a new perspective. "The new painting," Roh wrote, "separates itself from Expressionism *by means of its objects* . . . [The] fantastic dreamscape has completely vanished and our real world re-emerges before our eyes, bathed in the clarity of a new day . . . We are offered a new style that is thoroughly of this world, that celebrates the mundane."[8]

But, he added, "the new art does not restore objectivity by using all sensory potential *in the same way.*" In particular, it was not a return to the nineteenth-century naturalism that had pretended to portray objects as if they were being mechanically or empirically photographed. Instead, Roh wrote, what the new style "principally evokes is a most prolific and detailed *tactile feeling.*" This feeling that a painting was an experience of *touching* as well as *seeing,* Roh said, "almost always manifests itself in miniature form," the artist's elaborately detailed variations, rather than focusing on expanse.

In one of his most famous statements, Roh explained that "the extent to which the miniature can express maximum power *all by itself* can be explained by thinking of the greatest spectacle that nature offers us, a sight that contains the smallest units, almost simple points placed on the prodigious surface width of the picture: *the spectacle of the starry sky, through which we experience infinity.*"[9]

"The 'monumental' man," he explained, "piles up shapes in large groups while the 'microscopic' one establishes the largest possible number of subdivisions." They were two opposite poles each likely to be overdone, the monumental in danger of becoming a caricature of itself because of its "emphatic presentation" of categories and "its statuesque turgidity"; the miniature likely to plunge thoughts into "tedious minutia that scatter and confuse our attention." The opposite poles had to be held in creative tension, which, Roh suggested, was precisely what the new artists were doing.[10]

To name the new art, Roh chose a term that had been coined a century earlier by a philosopher of German idealism, Novalis, who had postulated that two types of prophets could exist outside of "enlightened" or established doctrines: a magical idealist and a magical realist.[11] Novalis himself had been more interested in the idealists. The new art, Roh suggested, was instead "magical realism."

Among its practitioners, Roh suggested, was the young artist Walter Spies.

In his book, Roh would reproduce three examples of Walter's pre-Indies art: the Romeo and Juliet *Farewell,* painted after Walter had left his lover Hans; *The Carousel*, painted while living with Murnau at Grunewald; and *Bashkir Shepherd*, completed just before he left Germany. The last showed a male shepherd tending two cows with a forest of miniature-needled trees glistening behind him. It was the fact that the leaves were rendered in such detail of light and shadow that made them seem radiant and tactile.

Roh had noticed and praised Walter's painting strategy even while the young artist was still in Berlin. Walter had written to the professor in September 1922: "Mr. Roh, you overwhelm me with splendor that I do not deserve."[12]

After he traveled to Bali, Walter had written to Roh that he did not have "the slightest desire to go back to Europe" but would instead soon move to the island to "be alone with the beautiful people there." He would study the gamelan music and the dances that accompanied them, he told Roh. As for future paintings, he said, "I'm actually doing very little."[13]

That latter statement apparently prompted Roh to express concern about the impact that life in the Dutch East Indies could have on Walter. The notion that tropical climates led to a degeneration of the European male's desire to work was well established in colonial thinking.[14] Roh sent along a copy of his book and his concerns in his next correspondence.

Walter was ecstatic at having been included in the book:

> What you write about the pictures is so correct, so correct, and I feel as if I am finally hearing what I have long awaited! It is an infinitely encouraging confirmation of my own approach . . . I admire the way you know how to make it clear . . . A friend of mine, who stood helpless and very stupid in front of some of my work, was all converted and enthusiastic after reading your book. It almost borders on magic![15]

By the late twentieth century, when Roh's term "magical realism" had begun to be applied more to literature than to art, scholars would recognize that the particular techniques of "magical realism" provided communication strategies for telling the stories of those in the colonial world who had been left on the margins by the narratives of progress favored by imperial storytellers. Among those techniques would be the presentation of different times as cyclical or as overlapping, treating cause and effect as subjective imaginations rather than as linear flows, and approaching the magical and the mundane as one and the same. These techniques would become the core of magical realism's strategic dissent from what was being presented as European values and as the monumental orderly categories within which thought was to be organized — solidified categories like homosexuality and heterosexuality, or masculine and feminine.[16]

Stephen Slemon, a scholar of magico-real techniques, would eventually argue that "a battle between two oppositional systems takes place, each working toward the creation of a different type of . . . world from the other." Because the ground rules of those two worlds were incompatible, he would suggest, neither could come fully into being in the particular art or the particular social geography of "real" life. Instead, he wrote, "Each remains suspended, locked in a continuous dialectic with the 'other,' a situation which creates disjunction within each of the separate discursive systems, rending them with gaps, absences, and silences."[17]

Magical reality, as a technique of communication and resistance, did not insist that one hierarchy be replaced with another. Both semantics existed together. The impact, as described by Lois Parkinson Zamora and Wendy Faris, two other scholars of magical realism, would be that "mind and body, spirit and matter, life and death, real and imaginary, self and the other, male and female: these are boundaries to be erased, transgressed, blurred, brought together, or otherwise fundamentally refashioned in magical realist texts."[18]

Bodies, desires, and genders would be revealed both as solid as the monumental categories proposed and as fluid as miniaturization suggested.

Of Roh's apparent concern that Walter's move to Bali might reflect some sort of sacrifice of painting — Roh may have used the word "paralysis" — Walter answered: "I have to quickly tell you that my most recent work is, in every respect, healthy and manly, much more so than my older work! It is not Java as a country or the Javanese who are to blame for my 'paralysis.'" Walter argued that Europeans were the problem. "There is nothing so crippling as putting yourself in front of the limp, flat, uncultivated Europeans here. It's a morass of people, inescapably dismal! The strongest, best ideas are crushed mercilessly here by sweetly crude and boorish snobs!"

> I beg you, dear Mr. Roh, do not think that the land and the local people could affect me badly in any way. The passivity and apparent indolence of the Javanese is nothing but the strongest concentration and uprightness. To the Balinese still come the demonic and the truth of life. God, the devil, the world and I, everything is there![19]

In early colonial representations, Bali had not been seen as paradise. The natives had been characterized as savages likely to run *amok*, a word the Dutch picked up in Malaya and Java. It described a peculiarity of males who, tranquil one moment, would suddenly seize a weapon and then surge into a frenzy trying to kill themselves or others. Some said it was due to possession by the evil spirits lurking on the island. Others attributed it to ideals of male honor, since women seldom went *amok*. It was the opposite of Laocoönian self-discipline that Winckelmann had celebrated as an ideal of European masculinity. The Dutch East India Company had even banned taking Balinese men as slaves because of the *amok* tendency.[20]

Geography also made Bali unattractive. Two volcanoes split the land, one rising more than 5,600 feet and the other a cloud-capturing 10,300 feet. They sloped southward and formed an amphitheater of volcano-enriched soil that supported one of the densest populations in the world. It was an ideal rice bowl sewn out of a lacework of terraces and irrigation ditches capturing rainwater moving downward. The large population and rich land should have been ideal for Dutch traders, but the puzzle was that dangerous coral reefs and a treacherous surf protected the south coast where the amphitheater ended. Those beaches had no natural harbors. The best trade routes between the Indies and China lay on the north side of Bali. But that meant trade had to climb over the volcanoes. Population and rice on one side, shipping routes on the other, two volcanoes in between meant colonial frustration. Coming straight east from Java was no help either. Streams coursed down the volcanoes and etched deep north-south canyons difficult to cross. Traditional Balinese politics had splintered along those north-south lines with different kingdoms either anchored along the beaches or stretching vertically up the volcano slopes between the streams. Thus, moving goods east-west meant building countless bridges and winding roads as well as mollifying many kings and village heads.

Having no central trade partner and only a fragmented *amok*-prone labor force available to press into permanent slavery or temporary corvée, the pragmatic Dutch had first opted for limited contact, preferring to create plantations on Java.

But there was one attraction. At the time of the first Dutch contact in 1597, the Netherlands was an infant nation less than twenty-five years old, a union of Calvinist provinces against the Spanish Catholic kings. Cornelius de Houtman, the Dutch captain who initially encountered Bali, knew two religious enemies: the Catholics and the Muslims. Along the coasts of Sumatra and Java, he pragmatically traded with the Islamic sultans to boost Dutch fortunes against the Catholics in Europe. Reaching Bali, he discovered what he imagined to be an island that might provide a two-for-one bonus: trade plus symbol. Unlike Muslim Java, he reported, Bali was a "heathen" kingdom, Hindu-influenced by ancient empires – a possible Calvinistic convert to serve as a barrier against Islam. An embryo of an idea was born: Among all those 17,000 pebble- and giant-sized islands in what would eventually be the Dutch East Indies, Bali was different.[21]

By the late 1800s, the Dutch had begun to move their colonizing across the mile-and-a-half wide channel that separated Java and Bali, seizing one kingdom at a time. The final collapse had come in 1908, just seventeen years before Walter first visited. The last royal court's male warriors, women, and children had marched straight into Dutch weapons fire. For the Balinese men, it had been a dignified death and a necessary magical battle of transformation. To the Dutchmen, it was an almost incomprehensible mass suicide, and, having been the complicit executioners, they immediately set about trying to find ways to rationalize their conquest by evolving a colonial policy that would seem compassionate to the other European empires. Looking civilized, as it turned out, was not just important at the other end of the Southeast Asian arc where Chulalongkorn ruled Siam but was important to the Dutch colonizers too.

Six years after the bloodbath, the Dutch steamship line KPM, which until then had mostly been transporting pigs from Hindu Bali to pork-loving Chinese on Java, issued a set of tourist brochures. Bali, the brochures suggested, was now a Garden of Eden, an island that one could leave only with "a sigh of regret."[22] Dutch administrators, in their writings sent back to The Hague, also laid the foundation for a new image. Rather than being a savage island, Bali was now a cultural treasure house of complex laws, economic relations based on irrigation commitments, unique musical and artistic traditions, and particularized social and gender relations. The Dutch adopted a dual legal system: one set of *adat* laws for the natives based on supposed traditions, another set for the Europeans visiting the island.

Four years after the Dutch had smashed the last Balinese kingdom, a young German medical officer named Gregor Krause arrived at Bangli, a village just northeast of Ubud. He had with him a camera. By the time he left seventeen months later, he had taken more than 4,000 photographs, about 400 of which he eventually published in 1920 in Germany, the same year that *The Cabinet of Dr. Caligari* was being premiered in Berlin. His two volumes, *Bali,* were effusive about this particular people living on the periphery of empire. Unlike what the British and Americans had written of the Siamese, Krause proposed, "The Balinese are inconceivably beautiful. Everything is beautiful, perfectly beautiful – the bodies, the clothes, the gait, every posture, every movement."[23]

Krause's women were often bare breasted, and that is what has drawn most notice from scholars who comment on how he influenced voyeuristic attitudes toward Bali. He wrote that the women had "strikingly slim" hips and "long, smooth black hair" and noted that they bathed naked, "not neglecting to massage every muscle and joint."[24]

But Krause also took striking photographs of males clad only in their sarongs or, in some cases, bathing nude beneath flows from fountains or river streams. One such photograph showed a male in his late teens or twenties crouched nude on a rock in front of a waterfall, facing the camera with his legs wide and holding his left hand protectively across his groin. Another showed a young Balinese male of high caste sitting in his sarong, head turned and high, in a pose almost identical to the one Walter would later use for *Hamid*. Still another dreamy, silver-toned print portrayed a slender, naked Balinese boy bent over washing his feet. Krause's men did not have the bulging muscularity of the new Nazi renditions of Winckelmann's Greek statutes. Instead, they were lean, toned, and confident.[25] In all likelihood, Walter had seen Krause's book either in Berlin or in Amsterdam at the Dutch Colonial Museum.

Krause's book signaled the impact that technological changes in photography were having. In the past, subjects had had to agree to stand still for bulky daguerreotypes, but Krause had carried a lightweight camera. He wrote, "I took the photographs with a small camera in such a way that nobody even noticed that I was taking them."[26] Europeans had given themselves permission to freeze a moment in the life of a colonial man or woman who was either clothed or naked and then to distribute that image throughout the world – with or without that person's permission. Although the Balinese were not intentional exhibitionists when they bathed nude in rivers, once Krause's book circulated, the Germans and the Dutch became romantic voyeurs, and from that erotic stance of the gaze would come their subsequent politics.

Adrian Vickers, an Australian historian of the island, noted that "the view underlying all these policies was that the natives were caught in some kind of primitive or less advanced stage of development, and so had to be 'protected' and preserved from the destructive effects of the twentieth century."[27] The Dutch policy would eventually get a name in 1917, when Jan Smuts, a future prime minister in Dutch-run South Africa, would coin the label *apartheid*. It was a colonial approach quite different from that being promoted at the same time at the other end of the Southeast Asian arc in Siam, where Vajiravudh had been trying to balance the expectations of "civilized" gender customs and laws with Siamese traditions. The Siamese had been berated for their sparse clothing, not celebrated for it, and European as well as the Siamese monarchy were pursuing change, not preservation.[28]

By August 1927, two years after visiting Bali, Walter was ready to move there. In Germany that same month, the Nazi Party gathered its first major rally at Nuremburg. Tens of thousands of the party's supporters staged a spectacular torchlight march and then attended daytime rituals marked with flames and trumpets and swastika banners. Adolf Hitler proclaimed that the power of Germany lay in the nation's purified blood and in its Winckelmann-sculpted men willing to be warriors for the sake of the new empire he planned to build.

"We are," he told the crowd, "marching already!"[29]

Once Walter had relocated to Sukawati's Ubud, he settled into a small cottage that leaked miserably in the heavy Balinese rain. It was a radical shift from his princely quarters at Kraton. Nevertheless, he wrote to his mother: "I am so happy to see no Europeans and to not hear the stupid talk! It goes with me how it always goes with me, endlessly good. I am over- and overjoyed."[30]

In Bali, Walter began to explore the possibilities of male bodies and desires freed from those being constructed by Hitler for imperial conquest. He would never become explicitly sexual about the male body itself. There would be no Krause-style males crouching and covering their genitals. One historian would write that Walter's "Balinese paintings are not overtly homoerotic" but rather "magico-realist landscapes of fishermen in boats, hunters stalking deer or, in his most often used theme, a peasant leading an ox, dwarfed by rice paddies, palm trees and mountains."[31]

One of Walter's earliest sketches in Ubud was of a mask carver titled *Ida Bagus Ketut Gelodog*.[32] In the head-and-shoulders drawing, some of the wildness of his discovery of Asian men that he had expressed in *Hamid* now gave way to a more cultivated sense of Asian male harmony and proportion. Gone was the wild bush of black hair. Instead, the young man's hair was now safely hidden beneath a handkerchief tied in front. The eyebrows were no longer as bushy or painted as the sharp horizontal ledges that had appeared on *Hamid*. Instead, they curved delicately above much more detailed oval eyes. The eyes themselves, instead of looking restlessly over the right shoulder, now gazed serenely downward. The *Gelodog* male presented more rest and contemplation, almost like the head of a Buddha statue.

Walter almost immediately complemented *Gelodog* with another sketch. Titled *Four Young Balinese with Fighting Cocks*, it became one of his most famous, most explicitly erotic male sketches – at least metaphorically.[33] In it, four lithe young Balinese men, nude except for loose cloths about their waists, sit on the ground with their fighting roosters, an ordinary social scene in Bali where cockfights were important rituals of masculinity.[34]

Walter decided not to render the moments of the cockfights themselves, although that approach would have been the logical choice for depicting male friendships built upon bloody contests. Instead, he sketched the moment of the social, more homoerotic circles of male friendship that could be witnessed in public. The mostly nude men, all of whom seem to be in their late teens or twenties, talk while all but one of their cocks wait patiently inside cages. The most prominent male in the circle holds his rooster outside of the cage, gently displaying it in front of his opened, crouched legs – an image that reversed Krause's portrayal of a young male hiding his genitals but did so metaphorically.

Each of the four figures in the circle emphasizes a different fragment of his body, almost as if Walter intended an anatomical study of the Asian male body from varying perspectives. Two sit with their backs to the viewer showing the flat planes of their slightly defined shoulder muscles held together by deep spinal curves. On the male closest to the viewer, Walter drew the arc into the young man's buttocks, which, unlike those of the others in the sketch, is exposed, split by a thong-like strip of cloth.

The circle's dominant male, the one facing the viewer and holding the cock, has a highly accented, horizontal ridge for a collarbone – an echo of *Hamid* – and sharply angled arms that give him a *contrapossto*-style dynamism even as he rests on the ground. Another male has his chest fully exposed. His pectoral muscles are outlined, his stomach softened rather than rippled.

Walter had represented Balinese men as lines and curves, not ellipses.

The first oil painting Walter made in Bali also suggests his evolving understanding of men and masculinity. *Banyan with Two Young Balinese* shows two males dwarfed by curving banyan tree roots that form a dense maze around them. Light streaks through the center of what otherwise is a dark forest with a small pale-golden pool. One man stands with his back to the viewer; Walter seemed more curious about the outlines of the more vulnerable male back rather than the Winckelmann emphasis on the male chest. The other male crouches. The natural swaying curves of the men's backs parallels the curves of the tropical palms and hanging banyan roots of the natural landscape. Walter drew both young men as long, slender, and androgynous, identifiable as male mostly because of the lack of any identifiable female characteristics such as breasts or rounded legs. He portrayed both in sarongs that leave their legs and torsos bare except for the wraps on their hair. Walter highlighted very subtle bicep and shoulder muscles on the standing figure and made his long horizontal collarbone an echo of *Hamid*. The young male stands with one leg slightly bent, his weight resting on the other, although not in a *contrapossto* style suggesting action. Instead, his hip thrusts slightly to the side and his knees touch as he angles his arms to untie his head wrap in what can be read as a slow, seductive but comfortable undressing with his companion. The two are posed much as female nudes in Europe were – amid trees and water – and so they contain what to the European eye would be visual codes of femininity. The standing youth in particular seems meant to be gazed at, an object of a viewer's desire. But by painting miniature highlights on his thighs and calves as well as on his shoulders and bent arms, Walter created edges that also gave him a distinctly male body, slowly moving in harmony with the light, like a dancer frozen on an icy pond.

Once again, he avoided plating the two with any Winckelmann-style muscles.

The representation was what could be called an orientalist stereotype of "delicate, lotus-eyed boys." But, viewed as a response to the Nazi-driven images of manhood sweeping his homeland, Walter's drawings offered a queering dissent. He seemed to be working on a subversive set of questions about how Greek classical representations of manhood had degenerated into Aryan male musculature and fears of racially different *nosferatus*. His male bodies are clearly delineated in their emphatic lines, but the Expressionistic-influenced light and shadow move fluidly around them. Male gazes and desires merge into landscapes and fraternal associations with other men; gender becomes more ambiguous, contest out of the question.

For Walter, the male body was less a column of power than an aesthetic conduit of magic.

Two years after moving to Bali, Walter began work on the painting he would call *Balinese Legend*. This time, he drew on a Balinese myth about a male duel but painted in such a way as to question the way moral duels between men had degenerated into a simple, unquestioning crusade for imperial supremacy.[35]

For *Balinese Legend*, Walter dropped the realistic sketches of men he had made of *Hamid* or *Gelodog* or of the four Balinese men with their fighting cocks, in which he had explicitly avoided portraying the cock duel itself. First he drew the natural landscape with what by then was becoming his signature style: bursts of light on miniature leaves and meandering lines. He painted a quiet stream curving past an open field and through mountains. Beyond lay a hazily visible volcano. Into this bucolic paradise, he then inserted a contrasting story. If the painting were viewed all at once – as most paintings were – the story seemed to be of a contest unfolding between two pairs of men on horses, a fifth having lost his seating in the stream and swimming to escape. Each male body is oddly attenuated, with extremely long slender limbs and torsos but radically shortened legs, almost like praying mantises with their forearms extended and their legs tucked out of sight. The men wear only red or blue cloths wrapped about their waists.

As he painted, Walter partly reversed the background and foreground perspectives so that smaller figures – the escaping swimmer and one man about to spear another on horseback –appear in front rather than to the rear in the more traditional perspective. He put the more dominant males in the center of the picture, challenging the Western notion of how parallel lines should converge in a painting to convey a sense of "realistic" distance. Instead of a smooth convergence toward a vanishing point where everything supposedly more distant would be smaller, Walter painted his perspectives as a diamond, tight and small at the front, enlarging in the middle, then returning to a "normal" convergence at the top of the canvas. It is as if one narrative explodes right into the middle of another.

In the dominant duel at the center, Walter painted the moment when a fierce yet boyish warrior dressed only in his red loincloth drives his horse over the neck of his opponent's horse, begins to spear the other young man, and then forces him to tumble backward from his horse. The falling man wears only a blue cloth. The spear point has not entered the young opponent's body – true to the form of the Balinese male trance dance in which men could be struck but not penetrated. Yet blood has already begun to flow from above the man's navel even though the spear has not entered. Walter drew the boy's face as if he was surprised by the yet-to-happen blow. The apparent victor rides a white horse; the apparent loser, a brown one.

Below, in the smaller duel, a very similarly drawn man on a white horse – but wearing a blue cloth – drives his opponent on a brown horse into the stream.

Because of the diamond-shaped perspective, the painting can be seen all at once as a single duel involving five men. But "heard" as music unfolding over time, it can be experienced as different rhythms overlapping within the same canvas –

that magico-real technique of holding oppositional narratives in tension, though not in hierarchy. The dominant duel at the center could be the effect of the same blue-clothed man's action below. Or perhaps it is the red-clothed warrior's actions at the center that would lead to the effects below. Or perhaps it is a contest taking place within one man only, constantly chasing and trying to slay his own fear of his mirrored image.

The three techniques of magical realism are all present: time overlapping, cause and effect as subjective perspective rather than linear connections, magic penetrating the ordinary moment. These are male bodies living a duel of oppositional narratives within a magico-realistic paradise.

In his letters, Walter termed the vision of men and landscapes and duels that he had painted in *Balinese Legend* as something "strange and unusual." He described it as having "something cruel and gruesome about it but nevertheless in an eerily cheerful atmosphere."

He also called it one of the best works he had created.[36]

This exploration of male bodies through unbounded, multiple-exposure panels and shifts of normal figure size and viewer perspective would continue to mature in Walter's later paintings. In another, completed in 1932 at the end of his first five years in Bali, Walter again subversively explored the issue of manhood. In a very non-orientalist fashion, he now assigned his "delicate, lotus-eyed, barefoot boys" roles of male-male penetration.

In *The Deerhunt*[37] he painted the loin-clothed, lined and curved form of the young Balinese male sitting symbolically at the margin of the canvas. Unlike *Hamid*, the male's chest now included nipples and a finely ribbed torso. Walter drew him aiming a long, phallic arrow across his groin into the center of the canvas into a watery opening that was magically sky, lake, and human body. Nothing soft or effeminate marks the archer, in contrast to the figures in the banyan oasis. Walter left no doubt about the penetrative potency of the Asian male arrow. But unlike Michelangelo's "David," whose young muscular male armed with a slingshot seemed to exist in a world of action, Walter's young Asian hunter emerges from within a dreamy world of warm colors and rippling water.

Different panels border the central watery diamond into which the arrow is aimed. A panel on each side is shaped like a rump, the left one portraying a deer after it is pierced and lies dying, and the right one a stag after it is born as a free, antlerless buck. Between the two, another panel shows the deer about to be shot. Walter elected to portray a stag that was not native to Bali but rather appeared more like a Siberian roebuck common to the Ural Mountains. As is true of the sketch of *Four Young Balinese with Fighting Cocks*, the painting is erotically suggestive and metaphorical but not photographically explicit: a male trope of penetration followed by rebirth, the Balinese archer penetrating a symbol of Caucasian manhood.

Walter seemed to be inviting a viewer to reflect upon the nature of manhood and masculinity, a man at the margins piercing a male symbol from the center. His mentor Murnau had used that same theme in *Nosferatu* with Orlock and Hutter. But Walter's narrative differed in its outcome.

In Walter's painting, the duel and the penetration had become an optimistic metamorphosis both in *Balinese Legend* and in *The Deerhunt*, a penetration that is life-resurrecting, not life-taking like a vampire confronting the morning dawn. It was to be embraced, not feared.

7
Men of the Dance

The European film director Victor Baron von Plessen arrived in Bali in 1931 to film a movie based in the South Pacific, a project Friedrich Murnau had hoped to undertake with Walter but had instead produced in Tahiti. Murnau's film, *Tabu*, celebrated both Polynesian paradise and Polynesian men, drawing on the customary Romeo and Juliet tragic romance. For Walter, von Plessen would provide the more intricate opportunity he needed to fuse celluloid and real life in a way that his hero Scriabin had sought, using not only light on a canvas but also blending sound and rhythm on the movie screen and then propelling those sounds and rhythm into an actual cultural ritual.

Walter had assisted on one earlier film about Bali, alternatively titled *Goona Goona*, and *The Kris*, and *Love Powder*. For that movie, Walter had found local actors and had recommended to the producer what he called "a marvelous simple story."[1] He had suggested the idea of a male duel between a Balinese prince and a Balinese peasant fighting for the same woman. At one level, it was a Hollywood-style plot about what appeared to be a reinforcement of the triple supremacy: a story about a romantic, heterosexual love triangle. But within that "marvelous simple story," as he called it, Walter had shaded numerous coded comments about conflicts among the various attempts to solidify a single type of male body, desire, or gender.

In the movie, his Westernized Balinese prince, clothed in both European coat and Balinese sarong, returns to the island and descends from a boat in a scene that directly recalled the way Murnau had positioned his own *nosferatu* entering the unsuspecting German village. The prince then falls in love with a peasant woman, Dasnee, and seeks to break his own prearranged marriage to another woman. His elders warn him that ideas of romance are "mad notions" from Europe, especially since Dasnee herself is already engaged – via arranged marriage – to the peasant male Wyan, the most muscular Winckelmann-style Asian male Walter would ever place into any of his images. An especially lengthy camera shot pans slowly across Wyan's elliptical pectoral muscles, bulging arms, and tight abdominals as he works in a rice field – a signal to a European audience trained in Winckelmann-style images that Wyan should be considered the male who is morally superior to the prince. In the contest that unfolds between the prince and Wyan, it is the Winckelmann-style Asian peasant who eventually triumphs over the European-influenced *nosferatu*.

But something is awry in Walter's story. Wyan himself treats Dasnee more like property than with feelings of romantic love. He assumes she belongs to him like a slave. The romantic prince is no hero either. He has Dasnee drugged with a love potion, the *goona goona*, and then implicitly rapes her.

Walter had insured that neither of the two male characters turned out to be completely satisfying. He also avoided any happy ending. Wyan stabs and kills the prince while he is vulnerably bathing in a stream, suggestively nude. Then Wyan himself is stabbed with the same *kris* by the prince's father, the final execution occurring in an erotic crucifixion with Wyan's arms stretched Christlike and the camera focused tightly on his bare chest so as to make him appear nude, just as the prince was.[2]

If *Goona Goona* had left a picture of manhood tortured, the new movie Walter suggested to von Plessen would offer a possible antidote.

For the plot of what would be called *Island of Demons*, Walter advised von Plessen to choose the central Balinese myth about the cyclic battle between good and evil. Paradise would be presented not as a salvific goal to be achieved, as in Hitler's notion of a Third Reich, or even as a place to be savored. Rather, paradise itself would become an aesthetic performance caught in tension between ideas of order and of unpredictable surprise. In the Balinese myth, neither good nor evil ever fully triumphed – a contrast to the messianic salvation myths in which good was supposed to ultimately win and human history be transformed.

The Balinese had personified the conflict as a fight between a scraggly witch named Rangda, and the community – a happy aesthetic village – that would ultimately have to turn to the leader of the forces of good, the Barong, for protection. Rangda sometimes worked alone or brought along her army, the *leyaks*.[3]

Into the plotline of the conflict between Rangda and the aesthetic state, Walter and von Plessen inserted the customary heterosexual love story about two peasants who lived in the village that was being disrupted. But the lavishness of the film imagery would be saved for the scenes that most interested Walter: rice terrace reflections of the sky, laboring male bodies in the fields, and what would become Walter's best-known expression of male ritual. He still remembered that dance that had haunted him ever since he had first traveled in Bali, the one of men and chants that he had described as "something strange I can never forget," and had said of it, "never in life have I seen or heard anything so suggestive."[4]

What happened varied from village to village and trance to trance. In some presentations, it was not a real "dance" at all but more of a communal exorcism aimed at protecting the Balinese against the *leyaks*. The *leyaks*, in response, would always try to disrupt the dance, so that any presentation was filled with tensions about what might come to pass as the dance itself unfolded. Sometimes the young dancers, called *sanghyang*, fell backwards into the arms of attendants or put their

Figure 7.1   Kecak Dance
Courtesy of Tropenmuseum of the Royal Tropical Institute, Wikicommons

hands into fiery embers. They might be thrust onto the shoulders of men, where they balanced as each of their extended fingers explored differently stitched planes of space. Sometimes boys in trances rode bamboo sticks between their legs with puppet horse heads attached to the front and tails to the back, the boys with their phallic stick projections considered both holy – and taboo.[5]

But there were commonalities: flaming torches, endless chanting by circles of boys and men, clouds of incense, sudden breaks in the sound, notes wavering and sliding up, a solitary voice spontaneously crackling above the group, arms broken into angled lines, thin fingers splayed in skeletal staccatos. In the haze of light and the blurring and yet distinct sharpness of every note, the entire village vanished into an odd liminal medium of monotonous repetitive miniature units.

Walter had found what Scriabin had suggested: an aesthetic ritual that fused sound, light, and rhythm in a transformation that occurred not only as art but also as real life.

For the movie, Walter drove from his home along the Tchampuan River east to the little village of Bedulu. There, it was said, a boy *sanghyang* had once fallen into a trance while simply talking to other boys in the village. He had immediately taken his bamboo stick horse from a nearby temple altar to chase *leyaks* away from the village. But the *leyaks* had had their revenge. They had lured him into a cemetery – an unclean space for the tabooed boy – and a few days later he had died.[6]

In Bedulu, Walter knew, lived a talented male dancer who specialized in a performance called the *Baris,* in which a single male danced the choreography of a warrior preparing for battle. His name was I Wayan Limbak. No one really knew how old he was. In fact, no one knew how old any Balinese man was, since the Balinese did not keep track of time like the Europeans. However, Walter and Limbak were probably about the same age, Walter then thirty-five and Limbak somewhere between his late twenties and mid-thirties, too old to cast as a boy *sanghyang.*[7] Walter had come up with a new idea for symbolically extending the power of the *sanghyang* against what, given conditions in Europe, must have seemed the global triumph of the *leyak* and their *Rangda* leader. In von Plessen's film — which was destined for European audiences -- Walter would insert a *Baris* warrior into an all-male chorus chanting "cak-cak," and the dance would come to be known as the *kecak.*

Bedulu's village elders had apparently been thinking similarly about the changes. To this day, scholars are unclear about exactly who had the idea, the Balinese or Walter.[8]

Years afterward, Walter would describe what emerged in the *kecak* in a book he co-authored with Beryl de Zoete, *Dance and Drama in Bali.* The two would paint the dance as an act of magical, fraternal manhood, rich with the sounds and rhythms of male bodies streaming, circling, erecting, pressing, spiraling, heaving, sinking, voices piercing and wailing against a chorus of "tjak-a-tjak," shuddering, trembling, fingers sparking, plunging, throbbing, sound curdling, all like "the full-blown flower of a volcano."[9]

Night has fallen, the two wrote, and . . .

> Down the lanes to the temple men are streaming, calling to one another out of the darkness, mustering in the temple-court. Already the circles are forming, one within another, five or six circles of crouching bodies, a hundred and fifty men under the flickering light of a great branching wooden torch. All sounds die away, there is silence and a feeling of suspense. Suddenly the motionless bodies grow tense, awaiting a signal. With a series of short cries, they lift themselves, then sink with a hissing sound of outgoing breath. They intone a rhythm, menacing, intense, all exactly together; then drop and muffle it, press it down into the dark hole between their crowded heads. They begin to sway; low inarticulate sounds break from them; their bodies gleam in the flickering flame, their eyes half close in dreaming faces. A slow chant rises from a single voice in their midst, a child's high-pitched wailing voice. The swaying grows and grows till suddenly the heaving mass bursts open with a roar, like a crater in eruption scattering fragments. Circle upon circle they fall backwards, the full-blown flower of a volcano.[10]

The dance has begun. There is another wave of sound, light, and body movement:

> Each new phrase begins with a stronger impulse of breath, as they
> sway from side to side with restlessly twining fingers. Suddenly
> they shoot up all together and sit erect with fingers spread, piercing
> the air like rays darting out of a thicket of thorny branches. Light
> plays on their stretching fingers so that these fingers themselves
> seem like flying sparks.[11]

This male dance with its thrusting and crackling and throbbing and sparking and splayed fingers and multiple layers of sound and light and bodies seemed as if it could go on and on and on all night. At a point, though, Walter's choreographed new *kecak* changes so that the actual narrative, now newly embedded in what had once been simply a trance-inducing chorus for the *sanghyangs*, can progress. Two males rise from the circles into the light and from that point on, the previously unified men become two groups locked in a duel between good and evil. In Walter's version, this was the point at which Limbak revealed himself as both a *sanghyang* and a *Baris*-style solo warrior.

Significantly, Limbak displayed not in the elaborately heavy *Baris* warrior costume but was nude except for a short *kain*, a cloth caught between his legs. Walter had stripped the warrior of his clothes to reveal the Asian male flesh in ecstatic and erotic movement.

Although the new *kecak* included an elaborate storyline, Walter and de Zoete wrote in their book that the plot was actually beside the point — merely one of many about good versus evil. Sounding almost like Scriabin intent on transforming or transcending stories through a fusion of sound, light, and rhythm, they added:

> To seek a consecutive theme in the wandering voices, the cracked
> strings and wailing cries, the various fragments of solo which
> occur . . . is a vain quest. It is like trying to find a meaning for the
> intricacy of melody, harmony, and rhythm in a musical symphony
> . . . the sound exists for itself . . . and is complete in itself.[12]

The purpose of this display of manhood was instead to forge a magical reality:

> The cries, the crowding, lifted hands, the devouring of single
> figures, the broken lines of melody bewildering to *boetas*
> [demons] who can only move straight ahead, all enhance the
> exorcistic effect. The words are less words than power-giving
> sounds, reiterated bird-like cries, lonely wailing voices, hoarse
> ejaculations, murmured bouts of fierce dialogue.[13]

Walter and the village of Bedulu seemed to have penetrated a truth about homoerotic relationships between men: that at the center of a male-oriented *culture* is not so much the behavior of men simply having duels or sex with other men. At the center is an exorcistic power in the act of men *dancing* with men and doing so in a highly eroticized arena of flashing lights, pounding repetitive sounds, and staccato movements of arms and legs. If Hitler had his ideal of a racially pure Winckelmann male in service to a salvific Third Reich, the *kecak* would be Walter's answer — built upon a visual explosion of Asian male flesh intended to protect the aesthetic village, the movements of an exorcism creating a "tremendous mood" of male unity, operating to "drive out evil as by an incantation."

There would be one historical irony. *Island of Demons* was a silent film. Europeans would see the visual impact of male flesh in a magico-realistic setting. But they would not actually hear the famous "cak-cak" incantation intended to befuddle evil with its multiple broken lines of sound. In Germany the audiences would be listening to a symphonic score added in the post-production phase by Wolfgang Zeller, the man who had become one of the most famous of German film composers and who would a few years into the future be musically scoring the Nazi's notorious anti-Semitic propaganda film, *Jud Suess*.[14]

Such were the oppositional narratives within which Walter lived.

One day, when Walter had been invited to a colonial banquet with several European friends, the servants accidentally tended to the person to his left first and then to the person on his right, skipping him entirely. He turned to one of his companions, and, as she would later recall, jokingly remarked: "It seems quite natural that I should be overlooked. I do not *feel* myself. It often seems to me that I am not there at all."[15]

It was not that Walter was alone. He knew many people. As tourism built on Bali and as his own fame grew in Europe, he became a tourist attraction himself. The well-known stayed at guesthouses he steadily added to his home at Tchampuan: Barbara Hutton, the heir to the Woolworth fortune, who gave him a Leica camera; Vicki Baum, a novelist who would include him as a character in her book about Bali; Charlie Chaplin, the actor and movie director; Margaret Mead, the anthropologist; Noel Coward, the playwright. Historian Adrian Vickers has written: "Single-handedly Spies made Ubud the alternative area for genteel tourism, the center of an artistic life."[16] Walter also counted as friends the Americans and Europeans that became his neighbors: the artist Rudolf Bonnet, the musicologist Colin McPhee, McPhee's anthropologist wife, Jane Belo. Dutch bureaucrats were friends too, most prominently Roelof Goris and archeologist Willem Stutterheim, the two men who led the Dutch study of antiquities on Bali.

Yet a friend remembered that Walter had once "sighed and exclaimed he wished he would meet a person whom he could revere with all his soul."[17]

Even if romance seemed improbable for a gay man living on Bali, Walter did forge a few deep friendships. In spring 1930, while traveling on a small ferry from

Surabaya, he met Rose and Miguel Covarrubias, the latter a Mexican painter and writer. Rose seemed fascinated by his garden in which, she would write, there were "orchids that looked like scorpions" and a veritable zoo of monkeys and flying foxes. The three traveled by outrigger to the west end of the island, camped, and frequented markets where she and Walter indulged in discoveries of delicacies – ferns, ants, bees. She thought him sometimes unhappy but only momentarily, until he could hear another gamelan playing. Sometimes, he would be cross until he could go to his studio and hide. Rose recalled, "None of us ever saw him place a brush on canvas." He always came out, she said, "seemingly relieved of a great task."[18]

Walter had also maintained his relationship with Murnau. Walter had often sent him paintings, and to an unknown extent, Murnau had helped bankroll Walter's dreams in the Indies. In March 1931, as *Tabu* was about to premiere in New York and Murnau was planning to return from the United States to Germany, he was killed in a car crash near Los Angeles.[19] Writing to his mother a few weeks later, Walter seemed resigned to the loss, the past possibilities of romance with the director now just a memory. "Did you hear the terrible message of Murnau's death? . . . Terrible, terrible! . . ."[20]

It seems easy to consider Walter an escapist, a dilettante simply living in and painting a version of paradise for men, like him, who sought out the margins of empires rather than their centers. But Joseph Chytry, a historian who has studied the Western idea of the aesthetic state and of the relationship of that poetic ideal to actual politics, held a different view. Chytry argued that Walter was not interested in the classical sense of beauty that such escapists sought, but in understanding the non-European criteria being used for an aesthetic life. "For Spies," he wrote, "this change implied jettisoning standard European notions of beauty and art." Walter "was looking for nothing less than 'a new *Heimat*'" – a new homeland – "that could contain the wealth of cultural life that he had tasted in his youth but found lacking in modern 'frightful' Germany."[21]

Chytry suggests that Walter had embarked upon a very deliberate "metapolitical activity," "a self-conscious form of modernist legislation" that would attempt to refix Europe's ideals, now degenerating toward Hitler's coming cataclysm, to a specific geography elsewhere at the edge of the empires – in effect fusing two different planes into a new magical reality that existed not only in art but actual geography.

Certainly, Walter worked strenuously as if he knew his mission on Bali would have a very limited duration. He was hardly the image of a man simply savoring paradise or out of touch with what was happening around him. He actively tried to influence the imaginative direction that both Westerners and Balinese were taking. "By his adoption of Bali as his *Heimat*," Chytry suggests, Walter "meshed the traditional art of its inhabitants with his own aesthetic sensibilities and philosophy, and took on the trappings of a modernist Brahmin in the town of Ubud."[22] Perhaps most important for the development of Balinese aesthetics, Walter tried to encourage local artists to experiment with their own thematically controlled traditions. Painting had been viewed as a lowly kind of art mostly for temple decoration and limited by the colorings of natural pigments like clay or soot. Walter showed some of the local artists the range of Western colors, the different effects of brushes, the impacts of woven canvases. He suggested to them ideas about vanishing line perspectives and, as he was already doing in his own art, ideas that also questioned those perspectives.

As Chytry and others have noted, Walter appears to have tried to mentor carefully, given Dutch concerns about interfering in the local culture as well as his own interest in learning non-European understandings of aesthetics. He did not strike the stance of a European master trying to lecture or convert. His role was as much cheerleader as innovator, since some Balinese artists had already begun to challenge stylistic conventions.

By 1931, Walter was working to restore the Bali Provincial Museum in Denpasar, which had been created in 1910 by a Dutch colonial officer concerned that Bali's artifacts would be shipped to Europe. The museum had been destroyed in a 1917 earthquake; Walter wanted to revive it. That same year, he and Roelof Goris also collaborated on a book of Walter's photographs to send along with the Balinese dance troupe to the Colonial Exhibition in Paris, the last international exhibition to be held in Europe before the start of World War II. Walter's photographs shimmered, creating silhouetted temple lines against distant volcanoes and showing the Balinese – men mostly – in ways that accented the sharp lines of their noses and bared shoulders and arms. The men were neither Winckelmann-like nor effeminate.[23]

Walter combed the island for artifacts and archeological sites to try to preserve them. He reported his discoveries to Stutterheim, often contributing his sketching skills. The month that Baron von Plessen arrived to film *Island of the Demons*, Walter enthusiastically reported one such find to a friend, Claire Holt, while also revealing his joy that a young cousin, Conrad, had come to join him:

> Sweet Clarity,
>   Since Balinese telepathy is very highly developed you will of course long ago have heard that my cousin Conrad the Silent, Con le Bon, has made a quite unexpected, fabulous discovery . . . One day when swimming . . . we were strolling around on the cliffs in our birthday suits, when Conrad saw a lump of stone sticking out of a Sawah bank with a pretty pattern on it . . . We dug and dug, and it just kept on coming, one piece after another.[24]

It was cousin Conrad who, by October 1931, had to report to Stutterheim why a certain archeological sketch Walter had promised had been delayed by the making of *Island of Dermons*, adopting a cheery tone Walter himself sometimes used for trying to set aside conflicts:

Dear little Stutti,

   May be he will find time when the film business is finished,
but I think that if he is not sketching, it is not a matter of distaste
or laziness, but that enormously important matters are keeping
him from it . . .There can be nothing worse than making films . . .
We spent two months looking for actors and arguing about them.
Since the end of July, we have been shooting and fighting.[25]

By early 1932, Walter had reached his creative peak. The Bali Museum had
reopened; the Balinese dance troupe had introduced Paris to the sounds, lights, and
rhythms of Walter's new aesthetic state; *The Deerhunt* was being completed; the
Island of Demons was being readied for movie theaters in Walter's other troubled
homeland.

   That spring, German voters re-elected the aging World War I hero Paul von
Hindenburg president of the Weimar Republic. For one brief moment, he held
enough power to ban the Nazi's paramilitary associations. Cousin Conrad wrote to
their very close friend, Jane Belo. "My dear . . . I just finished my preaching to A
Gusti, to whom I tried to explain in one hour's talk the bad influence of civilization
and what the Balinese should do to keep their happy state of some years ago. I have
to learn Balinese and then perhaps one could help to preserve them."[26]

   It was a quaint colonial notion riddled with the tensions and oppositional
narratives of manhood: that in helping "to preserve" the colonized Asian man, the
imperial European man might be able to save himself.

   It is easy to understand why Walter came to like Conrad so dearly. Conrad had
arrived in Bali in 1930 much like Walter had arrived in Java, young, enthusiastic,
curious, in his mid-twenties. To Jane Belo, he had written about learning more
of rituals and spirituality and the human body and how they all related. "May I
ask you something? Please try to find out books about 'reading in hands,' about
Physiognomy, Astrology, Prognosis, Mysteries, Spiritualism, and let me know the
editors. I have to cultivate my sixth sense. With my best love." He had signed the
letter as cheerfully as Walter "the Weed" sometimes did, except that he referred to
himself as "your Köslik," "Your Precious."[27]

   Conrad and Walter often enjoyed bathing or swimming together nude, either at
the rivers where the Balinese themselves bathed or, unlike the Balinese, at the ocean
beaches. Because of the possibility of evil spirits – the ocean, after all, was where the
cremated ashes of bodies were eventually delivered – the Balinese tended to avoid it.
Often when Walter and Conrad swam in the ocean, they went near the small town of
Lebih, about ten miles southeast of Ubud. The Balinese had built a temple there, Pura
Segara. It faced directly across a strait to the small island of Nusa Penida, which the
Balinese believed was the home of a particularly powerful demon worshipped by
practitioners of black magic.

On Saturday March 5, 1932, Conrad and Walter drove the famed German female aviator Elly Beinhorn to Lebih for a swim.

For weeks, Conrad had been in strangely alternating moods. Walter had noticed that he seemed even "merrier" than normal, as if in his various curiosities about Bali he had finally settled on a course for himself. But he had also begun to make odd comments about death. When they had driven past the European cemetery in Denpasar a few weeks earlier, Conrad had suddenly said, "I saw now where I will soon lie." He and his friends had consulted a Balinese astrological calendar and discovered that, for Conrad's birthday, the outlook was ominous: a young death.[28]

On the way to Lebih with Elly and Walter, Conrad started joking blackly about how he would soon be eaten by Kala Rahu, a Balinese *leyak* with only a head, who flew around eating the sun and the moon and producing eclipses. At the beach, the tide had ebbed and the water close to the shore was sandy, so the three waded into the waves. Elly asked whether there might be sharks. Conrad started joking as he waded ahead of them: "Yes, naturally, many!" He dipped and jumped in the waves, shouting, "There they come! There the sharks come!" Walter had never heard him teasing that way before. Conrad started splashing, striking at the water with his hands. Walter thought he was still playing.

Then he saw Conrad's face: "corpse-pale."

Conrad was about fifteen feet ahead and up to his hips in the ocean. He screamed, and then vanished. Walter hesitated. He was uncertain whether to run to the beach to get a boat. Conrad surfaced. Walter and Elly dashed through the waves as the water turned dark red. A shark had torn away the flesh on Conrad's right leg. "From the hip to the knee," Walter later wrote to Conrad's father, Rudolf, "only the bald bone remained."[29] The shark had also taken nearly all of his fingers.

Walter and Elly carried him to the car and started driving toward the only hospital in Denpasar. It was only fifteen miles away but along tortuously curving roads through village after village. To Walter, it seemed like hours. Conrad passed out, coming aware only to ask for water. The wounds stopped bleeding and Walter hoped that was a good sign. At the hospital, the doctor swiftly gave Conrad a shot for the pain and then amputated his leg. "All of my forces left me instantly," Walter would write. The wounds had stopped bleeding only because Conrad had so little blood left. Conrad "slept and slept . . . breathing ever more calmly, until he stopped and his body became cold and rigid."[30]

He was buried in the Denpasar cemetery, a gamelan playing softly. For Walter, the loss became a Laocoönian horror he would live and relive. To Jane Belo, he wrote:

> Oh Jane! Poor Köslik, it was so terrible! The only consolation
> I found was that he himself did not suffer much — he lost his
> consciousness immediately! . . .

Why, why had he to die? – he of us all had the bigger rights on life! He who was the purest, the most spotless human being that ever existed![31]

Walter seemed to have finally found someone he loved. To his friend Stutterheim, he wrote four weeks later:

Dearest Stutti: I am in a very bad way. I just cannot get over the death of Conrad. His non-existence is so utterly unimaginable. And then I keep seeing the whole thing pass before my eyes, everything just as it happened . . . The exposed bone of his torn-off leg; the mutilated hands; his face distorted by fear; the giant fish going at him; the water flowing with blood – O God how am I ever to forget it. I can hear his screams, smell the terrible thick smell of blood. And all of this happened to Conrad, dear quiet Conrad![32]

Surprisingly, Stutterheim would have none of Walter's grief. Instead, he wrote back with a fierce rebuke:

I would also rather sit like you and enjoy nature. But this same nature has concocted the cruelest things that we don't want and don't even care to look at when they happen to others . . .You don't want to see that the cruelest things happen everywhere in nature – that, on the whole, there is no peace for most people and danger is always looming . . .

You want to keep your childlike soul pure, and loved Conrad for that reason, because his soul had something pure and childlike, quite a lot of it, even. Nevertheless, your soul, too, has sometimes suffered a great deal and you, too, have sometimes been bitten by shark's teeth, if not in the actual sense. In any event, you carry such wonders around with you – that is clear – although you never quite want to say where they originate.

But you've never had the usual reaction most people do, namely, denying outright and protecting childlike fantasy so that it can't feel pain any more and so that you are more 'manly.' For the most part you've closed your eyes to reality, which is cruel and ugly and unsystematic and inhuman, and you've wanted to build your own world, a pretend-world, the like of which never occurs. I don't know if you're right; in any case, not everyone could do it, otherwise this whole thing would fall apart.

But maybe you can keep this pretend-world and continue to live in it, and never actually be mortally wounded by one of nature's cruel tiger paws. Hopefully never. I don't know.

The incident with our poor Conrad, however, is quite in keeping with the ugliness of nature – Reality.[33]

In Germany that summer of 1932, the Reichstag would be dissolved and bands of Nazi men would begin roving streets, chanting anti-Jewish songs, demanding the fall of the Weimar Republic, and provoking gun battles with communists. A new election would turn the Nazi Party into the most powerful in Germany and set the stage for Hitler to become chancellor.[34] On Java, Islamic nationalists were organizing, while on Bali, Dutch colonial officials defensively prepared *Balisering* – Balinization – a policy that could be viewed as enlightened protection or as benign apartheid. The Dutch had restored some limited powers to the old Balinese dynasties in 1929; now, the Dutch went further, trying to cut the aspects of Westernization that had crept in, by encouraging Balinese to shed the European clothing they had started wearing and to return to traditional methods of schooling, sitting on floors, for example, rather than at desks.

The German sexologist Magnus Hirschfeld, visiting the Dutch East Indies, made his way to Bali to see Walter. Hirschfeld discovered that, among many of those living in the Indies, sympathy was emerging for Germany and for Hitler as an underdog fighting against the colonial empires. "They saw Germany," Hirschfeld wrote, "struggling against the same great allied powers under whose pressure the Asiatic countries are themselves being crushed."[35]

In Batavia, a group of what one scholar called "ultra-right Dutch and Eurasian colonial diehards" who opposed any idea of independence for the Indies[36] gathered to form a new organization, the Vaderlandsche Club, translated variously as the "Club of the Supporters of the Fatherland" or the "Club of Patriots." Unlike many Eurasians who had tolerated or engaged in informal interracial relationships, the Vaderlandsche men believed in white supremacy and in protecting what they referred to as "European values" in the tropics – as well as the European right to own the tropics. Vaderlandsche members proposed turning parts of New Guinea into a safe homeland for white settlers should Java and Bali fall to either of two threats: Islamist nationalism or Russian communism. The Guinea highlands, they suggested, would be suitable for newly arrived Dutch whites, while "patriotic" Eurasians more used to the tropical heat could settle on the coastlines.

By the mid-1930s, a new whites-only colony called Hollandia would begin.

That idea of a white paradise at the east end of the Indies was also being supported by the Nationaal-Socialistische Beweging, the Nazi Party, which by now had clubs in the Indies as well as Holland.[37]

In Batavia, at the offices of one of the largest newspapers in the colony, *Java-Bode*, the editor Henri C. Zentgraff had joined in founding the Vaderlandsche Club. He had also begun meeting with the Dutch attorney general, H. Marcella, whose wife belonged to the local Nazi club.

Zentgraff would also hang a photograph of the local Nazi leader, A.A. Mussert, on his office wall.[38]

Reality was growing sharper teeth.

8
The Triple Taboo

Some believe Walter and other Europeans in Bali introduced homosexuality to the island, as if *nosferatus* were reverse-shipped from the centers of empires to pollute the peripheries. Others suggest Bali already enjoyed fluid male eroticism free of the monumental lines between hetero-- and homosexuality being drawn by imperial psychiatrists. A European observer in the 1880s, a voyeuristic doctor named Julius Jacob, who mostly commented on Balinese breasts and clitorises, included in his reports notes about men dressed as female dancers and offered to male visitors for sex.[1] And a respected Balinese leader, Anak Agung Made Djelantik, the son of a royal ruler of the kingdom of Karangasem who had been born just before Walter arrived, remembered male-male affection being common during his boyhood. He told an interviewer in 2003, "The boys kissing each other and hugging each other that is normal. And when they went to take a bath, nothing special about it. Among Balinese, nobody ever mentioned that homosexuality was imported from the West. It has been here since ancient times."[2]

After Magnus Hirschfeld visited Walter at Ubud in the 1930s, he touched on a conversation that the two probably had, writing: "Europeans who have lived on Bali for a long time agree that the love life there is very natural. On Bali, not only man, but everything that nature produces, can be the object of sexual desire and love. A youth who climbs a coco or sugar palm will kiss it as he would his bride. A real and far-reaching pan-sexualism reigns here." Hirschfeld remarked that when he went for nighttime strolls, he could hear men and women in various configurations fondling in the shadows.[3]

Yet the Balinese maintained a language about sex that was likely to point out its surprising *amok* tendency as well as its loving side. In Europe, St. Augustine had linked the two separate concepts of sex and sin, while in Bali the symbolic hooks ran between sex and magic. The sexual language, the Australian scholar Adrian Vickers wrote, used metaphors referring to the Balinese trance dance in which men could be "pierced" but, so long as they were in trance, show no wound.[4] Sex did not cause a fall from paradise, as in the Augustinian interpretation of the Eden story, nor did it necessarily create a romantic ache.[5] Instead, the penetrations and receptions magically transformed males in sometimes surprising ways that could not at all be ordered into monumental classifications.[6]

Anthropologist Margaret Mead and her husband, Gregory Bateson, commented on another aspect of male Balinese sexuality after they visited in the 1930s, relying on Walter to introduce them to the local villagers. Bateson wrote that Balinese mothers would often fondle their male infant's penis. "This will excite the child," Bateson wrote, "and for a few moments cumulative interaction will occur. Then just as the child, approaching some small climax, flings its arms around the mother's neck, her attention wanders." That would usually lead to a temper tantrum, which the mother would then ignore or even enjoy. Bateson speculated: "It is possible some sort of continuing plateau of intensity is substituted for climax as the child becomes more fully adjusted to Balinese life." Bateson thought that such a tendency to avoid quick climactic intensities and instead substitute long-lasting plateaus of ongoing erotic sensuality was characteristic of other aspects of Balinese life as well, including the hypnotic gamelan music heard everywhere. "It does not have the sort of rising intensity and climax structure characteristic of modern Occidental music, but rather a formal progression" through various relations between the notes, Bateson wrote.[7]

Training in sensual teasing and edging, not climaxing, was a possible key to understanding gender role, sex, and art all fused.

Hirschfeld had also commented on gender expectations, writing that Balinese men's "clothes are far more colorful than those of the women [and] the custom of wearing pretty flowers, which they usually put into their mouths or behind their ears, also tends to give the men a particularly coquettish appearance." When it came to dancing: "Many male dancers in Bali showed signs of striking femininity, and many female dancers of masculinity."[8]

In some dances, males dressed as the highest-ranking queen, princess, or female demon. Clothing and mannerisms — two key components in gender performance — did not stop at the stage edge. In their book on Balinese dance, Walter Spies and Beryl de Zoete described males with "their homely faces under flower-laden crowns" gliding about "with such delicate inflexions of body and lovely turns of wrist that before they have been dancing for five minutes the illusion [of them being women] is complete." Off stage, the males continued to appear "curiously effeminate . . . though entirely without the nuance of affectation that we associate with effeminacy, the male and female types being certainly much less differentiated."[9] Men would sometimes take turns flirting with a young male who had dressed as a female and who after the dance would perform sexual favors. The Balinese seemed to make no negative judgment.[10]

Besides homosexuality, Europeans sometimes were concerned about the increased possibilities for cross-race sex.[11] Historian Tim Lindsay, who studied Europeans in Bali in the 1930s, suggested that interracial sex "was seen by many Whites as wrong and something of which to be ashamed."[12] Centuries of mingling had already occurred on Java but not yet on Bali, and if the island were to be saved as a kind of living museum, then the presumption was that cross-racial relations should not occur. Too, eugenic theories had grown more popular by the early twentieth century, and racial purity was a rallying cry to protect not only the center from the periphery but vice versa.

Completing the triple taboo that contrasted with the triple supremacy of monogamous, romantic, heterosexual relations, Europeans had also turned cross-age sexual desire into a scarified emotion and legally forbidden action. By the end of the nineteenth century and start of the twentieth, such desires – particularly between males – were being increasingly defined as both psychologically perverse and criminal. In Britain and the United States, age-of-consent laws had begun to replace biological ages of sexual maturity, defining a new legal category of adolescence that was supposed to remain asexual. Imperial laws also presumed the newly defined "adult" to be the one with perverse sexual desire and thus the one at fault; the newly defined "child" – who could be as old as twenty – was presumed innocent and thus the victim.

Although little seems known about expressions of Balinese cross-age desire before the Europeans arrived, one of the most famous images of such sexual expression was drawn by an artist who became highly regarded by Walter, Gusti Nyoman Lempad. In the 1930s, Lempad sketched an older Balinese man naked except for a headscarf and opened sarong. The man fiercely concentrates as he enters what appears to be an adolescent Balinese male anally, seemingly sending him flying through the air. With one hand, the older man grasps the younger male's neck while with the other he holds a portion of his own waistcloth, drawn to resemble an undulating *kris* dagger.

The younger male in Lempad's drawing does not seem to object to the penetration but rather fully participates. He, too, is naked except for a small part of his own sarong, which falls to the ground revealing his own sizeable penis. The younger male is not a pre-adolescent "boy" in European terms but fully sexually mature. He is suspended in mid-air – left hand on the ground, buttocks hooked onto the older male's penis, right hand grabbing onto the older male's chin. The younger male appears to have willingly adopted a ritualistically sexual position in which he is about to be transformed by his older mentor into a future toward which his eyes are focused.

In Lempad's image, cross-age sex between men became an intertwining of sexual desire and of male magical power. Balinese men might wear flowers in their hair and appear feminine or androgynous to Europeans like Hirschfeld, but their gendering – both as versatile recipients of the arrow or *kris* and as archers or *kris* wielders – was a different performance of idealized manhood. Adrian Vickers, the Australian scholar, suggested the scene was one of "emotional extremism" reflecting a now-public tension about cross-race and intergenerational male sex that was arising from encounters between the Europeans and the Balinese during Walter's years on the island. Both males in Lempad's drawing are Balinese, suggesting he may have been sketching publicly a desire or behavior already present – something that could now be talked about openly. With the arrival of the Europeans, Vickers noted, "homosexuality had been made into a topic of public interaction."[13]

Lempad had symbolized the magical and transformative power of sex as a male "piercing" of one another, much as Walter had done metaphorically in 1932 in *The Deerhunt*, but Lempad, the Balinese, was more explicit.

When Walter arrived in Bali in the late 1920s, the Dutch governor of the island, called the Resident, was H.T. Damste, who viewed Bali as a unique land that needed protection. "Let the Balinese live their own beautiful native life as undisturbed as possible!" he had written, overlooking the obvious intrusion of his own government. "No railroads on Bali, no Western coffee plantations; and especially no sugar plantations. But also no proselytizing, neither Mohammedan (by zealous natives from other parts of the Indies) nor Protestant nor Roman Catholic." He had used a telling metaphor that equated Bali with a woman who needed to be saved by Dutch men: "Let the colonial administration . . . treat the island of Bali as a rare jewel that we must protect and whose virginity must remain intact."[14]

But not all agreed. Others thought that a previous assistant resident named A.J.L. Couvreur had been right. Couvreur had proposed a different kind of symbolic Bali founded on pragmatic geopolitical goals. Bali was strategically positioned between Islamic Java and Islamic Lombok, Sumbawa, and what was then Celebes (now Sulawesi). The sheer numbers of Muslims surrounding Bali doomed its culture, Couvreur argued. Its governance had to be separated from Java so that its separate interests could be promoted and Islam offset by Christian conversion. Catholicism would be best, he believed, since the Catholic emphasis on ritual seemed akin to the Balinese interest in drama and performance.

By the mid-1930s, half of Couvreur's argument had won. Bali would be linked to what was called the "Government of the Great East" – the eastern Indies, rather than to Java – and Damste himself would be replaced by a new resident who supported Couvreur.[15] But Damste won what seemed to be the more important religious argument. Christian missionaries would still be excluded, in order to try to preserve the unique brand of animist and Hindu traditions existing on Bali. Damste's partial victory of promoting Bali as a "living museum" seemed aligned with Walter's imagining of Bali as an aesthetic state. But it also held its own latent danger: Europeans like Walter, who had moved into the villages and befriended the Balinese, even at their invitation, now looked like cultural intrusions.

At the beginning of his second five-year period in Bali, in 1932, Walter seems to have been on good terms with the local Dutch administrators. One, Christian Grader, noted that "Spies' influence on the Dutch authorities was considerable and he gave valuable advice on many occasions. An essential ingredient of the influence he exerted was the absence of any formal constraints. You could ask his advice at any time, and he often called on us to raise some point or other." One of Grader's colleagues had similar praise: "Spies had been to the most remote and almost inaccessible villages, and since he always had a receptive ear for what the villagers had to tell, he heard of many things the administrator was never told. But when the people saw me traveling regularly in his company, I too gained their trust. My work of administration became easy."[16] Walter had even been asked to help prepare a reception for the Dutch Viceroy, showing him the artifacts at the Bali Museum that Walter himself had helped save from souvenir hunters.

Walter's second five years on Bali would also mark the height of his "anthropological" work: his photography for the book with Beryl de Zoete about dance and drama in Bali, his assistance to Mead and Bateson as they conducted their field research, his close relationship with Jane Belo and her musicologist husband, Colin McPhee.

In this period Walter's thoughts about the aesthetic state and aesthetic manhood also matured as he pushed toward what would be his best expressions of male lives carried out across multiple intersecting planes of time and space, fusions of sound, light, and movement in different media. A panorama of rice fields in arcs reaching toward a volcano in *View across the Sawahs to Gunung Agung*; a burst of mysterious tropical light within multiple planes of men at work in *Vista through the Palms*; a gauzy and silvery view of a village watched by a distant male observer in *Iseh in Morning Light*.[17]

Then had come an odd painting that would prove to be transitional. Walter had called it *Landscape with Shadow Cow*. His horizons and his men with cows and their strangely magnified or shrunken shadows multiplied so much within the single canvas that the pictures became a set of individual miniature notes flowing into one another — but the passage of time was also apparent. Some of the trees resembled those he had painted in Germany; others, including huge shadows cast against the sky, looked more like surrealist metal cutouts. A biographer suggested they corresponded to "the gloomy shadows of approaching war."[18]

By then it was 1938 and a new Dutch resident for Bali had arrived: H.J.E. Moll.

The campaign against the triple taboo that reached Bali in 1938 had actually begun two years earlier in the Netherlands in the so-called Ries affair. Then it had flowed into Batavia. The catalyst had come from Germany after Hitler had worn down the president, Paul von Hindenberg, and had forced the aging war hero to name him chancellor. In 1936, the Netherlands' chief treasurer, Leopold Ries, had begun financial negotiations with Hitler's government.

An anti-Nazi lawyer and a Jew, Ries had little liking for the government with which he was dealing. He was known as a shrewd negotiator as well as coolly analytical, a trait that had helped him accept his own homosexuality at a young age. He had been a contributor to the Dutch branch of Magnus Hirschfeld's Scientific-

Humanitarian Committee promoting more tolerance for homosexuals. At The Hague as a young lawyer, Ries had risen to prominence, receiving a decoration from Queen Wilhemina when he was only 28, becoming acting chief treasurer by 1927 when he was in his mid-30s, and then being assigned permanently to the post in 1935.[19]

Unknown to Ries, on May 9, 1936, while he was in Germany, a seventeen-year-old in The Hague named Hank Vermuelen falsely told the Dutch police that Ries had been paying him ten guilders a week for sex. Ries, Vermuelen claimed, was only one of a number of senior Dutch civil servants who were part of a homosexual network he was supposedly servicing. It seems likely that the police, who had Nazi sympathies, knew Vermuelen's accusations were false; he had already confessed previously to charges of swindling and was on court-supervised probation. Because Ries was in Berlin, the police waited but did almost no investigation. On May 24, Ries returned and the next day briefed the Dutch president, Hendrik Colijn. The following day, the police arrested him, but not for supposedly paying for sex, which was legal in the Netherlands, nor for homosexual sex, which was also legal. Rather, Ries had violated the new age-of-consent laws meant to define who was an adult able to consent to sex and who was a "child." Under pressure from conservative churches, the age of consent for male-male sex in the Netherlands had been set higher than that for male-female sex, at age twenty-one rather than at age sixteen. Even though Vermuelen was seventeen and considered an adult for sex with women, he was not old enough to consent to sex with men. Ries now stood accused of pederasty, something that allowed the newspapers to quickly smear him as a "child exploiter" and a "boy lover" – despite the fact that, as a street hustler, Vermuelen was in no way a child innocent of sexual desires or sexual experiences.

The police searched Ries's house for letters. Quickly, details leaked to newspapers, details that, as it turned out, included such supposedly "lurid" items as Ries contemplating having homosexual sex with an adult soldier thirteen years earlier – but not actually doing so. He had also attended a party at which other homosexual men were present, the simple fact of association with other adult homosexuals somehow making him even more tainted as a "boy lover."

The first court hearing the accusations against Ries ruled that the police investigation was so shoddily done that there was little evidence and insufficient description of any illegal act that he was supposed to have committed. But the investigation proceeded and throughout the summer, the prosecutors lingered, letting the newspapers play the so-called scandal's details not only against Ries but also against eight other civil servants. At one point, the prosecutor claimed he was too busy with other affairs to move forward, and then he took a month-long holiday. Vermuelen eventually recanted his testimony, but under pressure from the prosecutor later revoked the recantation.

Only two men were ever convicted. They were given suspended sentences, but one committed suicide because of the publicity. The other six, along with Ries, were found innocent.

But the damage had been done. Ries had to seek refuge in New York.[20] Opponents of the Dutch government had found a potent new rhetorical weapon. Relying on a law that set varying levels of consent for male-male and male-female sex, as well as on blurry distinctions of age between a "man" and a "boy," accusations of cross-age sexual desire could be used to bound appropriate manhood and to weaken governments the Nazis were preparing to attack, even if the accusations did not involve desires for actual children – and even if they were completely false.

By October 13, 1936, the tactic arrived in Batavia. A small newspaper, *De Ochtendpost*, began by publishing sensationalized reports about homosexual meeting places in the Dutch colonial capital as well as rumors that colonial officials were engaging in homosexual sex with underage Javanese "boys." The local Christelijk Staatkundige Partij, a moral reform group with contacts to the right wing in the Netherlands, demanded the Colonial Governor-General, A.W.L. Tjarda van Starkenborgh Stachouwer, launch an investigation, which he did. In January 1937, the Batavia police commissioner and the city's Dutch Resident, H. Fievez de Malines van Ginkel, reported that, although homosexuals certainly lived in the city, no particular scandal was occurring. Rather, the two said, *De Ochtendpost* had made it look like a problem by focusing on the activities of a few men. In the Netherlands, Dutch President Colijn said he doubted any fall in European morality among the Dutch officials in the colonies.

For a time, *De Ochtendpost* quieted. But only temporarily.[21]

When 1938 began, it had seemed like it would be the best year yet for Walter. Miguel Covarrubias, the Mexican writer and artist who Walter had befriended, had published his guide *The Island of Bali* late the year before, and it was beginning to be circulated in Europe and the United States. The book had made Walter even more internationally famous. In the introduction, Covarrubias had written: "In his charming devil-may-care way, Spies is familiar with every phase of Balinese life . . . An authentic friend of the Balinese and loved by them, I feel he has contributed more to the prestige of the white man than the colonial despots who fail to impress the discriminating Balinese by the policy used to bluff natives into submission."[22]

Walter bubbled when he got his copy in April. "The book arrived. Thanks, thanks, thanks, it is lovely!" he wrote. "It reads so easily, and all the questions which everyone asks, are all answered . . . I hope you make millions. I see every tourist with it . . . and to everyone who asks me something, I say, look in Covarrubias." As for the introduction, Walter remarked: "I am very ashamed to read all that glorifying nonsense about me in the introduction and I must say that it has already added to my publicity! Every new tourist coming in knows everything about me, and I had already two orders for pictures again through your book!"[23]

Little did Walter seem to realize that having his name associated with Covarrubias's attack on Dutch colonial policies – a criticism now arriving with "every tourist" – might not be in the best interest of someone who, technically, was still a citizen of Germany.

Covarrubias's work was not the only one to enhance Walter's fame that year. Vicki Baum's novel, *A Tale from Bali*, had also just been published. In it she had converted Walter into a wise fictional character named "Doctor Fabius," of whom she had written that he was "the oldest Dutch resident and an eccentric with an unrivalled knowledge of Balinese life." The novel was framed as a retelling of Fabius's notes on Balinese life during the years 1904–06, just before the 1908 battle in which the Dutch had put a bloody ending to the reign of the Balinese kings. General readers may not have known the supposed narrator was Walter, but certainly his friends – and enemies – did. Unlike Covarrubias's attack on the "colonial despots," Baum had praised the Dutch for trying to protect Bali. She credited "Doctor Fabius" – Walter – with the belief that, after witnessing the Balinese magical self-sacrifice in the *pupatan*, the Dutch had learned "the need of ruling this proud and gentle island people as considerately as they have, and so kept Bali the paradise it is today."[24]

While Covarrubias and Baum had authored contrasting sentiments, since Walter had influenced both writers, their divergent rhetoric may have reflected separate pieces of his own thoughts. Walter seldom spoke directly in his letters about the situation in which he found himself: the political disintegration in Europe, the nationalist challenge to colonialism throughout the Indies, the magico-realistic refuge for aesthetic ideals he was promoting but that was being transformed by global tourism. When the two books by Covarrubias and Baum are placed together and interpreted as a voice of a primary informant named Walter Spies, it seems as though Walter may have been struggling to make some sense out of the divergent planes of political, magical, and sexual existence he was leading in Bali.

A third book, Walter's own, would also be published that year. To his mother he wrote: "Our book – Beryl de Zoete's and mine – is coming in the spring. I'll send you a copy, because I know you want to know what kind of son you have. It will be the best book in the world."[25]

By June, in order to concentrate on his painting, he had moved from his house in Tchampuan to a retreat cabin at Iseh, leaving the larger house in the care of two gay friends, Walter von Dreesen and Fritz Lindner. He told his mother that they "look after all my 'guests,'" placing the word "guest" in quotation marks as if he were not sure he wanted all of the visitors who were now coming to see him. Still, he noted, "Some of them come as paying guests, and we can live well from that."

But there was a danger. Critics would begin to argue that Walter's home at Tchampuan was a pseudo-hotel in the heart of a Bali that was supposed to be protected. Now that it was in the day-to-day control of two homosexual men who did not have Walter's reputation, the home at Tchampuan could easily be transfigured into a piece of symbolic geography, a home of *nosferatus,* where the feared triple taboo regulating relations between males, between races, and between ages was regularly broken.

Figure 8.1   Walter Spies's controversial home near Ubud
Courtesy of Tropenmuseum of the Royal Tropical Institute,
Wikicommons

Walter's friend Willem Stutterheim, the Dutch official in charge of protecting Bali's archeological discoveries, apparently saw the danger first and tried to caution Walter. On June 10, 1938, Walter responded with what for him was a rare, defiant tone:

> I've been hearing that there is a rumor going the rounds in Java that I have opened a hotel, that I am ruining Bali and such like rubbish! Because I have at last come to my senses and no longer put up everyone for free, as was formerly the usual thing, is this to be held against me? . . . Call it a hotel if you want to. I don't give a damn . . . The tiny trickle that Tchampuan brings in with paying guests is just enough to keep it alive. And it would have been much nicer if you had defended me just a little, instead of listening to stupid gossip.[26]

On June 15, Stutterheim reacted severely, just as he had after Conrad's death:

> From different sides – different also in the nature of the messengers – I have learned that the Balinese who come in contact with tourists are more and more willing to prostitute both their spiritual and material possessions for money . . . [Tchampuan] has become more of a tourist center than it used to be and that is exactly the point. [Balinese] come into contact with rich, at least by their standards, people who don't feel they are part of a society, who are often eccentric and have an incorrect image of Balinese society and who pull the Balinese completely out of balance by their remarks, their actions, etc. after which they leave without

any concern about the consequences. They use the Balinese for
their pleasure and entertainment, the way they use a prostitute
and leave her (him) to fate.

Stutterheim had used the word "prostitute" twice, as if to send a clear signal
to Walter about the sexual nature of the gossip. Then he drove the point again,
practically referring to Walter as a *nosferatu* — although framing it with a different
metaphor, the Homeric Trojan horse, and assuming a bit of a Laocoön-like role of
agonized warning:

> The fact that you have now fled from the Tchampuan house,
> which has become such a tourist center for prostitution, in order
> to paint . . . does not make a difference. You will certainly not be
> fleeing from your responsibility in the eyes of the Balinese once
> they come to realize what a Trojan horse they have let in with the
> tourists . . .
>
> I am powerless although I sincerely wish I could put a stop to
> it [the gossip]. It is unstoppable.[27]

Walter's response to Stutterheim's dose of stern fathering was to ignore the
message for almost two months, stay at Iseh, and continue painting. At the end of
July, he wrote to his mother. "I've been sitting for over a month in my studio on the
little hill and have been painting with utter abandon."[28]

Not until mid-August did Walter respond to Stutterheim. Then, he deflected the
possibility that Tchampuan was becoming a sexual Trojan horse with lighthearted
rhymes:

> Dear Stroppiproppity,
> I began this letter, or so it would seem, a terribly long time ago,
> but so many things intervened . . . What a pity I didn't hear
> all this personally and directly from you. And I'm grateful, but
> I'm hateful and I'm baleful about the pail full of nastiness which
> makes up the world. I'm neither a fool nor cool in this role . . . I
> admit that you are almost right in all that you say . . .
>
> For the present I can reassure you on the point of my own
> pure, calm and clear conscience. I will surely never do anything I
> would have to be ashamed of . . . I earnestly beg you if you should
> ever hear anything positively bad about me or us, write to me and
> tell me, for I must say I find it a poor thing when you learn that
> all the good you have attempted to achieve in this world can be
> doubted by even your best friends. Nobody is without stain, God
> knows, and it would be nice if one's friends at least could draw
> attention to one's failings.[29]

On September 15, 1938 Walter celebrated his forty-third birthday, still writing from his Iseh retreat rather than from his Tchampuan house, and still ignoring the threat. Perhaps he was being naïve staying in Bali, or perhaps courageously insisting on the right to his own narrative. Returning to Germany was out of the question anyway. That same September 15, Neville Chamberlain left London to meet Adolf Hitler at Munich and trade part of Czechoslovakia for peace.

Walter wrote to his mother that five gamelan orchestras had gathered to play at his birthday party – or, as he phrased it, in honor of his mother for giving him birth.

"We're celebrating in ecstasy . . . the champagne flows with every pop of the cork!" Walter told her.

He pleaded: "A thousand kisses to all, stay sensible and don't make a war."[30]

9

A Pivotal Year

By 1938, the refuge for whites being promoted by ultra-right-wing Dutchmen, especially the Vaderlandsche Club in Batavia, had faltered. The movement had stated its goal was to form a new Hollandia, "a fatherland for all Dutchmen in the Netherlands Indies and an area to absorb Holland's own excess population."[1] The number of white colonists had reached 102 in 1936, but in the following year, only 50 new migrants arrived to set up their segregated homeland. The crusade for the protection of "European values" in the Indies proposed by the Vaderlandschers needed a boost. Vaderlandsche Club founder Henri Zentgraff, the editor of the *Java-Bode* newspaper in Batavia, would provide it.

That autumn, both his newspaper and *De Ochtendpost* began reporting that a navy officer, a judge, and a doctor in Surabaya, on Java's north coast, had been recalled because of sex with underage native "boys," although the newspapers did not state the ages of the males involved, preferring to blur the meaning of the word "boy." Zentgraff coupled his report with an editorial attacking the Dutch Scientific-Humanitarian Committee, the homosexual rights group in the Netherlands that was supporting Magnus Hirschfeld's civil rights efforts in Germany. The Dutch committee had no local affiliate in the Indies, but Zentgraff pressured the police to act, and they soon began spying on the sole male in Java who was receiving mail from Jonkheer Jacob Schorer, the founder of the Dutch committee. As Walter had long ago warned his mother, one always had to worry about colonial postal inspectors.

That local man would be known in the press reports as "Van E." On November 28, 1938, when he invited men who seemed to be under the age of twenty-one into his hotel room, the police arrested him. The police never presented proof that sex had occurred in the hotel room and, at any rate, the so-called "boys" might likely have been considered adults for the purposes of heterosexual sex. As had happened to Leopold Ries in Holland in 1936, the police raided Van E.'s personal belongings as they were arresting him, and seized his letters to other men in the colony. That provided them with a first list of people they considered suspects, good enough for Zentgraff to then claim that a network of men throughout the Dutch Indies might be having sex with the native "boys."

A media-based *Zedenschaandal* – a morals scandal – was born overnight.

The effects spread quickly. The investigation started the very next week of December. By the second week, *Java-Bode* reported that the morals police had expanded their questioning due to an "increase in illicit, abnormal sexual acts." Parts of Batavia, the newspaper warned, no longer seemed safe from prowling European pederasts.

But it took almost a month, until December 21, for the next actual arrest to come: a teacher. Six days later, *Java-Bode* turned over two columns of its six-columned front page to breathlessly report:

> During the Christmas holidays the investigation into the vice scandal – certainly the largest ever in the history of the East Indies – has been pursued by officers of the Public Prosecutor's Office in Batavia and the General Investigation Service with tireless enthusiasm.
>
> While ongoing business has to be attended to during the daytime, this inquiry mainly takes place in the evening and during the night. In the past days the interrogations of suspects and witnesses has also started at 7 p.m. and lasted until the early morning hours. The end is nowhere in sight and more arrests are to be expected.[2]

Java-Bode listed thirteen men who had either been arrested or "temporarily detained." One man's questioning had begun at 8:30 p.m. and had lasted until midnight before he was taken to Struiswijk Prison. *Java-Bode* coolly reported that another was a school headmaster who, after being arrested, "took his own life."[3]

The *Java-Bode* stories avoided listing the ages of any of the Asian "boys" supposedly being victimized. Zentgraff would never mention the well-known difficulty that ages of native males were often not known because the Javanese did not use European calendars. It could be quite impossible to distinguish physically between a twenty-year-old and a twenty-one-year old who had no idea or record of his birth. Zentgraff's articles also failed to note that the Dutch colonial law being used, Article 292, had different interpretations. Some believed it applied only to European males having sex with other European males under age twenty-one, not to sex with native men governed under their own local laws, such as the Balinese *adat*. Those local customs typically held that a male became sexually mature when he was biologically mature, and he was then free to consent and to make choices about partners. That could be at an age closer to puberty, such as thirteen or fourteen, and certainly by ages seventeen, eighteen, nineteen, and twenty.

> The vice crime interrogations continued last night . . . Among other things, two new suspects from Bandung were taken before the public prosecutor. However, no decision about their fate has been made yet.

During the course of the night the public prosecutor ordered the arrest of P.J.C. Willems, chief constable of police in the area, for sexual abuse of a person subordinate to him in his position as a police officer.

There were no further arrests last night, but the inquiry continues . . . the evidence for the justice department is piling up by the day.[4]

The articles highlighted the Dutch trinity for exercising power in the colony: the combination of the public prosecutor's office, the prosecutor's own secret investigators, and a string of prisons. The office of the public prosecutor was then held by a man named de la Parra, operating under the aegis of the Dutch attorney-general, H. Marcella, the official whose wife belonged to the local Nazi club and with whom Zentgraff often chatted. That de la Parra had had a local constable arrested suggested his willingness to use his own secret investigators to intimidate local police when necessary.

At first, *Java-Bode* did not report the names of those arrested, using only the initials of their last name, such as "M." or "L." But Zentgraff soon began go further, apparently at de la Parra's request. Referring to a news service report that had contained only the initials of the men being arrested, Zentgraff attached a note to the December 28 article: The news service, he wrote, "is being very foolish by mentioning only the first letter of the last name. This is contrary to the public prosecutor's wishes, who wants the initials of the first names published as well." Zentgraff told his readers he would go even further and now "give you the complete name of the arrested man."[5]

Still, the newspaper reported only what had happened to Europeans, displaying its primary interest in regulating European male sexuality rather than native male sexuality. In *Java-Bode*, the young Asian males would remain anonymous and silent, their fates left generally unreported, and they themselves given no voice to explain their side of the encounters. Of these silent "victims," *Java-Bode* reported only: "The measure is being considered of putting the underage boys, who offered themselves as objects of seduction, in a work camp so as to teach them to work under strict discipline." The newspaper does not seem to have considered the illogic of its wording. Whoever these anonymous Asian "boys" were who were supposedly "underage," they also had been old enough to be able to choose to "offer themselves" for "seduction" — in other words, to act on their own attraction to the European men. The so-called "boys" were not being charged as prostitutes. Yet they were apparently old enough to be sent to forced work camps rather than be sent home as children. The *Java-Bode* article noted that they could be put into a work camp only "if they are a nuisance to society or if they refuse to work" by rebelling against the forced *corvée* system that the Dutch were imposing to construct roads and irrigation systems throughout the islands.

"In fact, these terms [nuisance and rebellious] are considered to apply," the article said.[6]

Steadily, arrests spread. In 1935, only three Europeans had been charged in court with such violations of Article 292. In 1936, the number had barely risen – to six. In 1937, it had dropped to five. In the months of 1938 before the renewed campaign by Zentgraff, another five had been arrested. But within the two months of December 1938 and January 1939, at least 223 European men were arrested. More than 100 native males were also detained. Three European men committed suicide because Zentgraff published their names in *Java-Bode*. No one knows how many Europeans chose to flee nor what the impacts were on the native males.[7]

In Bali, meanwhile, the new resident, H.J.E. Moll, waited to make his move.

She was not what you would imagine a Dutch daughter of a Christian evangelist to be, at least not in appearance or demeanor. With long curly hair, a radiant smile and what one writer called her "sensual persona," Mary Pos seemed more the Hollywood star than the missionary. She worked as journalist and lecturer, and in the late 1930s, she traveled throughout the Indies, bringing along both zeal to help save the natives and conviction that the Indies belonged to the Dutch and should always remain so. She believed in emancipation for women, even native women, but her concept of masculinity was more traditional. Supposedly she loved rugged men in uniform. One of her books would be titled *The Reality on Bali*, and by that she had something quite different in mind from the "paradise of Bali" imagined into being by Walter.[8] If in Walter's Bali, masculinity and men lived harmoniously with nature, in Pos's Bali, masculinity was rapidly degenerating and its victims were both women and men.

Christian missionaries had long been angry about being banned from the island by colonial officials, but it had proven fruitless for them to directly assail the notion of the "living museum." Missionaries like Pos had settled on an alternative strategy. Bali, they would argue, had begun to decline morally under the impact of the Westerners who were already there. For proof of that, they contended, one needed to look no further than the voyeuristic photographs of bare-breasted Balinese women or Miguel Covarrubias's artwork in various magazines. The cover of the April 1937 edition of *Asia* magazine had featured one of his paintings of a slender Balinese woman wearing a bright sarong topped by two sharply pointed breasts, while another appearing in *Life* in 1938 had shown fourteen bare-breasted women carrying elaborate offerings atop their heads while naked children stood and watched. Covarrubias had also painted males; his *Balinese Fishermen with Outrigger* showed seven naked men launching an outrigger.[9]

Krause, McPhee, and Covarrubias had intended their images to be reflections of a Bali innocent in its nudity and pan-sexuality. But with little effort, that image could be twisted by missionaries into a horror of any mingling of naked adults, teenagers, and children. Their goal became demonstrating that the Dutch policy of preventing Christian missionaries from converting Bali was leading to moral decay and child sexual exploitation.

In December 1938, as Zentgraff's *Zedenschaandal* was beginning, Mary Pos lectured in Surabaya. While no one seems to know exactly what she said, her later memoirs are clear about imported Christianity needing to trump the preservation of local culture:

> Everything was allowed and everything was possible on Bali but the Christian doctrine. . . People forget that there is something more important than art and culture, but how could they see that, if they show nothing but the greatest indifference for their own soul and bliss.

Europeans on the island, she continued, slandered God and pursued "unnatural" sins. She targeted one man in particular:

> I have seen myself how one of the most well-known Europeans on Bali – in this case no Dutchman – arrived at the market in a convertible, surrounded by six of his favorite Balinese boys! A mockery and a tearing down of morality, a degeneration of the highly prized virtues of this people – not to be spoiled by the work of missionaries![10]

One European on Bali was well-known for driving a convertible: Walter.

Walter's friend Colin McPhee had readied his escape from Bali soon after the arrest of "Van E." McPhee, who always seemed to show on his face the pain of dealing with his own homosexuality, had come to Bali to study its gamelans, and by 1938 had already separated from Walter's closer friend, the anthropologist Jane Belo. On December 2, he signed over one of the orchestras he had been sponsoring to the children of Kutuh and told them they should practice so as to make their village proud. He had booked passage on a Dutch freighter leaving Batavia on Christmas Day. In the book he wrote later, *A House in Bali*, McPhee did not mention the *Zedenschaandal*. He wrote obliquely, using the last pages of his book to link stories about missionaries like Pos with omens that paradise was ending. The night he signed over the gamelan, he wrote, he awoke to a bright light shining in his doorway, but it vanished when he reached for a flashlight. *Leyaks*, his Balinese friends said. Another night, he saw lights oscillating, and then lining perpendicularly. Again, his Balinese friends warned, *leyaks*. They came "from somewhere in the north," they told him.[11]

The night before McPhee left, he drove his favorite roads in Bali, stopping in the moonlight to watch a dance by an oddly dressed troupe of Balinese girls and boys. Instead of traditional costumes, they wore cotton stockings and tennis shoes. They gesticulated "aimlessly," McPhee noted, "singing the dreariest of tunes." When the time came for the young male hero to appear, two boys emerged, one dressed in a "sports shirt, white pants, black smoked glasses," the other wearing "gold brocade and a soldier's hat." They argued stridently. "Back and forth, "McPhee wrote, "the voices cried, harsh, furious, in fancied imitation of important colonial officials." McPhee was entranced. But then his Balinese guide touched him on his arm and warned him, as if he himself were a *nosferatu*. "It is time to go; it will soon be dawn."

The next day, McPhee boarded the ferry that operated from the west tip of Bali across the short strait to the Javanese port of Banjuwangi. In the last paragraph of his book, he wrote that, as the ferry reached the middle of the channel, rain fell in a "heavy silver sheet" and in a quick moment, the paradise of Bali had been blotted "completely from view."[12]

New Year's weekend turned out to be even busier than Christmas had been for police throughout the islands. On Friday, December 30, *Java-Bode* reported:

> In Bandung the investigation is being continued vigorously and much more is to be expected. The arrests in Medan followed the apprehension of a native in the house of a European who lives there, and from whom photographs and letters were confiscated . . .
>
> It can furthermore be reported that the linguist Dr. R. Goris, adviser to the "Kirtya Liefrinck van der Tuuk" Foundation at Singaradja, was arrested in Bali.[13]

Roelof Goris was another of Walter's friends. He had collaborated with Walter on the book of Balinese photographs that had been sent to the Colonial Exhibition in Paris. He was also one of Bali's foremost cultural specialists, working for the Dutch Antiquities Bureau. As such, he had argued strenuously against the missionaries who wanted to convert the Balinese, saying "Calvinism is an enemy of art."[14] Once, he had allied with a Dutch journalist, J.A. Houbert, who had discovered a package of Bibles being mailed to a missionary, thereby apparently breaking the promise to be only an observer, not a converter. Goris and Houbert had forced the missionary to leave.[15]

On Saturday, December 31, *Java-Bode* reported that from Batavia the public prosecutor, de la Parra, had extended his reach:

> Besides the arrest of the linguist Dr. R. Goris on Bali, whose apprehension we already reported yesterday, the Public Prosecutor in Batavia has ordered the arrest of the painter Walter Spies, also in Bali.

Walter, though, had "avoided precautionary detention by fleeing."[16]

Walter's letters do not make clear when he would have left his retreat cabin at Iseh to return to Tchampuan. Normally, he would have been at Tchampuan on Saturdays to see any new works by the Balinese artists of the Pita Maha guild he had helped to form. At some point around New Year's Eve, he appears to have made a last-minute decision to escape Bali. But, like his father in Moscow decades earlier, he had delayed too long.

Published details about his attempt to flee are sketchy, but one historian who later interviewed K'Tut Tantri, one of Walter's friends who had helped open a hotel on Kuta Beach, said K'Tut claimed that a wealthy friend who had been staying at Tchampuan − Marianne van Wessem − had suggested a hastily arranged marriage might save Walter.

He had declined.[17]

In a film script that K'Tut Tantri wrote years later, based on her autobiography *Revolt in Paradise*, she included what she claimed was a conversation she had with Walter. He had supposedly showed up at her hotel in Kuta, hiding behind a palm tree.

"K'Tut, "he supposedly whispered, catching her attention. "The Dutch are looking for me!"

"But what on earth have you done?" she asked.

"They're rounding up homosexuals. No one is exempt," Walter supposedly said.

"Where will you go?" K'Tut asked.

"To the western part of the island. I may be safe there 'till this all dies down."

K'Tut volunteered to drive him.

"You must not be seen with me. It's too dangerous."

"Then Wayan will drive you," she is supposed to have said, offering the services of a Balinese servant. "You are too good a friend of Bali to be allowed to suffer at the hands of the Dutch."[18]

How likely it is that any such conversation occurred is unknown, but it does seem clear that Walter did head west across Bali. There are two accounts of his eventual arrest. One has it that he was arrested in Tabanan just a few miles north of Kuta on the main highway to the west and that he was in K'Tut's car at the time.[19] The other account, based on news stories in *Java-Bode*, suggest that Walter decided to embark on the same ferry to Java that McPhee had chosen for his escape. Like McPhee, according to the news stories, Walter made it all the way to the western tip of Bali and boarded for the port of Banjuwangi on Java, undoubtedly watching Bali disappear on the horizon just as McPhee had. Unlike McPhee, however, he never made it past Banjuwangi. On New Year's Eve, according to the *Java-Bode* stories, the Dutch arrested him there.[20]

On that same last day of the year, Walter wrote to his mother, telling her that he had heard that she had received a copy of his book, *Dance and Drama in Bali*. He admitted to some conflicts with Beryl, his co-author, but added that the harmony he always sought in his life had prevailed. "We continuously argued and fought over it. But now all is well, and I even have the courage to write any book with Beryl de Zoete. Her style is so unbelievably good. So alive and very nice."[21]

In that last letter for the year he also wrote excitedly about two gamelan orchestra clubs he had assumed sponsorship of, paying the musicians monthly salaries. "You think probably now, oh god, he must have a lot of money to pay for something like that, but you will be surprised. One gamelan survived on only three gilders, the other on five." He joked, "Tell Ljowa" – his brother, who by then was a symphony conductor in Europe – "he should try that with two orchestras in Germany, one that concentrates on pre-Bach music, and the other one maybe Bruchner, maybe Mozart . . . How much would that cost?"

Cryptically, he noted, "I took them over from McPhee, who is absent for a while from Bali."

He did not explain why his friend had disappeared. He also did not explain why the letter he was writing was coming from Denpasar rather than from his customary home in Ubud.

Left unsaid was that Walter was being held at the Dutch jail near Denpasar, in the nearby village of Kerobokan. He had been charged with violating Article 292 of the Dutch-Indies Criminal Code, the homosexual seduction of a minor, "minor" being defined as any male under the age of twenty-one.

In a later lengthy, secret report to the colonial ministry in Batavia, the Bali Resident, H.J.E. Moll, described how the investigation had unfolded and had eventually captured Walter.[22] Moll had assumed oversight of Bali in June 1937. Aware of the stir the newspapers had created after the Ries affair, he had apparently begun questioning the presence of the Europeans on Bali almost immediately:

> Originally, I was of the opinion that the immoral lifestyle of certain European residents of this District should be understood to include in particular: excesses in the form of alcohol abuse; consorting with the natives in extreme fashion; "would-be" art, where the natural nakedness of Bali has been lowered to shameless posing for the taking of all kinds of pictures and photographs of dubious character; [and] (normal) unbridled sensuality.

Under pressure from the newspapers and moral reformers, he had "discovered" something else.

> [I too] heard rumors of homosexuality among Bali residents. In general, rumors and communication about a subject like this coming from the umpteenth hand should be considered with the greatest of reserve; however, these coincided with the newspaper report from a source that cannot be dismissed off-hand.

Moll complained, "I did not receive communications from any party that would have provided a hook on which to hang any solid investigation against persons residing in Bali." He criticized Mary Pos in particular.

> Even a known publicist such as Mary Pos, who isn't exactly accustomed to hiding her opinions, provides her generally known information during a lecture in Surabaya, but neglects to come clean, facts and all, to the European administration. Why?
>
> Because it is hard to assume that this lady could believe that the administration would knowingly tolerate the evil, there is only one answer: In the small European society in Bali, nobody – stranger or resident – wants to be the spokesman for facts that would provide direct leads to the administration for aiming its investigation in a certain direction. After all, if such an investigation didn't lead to the desired result, one could wind up entangled in unknown difficulties.

In fact, of course, it was in the interests of Christian missionaries to make it seem as if the Dutch administrators were tolerating the so-called "evil" of homosexuality and promoting it through their policy of not allowing Bali to be Christianized. Moll seems to have failed to recognize the strategy.

> Some Europeans who were involved in homosexuality here held a prominent position in this small society. Outsiders or residents don't like to antagonize people like Walter Rudolf Spies, who must have a wide net of connections. A journalist like Mr. J.A. Houbolt in Denpasar, who enjoyed little sympathy to be sure, often wielded a sharp pen, with the result that people didn't want him as an adversary.

Moll rationalized away the fact that the Balinese themselves were not turning over evidence of "abuses," and then hinted that it was only because of some competition between the Sukawatis of Ubud and another Balinese ruler in the area of Gianyar that he had been able to obtain any evidence at all.

> It is evident how extensively people who have since become indisputably known as homosexuals in the Gianjar area (Ubud and Bed(ah)ulu) had bound the local population to themselves with "silver ties, " especially including Messrs. Spies and A.V.M. Bonnike, whose group also partially included Mr. Houbolt who resided in Denpasar. For this reason there has hardly been any cooperation by the residents in the investigation. We could even call it passive resistance, so that only by involving the influential Self Governor of Gianjar have we been successful in obtaining material against the above-mentioned persons that turned out to be reliable. The population of Gianjar is the opposite of rich, and

the advantages offered by the association with the unfamiliar area
of homosexuality were certainly not unwelcome to the population.

Moll criticized Walter's friends for trying to derail the investigation, providing
the detail that the Dutch artist Rudolf Bonnet might have tried to secure safe passage
for Walter.

> I should not fail to mention here that when the above-mentioned
> preliminary investigation was in full swing, apparent outsiders,
> and even those included in the suspicions, tried at times in very
> bold ways to intervene in favor of the oft-mentioned Mr. Spies,
> which at times had the appearance of hindering civil servants. I
> refer you in this regard to the secret telegrams, written by myself,
> of December 31 (Miss M.J.A. van Wessem) and of January 2, 1939
> (Professor Wolff Schoemaker) and can add the oft-mentioned
> name of Mr. Bonnet to this, who went so far as to sound out
> the Assistant District Administrator on December 29, 1938 about
> letting Mr. Spies leave unobstructed.

Goris had been the first and easiest target, because, Moll said, he had "completely
lost sight of being careful in his actions." But the police had deliberately delayed
his arrest. The government linguist was based in north Bali, in Singaradja, but he
had extensive contacts in south Bali, where Walter and others lived. The police first
wanted to cultivate witnesses against Walter without Goris's contacts immediately
alerting them.

Moll wrote: "The police didn't have much more than a list of names – which
later turned out to be incomplete – connected with homosexuality in South Bali, but
no useable information at all." So Moll suspended action against Goris, not wanting
to "muddy the evidence that I believed could be obtained in South Bali."

By December 26, he was ready to move, first against a man named J.R.
Gockinga in Denpasar, as well as against another, A.V.M. Bonnike, living in Bedulu.
On December 27, Moll received a telegram from the public prosecutor in Batavia
insisting that he act.

> The result of this telegram was, obviously, that the planned
> scheme had to be executed more quickly, without losing sight of
> the caution required. The house search after Mr. Bonnike's arrest
> already showed that a start in destroying evidence had been
> made. Mr. Spies' foolish effort to flee caused further acceleration
> of the action against Mr. J.A. Houboult in Denpasar . . . However,
> these last-mentioned persons must still have had the opportunity
> to dispose of potentially valuable material.

As far as Moll was concerned, he was breaking up a secret homosexual network in which at least ten men were prominent. He listed them by number, and then described their interactions.

1. Dr. R. Goris,
2. J.J. Blans, a former planter who before his stay in Singaradja stayed with Mr. Bonnike in his house for several months,
3. W.J. Dorgelo, school principal, all from Singaradja.
4. J.R. Gockinga,
5. J.A. Houbolt, both from Denpasar or its environs.
6. Mr. A.V.M. Bonnike, from Bedulu (Gianjar),
7. W.R. Spies residing in Ubud (Gianjar) and Selat (Karangasem).
8. W. Dreesen, painter,
9. F. Lindner, artists-photographer, both of Ubud.
10. E.H. Siebs, K.P.M., employee, of Singaradja.

The last three, he said, had been allowed to leave because they had had sex only with adults, a revealing comment, since Dreesen and Lindner had been among those helping to take care of Tchampuan when Stutterheim had first expressed concerns about the activities there.

Moll noted there was much hostility between Spies and Houbolt, but Houbolt often "kept company" with Goris and Bonnike. Gockinga was said to have known Bonnike, as well as Houbolt, Dreesen, Lindner, and Bonnet. Goris and Blans had "kept in close touch," while Goris and Dorgelo "were often seen together."

"This," Moll declared, "is an approximate overview of what could be considered 'club forming.'"

Associations of homosexual men, perhaps for nothing more than socializing, had suddenly become suspicious and demanding of government surveillance. Moll concluded his note with additional reasons why he had not acted sooner to arrest the "club" members: "Every effort [by the police] failed to find definite public places for rendezvous, where like-minded people met each other and the targets of their intention."

In other words, although a social network of homosexual acquaintances seemed to have formed – certainly to be expected among like-minded Europeans on a small island – there really did not seem to be any particular place where these Europeans actually gathered to pursue sex with the local Balinese.

Indeed, Moll admitted, the police had discovered only that the hotel in Denpasar used by traveling civil servants "was a hotbed of this unnatural activity." Despite Stutterheim's earlier concerns, Tchampuan had not been proven to be a center of adult sex with boys.

It had been especially difficult, Moll said, to gather any evidence against the Europeans, such as Walter, who were living in villages. This he blamed on the relationships that had formed between the villagers and the Europeans like Walter.

These relationships, Moll claimed without citing any evidence, were based more on money than on friendship.

> This investigation showed that in most cases abuse of persons of the same sex was performed with people living on the same premises or in the same house (including boys), who were bound to the homosexual, in Balinese eyes, by rich rewards and because of the potential of sharing those advantages with their family. To the extent that the guilty parties devoted themselves to the evil in other ways, it was most often done with extreme care.[23]

Despite the length of his report, Moll cited no specific evidence against any of the men. Simply the fact that they were homosexual and were involved in cross-racial as well as mixed-age friendships with Balinese males seems to have been enough to justify their surveillance and then arrests.[24]

The year Walter would enter the Kerobokan jail, lawyers' magazines in the Netherlands – which once had published arguments in favor of equality for homosexuals – would now instead print one that suggested homosexuals should be considered aliens with neither a state nor a society to call home. The article concluded that they therefore had no civil rights of citizenship.[25]

They were *nosferatus* with no home.

The year 1939 had arrived. Hitler was readying his new German men for their September invasion of Poland.

10

A Final Chord

The Dutch colonial jail in Kerobokan, west of Denpasar, sat on flat land, a dull contrast to the terraced green hills Walter loved in Ubud. Legend has it that adults in Walter's favorite gamelan orchestra gathered at the jail to serenade him after he was arrested for supposedly seducing their Balinese "boys." Scholars do not seem to have footnoted any documented source for this particular story, but the tale is often repeated to explain that the Balinese continued to hold Walter in high esteem and that they, with their own understanding of sex, were baffled by the sudden Dutch crackdown.[1]

After Walter's arrest, *Java-Bode*'s editor, Henri Zentgraff, let loose his most vicious rhetoric. All of it promoted an ideal of manhood he claimed the Dutch had failed to enforce: that of the superior European male who adhered only to a particular understanding of heterosexuality . Other men were "scum" and "lived like pigs." On Thursday, January 5, a few days after Walter was arrested, *Java-Bode* published an editorial on its front page, using a Dutch spelling for Walter's last name:

> Just how long they [colonial officials] remained deaf to obvious complaints and indications should become clear by consulting the articles in various magazines over the last years. To cite a single example: we have repeatedly called attention to the formation of an illicit group in Bali, for the most part foreigners, and we insisted that the government clean up the international scum that washed ashore there . . . They were partly "artists," degenerate individuals who lived like pigs, and when the famous Walter Spies — now arrested — drove around in a seven-seat car with five Balinese boys, people would exclaim: "There goes Spies with his harem!" Thus, all this was known for a long time and no one tried to put a stop to it. Many months ago we published all sorts of details, but nothing happened. Who is responsible for this most grave neglect?[2]

Zentgraff also quoted a supposed account of a dinner with Walter: "The food was Balinese . . . and it was served by two magnificent Balinese boys, naked down to the waist." A traditional Balinese male way of dressing and serving food — in sarongs — had become evidence of degeneracy.

> The Balinese government of that time left everything the way it was, never intervening to clean up, and so Bali derived a reputation that seemed very attractive even to the abnormal . . . A serious deficiency in the government's fulfilling of its duty — to watch for and act against this evil — was evident. Then suddenly the bomb bursts and after a short while even he who applauds the current actions of the judiciary must conclude that the avalanche of filth is too powerful for society. There is a need for peace and quiet again, so people can think and talk once more about less nefarious topics.[3]

While Zentgraff pummeled the government, Walter passed his jail time in Kerobokan writing letters. Often they went to his close friend Jane Belo, who had been away from Bali but now hurried back to try to help him.

> January 18: My dear, dear beloved Jane! I can't believe it that you are here. How marvelous, how incredibly beautiful! But how agonizing that I can't see you yet. I can't wait! . . . This whole mess is most dreadful and tiresome, but I hope this state will end soon!![4]
>
> January 19: My dearest dearest Jane! How marvelous to have real letters from you, and two at the same time. Now I really believe you are in Bali and very near somewhere, and there is hope that I shall see you very soon . . . Darling Jane, please, please write very often. It makes all the difference.[5]
>
> February 4: If only I knew how long I will be staying here in Denpasar! I would love to begin another picture . . . I have such a certain feeling somewhere round my navel. But what it will be, God knows. I know only that it will be quite different from anything I have painted — something you can stay in and walk round in, and have all sorts of fun discovering things! [He had forwarded a detective story to Roelof Goris, also in jail.] Poor Goris; I had asked him if he wanted to read one and he was furious it seems. He could not imagine reading such stupid stuff in such serious times . . . I simply can't understand how it could possibly help to see everything so black and feel so crushed and down. What does one gain by it?[6]

By February 5, the dreaded had happened. The news had reached Europe and Walter had received an inquiry from his mother. He had written to her from jail on

January 12, being careful not to mention anything about the arrest. Now he wrote
to Jane:

> Today I had a miserable time − I had to write a letter to my
> mother. You can imagine how it was, her not knowing, not even
> guessing about whatsoever! Yesterday I had a letter from her, a
> worried one; she had read something in the papers . . . So I had to
> begin to write something − not just about dragonflies, gamelans,
> and virgin forests!
>
> I prepared her for the possibility that perhaps I will have to
> leave Bali for a time. I gave all kinds of explanations and reasons
> − of course not mentioning the most serious one. She would
> never understand it, I am afraid. She still thinks I am the purest
> angel . . .
>
> But she will have to know it sometime; there is, I suppose,
> nothing to be done. And chiefly I wrote of course that nothing
> that ever happened to me could ever make me miserable and
> unhappy, and she must never forget that luck is always with me
> and round me and in me − that everything in life has a reason to
> be and nothing ever happens which is not to the good!
>
> Isn't it so, Darling? So now enough of those lamentations.[7]

He changed the subject and wrote about his fascination with small details of
sound. He was able to sit in jail now and simply listen.

> You know, Janechen, I am improving in listening to things! Every
> evening when the light has to go out at 8 and I am in bed and
> not very sleepy yet, I am just listening and enjoying all the full
> orchestra of sounds round about me, and trying to hold them
> separate and determine them and visualize their source . . . There
> is water running, deepish gurgling through my toilet, there is the
> rain falling softly on the tile roof, a different sound from the
> rain on the corrugated iron-covered verandah. Water falling or
> trickling from the roof into mud or puddles; very staccato, jumpy
> things, all different in pitch and rhythm. Then somewhere frogs,
> and somewhere else toads with their hollow barking . . . Inside
> our own walls, the soft and melancholic singing of some prisoner
> − snoring of somebody already asleep − the periodical bell of
> the clock . . . And then of course all the noises one is able to
> produce oneself, scratching one's nose or sneezing, coughing −
> or even the squeaking of the bed . . . Oh Jane, there is such an
> incredible lot − and everything goes beautifully together in the
> most extraordinary sonorities, rhythmisations, syncopations.[8]

Eventually, Zentgraff and his allies would fell their biggest political prize:
H. Fievez de Malines van Ginkel, the Resident of Batavia himself, the man who

two years earlier had turned aside their accusations as overblown. Supposedly, the Resident had sought out young men in the native villages on nighttime walks and then had taken them to his country home. Allegations in hand, the Dutch attorney general for the colony, Marcella, advised van Ginkel to leave quietly. Van Ginkel agreed, but aboard the steamship that was to carry him away, the former Resident found himself stopped as if he were a common criminal fleeing. Zentgraff used the arrest for his most thoroughgoing attack and issued his strongest proclamation against homosexual behavior of any sort by any European.

Significantly, all of his rhetoric was about upholding European concepts of "civilized" manhood, not about any actual harm done to the supposed Asian "boys," who remained silent in *Java-Bode's* columns. Zentgraff continued to allow no hint in the newspaper that the ages of the Asian males involved were indeterminate and that, even if they were under age twenty-one, many would likely have not actually have been labeled "boys" if they were engaging in heterosexual sex.

Instead, Zentgraff called for stringent investigations to prevent what he called "morally impaired" and "psychologically abnormal" men from ever entering the Dutch civil service:

> In every instance of doubt, certainty must be strived for in every way . . . to dig in the private lives of civil servants who are ready for promotion, but also − and more so − for the appointment of morally impaired people who can sooner or later damage the entire society and the Western Authority. Because, no matter what, such elements must be prevented at all costs from holding high and trusted positions. Ways of doing this must be found; it is more important to know their psychological interior than the interior of their houses . . .
>
> Do not let us and this country be ruled by pathological individuals, by homosexuals, but by men with a healthy soul . . .
> [signed] Z.[9]

In the letter that Walter dreaded writing but finally did send to his mother in February 1939, he did not come out to her as a homosexual, if indeed he even needed to. He instead focused on the context in which he found himself. He had gotten trapped in a world where the imperial center was collapsing, even while those empires still asserted that only their notions of romantic heterosexual monogamy could be moral. He focused on the aesthetic state that he had tried to foster in Bali, a place where, he said, men would not have to wear "gas masks, and tanks aren't necessary." Walter wrote almost 1,700 words, six pages of cursive handwritten script, a length highly unusual for him:

> Dear Mom,
> A heartfelt thanks to you . . . Yes, it's true what you've read in the papers. Circumstances are very unpleasant and painful here . . .

You know how many wonderful peoples and entire islands have already quite irresponsibly been spoiled or even completely ruined by coming in contact – and disadvantageous contact at that – with so-called European "culture" . . . Now it seems the Dutch Government has decided to go ahead at this time and intervene, before it's too late. Somewhat suddenly and drastically perhaps, but nevertheless understandably. And all of us who live here in Bali and love Bali will, I suppose, stand to suffer from it . . .

You mustn't be too surprised if I one day write you that I will be leaving Bali . . . That would be very sad for me, naturally, since I've always tried to do my best, insofar as it seemed right to me, to help the Balinese and show them the value of their own culture. In any case, I feel no guilt that I may have exercised any kind of bad or negative influence on them . . .

And if it so happens that I have to leave Bali – What then? I can certainly reassure you here! Because you know me! The world is big and wonderful – and weeds grow tall! There'll be another corner left somewhere where there are still no gas masks, and tanks aren't necessary. If not here, then somewhere else! I've always had luck in life, and have only to wish for something and it just happens – without my needing to put forth much effort. The world has always been like a fairytale for me. Everything always shows up just as good as it gets! . . . It can *never* go badly for me!! What could happen anyway! . . .

Greetings, kisses [for] everyone and everything.

Your Weed.[10]

By early February, Jane Belo had swung into action using her skills as an ethnographer to try to help Walter. On February 14, she talked with a young male named I Seken, who appears to have been one of Walter's ranking servants, a *djongos*. I Seken talked about the tactics a *mantri* (a top official) had used to try to get him to "confess" information about the artist:

He talked menacingly, he said he would put me in jail, in the kawerglap, if I did not mengakoe [confess] . . . Then I said I had nothing to confess, if he ordered me to confess something I would obey, but not because it was the truth, only because he ordered it. And if I was to take an oath, I was ready, he could lock me up for a month if he liked, even if I had to die . . . and it was better to die not having told an untruth.

Seken told a story about a second attempt at coercion.

There was a boy called I Tedoen from Sangai, Singpad, who came to teach the gamelan. He was called before me, and he was threatened, he was very frightened . . . The Mantri told him

that Master was in jail in Denpasar and had already confessed to
sleeping with him. If he now confessed he could go free, but if he
did not he would be put in jail. He then confessed he had slept
twice with Master.

The next day I was called. I was asked if I knew someone
called I Tedeon. I said I did not. I was asked how long I had worked
for Master. I said a year . . . Again I was asked if I did not know
Tedoen. I said no. Then Tedoen was called, asked if he knew me.
He said yes, that's I Seken. Mantri then got very kras (cross) and
asked how I could say I did not know him. I said, I am the Djongos
of Master, many people know me whom I do not know . . . Then
he was quiet for a while. Then he began again, speaking politely
– that's the way it was, kras (cross) for a while, then politely so as
to confuse us. He said I must have [served] Tedoen to eat. I said I
was the Djongos of Master, not the Djongos of that boy there, and
if anybody gave him rice it would be the cook, not me . . .

So they kept me overnight and questioned me three times. I
was asked if I had thought over what I had said, and if I wanted
to say anything different. I said no, I would say the same thing
again, as it was the truth.[11]

Walter's friends found him a lawyer named Witsen Elias, who advised everyone
to not create much of a stir, precisely because of Walter's prominence. "The
difficulty," Jane Belo wrote to a friend, "is that the whole mix-up has political
complications which are rather beyond our ken, and we dare not do or say anything
which will injure his case." Judges in Java were being harsher on more prominent
men. "Everyone seems to think that in a month or so, the whole scandal will have
simmered down somewhat," Belo added, "and the cases which come up the latest
will be most leniently dealt with."[12]

Elias contacted both Margaret Mead and her husband, Gregory Bateson, and
asked if they would be able to testify, but both declined because they were about to
leave the Indies. Instead, they wrote lengthy letters that Elias submitted to the court.
The attorney asked them to answer three questions: What was the likely age of the
Balinese "boys" that Walter had been accused of seducing? What was the nature of
his desire for them? And did he pose any threat to them?

Gregory Bateson answered first in a ten-page letter dated February 28. His tone
was that of an expert witness rather than a personal character reference.

It seems best . . . that I should write down for you all that I have
to say on the subject of guessing the ages of Balinese boys. I am
afraid that some points in what I have to say may be used against
Walter Spies but I do not think any of these are very seriously
against him and I am happier as a scientist if I set down the whole
matter as I see it.[13]

Like a good social scientist, Bateson first defined the term "age," suggesting it could be understood three different ways: chronologically as a date of birth, medically in physical development, or socially as maturity and responsibility. The law, of course, was concerned only with the chronological. About that, Bateson wrote, it was "in general impossible" to prove the age of any man or boy in Bali both because birth certificates simply did not exist and because the Balinese did not calculate time or ages as Westerners did.

> The Balinese do not know their chronological ages and they are not interested in the subject. Under stress of questioning, they will mention as their age whatever figure seems likely to please their questioner. If the questioner is careful to give no hint of what answer he expects, the Balinese will answer almost at random.[14]

Later Bateson sent Elias a seven-page study he and Mead had conducted of Balinese parents to see if they knew the ages of babies whose births he and Mead had been able to actually date. None of the parents did. In one case, for example, the parents of a seven-and-a-half-year-old child said he was only five; in another, the parents thought their three-year-old was less than two.[15] If that sort of error could occur even when the birth was so recent, by the time adolescence or young manhood was reached, few could remember or tell who was sixteen, nineteen, or twenty-one – the kinds of categories the Dutch law was using to determine the legality of sexual relationships.

That left the male anatomy and male physical development to be examined. For that, Bateson offered what amounted to a social scientific explanation of the Asian male body: that, however old the Asian may be, in his late teens through his thirties he would almost always look younger than a European male of comparable age. Bateson's explanation was only slightly hedged. Balinese males, he explained, seemed to initially develop their physical bodies faster than Europeans, but at a certain point in adolescence, they leveled off and began to develop more slowly than Europeans. In other words, he wrote, "If a boy looks like 'European 10' his real chronological age is probably less than 10, [but] if a Balinese boy looks like 'European 17' his real chronological age is probably more than that." Specifically, Bateson noted, the body of a twenty-five-year-old Balinese man "would in many particulars correspond to a European eighteen-year-old boy." That would be especially true, he wrote, if a man's secondary hair was examined. "If you argue from hair," he wrote, "you will get an answer [to the Balinese male's age] that is too young."

He drew a rudimentary graph for the attorney, little more than two lines crossing one another. On one side of the graph, Balinese males would look older than European males; on the other side, they would look younger. Bateson acknowledged, though, that no one really knew the average age at which the lines crossed, much less when they crossed for a specific individual. Again like an academic social scientist, he suggested a study be undertaken of fifty young men whose chronological ages were actually known.

"Be careful," he warned Elias. "If they have any cases against Walter Spies of homosexuality with very much younger boys e.g. with boys right at the beginning of puberty, then the bend of the curve [of bodily changes] will be against you."[16]

A few days later, Bateson apparently decided his social scientist stance had been too detached. He decided to also offer what he knew personally about Walter and so wrote a second letter:

> I do not expect that there are any cases like this [of younger boys] against Walter. In fact I should be very surprised if any cases in [the] first half of puberty are brought up. My estimate of Walter's character would be "a homosexual, but the sort of homosexual who is a man-loving man." And this is a very different picture from the type of homosexual who loves little boys. The man who loves little boys is generally either a frightened rabbit or a bully and the little boys are substitutes for women. I do not think Walter was of this type and I shall be surprised if it is shown that he ever loved little boys.[17]

He went on to suggest that any evidence of that sort should be closely questioned as a possible "'frame up' of some sort," either intentional or accidental.[18]

On March 2, Margaret Mead wrote. Like Bateson, she quickly dismissed the notion that Walter had been sexually involved with any actual "boys," as opposed to older Balinese males whose ages were in the early twenties or were completely undeterminable.

"He has no interest in children," she declared.

For five typewritten pages, Mead the anthropologist explained her own understanding of the causes of homosexuality, ranging from being born with a hermaphroditic body to "traumatic occurrences in early childhood" to dissenting from the sex role that had been prescribed by one's culture or religion. By page six, she had started writing about Walter specifically. His homosexuality, she argued, was neither abnormal nor pathological — but "rare" — rather, she said, like the difference between a boy whose voice failed to change at puberty ("abnormal") and one whose voice was a "high tenor" (normal, but rare).

> This type of homosexual, to which Walter Spies belongs, is an individual who is at once less and more dependent upon other persons [than] are most people in the world. He or she is dependent upon some warmth, some social contact with others, at the same time that they wish to keep their individuality intact, to remain uninvolved with the world of personal relations. In many cases, this urge towards uninvolvement is joined with some special artistic or intellectual gift; the individual feels that he has special

things to do in the world, and things which he must do alone. He
wishes to be close to others and yet not too close.

Bali, she argued, had presented Walter with the ideal setting for such "light"
connections.

> [Balinese relations] to kindred and neighbors are formal and
> impersonal, combined with an ease and frequency of light physical
> contact, the arm on the shoulder, the group of young people,
> sometimes of one sex, sometimes of both sexes, who sleep all
> curled up together, like kittens in a new-made nest. The Balinese
> are capable of standing an amount of physical contact, especially
> close physical contact between adult men, which is unthinkable
> to the European who is not a homosexual. And the Balinese can
> do this because they are not concerned with that aspect of the
> relation between man and man which so preoccupies European
> males at present.

Then she argued that it was, in effect, the trinity of religion, law, and medicine
that was forcing Walter's sexuality to be defined in one of two boxes: heterosexual
or homosexual.

> If W.S. had been born a Balinese, there is every probability that
> he would never have become a homosexual. He would have been
> left free by his society to do his own work, to paint and compose
> music, and he would have been provided with the kind of
> impersonal warmth from men and impersonal sex relations from
> women which would have been congenial to his temperament.
> But he was not born a Balinese, and he came as a gifted unusual
> boy, who had developed his special talents almost unaided in the
> Tartar wilderness, to Germany in the early twenties.

He was a "rare artist type," with no interest in aggression or domination, who
wanted only "casual, graceful, warm physical contacts with other individuals who
are like himself." That, she added pointedly, he could never have found in Europe,
either within romantic, heterosexual marriage or within the kind of homosexual
community that had evolved in Berlin.

> [In Europe] women made demands upon him which were
> completely alien to his spirit, which would have interfered with the
> free development of his spirit. But if he turned to the men, he met
> either the[ir] desire to dominate him or the desire to be dominated.
> And he wished for neither; he wished merely to be free of too
> exacting personal relations, to have the warmth of casual slight
> physical contacts in which there was no possibility of degrading
> either partner to a subordinate position. And HE LEFT BERLIN, for

there was nothing in the rampant homosexuality there which had any meaning for him. He came to Bali and found a people whose personality type was like his own, who would accept him easily and casually, give him affection without demands, leave him free to do his work.

She argued that the number of Balinese men he had socialized with actually argued in his favor:

> He has been criticized because he has had so many slight sexual contacts with different Balinese young men. But in the very number of these fleeting contacts lay their protection and his; they ran no risk of permanent fixation, he ran no risk of a sort of relationship which would tie him down, become an enslaving habit, instead of a gay and careless adventure. The young men who have known Walter Spies marry and are happy, they have children and are proud of them; they continue to serve and paint and make beautiful things as Walter Spies has taught them to do.

Finally, Mead, the great anthropologist, saved for the end of the letter her greatest praise. She wondered at the plane of magical reality that Walter had not only found but had founded in Bali.

> Walter Spies has been able to do what very few gifted people . . . have been fortunate enough to do. He has found a country of the spirit, a country which is so congenial to him, that his rare gifts have been able to flower there . . . He has been able to preserve the best in Bali because Bali has preserved the best in him.
>   In Bali, therefore, Walter Spies, who felt no guilt about his relations with men himself, was not forced by public opinion to feel guilty. The Balinese thought it was too bad the Toean [white master] did not have a wife, but then he painted such beautiful pictures – just like a God, and perhaps had no time for it.[19]

Walter stayed in Kerobokan until mid-March. Then he was sent for trial in Surabaya. Almost immediately, he had to respond to his mother, whose letters must have been growing increasingly distraught and angry. He responded with an unusual peevishness, as if the jail time had become wearisome, going so far as to tell his mother to send all of her future letters to his lawyer:

> Why can't you let up needlessly upsetting yourself? . . . I ask you strongly and once again to stop it! What sense is there in it?! You've already known, for I don't know how long, that nothing can happen to me that's not for my best. Why don't you believe that!! . . .

Something else *very* important!! For God's sake, contain
yourself and don't write *objectionable* things about the Dutch in
your letters . . . Totally innocent statements, as in your first letter,
can be misinterpreted quite easily – and then we'll be sitting with
our pants down!! After all, you must know that *all* letters, *here
too*, are read by the various authorities before reaching a person . .
. don't mention names, titles, positions of people . . . [these could]
become dangerous for a person in these joyless times! I'm now
having all my letters addressed first to my lawyer and ask you to
do the same as well . . . I can't write anything more specific, but as
mentioned, as soon as it's all straightened out – and that can't take
very much longer – I'll inform you immediately" . . .

Be reasonable. Don't make me unhappy . . . By the way, I'm
writing from Surabaya.[20]

Throughout those weeks of March, Jane Belo continued to write letters to
friends. On March 9, she contacted the archeologist Stutterheim, who had warned
Walter months earlier that rumors were building against him and that he was likely
to become a political scapegoat:

You can imagine Walter has amazed everyone by the continued
joyousness of his spirit even in jail. He has made two paintings,
translated a stack of folktales, managed to go on directing the
activities of gamelans
. . . Balinese and Europeans alike said, "He must not have a
guilty conscience if he can take it so calmly, and go on just as
he always has". . . And of course he <u>has</u> got a free conscience,
because he knows that he has not done anything ever that would
harm a Balinese . . .

That the charges against him are dubious, to say the least,
is quite clear. Certainly he has never cared for the young, and it
becomes a mere quibbling point when the lawyers have to make
a great fuss debating, with the aid of X-rays, Balinese calendrical
computations, etc., the age in years of Balinese who are obviously
mature . . . and on this it seems will hang the whole trial.
You know, it's nonsense.[21]

The circumstantial evidence for Walter's sexual attractions also pointed in a
direction opposite that of "boys." His paintings and photographs typically showed
not prepubescent boys or even young teenagers, but laborers or men like those in
Hamid or *Gelodog* or those waiting with their fighting cocks or bathing amid the
banyan trees – all of whom seemed to be at least in their twenties or thirties. The
male dance Walter had choreographed, the *kecak,* was performed mostly by men in
their twenties or thirties; he had not chosen to feature the *sanghyang* with younger
boys in *Island of Demons.* And his known affections with European men – with

Hans Jürgen von der Wense, or Murnau, or even his close friendship with Conrad Spies – were with those in their twenties or thirties at times when he himself was either of a similar age or within a decade of theirs.

Walter's lawyer, Elias, also contacted the families of those whom the artist had allegedly "abused." When the attorney asked one father whether he was angry, he was said to have replied, "But why? He [Walter] is after all our best friend, and it was an honor for my son to be in his company, and if both are in agreement, why fuss?"[22]

Few details would be reported about Walter's trial in Surabaya that spring. *Java-Bode* carried no stories; by April its comments on the *Zedenschandaal* had dwindled to minor, scattered paragraphs.[23] If a transcript was made, it was likely destroyed during the later Japanese occupation or by tropical decay in neglected archives. Surprisingly, a transcript or thorough report also never seems to have surfaced in the extensive correspondence that Dutch bureaucrats forwarded to the colonial ministry at The Hague. Published histories about Walter lack any testimony by witnesses or by Walter himself. They also do not contain the statement that was apparently made by the judge at the end of the trial, and are absent of any descriptions of what kind of actual seduction or sex is supposed to have taken place between Walter and any Balinese "boys" – whether it was actually sex or simply the "light physical contact" Mead had described as customary among Balinese men, the arm on a shoulder, the casual sleeping together.

Because the Dutch judge sitting in Surabaya ultimately convicted Walter, most current writers automatically assume that he was, in fact, guilty of seducing children or at least young teens.[24] They ignore the also likely possibility that, as with Leopold Ries in the Netherlands, Walter may have been turned into a scapegoat by Nazi and white supremacist sympathizers like *Java-Bode*'s Zentgraff and by angry Christian missionaries like Mary Pos.

The fact that Walter did not appeal his sentence is no evidence of guilt. His lawyer knew better than to do so as a matter of strategy. The Dutch colonial judicial system allowed appeals courts to actually increase lengths of sentences. If a relatively light sentence was given by the trial court, and if much of that sentence had already been served by the time a trial occurred, then the practical thing to do was to not appeal. Both factors – a light sentence and much of the time already served – happened in Walter's case.

By early April, the trial had concluded. Walter had been convicted, but the sentence was relatively short.

Elias would write to Bateson and Mead that their letters had helped when presented to the court:

> The eight months which Spies got, luckily were not such a blow
> and Spies, very philosophical and sensible, took them with easy
> grace. Also, thanks to your good work – photos, reports on

Balinese customs and inability of precision re ages and estimation
of time — we managed to obtain an acquittal in four out of the
eight cases. The prosecutor had asked for an imprisonment of
twelve months and the Court gave eight. I also could make a very
good use of Mrs. Bateson's essay on homosexuality, especially
applied to Spies' case.

Spies' imprisonment will be finished on the 28th of August
as all the months he has been in jail before his case came up,
were deducted. He still is in Surabaya, where he may receive
visitors and is able to paint. In fact he has made three pictures
and appreciates it no end to be able to paint without any of the
usual disturbances![25]

Walter himself described the trial only briefly in one of his letters to Jane
written on April 13:

There we are at last! 8 months. 3½ are gone already and so it
seems not quite as disagreeable as it seems. The only disagreeable
and very disagreeable thing is that I will miss you.

In the "sentence" which the President of the court read, it
was mentioned in some "flowery words" that I was liked by the
Balinese and did a lot of good to them and about them; at least
I understood it like that (it was read very quickly and not very
clearly) so I am very happy that my "sins" were looked upon as
not too dreadful and too "destroying." And it was also specially
mentioned that although I had lived in Bali more than 12 years,
and everyone "knew," nobody had ever "warned" me, or expressed
any displeasure about it, pointing out the "restrictions" which
could become so unexpectedly dangerous.[26]

He continued, "3 of the 8 witnesses were 'fired,' I think." Walter seemed to be
suggesting that their testimony had been discounted, or they had not been allowed
to testify at all, or they were obviously much older than twenty-one: "Ali, Djenak
and Kadja, as being possibly older, or in the case of Kadja, improbable. There were
hundreds of other things said, but I can't remember them now and didn't hear them
clearly enough, and I haven't got the sentence to read yet because it wasn't quite
finished."

He wanted to stay at the Surabaya Jail rather than move to one in Bandung.
"I'll try to stay here as long as possible . . . I am just feeling like painting." He added
cheerily, "And here I can eat apples, and there none!"[27]

In the Surabaya Jail, Walter surrendered to his newly imposed solitude, but he
also strengthened his resistance to the world invading his.

Margaret Mead wrote in June. She did not "have a very big supply of anything cheerful to say, except how much we love you . . . This western world is not a very good one these days; the newspapers are nothing but scareheads, sunk submarines, and new purges. We are not pleased to be back where we have newspapers every day. Maybe you do not, and if so you are lucky."[28]

In Germany, his sister Daisy's dancing career had begun to flourish. Ironically, she would become one of Hitler's favorites. "My dearest DéSie!" Walter wrote in July, "write me sometime about your dancing! . . . I really would very much like to know how it's done! . . . What and how do you prefer to dance, do you dance by yourself? And what is the process? Does it begin with the music (if so, to what extent and following what is the music danced?) or does it begin with the movement of the dance itself, and is the music only a medium? . . . Oh God, there are so many questions!"[29]

A letter to his mother the same month began lyrically, "I am chi-chipper. To-tomorrow too! For m-me it's going splendidly. Mo-mother doesn't have to get upset any mo-more."[30]

In two of the paintings Walter completed at Surabaya, he expressed his gentle defiance of the values of the world around him.

The first sang homage to the Bali he had both experienced and imagined into existence. Titled *The Landscape and Her Children*, it shows Walter's signature slender male peasant walking through a tropical forest followed by his cow, the two of them slightly off center.[31] An exact, smaller pair repeats them in the distance. The landscape dominates, sunlight glittering from the edges of each frond, and rhythmic waves of palms rolling into the distance toward the island's revered Gunung Agung volcano. Above that, cumulus clouds spiral. Farther into the distance, the visual planes shift and yet another volcano appears, surrounded by boiling clouds.

Walter is said to have joked that, in the painting, the "mother" − the land − seemed to want to call its children toward home "because there is a storm brewing."[32] To Walter, the children in the painting were not just the humans but also all the plants and animals. Around them, the light, he wrote, was "threatening and heavy."[33] His concern with constructing a sense of home in the face of danger seemed to have intensified.

In a letter to an art critic, Walter wondered why it was that viewers of the painting often saw only the landscape. They did not seem to perceive what he called the "family complications" of the desires of each of the palms and each of the humans. Walter's biographers Hans Rhodius, John Darling, and John Stowell later wrote that the painting was the "crowning work of his 'magic-realist' style."[34]

The second painting Walter composed turned in an unexpected and, compared to his previous work, an almost incomprehensible direction. While it could be seen as a revisit to the melancholy Expressionist farewells he had painted at the end of his stay in Germany, it seemed more like an extraordinary Scriabinesque plunge forward into a fluid world of body, desire, and gender, a world that was both in dialogue with and in contrast to the social reality in which Walter now found himself punished. He would deliberately try to turn sound into light and rhythm, not simply as waves of palm trees or developments of certain tonalities of shadow but as something that focused on the kinds of human family complications that various solidifications into bodies and desires posed.

He was at work on it within a week of the conclusion of his trial. He tried to explain to Jane Belo what he had in mind by comparing it to a piece of music that he said he had heard. Imagine objects of different forms, he wrote to her, all in relationship to one another in space and "forming a kind of stereometrical figure in a three-dimensional space," just "hanging in air." Nothing would be moving, but there would be a "certain tension of color in the planes between those objects." It would be as if there was a "magnetic radiation" holding them to each other. "But don't forget," he warned, "everything is in a state of repose." Nothing would move – except the viewer, who would go in and out, up and down, and pass not only between but – he underlined this – "*through* the figures" with the result that they would "enlarge perspectively and become more brilliant in color." After going inside the objects, the viewer would "fly higher and higher" until outside again, not only circling around perpendicularly but then at an inclined angle and then at the horizontal, and finally it would then be time to go back inside but "perhaps with a different speed now."

> One has only to follow one's own feeling, one has to become quite
> a mindless "medium," just feeling intensely where the best way
> is to go, where to stop, to turn a corner, where to rush through
> quickly, where to fall suddenly or to make a somersault perhaps
> where there is need for one![35]

That, he told her, was what life was and what he wanted to paint. He titled the canvas *Scherzo for Brass*.[36] In classical European symphonies, scherzos are the third, lighthearted, fast-paced, and dancelike movement intended as contrast to the slow adagios of the second movement. It was as if Walter could now see his time in Europe as his allegro, his time in Bali as a slow and graceful unfolding, and the time he was now entering into as an uncertain, fast-moving one. In Italian, scherzo means "joke," although some composers had turned their "jokes" into very darkly veiled rhythms. Walter's purpose, as always, seemed to be to teach about the different experiences of a surprising nature that fit no one's rigid conceptions. He seemed determined to comment especially on the relationship between that part of a human that was body and "animal" – the part he had been imprisoned for – and that part which was face and soul.

In the painting, what appears to be a family of centaur-like beings with human face and animal bodies frolics upon a tropical beach. Many of the figures are tiny like children, two are moderately sized as if adolescent, and two others fill the painting from top to bottom as if they were parents of the family below. Unlike European centaurs, though, none of these shows any muscle. All have rounded faces and smoothly elongated, curved bodies similar to the roebucks Walter had painted in *The Deerhunt* seven years earlier – the effect being to treat them more like sweeping musical notes pouring across the page rather than actual physical beings. A single "centaur-note" dominates the center of the picture, splitting it into two halves. In his letters, Walter referred to it as "The Animal" or "The Big One." Its face, with angular nose, almost feminine lips, and wide doe eyes sadly staring at the viewer, resembles Walter in that photograph taken when he was a teenager at Nekljudovo the summer that his adolescence turned into contest-driven journeys. In the photograph, he had stared off to the space in front of his right shoulder; now the musical note turned to look directly at the audience.

To the left of "The Animal," the two smaller, adolescent-size figures stand parallel to each other, their necks crossing, their faces also staring directly at the viewer. With their own sharply angular noses, one bears a resemblance to Walter's sister, Daisy, while the other taller, somewhat more masculine one, could be his brother Leo. To the right of "The Animal," is the other large "note," a graceful, crescent-moon curved figure Walter referred to as "the Mona Lisa Mother," looking gently down at three smaller "centaurs" that have climbed aboard her back.

Small ones rush and tumble at the bottom of the left side of the picture. But on the right side they form themselves into doubles and triples. "The Animal" himself becomes the most three-dimensional, a "stereometrical figure hanging in three-dimensional space." Adjusting perspective, moving around and *through* the figure, what appears to be an ocean bordering the island becomes instead "The Big One's" torso and body. What had been curved palm fronds with curious dogs standing between reveal themselves as the balustrade of a spine.

Aspects of the painting resemble a Hieronymus Bosch garden of delight, although without any overtly sexual aspects. Other parts evoke a *Guernica* sadness. It recalled a comment Walter had once made when he and Hans Jürgen van der Wense had loved and played music all night: "I do not hear the music," he had commented. "I am entirely little and I go around between the notes and the lines. I am inside with it."[37]

Walter tried to describe the painting to his mother in July and eventually sent a photograph. Even he seemed to be having trouble explaining exactly the fusion he had painted. The "clangorous trumpeting in this Picture of Light can't so readily be heard so I suppose I'll have to word a harmony and color legend for it." He tried to explain this magical realist understanding to everyone in words. He wrote, "This is already (it's going to make me puke) the umpteenth time I'm doing it, since naturally everyone wants to be informed."

First, the colors: the heavens were black with a tinge of blue. The light behind the "Big One" at the center was "glistening yellow," as well as "frightful" and "overbearingly sharp." Everything that resembled a bush, a shrub, or the forest was painted red-bronze-copper "so it has a metallic glitter and sparkle." The creatures, although having human faces, were "poisonous green" and "steely blue in brilliance," best compared to "beetle wings shimmering like 'shangjang' glitter." The earth and soil were "pink and orangy brown" and then turning black-blue in the shadows.

The left-hand side of the painting has the tumbling centaur-notes he described as "quite normal." "A certain naturalness and randomness reign there. There is arguing, anger, astonishment, staring in boredom or running away."

But once the viewer arrived at "Big One," "right there it goes crazy." The comment is telling, especially since the "Big One's" face so resembled Walter himself.

"There he stands – and something has snapped!"

"A kind of obsession, a kind of ridiculous rhythm overcomes them all . . . Objects double themselves, triple themselves or dislocate themselves into wacky arrangement. Perspective heeds no counsel; colors run wild. The creatures chameleon themselves into ultramarine and magenta-violet. The three sisters on the back of the Mona-Lisa mother are behaving themselves in such a way that they're quite ridiculously pink."

The light also changed on this right side of the *Scherzo*. "The light, which sneers there behind 'the Big One,' has become very cold, cold turquoise green-blue, and shines on the line of leaves that has taken form, with the Balu dogs in between and mirrored in the sea of its body – with the coldest paleness of a corpse." Even the foliage had shifted. The palm fronds had grown "quite fleshy, like drooling tongues."

He warned his mother that many of the "crescendos, diminuendos, accelerandos" would be lost in the black-and-white photograph that he was sending – the photograph that would become the sole record of the *Scherzo* when the painting was later lost.

"A better reproduction," he added, "would probably be attained in radio."[38]

To Jane, he had written: "There are so many faces in it, many looking right into your eyes, so very disturbing that you have to look away, otherwise you blush!" He had added: "Every morning when I uncover the thing, I have to close my ears first against the noise it makes."[39]

In a long letter to an art critic, Walter explained:

> The peculiar form [the *Scherzo*] has is similar to some of the later compositions of Scriabin, I think especially in the Ninth and Tenth piano sonatas which I really don't like that much but I always get sucked into it because I hope something funny will happen. Somewhere in the middle of the composition there is an infection of some dancelike rhythm that gets stronger and stronger until all the themes are infected with it – crazy and terribly grimaced. And at the end it's a trancelike dance ecstasy.[40]

Scriabin's Ninth Sonata had been termed the "Black Mass Sonata," built around the instability of a minor ninth interval, its final chord the tritone that had come to be known as the "devil's note." The Tenth Scriabin had been called his sonata of insects.

Walter's most telling comment came to his friend, fellow composer Leopold Stokowski:

> Everything seems concentrated into a kind of final chord and he [the "Big One"] again is looking out from the picture straight into your eyes in a sort of melancholy fashion, while trying to be understood and perhaps even forgiven.[41]

11
Dancing with Ezekiel

On September 1, 1939, the Dutch freed Walter from the Surabaya jail. The trial judge had ruled he could remain in the East Indies. It seemed that, at least as far as the judge was concerned, Walter was not an exotic foreign threat who had to be banished from the colony back to the center of the empire. Unlike other Europeans caught up in the *Zedenschandaal* who were being sent away, Walter was apparently not considered a continuing threat to Bali's "boys." Perhaps the judicial conclusion was that he had never really been much of one.

The same day Walter walked free, half a world away three German army groups launched their blitzkrieg against Poland. Unfortunately for Walter, he was still a German citizen.

Walter wrote to his brother Leo later that month, explaining his approach to life as he now reached his forty-fourth birthday:

> This whole life is another birthday for me! . . . Every day I feel like I am reborn, and my table of life is overflowing with presents, most of which I wished for or gave myself. And there is so much beauty that I can hardly find the time to regard or play with it. So much is left unplayed with! . . . I lament people who do not love life, who do not play with life![1]

At first, he sought a respite at the botanical gardens at Buitenzorg on the outskirts of Batavia, invited there by friends. Walter briefly departed from his landscapes and Scriabinesque scherzos to sketch in minute detail the hair on spider legs, the stream-like arms of sea stars, and, in a possible bit of deference to Scriabin's Tenth Sonata of insects, the wings of dragonflies.

Realistic, glimmering miniaturization. It was an exacting practice of one technique that made magical realism work.

Walter seemed to now want greater simplicity: drawings pinned flat to whiteboard like specimens, with no depth and with the viewer looking straight down upon them.

In November, he returned to Tchampuan, and while Bali the island had not changed much, the Bali of the imagination that he knew had. Most Europeans had gone, except for the Dutch officials who had treated him so badly. By May 1940, Hitler had turned his attention to the western frontier, his army rolling across Belgium, Luxemburg, and into Holland, for Walter creating a repeat of the situation he had found himself in as a teenager in Nekljudovo in 1914: a German citizen in a country now invaded by Germany. On May 15, The Hague surrendered and the Indies became a free-floating piece of a former empire.

Margaret Mead wrote from New Hampshire in August. Her husband, Gregory Bateson, had just gotten back from England, where the military had refused him since "they have no use for anthropologists." Jane Belo had gone off to Central America. Colin McPhee had traveled to Pennsylvania to eat German food and "treat the local inhabitants as if they were Balinese"– a comment she left tactfully unexplained. She was still assembling her reports about Balinese culture that would add to her fame.

"It seems incredibly odd," Mead wrote, "to be working on details of the ritual behavior of the Balinese with all the world cracking about our heads, but on the other hand sometimes it seems the only sane thing to be doing . . ."

"Dear Walter," she closed, "I hope you are still being happy in Bali."[2]

By then, Walter had again been detained.

The day the Dutch packed Walter onto a wagon, a friend in Bali, Marianne van Wessem, caught her last sight of him.

> By chance I saw him. Walter sat on the last wagon on the edge, like he so often sat, with his arms resting on his legs. I could only give him one piece of chocolate and then they drove on. That was our farewell.[3]

He had had to leave all of his belongings at Tchampuan, including artworks such as his *Scherzo*. Van Wessem paid the Dutch for all of them rather than see them dispersed, but her hope of saving them would be futile. Only one storage cabinet would survive the war. The rest, including the one with the *Scherzo*, were destroyed.

Distrusting all Germans, the Dutch first sent Walter to Ngawi on Java.

"Each day here," he wrote, "is like yesterday, and that like tomorrow . . . I do not paint here because of all the people and because of the missing quiet." But he was determined to remain alert and creative. Send books, he told friends.[4] Later his list would expand: Send paint brushes, an easel. He gave six students instruction in Russian. He found a piano to play and began practicing fugues. By the end of summer, he heard he would be moved to the island of Sumatra, to a place called Kotatjane, "the central internment warehouse," he called it, "somewhere in Aceh."

He kept his optimism: "It should be a pretty area, and a cool climate."[5]

The letters soon turned into postcards.

"Only 100 words!" he wrote from the new camp in October 1940. "Pencils and ink vanish." The weather was actually worse. "Every day, rain and rain, and that is very depressing."[6]

A Dutch guard, Cornelius Conyn, who had met Walter in Bali years earlier and had viewed male dances with him, was accidentally assigned to guard him, their fates now separated by the different citizenships into which they had been classified.

> My loaded gun on me I went over there [to the cell block where Walter was kept]. Suddenly I saw a recognizable face! . . . A long thin white appearance, the eyes of a seer, eyes that shined with all the knowledge and good of this world . . . Walter sat alone, with his knees raised, his long back leaning against a little palm, and drew. He smoked his cigarettes that he rolled himself with quick and nervous puffs. I recognized him at first through his characteristic gestures because he had changed his appearance during the years since my visit to Bali. He let a beard grow — thin yellow stubble that was in its first stage. His crumpled straw hat, his provocative red shirt that was open, and above all his remarkable dark, all-seeing eyes that gave his face a look like the self-portraits of van Gogh . . .
>
> In this instant he looked up and our glances crossed each other. He recognized me. I believe that I blushed down to the roots of my hair, a childhood habit that I thought was long gone. I felt deeply ashamed, but what could I do? Behind me native soldiers and my comrades, who were on the other side of the wire, were coming near.
>
> Walter found the best solution. He obviously stared in my direction, then turned his head and shrugged his shoulders. But his lean face with those deep folds around his mouth suddenly illuminated from an inner laugh, a mild and wise laugh that touched me emotionally. I felt that he, as well as myself, remembered back to our last meeting and remembered that unreal moonlit night in his garden, when the two boys did that trance-dance for us.[7]

Another German, F.W. Block, had also been interned in the camp with Walter and remembered him in a later letter to Walter's brother, Leo:

> I learned of your brother from behind the barbed wire. He was like many others in a tennis shirt and washed blue gym pants. His long blonde hair was bleached from the sun. His narrow face with those striking lines, those big eyes, could see so much. Mostly he was happy, often sunny, but always loveable. For weeks, led by Walter, we built a badminton court, first thirty of us, then only four . . . And after a long time without proper music, a piano came into the camp. I saw your brother's happy face as he sat before

it for the first time. He practiced daily, sometimes imitating the gamelan. It sounded very genuine and put us in a wistful mood.[8]

Months in the jungle passed slowly.

"Saturday I played in a concert," Walter wrote in April 1941. "If the piano were better, it would not have been quite so bad . . . Otherwise, the life here is terribly monotonous. No quiet to concentrate really. With the paintings, it does not go so good. Two pictures had to be destroyed again!"[9]

July: "The same monotony and useless boredom."[10]

September: "The only piano in our block is old and broken." Could someone send an old one? His Russian language students had celebrated his birthday. They had danced. "A sigh escaped each, colored with some hope."[11]

By autumn 1941, rumors reached the camp. The Japanese, it was said, were eying the Indies for their own empire. Britain, supposedly, was preparing a safer detention camp, "somewhere else," Conyn wrote, perhaps in India or Ceylon. The prisoners at Kotatjane would have to be moved.

Walter continued to paint, even building a small studio next to his stone barracks. His choices of what he wanted to communicate in his final days in the Indies sharpened. All the brutality of the empires was converging on what he had been able to imagine into a home.

First, he painted a tight canvas overwhelmed by foliage that he called *The Jungle*. Block described it:

> There were light and olive-green contours, trees, bark, grass, and a stream in the pebbles. He painted in bright and dark green-blue colors. With unbelievable authenticity he drew different trees, lilies, moss, lichen, ferns. Every part was like a botanical work of art. He endlessly painted out in the open, incredibly firmly, and almost always in black and white. The dark trunk of a huge tree cut through the painting, hard stripes like rays of sun.[12]

It was a dark rendering broken by only small amounts of light. Walter managed to send it to Marianne van Wessem in Bali, who noticed that, within its darkness penetrated by a hardened trunk, it had also "a clearing full of nice light."[13] She hung it in her bungalow at Tchampuan.

The second painting was a memory of his own Balinese house at *Tchampuan* — now, he knew, lost forever.

For his other work, Walter chose an unusual theme for him: a Biblical narrative from the story of the prophet Ezekiel. He had been concerned with the dances the Balinese used to ensure the ongoing balance between the good Barong and the evil Rangda, and with the mix of what was considered magical and what was considered real. But he had never so explicitly assumed a Christian theme in his paintings. Portrayals of the Ezekiel narrative had extended across hundreds of centuries of Western art, from Fra Angelico through Raphael to the mystic William Blake, and onward through one of Walter's earliest influences, Marc Chagall. All had tackled the challenge of visually expressing the vision, and now Walter chose to do the same.

The Biblical story goes this way:

When the first of the Jews had begun to be exiled to the land of Babylon, a revelation had befallen Ezekiel. In it, an angry God had condemned all the empires for their hardheadedness, promising that mischief would come upon mischief and the cities would fill with blood. According to some stories accompanying the main Biblical account, Israel's young sons would be forced to choose whether to die by fire or to comply with the demand of King Nebuchadnezzar of Babylon that they worship him and his imperial idols. The sons would choose to die. But then they would be reborn.

In Chapter 37 of the book, Ezekiel prophesizes to dry bones that from them a new life would arise, the Lord proclaiming: "I will put my Spirit in you and you will live, and I will settle you in your own land."[14]

A homeland was promised for those who had been driven into exile. The final chapters of the book detail a blueprint for constructing an aesthetic temple to anchor the center of the new home.

Of all the revelations in the Bible, Ezekiel's first vision in his encounters is one of the most complex and colorful, told in far more visual detail than is the case with the simpler burning bushes or skyward ladders of other books in the Hebrew Scriptures. Ezekiel's vision is of "a windstorm coming out of the north" – just as the empire of Japan was – "an immense cloud with flashing lightning" and four living creatures in the center of a fire, each having the face of a man, an ox, a lion, or an eagle. The four had wings. Beside their legs, wheels intersected other wheels sparkling like yellow-green gleams of chrysolite, the mineral that supposedly turns dreams into reality. Together the four figures and their wheels form a base of fire, cloud, and light, and above them rises a single "throne of sapphire" and "a figure like that of a man." Around him glows a brilliant light "like a rainbow in the clouds on a rainy day."[15]

Each artist treated the vision differently. Fra Angelico had placed sexless Gospel evangelists inside the wheels to make it seem as though the vision was a precursor of the Christian New Testament stories. The more sensual Raphael had instead used two naked cherubs to frame a highly eroticized male God with strong pectoral muscles and powerful shoulder and biceps muscles. William Blake had focused on a nude, multifaced, muscular male beast carrying a clothed and ancient sage.

For Walter, now ending his own quest to find "a new homeland," the vision appeared to have taken on special power.

His canvas would fuse the landscapes and the power of light and shadow that he had been exploring for years. The only information about the details would come from one of Walter's fellow prisoners at Kotatjane, who remembered that Walter's *Vision of the Prophet Ezekiel* would be drawn — as was Walter's custom — as three independent planes of narrative stitched together. One plane held fire playing in the sky and reflecting onto the landscape. Another held a solitary male hermit at a magically lit refuge in a cave on a hill. The third plane held the wheels of Ezekiel's vision spinning.[16]

Little else is known about the painting or why Walter chose its theme. Perhaps one hint is the positioning of the male as a magically lit hermit. In the Bible, the prophet is warned:

> Son of man, with one blow I am about to take away from you the
> delight of your eyes. Yet do not lament or weep or shed any tears.
> Groan quietly; do not mourn for the dead.[17]

On December 9, 1941, Walter sent a postcard to a friend, the final one that would survive.

> I hope it will be possible to send you my two last paintings. But I
> must wait, because the paint is not entirely dry.[18]

The day before, local time, the Japanese had bombed Pearl Harbor and launched their thrust toward the Indies.

By January 1942, the Japanese were pressing toward Singapore and their bombers were patrolling the Straits of Malacca, looking for any airfields the Dutch might have on Sumatra. The German prisoners at Kotatjane prepared for a long ride south down the island to the port of Padang. Fearful that the prisoners might escape and assist the Japanese, the Dutch planned to move them to Ceylon. The Dutch guard from the camp, Conyn, remembered seeing Walter as he left the camp. He was, Conyn wrote, "long, haggard." But still he wore his red shirt "as a defiant fleck of color in the bleak monotony of the terrible khaki that most wore."

"To the very end," Conyn wrote, "he remained striking. On top of his bags lay a piece of canvas to paint and under his free arm he carried a sketchbook of witty drawings."[19]

A few days later, Walter and several hundred other prisoners were ferried aboard bamboo rafts to the *Van Imhoff*, an old merchant ship that the Dutch had pressed into military service. The ship had limited lifeboats and life jackets. The captain, M.J. Hoeksema, apparently protested, only to be ordered to embark anyway. Walter and others were locked into the holds. On January 18, the ship sailed from Padang north toward Nias Island.

One of the internees on board with Walter, a missionary, would later remember:

> We had lost all our belongings. We possessed no more than a towel, a bar of soap, and the clothes that we wore. The ship offered little space for 200 people; therefore, 111 internees were sent back to shore. We lay the remaining 366 in the bottom of the storage vessel like herrings in a barrel. All entrances and hatches were secured with heavy barbed wire behind which stood the sentry. We could not see anything because we were deep under the water line, and had the feeling of sitting in a rat trap. An unbearable heat and a terrible stench filled the room. We did not know where we were going.[20]

About noon the next day, January 19, not far north from Nias Island, a Japanese bomber pilot swept low along the hills of the western Sumatran coast. An unarmed merchant ship from an enemy empire was easy prey. That much of one plane of reality the Japanese pilot knew. Another plane of reality, that the ship was carrying citizens of his empire's ally empire, Germany, he likely did not know.

The Japanese pilot aimed either a bomb or a torpedo. The missionary aboard the *Van Imhoff* remembered:

> An explosion shook the ship. We did not know what it was. Before we could ask the reason, a second, even worse explosion came . . . The ship reared like an animal. The engines stopped. Among the internees, a wild cry arose from fear. We were tossed back and forth, heard hissing steam and felt the ship incline to the side.[21]

As the ship began to sink, most of the Dutch guards and crew filled the lifeboats and rowed away. But they did not tell the prisoners.

> When the plane was gone, the Dutch guard commander came to the door and tried to calm us. He praised us that we had behaved calmly and said the ship had no serious damage, they would check the engines, and then the journey could continue. We should not worry. They would care for us . . . If a disaster actually happened, the captain would be the last to leave the ship. His words were only lies, so we would not mutiny. They had already given up the ship.[22]

One guard who had stayed behind released some German prisoners and helped them into what few life jackets remained. Other prisoners plunged into the ocean, most drowning as they attempted to swim ashore. Whether Walter drowned still on the *Van Imhoff* or trying to make it to shore, no one knows.[23]

Seventeen years earlier, when Walter had first landed on Java, he had pretended in the letter to his mother that he was afraid to return to Germany in winter because he might be lost at sea in a storm. Now the storm had come, and Walter's life was over. He was only forty-six.

For anthropologists, Bali had been a museum; for photographers, a voyeurs' delight. Dutch bureaucrats, missionaries, and Nazis had insisted on fitting the island's bodies to the monumental categories favored by their empires.

For Walter, though, Bali had been a different homeland, one for the aesthetic ideals of a manhood that had gone dry in the face of imperial contests. In Bali, males could move sound and light and rhythm into their own "cloud of flashing lightning," their chests bare, their long slender fingers wheeling in the firelight on dark nights, their legs dancing magic and reality together, forever resisting *leyaks*.

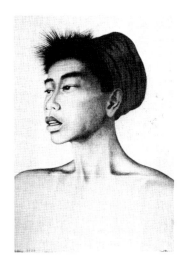

Plate 1   *Hamid,* 1923
         Walter Spies Foundation/Leiden

Plate 2   *The Farewell,* 1921
         Walter Spies Foundation/Leiden

Plate 3   *Four Young Balinese with Fighting Cocks*, 1929
         Walter Spies Foundation/Leiden

Plate 4   *Balinese Legend*, 1930
         *Walter Spies Foundation/
         Leiden*

Plate 5   *The Deerhunt*, 1932
           Walter Spies
           Foundation/Leiden

Plate 6   *Iseh in Early Morning*
           Light, 1938
           Walter Spies Foundation/
           Leiden

Plate 7   *The Landscape and Her Children,* 1939
Walter Spies Foundation/Leiden

Plate 8   *Scherzo for Brass,* 1939
Walter Spies Foundation/Leiden

Plate 9   Stuart Koe as Fridae.com CEO, 2005.
Courtesy of Stuart Koe/Photograph by Chris A.

Plate 10   A masculinity of feasting:
Khun Toc's dining table at Babylon.
Courtesy of Adrian Parry/Babylon.

Plate 11   Entryway at Babylon.
Courtesy of Adrian Parry/Babylon

Plate 12   Winckelmann-style statue at Babylon.
Courtesy of Adrian Parry/Babylon

Plate 13   Screen shot of Fridae 2005.
Used courtesy of Fridae.asia

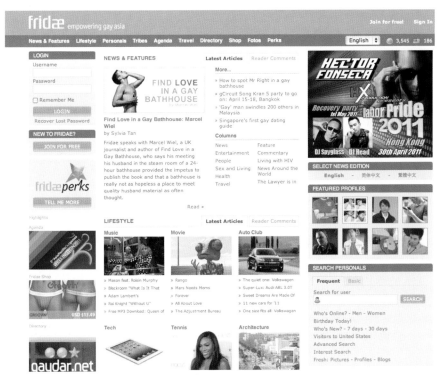

Plate 14   Screen shot of Fridae, 2011.
Used courtesy of Fridae.asia

Plate 15   Photograph from
           Nation V party,
           2005.
           Photograph by Victor
           Chau/Fridae.asia

Plate 16   Photograph from Nation V party, 2005.
           Photograph by kit/Fridae.asia

12

Transition: A Murder for Paradise

The year the Dutch prosecuted Walter in Bali, 1939, Darrell Berrigan left the United States, twenty-three-years old and, much as Walter had been, a restless young male in search of a new homeland. Wiry, witty, and in his later years given to showing up at dignified occasions in flamboyant sports shirts, he had grown up in Bakersfield, California, attended junior college, made his way to the Detroit auto factories, served as a schoolteacher in Colorado, and then had returned to California to become a social worker. He was broke when he arrived in Shanghai. Japan had occupied most of coastal China, but Pearl Harbor had not yet occurred, and so the Americans and the Japanese were still at peace and Berrigan was able to hire on with the United Press wire service. For two years, he had reported on the ongoing Sino-Japanese War. In 1941, while Walter was being detained again, Darrell – or "Berry" as he was sometimes called – transferred to Bangkok before the Japanese attacked Pearl Harbor and invaded the Indies.[1]

In Bangkok, he had had plenty to write about.

Absolute rule by a Chakri king had not long survived Vajiravudh's sudden death in 1925. In June 1932, the government headed by his brother Prajadhipok had fallen to a coup led by the newly educated class of civil servants that Chulalongkorn and Vajiravudh had created and by the military officers who had lost their faith in the monarchy's potency. Prajadhipok had reigned as a constitutional monarch for three years but then had abdicated in the face of ongoing contests with the anti-monarchists. The new rulers replaced him with a nine-year-old king, Ananda Mahidol – Rama VIII – who would stay safely far away, studying and living in Switzerland.

By then the politics of gender and power in Siam had grown even more complex than during Vajiravudh's reign. The course toward greater distinctions between male and female as urged by the Europeans had continued but had begun twists describable only as uniquely Siamese.

Polygyny would finally be officially banned in 1935, the year of Prajadhipok's abdication. Siam's family law would henceforth tolerate only the triple supremacy as an example of modernity, *siwilai*. But there were two careful twists. A Siamese man could officially marry only one woman, but he could still register all of his children by any woman for inheritance. As Vajiravudh had warned, to do otherwise would have suddenly created a new social problem in the country: thousands of illegitimate and likely impoverished children. But it also meant there was no effective legal sanction against having children from more than one relationship. The second twist was that adultery was legal cause for a husband to divorce his wife but not legal cause for a wife to divorce her husband. Thus, a married woman could only tolerate her husband's mistresses and concubines, who could be used to continue to produce heirs and pleasure. Some argue that the legal standing of the major wife and the mistresses actually worsened under the new family law.[2]

By the late 1930s, what constituted the symbol of ideal manhood in Siam seemed to be up for grabs. Was it the animist king attending plowing rituals for fertile rice fields, or the Buddhist king supporting temples and making merit that could be bestowed on others? Was it the middle-class and military "founding fathers" of constitutional democracy? Was it still the sexually fluid Siamese male with largely unregulated rights to sexual desires and behaviors? Was it the newly romantic, monogamous, and thoroughly heterosexual male who, in selecting partners, also kept to his own age group and his own race?

As Darrell Berrigan headed to Asia, some answers had begun to emerge. Phibun Songkhram, a young army major who had participated in the original coup in 1932, had grown weary of the battling between royalists and democrats and had ordered his soldiers to sweep the capital of opposing princes and politicians alike, summarily executing some, while trying others for treason or sending them to remote islands. Phibun had been trained in France during the years when Vajiravudh was ending his reign, and because models of manhood were in some dispute in Siam, he had taken to admiring the Winckelmann-derived manhood represented by the nationalism already taking hold of Germany – the very ideas Walter had sought to escape by going to the other end of Southeast Asia.

For Phibun, the fascist "new man" being constructed by Adolf Hitler was especially appealing. Just as Hitler was calling himself *der Führer*, so Phibun would call himself *phu-nam*, "the leader." The king's portrait came down; Phibun's went up. Not surprisingly, he would eventually ally with Germany and Japan. In June 1939, he helped rename the country Thailand. "Thai" is a word that refers both to an ethnic group occupying the central plains and to the idea of being a "free man."

Soon, Phibun aimed the Chakri project in gender re-engineering toward its climax.[3] Some reforms he pushed remained from the days of Mongkut, Chulalongkorn, and Vajiravudh but simply had never been well implemented. Men were ordered to wear trousers and socks. Anyone wearing the traditional sarong-like *jong-baren* was to be refused service in a government office. Even the poorest had to engage in a new form of consumerism: going to stores to buy Western clothing rather than making the *jong-barens* at home. Phibun also promoted national beauty contests like "Miss Thailand" in order to solidify the new concept of highly gendered, feminized beauty for the Thai women who had once been decried as too masculine or too androgynous for European eyes.

He created a Committee for Establishing the Principles for Giving Personal Names, an extension of the project to create surnames that Vajiravudh had launched. But Phibun's program was aimed at actually gendering first names, which Vajiravudh had not tried to do. Under Mongkut and Chulalongkorn, Siamese had attached the sounds *ee* to female names and *ai* to males to distinguish them. Vajiravudh had then encouraged more formal titles like *nai* for men, the equivalent of the British "mister," and *nang-sa* and *nang* for Miss and Mrs. Instead, Phibun directed the committee to draw a list of specific male and female names so that additional words would not be necessary. Thai names were to become more like the gendered European ones, "Dick" or "Sally." By 1941, when Germany was readying to invade Poland and Japan to bomb Pearl Harbor, Phibun's list of approved names had begun to be sent to district government officials to share with parents so they could name their infants appropriately.[4] Phibun insisted that state agencies, including all schools and colleges, enforce the new gender norms and names.

Even pronouns began to change. For the English first person "I," female speakers adopted the pronoun *dichan*, while males used *pom*, effectively gendering any statement referring to themselves in ways they had not done before. Just in case there was still any doubt, each also then ended sentences with gender-distinguishing words of politeness: *kha* for women and *krup* for men. Under Phibun, the Thais would go even further than the British had. A simple ungendered "hello" for the British – *sawatdee* for the Thais – now needed a gender ending in *kha* or *krup*.[5]

In place of a culture that Europeans had criticized for not being gendered enough, Thais under Phibun began to exaggerate in the opposite direction, insisting on clear-cut monumental classifications.

Explicit erotic images, which had been common in Siamese art and literature, were steadily stripped away. That had begun during the monarchy as part of its campaign for *siwilai* but expanded during Phibun's rule, the result of the elite acknowledging that British and American sensibilities about explicit displays of the body differed from the Siamese tradition. In contrast to the celebration of nude Balinese bathing occurring in media images of that part of Southeast Asia, the Thai government would condemn as "impolite and disorderly" the old tradition of wearing only a light sarong-like cloth while bathing in rivers. Public nudity, once no cause for shame except to European commentators, became outlawed.[6] What some missionaries were trying to do in Bali, they were succeeding at doing in Thailand.

The practical effect of all the social engineering was a hyperawareness of gender. It was as if the waning days of colonial geopolitics had birthed a ground on which the players were not only aware of the expected colonial rules but also of how fluid the rules could be – how easy it was to consciously adopt or bend fashions, to create new gender identities, or to forge special events like beauty contests that quickly altered a particular definition of beauty.[7]

Leslie Ann Jeffrey, an American political scientist who studied the history of gender beliefs in Thailand, described the impact on manhood this way: "For years," she wrote, the model of the new manhood would become "the military man . . . complemented by his beauty queen wife."[8]

On the day the Japanese attacked Pearl Harbor, they also landed on the southern coast of Thailand. The Japanese needed to cross the country to seize British Burma and its famous road used to supply Chinese troops. They also needed Thailand as a base for invading rubber-rich Malaya and moving south to Singapore and onward to the Dutch East Indies.

Phibun offered no resistance, and so Darrell Berrigan, now a new American enemy of the Japanese, fled his United Press bureau only moments before the Japanese arrived, grabbing one of the last trains out of the country. By early January, *Time* magazine was reporting that he was in Rangoon. "He had come through the jungles from Bangkok," the magazine said, and "outwitted the Japs who arrested him as a spy on the Thailand-Burma border." A later story would say a friendly Thai captain had helped him escape.[9]

Once in Burma, he began sending dispatches lauding the courage of the departing British defenders. A typical article, written just four months after the Japanese had launched their attack, read: "The British Imperial Army in Burma is in retreat, but it is a glorious retreat, marked by almost superhuman courage and endurance."[10]

Darrell himself would also become famed for manly adventures, such as his escape from Bangkok. One story had it that he and another journalist had driven their jeep 1,300 miles out of Burma into India after the capture of Mandalay. When they arrived and were told that what they had done was impossible – because there were no roads where they had traveled – one of them told the *Chicago Daily News*, "Sh-h! Not so loud. Our jeep hasn't found out about roads yet and we don't want to spoil it."[11]

A historical oddity then occurred that would reshape Thailand's future as well as give Darrell a notable footnote in it. In Bangkok, the regent of the new young king residing in Switzerland secretly began aiding the allies, adopting the code name of "Ruth" and radioing out information.[12] When Phibun declared war against Siam's long-time tutor Britain, the London government immediately responded with a similar declaration of war. But in Washington, DC, the ambassador loyal to the young king and his regent only half-heartedly handled the declaration. The US secretary of state then cleverly rejected the declaration as the coerced act of an occupied country. Thus, Britain would consider itself to be at war with Thailand, while the United States would think of the country as an occupied ally like France. That left the Thai ambassador in the United States the freedom to recruit Thai students in America to form a resistance. In turn, from his post in Burma, Darrell began working with US intelligence services to channel information and money to the Seri Thai (Free Thai) insurgents.

After the war, Darrell helped the Thais even more directly. The British had secretly demanded that "enemy" Thailand pay reparations: half of what the British said were 1.7 million tons of surplus rice to feed the colonies the British were restoring in Malaysia, Burma, and Singapore. According to American estimates, only 800,000 tons of surplus rice was in Thailand. That meant the British, by overestimating, were demanding all of it. Not wanting to open an obvious split with its main ally, the US State Department first remained mum even as the months dragged without a settled peace treaty. The US-friendly Thai ambassador in Washington – who by then had returned to Bangkok as the country's new prime minister – called in Darrell, and the young journalist made the British demands public while also revealing the cooperation that had been occurring during the war itself. In December 1945, Acting US Secretary of State Dean Acheson used Darrell's reports to try to change what, in diplomatic cables, he termed the "completely intransigent attitude" of the British negotiators. A secret cable from Acheson to the US ambassador in London on December 13 specifically noted Darrell's articles, saying that "the press has given wide publicity to a UP dispatch from Bangkok giving a harsh interpretation of reported British terms. Strong editorial comment adverse to the British is spreading and there is heavy pressure on the [US State] Department to state publicly what it is doing to . . . secure fair treatment for Siam." If the British did not change, Acheson suggested, the United States would unilaterally recognize the new Thai government and denounce the British demands.[13]

A *New York Times* editorial then argued, in contrast to the British views, that "Siam [should get] off with her honor and her possessions in fair condition."[14]

Under the pressure, the British would eventually relent. At the highest levels of the Thai and American governments, then, Darrell Berrigan would be considered a special friend who had helped a new alliance.

For that reason, his homosexuality seems to have been overlooked – at least until he was brutally murdered for being a homosexual in the city that was becoming known as Southeast Asia's erotic paradise.[15]

During the postwar years, Darrell had continued to cover what now became the tense attempt to re-establish the colonial empires in the lands that the Japanese had occupied but had also freed from European control. By 1954, he had moved permanently to his favorite Asian city, Bangkok. There he found a comfortable social circle, mingling with other Americans such as the soon-to-be legendary Jim Thompson, who was often rumored to be gay himself. Thompson's own family ties with Thailand extended to his grandfather, who had entertained Vajiravudh at the family home in Delaware while the crown prince was on his way home from London. Young Jim had grown up looking at pictures of the crown prince, and, like Darrell, he had supported the anti-Japanese Seri Thai movement. After the war, he had created a Thai silk company, sending the fabrics for the costumes that would be used in the *King and I*, the story about Anna Leonowens and her encounters with Mongkut and the young Chulalongkorn.[16]

After World War II, the Siam that Vajiravudh had once led had begun to transform economically. It fell to Darrell to report in 1959, for example, that the country had "started on her long-delayed march toward becoming a modern economic state" by trying to diversify and "take some of Thailand's eggs out of the rice bucket."[17] Part of the strategy was to develop more tourism. Twenty-three airlines served Bangkok's airport, Darrell wrote, "but not enough leave passengers here."[18] Instead, the travelers passed through bound for India, Hong Kong, and Singapore. To retain more tourist dollars, the Thais and the Americans had decided to finance tactics to expand tourism.

One such tactic, Darrell wrote, was to be the deliberate revival of what the reporter called "numerous ancient ceremonies" abandoned after the coup had sidelined the monarchy in 1932. After World War II, a new, young and handsome king named Bhumibol had ascended the throne at the age of nineteen, replacing his brother Ananda, who had been killed in a gun accident. Born in Cambridge, Massachusetts, and educated in Switzerland, Bhumibol bore his globalized status much more easily than Vajiravudh had. He not only spoke Western languages but enjoyed Western music and media. He played jazz, wearing dark glasses and hanging a saxophone around his neck. He carried his camera wherever he went, like the tourists the country was hoping to attract. He lined his office with short-wave and long-wave radios, listening to international broadcasts and military and police channels. He joined games of badminton and tennis — individual competitive male sports rather than the male team sports Vajiravudh had emphasized. He showed a knack for technology and science, promoting water and health projects in villages as avidly as Vajiravudh had written plays. By the 1960s, Bhumibol was becoming a king of the arts and the sciences, as well as of the Buddhist and Hindu and indigenous beliefs in Thailand.

By the time of Darrell's stories, Bhumibol was in his prime twenties and early thirties. He had married a beautiful queen named Sirikit, whom he had met while in Europe. Along with the still young Queen Elizabeth II of Britain, born only a year earlier than Bhumibol, Thailand's king and queen were among the most photogenic royal couples in the world. Most importantly, they seemed to exuberantly embrace the new plotline for Chakri royalty that had initially been composed decades earlier by Vajiravudh. They were romantic, they were heterosexual, and they were monogamous.

In 1960, Darrell wrote:

> To dramatize what Thailand has to offer, numerous ancient ceremonies were revived last year, most of them centering around the handsome young King Bhumibol and his beautiful queen . . .The first of the ceremonies was that surrounding the

inscription of the King's white elephant into the Roll of Royal White Elephants, which called for three days of pageant. Then, in December, for the first time in thirty years, the King mounted a gilded throne set in the center of the golden Royal Barge and, escorted by a flotilla of other golden barges manned by sailors in ancient dress and accompanied by the music of pipe and drum, was rowed down river to the Temple of Dawn to present robes to the priests.

Later in the same month, illuminations once carried out annually in honor of the King's birthday but long since abandoned, were revived and the city burst into colored light and fireworks flared above the temples, throwing their light on the gables and golden towers. Then there was the annual trooping of the colors, with the royal pair reviewing the troops, led by the Prime Minister in a plumed helmet.

All these, with the exception of the white elephant ceremony, will now be annual ceremonies again – exotic, colorful pageants probably unrivaled anywhere in the world.[19]

Henceforth, Darrell wrote, the royal barges would no longer sit in their "rickety boathouse" but would be placed astride the Chao Phraya River – for easier photographing by international tourists. Other kinds of details were being tended to as well: "The city's face is being lifted... its public buildings painted, its monuments restored. Tour guides are being trained. Taxis will be required to carry meters."[20]

Bhumibol was becoming a new model of Thai manhood and kingship. He was popular with the Western media and in Europe. He could move fluidly among the rhythms of manhood now being expected in Thailand. He could gracefully code-switch, whether he was performing the animist male rituals honoring the good luck of finding white elephants, or claiming the Hindu gilded thrones of divine essence or performing the Buddhist merit-making patronage of monks and temples. He could engage the new global arenas of technology and science of everything from music to image-making to metered taxis.

In the 1950s, Darrell became editor of an English-language newspaper, the *Bangkok World*, turning it into a stable source of income to complement his continuing freelance stories for the *New York Times*. *Time* magazine noted that he had gotten the position "through an orientally inscrutable tactic" – charging in a story that Thailand's chief cop, who owned the newspaper, was also Thailand's biggest opium smuggler. Instead of being outraged, the general in question had "reasoned that any newsman intimate enough with the country's boatmen, taxi drivers, prostitutes and businessmen to put together such a report would make an ideal editor."[21]

Eventually, Darrell bought the paper, becoming, according to *Time*, "such a national institution that diplomats phone him openly for guidance and Thai officials consult him on politics – foreign and domestic." Darrell, it added, had "turned his *World* into one of the genuinely cultured pearls of the East" – relying on Thai compositors who spoke no English, a favored taxi driver for general manager, and a former houseboy for his star photographer. "A bachelor," *Time* notably added, "Berrigan works seven days a week 'from early morning to early morning,' is likely to show up at a dignified party in an outsize, loud sports shirt, and is famed among Bangkok's beggars of high and low degree for being the softest touch in town."[22]

He wrote a regular column called "This Wonderful World." It was a cheery title considering that, by the mid-1960s, Thailand had begun to be used as a base for American bombing runs over Vietnam and Laos, a long-lasting Indochinese conflict having broken out as France tried to reassert its colonial control after World War II.

In his column on Friday, October 1, 1965, Darrell joked about a visit to a cigar club:

> We smoked round cigars and square cigars and long cigars and short cigars and cigars that were fat and cigars that were lean. In the process we began to develop a taste for cigars. We were a connoisseur. We could detect immediately the kind of cigar we were smoking simply by looking at the label.[23]

The next day, Saturday, October 2, he chatted in his column with a fictional gecko, "Oscar," who he often included in his writings. "Oscar" complimented humans for paving Bangkok with concrete. No longer, Oscar said, did he have to dodge elephants or buffalos to avoid being squashed. Instead, Bangkok had become a paradise for all geckos. All he had to do was to wait for the mosquitoes to fatten themselves up on humans before he ate them.[24]

That Saturday afternoon, Darrell drove his Volkswagen station wagon to the Bangkok airport to meet a Thai man special to him. Darrell was fifty-one at the time; Ari Sriburatham was thirty. The age difference between the two male friends was not uncommon in Thailand. Long-standing friendships between men often bore an element of "senior" and "junior," what was known as *phuyai*, or big person, and *phunoi*, or little person, the distinction based on any of several of factors: age, wealth, education, or just personality. The junior man generally deferred in decisions, but much of the ethical obligation of the relationship fell on the senior man, who was expected to be a mentor or assist with finding jobs or paying the tab at a restaurant.

Ari had been a particularly idealistic village teacher from a province northeast of Bangkok when he met Darrell a few years earlier. Darrell had treated him like a foster son. That October Saturday, Ari was just returning from a trip to Hawaii, where he had taught Thai language to the new US Peace Corps volunteers who were about to be sent to Thailand, another sign of the deepening cooperation between the two nations as well as of the US concern about offsetting any possible Communist insurgencies. After Darrell and Ari met, the two drove to the Patpong district of the city, ate dinner at a Chinese restaurant, attended a band performance nearby, and then walked down a small Patpong *soi* to a late-night snack at Mizu's Japanese Restaurant. Then Ari left.

Early Sunday morning, October 3, had begun. Darrell was planning to meet another young Thai man.

Twenty-four hours later, the *World* led its front page with the grisly story of that encounter:

> Darrell Berrigan, 51, was shot dead yesterday and his body was found in his Volkswagen station wagon about 50 yards from his Soi Lue Cha residence at 6:45 a.m.
>
> After an extensive investigation, police said last night that the motive for the murder arose from personal affairs. Police eliminated robbery and political motivation.
>
> Berrigan, editor of the *Bangkok World*, died as a result of a single shot fired at close range from a .38 revolver, police said. The bullet entered his head at the base of the skull . . . Berrigan's body was found in the back seat of the car with his hands twisted behind him.[25]

The Thai-language press that day had more notorious details to report. The newspaper with the largest circulation, *Thai Rath*, wrote that Darrell had not simply been shot in the head, but that he had been "stripped and murdered," using a Thai phrase that implied he had also been raped. Darrell's arms, *Thai Rath* said, had not only been twisted behind his back, but his lower body "could almost be called naked, because both his trousers and underpants had been pulled down to his shins."[26]

At first, the two English-language newspapers in Bangkok, the *World* and the competing *Bangkok Post*, focused their reports on the possibility that Darrell's contacts with American intelligence services had prompted his murder. Ari also suggested that might be the case, speaking after the police had checked him for gunpowder residue and had found none. Police also checked for gunpowder on another Thai man whom the press was referring to as Darrell's "adopted son," Vichai Chaicharoen, an advertising manager at the *World*. US Embassy representatives urged the Thai police to study the possibility of political motives. The condition of Darrell's half-naked body in the back of the Volkswagen might be a ruse to throw off the search, they suggested.

Only gradually and reluctantly did the English-language papers begin to consider the homosexual element, although not by reporting it directly. Instead, in their daily summaries of what could be found in the Thai press, they would report that in such-and-such a Thai newspaper, a reader could find the headline "American

FBI on Berrigan's Case, Robbed by Homosexuals."[27] For the next ten days, story after story tracked the police effort to find Darrell's murderer. Like a TV soap opera, the details of what had happened that early Sunday morning only gradually snapped into place.

Peter Jackson, a Southeast Asian scholar in Thai history, later researched and translated the Thai newspaper texts:[28]

> After leaving Ari, the editor had met two Thai men, one of whom lived near Darrell and who introduced him that night to a fourth man, Jayant Maksamphan. The *Bangkok Post* would describe Jayant as "a strapping, handsome youth" of twenty-two who enjoyed hanging out in bowling alleys not far from Darrell's house.[29] Both the English and the Thai press would settle on a description of him as a *jikko*, a member of one of the urban street gangs beginning to appear in Bangkok. The gangs seemingly took as their model those they had seen in *West Side Story*, the then-popular US movie about racism and mixed-race romance. *Jikko* possibly referred to "Chico," the slur the white-skinned Jets had hurled at the brown-skinned Sharks.[30]

The three Thai men joined Darrell in his Volkswagen near the editor's home, and then drove around until after midnight. The original two Thai friends left at a market. Darrell drove Jayant to Bangkok's Playboy Club for drinks. Then he and Jayant returned to the street where Darrell lived.

Both men were drunk, Jayant would claim, and Darrell began to make sexual advances. Jayant said the advances upset him, although his account never explained how, if he did not want to have sex, the two traveled to the backseat and then Darrell's pants were pulled down and his arms twisted behind his back. Jayant drew a .38 caliber Smith and Wesson pistol – which he apparently happened to have handy – and then shot Darrell in the head.

The Thai police figured the truth was different: that Jayant had had sex with Darrell and then, according to a plan hatched by all three of the Thai friends, had shot him in the head in order to rob him. Apparently surprised that Darrell carried little cash, Jayant escaped only with the editor's Rolex watch.

The Thai police would find Jayant at a railroad station outside Bangkok and charge him with premeditated murder and his two friends with being accessories.

Thai Rath headlined that Jayant had murdered Darrell "while making love."[31]

After Darrell Berrigan was murdered, a new public conversation about male-male love in Bangkok transpired. The Bangkok press had to make sense of who – or what – kind of men Darrell and Jayant were. The description in *Thai Rath* of their lovemaking had used a Thai phrase that suggested Jayant had played the masculine role of male suitor while Darrell the feminine role of a courted woman.[32] But the descriptions grew more complicated.

A few days after the murder, *Thai Rath* bannered a headline that suggested a different gender for Darrell:

> *Kathoey* Reveals Berrigan's 'Transvestite' Life — Says He Raised
> Young Men as Husbands.

"It was general knowledge," the newspaper said, "that Berrigan loved young men the way other men love young women."

According to *Thai Rath*, Darrell had "kept" both Ari and twenty-nine-year-old Vichai as his "young adopted sons." He had given them a good education and "loved them as if they were his own sons," clearly ascribing to him a *phuyai* role. Darrell's chauffeur had not been with him the night of the murder, *Thai Rath* reported, but he had since undergone an anal examination to see whether the editor had sexually penetrated him. Yet the headline had also used the word "transvestite" for Darrell.

Thai Rath reported that police had been questioning two teenagers whom it described as Darrell's "sleeping partners." Those it described by using a different gender term: *kathoeys*. From them, it said, police had learned that the editor supposedly had "degenerate sexual desires."[33]

Kathoey loosely means a man who cross-dresses and so, in Western terms, might be considered any of three categories: a transvestite who enjoys women's clothing, a transgendered man who is more feminine in his speech and gestures than "normal" masculinity demanded, or a transsexual man who feels he has been born into the wrong biological body.

On October 9, *Thai Rath* reported that its journalist had "penetrated" what the newspaper called "a jungle of *kathoey*" living in the middle of Bangkok in search of "facts behind the 'transvestite' life" of the murdered editor":

> At every locality . . . all of the interviewed transvestites, who are
> born with a male form but who feel that they are women, were
> unanimous in insisting that, while Mr. Berrigan was a man, he
> had the feelings and desires of a woman and that he had a special
> liking for teenage youths, whom he loved as his "husbands," not
> as his "wives."[34]

Darrell, who in the earlier account had been portrayed as adopting "young sons" and mentoring them like a father or a *phuyai*, was now being re-categorized as a man with "the feelings and desires" of a woman who wanted young "husbands" who would sexually penetrate him. That seemed consistent with the position in which he had been shot and left in the Volkswagen.

In a signal of a tension in categories about how to label the editor and his murderer, the report claimed that Darrell himself had a "transvestite mind" and "transvestite feelings," which suggested he had been the receptive *kathoey*.[35] Here, then, was an extraordinarily masculine man who had not been known to cross-dress, who been in combat with the most courageous of British soldiers, and who had helped liberate Thailand from Japan. He did not outwardly behave as a *kathoey*, but he seemed to have an identity ("mind") as well as desires ("feelings") that somehow needed to be categorized as *kathoey*.

Gradually, the reporters and their sources started to employ a series of words that seemed to show how individuals in 1960s Bangkok had begun to work with – or play with – new gender categories. Sometimes the *kathoeys* called themselves "low-grade," which meant they were either too poor or too unfeminine to cruise for clients in the kind of upscale neighborhood where Darrell lived. Others were so "high-grade" in their femininity and cross-dressing that they bore the word *kathoey* in front of their personal names, much as a man might be called "Mr." and a woman "Mrs." Some were *kathoey phu-chai*, meaning "masculine *kathoey*" who had sex with "normal" feminine *kathoey* or, possibly, with other masculine *kathoey* or even *phu-chai*, who were the "real" men.[36]

On October 11, two days before Jayant was arrested, *Thai Rath* discovered a new kind of "den" in Bangkok:

> *Thai Rath* has found a den of "men who sell themselves" and who call themselves gay. There are two hundred members and they make a sizable income from being *farang's* sleeping partners.[37]

Farangs were Caucasians like Darrell, an important racial categorization, since it was *farangs* who had always represented *siwilai* and who, thus, were expected to express particular kinds of civilized erotic desires or exhibit certain gender behaviors.[38] The discovery of men who called themselves not *kathoey* but *gay* was immediately associated in the news story with several other pieces of damning rhetoric: prostitution, cross-race sex, and, since Darrell and the other *farangs* were older than the Thai men, with cross-age sex. There was one other association: These Thai gay men, *Thai Rath* told its readers, "have unbelievably high incomes" derived not from the direct sale of sex only but from their *phunoi* relationships with the older, white men.[39]

Nowhere in the story were the men described as *kathoey*. Instead, they "call themselves and are known as the 'gay group' [*phu-ak gay*]."

The *Thai Rath* journalist had found what he considered a new phenomenon:

> It is almost beyond belief that a den of these *gays* or men who sell themselves has come to exist in Thailand, and at their meeting place the *gays* or men who sell themselves confirmed that Mr. Berrigan and his adopted son . . . used to associate with them. All of the teenage youths who have this surprising occupation are handsome and of smart appearance and can be called attractive men. They have the minds of complete men, not of *kathoey*, and never dress as women. All their clothes are fashionable and come from famous stores.[40]

Two days after Jayant was arrested, *Thai Rath* began to publish six editorials in a series entitled "Civilized People in Dark Corners." It would repeatedly attack *farangs* for bringing *gay* to Thailand — a use of the *nosferatu* metaphor as a threat to the long-standing concern with being "civilized."

One editorial picked up the defense that Jayant himself was trying to promote, that what had happened was the editor's fault. The cause of the murder, the writer fumed, was Darrell's "own sexually perverted behavior."

> We need to consider another group of people, namely men who sell themselves or who call themselves *gay*. If the activities of this group are left to run wild, they will present a danger to the country, both in terms of public peace and order and also, without a doubt, in terms of the good morals of the people.[41]

In another editorial, the *Thai Rath* writer warned "these people have degraded, perverted, and abnormal minds and may commit other serious crimes against society, such as the murder of Mr. Berrigan, or they may become a criminal element if they congregate in large numbers."

Another column by the writer urged the Thai government to "draft a law to control those activities, define them as wrong, and lay down punishment for anyone who engages in them." *Gay*, the writer argued, could never be welcome in Thailand.

The *Thai Rath* columnist concluded:

> Individuals who call themselves civilized may think that such things are ordinary and everyday. Nevertheless, given that we are an independent country, we should be able to proudly enforce a law that cleans up and wipes out filth from our land, because such a law not only would protect and enhance Thailand's high mental culture but would also maintain public order and uphold the good morals of the people.[42]

Fifty-five years had passed since that October 1910 when Vajiravudh had ascended the throne. The rhetoric of the triple supremacy and the triple taboo had now become fully deployed in the land that Vajiravudh had once ruled.

Halfway between Bangkok and Bali, a new paradise was being envisioned. It would be one where — eventually — Walter's silent "delicate, lotus-eyed" men would finally assert a public and gay voice.

Part Two

The Hope for a Better Age

13
Nanyang Family

Centuries before the British took the island that would be Singapore, the land had already been used for monitoring cargos moving through the narrow strait of ocean between the Malay Peninsula and the island of Sumatra. That slender strait linked the Indian and Pacific Oceans and with them the rich lands of India and China. What would be Singapore was little more than a pebble, just twenty-five miles long and fourteen wide, but it was a strategic pearl. Like Bali, the island had alluring beaches and green hillsides, but after the British converted it to a free-trade zone in 1819, Singapore's image did not focus on beauty but on business. Its culture would become a stew of the dominant economic forces in the strait: the British, Chinese, Hindu, and Islamic. Its population would rise to more than 200,000 by the end of the nineteenth century and then nearly double as Edward VII's reign ended and World War I neared.[1]

During those decades, the British reconfigured the island from its role as a tidy spice cabinet for trading nutmeg, cinnamon, and cloves into the world's largest warehouse for sorting and exporting rubber, transported from the plantations being created in Malaya. The rule became that a national metamorphosis would have to occur every few decades in order to keep up with the trading demands.

Along the way, the incoming male labor force added a second reputation to the island. By the 1920s, when Walter Spies sailed for Southeast Asia on the *Hamburg*, Singapore had become a booming brothel for Asian women who thought they were coming for jobs but instead ended up in the sex trade, some deliberately trafficked and some slipping into it as a matter of either temporary or permanent survival.[2]

Their children were sometimes pressed into those trades offered by the brothels, the girls following in their mother's footsteps, the boys marketing in secret brotherhoods to find additional profit. These children, along with the sons and daughters from marriages among Chinese laborers, had no schooling and, being poor, made weak candidates for the elite British school system set up by the man who had negotiated British control, Sir Thomas Raffles.[3]

That was where Singapore's Nanyang Primary School came in. In 1917, the school was created as a piece of the Nanyang Girls' School to help break the cycle of illiteracy and poverty for the children it could gather into its classrooms. It was a private school, not government, and it was specifically for the Chinese. For decades, Mandarin was the language of instruction. The first year that Nanyang opened in a rented shop house next to a Chinese movie theater, 100 children came.[4]

Over the decades, the Nanyang School's fortunes would follow the path of the city growing around it. In 1927, the school's faculty moved to a section of Singapore called Bukit Timah, along the slopes of what was the island's highest hill. During World War II, the British used the school as a field office until the Japanese chased them out and destroyed Nanyang. After the war, Chinese alumni, grateful for how the school had helped them, rebuilt it. As the island's economy once again transformed, this time from rubber transport to manufacturing, Bukit Timah became a center for industry, and Nanyang's children changed into the sons and daughters of blue-collar factory workers.

The school became its own metaphor for Singapore. As a result of education, Nanyang helped the children and grandchildren of the original migrant Chinese workers move toward middle- and even upper-class economic paradise. These days, Nanyang maintains a website on which it flashes its values in both Mandarin and English characters: "Diligence, Prudence, Respectability, Simplicity."[5] The school song, sung in Mandarin, takes only one minute to assure seven- to twelve-year-olds that "Nanyang gathers glory," and "Nanyang produces distinguished students," and "We become complete by working hard together pursuing glory, building up our country and developing our mind and body."[6]

The Nanyang School also imposed a dress code of gender propriety. Girls cropped their hair above their shoulders and wore white box-pleated skirts stretching below the knees. Boys wore white shirts and khaki shorts.[7]

By the late 1950s, when the island's most prominent married couple, Prime Minister Lee Kuan Yew and his wife, Kwa Geok Choo, was deciding where to send their firstborn son to primary school, Nanyang seemed a logical choice. Both parents took education very seriously. Lee Kuan Yew's father had acquired a British education in the colony, while Lee Kuan Yew himself had attended the Telok Kurau English School in the years preceding World War II. Telok Kurau sat on a vast coconut plantation distant from Singapore's noisy wharves and brothels, and it was a school where a photograph from the time showed Chinese schoolboys dressed in crisp white shirts and shorts, playing pianos and violins, the coconut trees forming a backdrop.[8] From Telok Kurau, Lee Kuan Yew had won a scholarship as one of the island's brightest students and had then graduated from Singapore's leading British high school, the Raffles Institution, begun by the city's colonial founder himself, Sir Thomas. He had then traveled from the edge of the British Empire to its center and had graduated from Cambridge University as a lawyer. His wife had excelled too. She had taken a spot as the only girl at the all-boys Raffles in a special class set up for students hoping for a Queen's Scholarship to study at either Oxford or Cambridge. Winning one, she too had moved from the periphery of the Empire to its center and, as would her husband, had graduated from Cambridge Law School. Back in Singapore, they along with Lee Kuan Yew's brother had formed the law firm of Lee and Lee.[9]

Their first son, Lee Hsien Loong, was born in 1952, and as he moved through his infancy and toddler years, his father entered Singaporean politics. By the time the son was just two years old, Lee Kuan Yew had joined other British-educated and middle-class Chinese to launch the island's People's Action Party, lobbying for independence from a Britain that had been driven out by the Japanese but had then reasserted itself as a colonial master once the war had been won. Well-educated Chinese like Lee Kuan Yew linked with socialist-oriented trade unionists. The intellectuals understood British law; the unionists knew the masses working in Singapore's new factories. From the alliance emerged the particular characteristic of Singaporean political life: the British-educated Chinese elite provided guidance, while the masses gained a social welfare state. By 1959, Lee Kuan Yew had become the first prime minister of a Singapore moving toward full independence.

And his firstborn son was ready for primary school.

Nanyang was the choice. It neatly symbolized the link between Chinese intellectualism and the aspirations of the Chinese working class.

Like the father, the son would eventually study in the center not only of the British Empire but also of the new American one, graduating from both Cambridge and Harvard, and by August 2004, Nanyang Primary's most famous alumnus would assume his father's mantle and become Singapore's third prime minister. In his inaugural address, Lee Hsien Loong would sound at times as if he was reciting the Nanyang Primary School pledge.

"We always want to move on, do better," he told his audience. Singapore needed to be "a community where every citizen counts, where everyone can develop his human potential to the full, and where everyone participates in building and repairing and upgrading this shared home." Alluding to changes that were underway as a result of the government's pursuit of new communication technologies, he said that young Singaporeans, that next generation after his own, had been groomed to be "a strong generation ready for the future."

But the Nanyang graduate also acknowledged that a problem shadowed the island. Paradoxically, many of the young and most creative of Singapore's citizens were leaving. They were different, he said, this "post-independence" generation, especially the males.

"I was in Korea recently," Lee Hsien Loong explained. "They gave me a definition of youth. They said, 'A young man is somebody who can do an SMS (a text message on a cell phone) with one hand on the phone in his pocket.'"

It was a different kind of masculinity, a different blending of male body and desire and performance of gender not exactly described in the Nanyang School code.

"In Korea," Lee Hsien Loong said, "young men like that changed the government."[10]

A decade after Lee Hsien Loong attended Nanyang Primary, another Singaporean family, the Koes, faced the same decision as the Lees had: where to send their firstborn son to school.

The senior Koe ran a successful pharmacy company; the son, part of that first generation of Singaporeans born after independence, was skinny, bookish, and perhaps a bit on the hypochondriac side – although that seemed somewhat justified given that his male relatives tended to die of hypertension at an early age.[11]

His Chinese name was Koe Chi Yeow, born September 6, 1972. Unlike Lee Hsien Loong or Lee Kuan Yew, however, he would hardly ever use his Chinese name. Instead, he preferred his English first name: Stuart. Even better, as he would come to sign it on his Internet blogs, he preferred "S2" which sounded like "Stu." Perhaps not just coincidentally, it was also a pharmaceutical reference to the asthma inhalants used to open constricted airways.

Like the Lees before them, the Koes picked what they thought would be the best school. Once again, it was Nanyang Primary.

Young S2 seemed less than thrilled – at least when he later looked back and blogged about his years there. "I learnt later in life," he wrote, "that [Nanyang] was where lots of snotty Chinese parents who ran large Singapore corporations or came from large snotty rich families sent their kids."[12]

At Nanyang, Stuart quickly found himself mostly attracted to playing with the girls at recess, but not because of any early blooming sexual desires. Just the opposite. For Stuart, the Nanyang dress code requiring short-cropped hair made at least some of the girls seem "butch" – "butch in a big way, even before they were 12," he would write. His mind had quickly noted the kinds of gender differences that being a girl or a boy made. The girls used words more precisely and, sometimes, more cuttingly. He liked that. He was interested in words and language, so much so that he would eventually list the linguist Noam Chomsky and the anarchist poet Arthur Rimbaud among the authors who changed his life. Ditto with John Rechy and his *City of Night* novel about a young male hustler's journey through a marginalized world of prostitution and sex.[13]

S2 wrote that, compared to the girls at Nanyang, the Singaporean boys were "timid, wimpish, and general bores."[14] He longed for creative playmates, later writing that his likes included "good company, good food, good books, good films, beauty and creativity." He described his "mission on earth" in a single verb: "create." The type of person he liked was "someone I can go exploring the world with, someone intensely self-aware and earthy, equally grounded in the arts and sciences."

His dislikes: "People who only add to the negative energy of the world" and those who favor the "status quo."[15]

Shortly after Stuart enrolled at Nanyang, Singapore's government, then still headed by Lee Kuan Yew, made a fundamental decision that would shape much of the rest of S2's life. Manufacturing jobs, the government believed, would no longer be enough to insure the future of the island's social welfare state. Too much competition was coming from elsewhere in Southeast Asia and in that gradually opening behemoth, mainland China. The island's commerce needed to metamorphose again. Singapore would instead engage the emerging global market for computer and information technology: chips and disks and all the accoutrements of knowledge and communication that went with them.

If Bali had developed the reputation in Southeast Asia of being the aesthetic paradise imagined by Walter Spies, and if Bangkok was the erotic paradise thanks to decades of fretful Europeans worrying about promiscuous Thai men, Singapore would become the smart paradise.

The monumental change was planned to unfold in a very orderly fashion. From 1981 to 1985 – when Stuart and others of his age were still in primary school – the National Computer Board would be established and a Civil Service Computerization Program begun. Government ministries would be computerized first, seeding a cadre of Singaporeans who would become computer-savvy professionals. The second phase would begin when students S2's age reached high school, in the late 1980s. Then, what was called the National Information Technology Plan would kick in, funneling government money to private businesses working in communication technology. The finale was to begin in the 1990s. Under the so-called "IT2000" master plan, computer-based information technology would be placed into every niche of the nation's culture: at home, at work, at play. In this new high-tech Singapore, the city's architecture and cyberspace were to be seamlessly stitched into a magical web of "smart" homes, "smart" office buildings, "smart" transportation hubs, and "smart" community centers.[16]

It would all be a bit like the "modern kitchen, all white and shiny" that Walter Spies had suggested his jail mate wanted.

A smart, orderly paradise.

A part of the IT2000 report described what would happen by presenting a hopeful novella. Each morning, the story ran, the fictional Tay family living in this smart paradise would awake to run its life through voice-controlled high-definition TVs hanging on the walls. The TVs would serve as picture telephones as well as interactive tutors for the fictional Tay children. The Tays would use smartcards with personal and medical histories. Because money could get dirty, the smartcards would also replace bills and coins. At Mr Tay's tailor shop, customers would study different shirts on a screen, without touching or trying them on. Mr Tay could use an electronic scanning pen to change the designs to fit each body. Conveniently, that also left him a database with the physical construction of the body of each of his customers and how they did or did not fit certain norms. Some might be slender and toned; others muscular; some fat; some with big shoe sizes, some with small. Meanwhile, Mrs Tay ran her insurance business from home on one of her wall screens. Whenever she needed a break, she played mah-jongg digitally with her friends, who were also taking breaks in their own homes and becoming pioneers in a new, imagined world of virtual gaming.

Most important for school-age children like S2, the fictional son in the report – named Tay Leng Meng – would find his way home from school by tapping into public information terminals to locate bus routes. Tay Leng Meng would then sit in front of the wall screens to use multimedia databases, working on school assignments about what the "old" Singapore was like – with its brothels and rubber warehouses.[17]

A year after the IT2000 master plan was released in 1992, a writer for *Wired Magazine* asked a provocative question: What would happen if Mrs Tay decided to trade her insurance business for a more lucrative out-call sex trade? Clients like those at Mr Tay's tailor shop could then use her husband's databases and the wall screens to pick the bodies of the women – or the men – they most desired, shopping for those who were muscular or those who were lean, those with impressive shoe sizes, those with less. And what if the young Tay Leng Meng, instead of innocently finding his way home from school and dutifully working on his assignment, turned into what *Wired* called "a disaffected teenager who spends almost all his free time cracking private and governmental databases."[18]

That, the magazine suggested, was the kind of surprising scenario the government of the new smart paradise might not anticipate: the matchboxes Walter Spies had described gone to moving in surprising and disorderly chords.

Singapore's official plan for students was simple: Stuart and his Nanyang schoolmates were to become pioneers in that brave, new cyberspace where a transformative Scriabin-like symphony of sound, light, and rhythm lived online.

But the last thing the soon-to-be S2 wanted to become was a fictional Tay Leng Meng writing a term paper about the old Singapore.

S2 wanted a new Singapore. And that database of men held the key.

In the late 1970s, while Stuart was still attending Nanyang Primary, *Spartacus*, the international gay travel guide, was proclaiming Singapore a hostile land for any men who defied the dictates of the triple supremacy.

In Singapore, the guide reported, such men could find only a very limited geography within which to lead their lives. Institutions that symbolized most of the public life of a citizen had been barred from any expressions: the churches, mosques, and temples where citizens explored their individual religious faiths; the legal chambers where the body politic harmonized its understandings of governance; the schools and museums that served as repositories of what society had judged to be important historical knowledge; the theaters that provided stages for exploring human passions; the commercial markets where identities could be expressed through individual purchases; the hospitals and medical understandings that defined health and nurturing; the individual homes that sheltered and helped define families. Public announcements about being gay, homosexual, queer – any label other than heterosexual – were not welcome anywhere.

Spartacus reported:

> Homosexuality is illegal in Singapore and social attitudes make it very difficult for the Singapore gay to be open about his gayness. One can meet gays of 25 or 30 who have never met another gay person – even in such a small island.
> From a gay point of view, Singapore is not really worth spending time in.[19]

Singapore had only four gay-friendly bars, and even those mostly served heterosexuals. Typically, gay men gathered only on one particular night at each bar. *Spartacus* recommended only two spaces worth actual visits: the Pebble at the Hotel Singapura on Orchard Road and the Treetops at a Holiday Inn. The guide warned, "Don't be too obvious."

Rent boys could be had on what *Spartacus* referred to as "Johore Road" at "several rather dirty male brothels." "Go only if you are desperate," it advised, marking them with a symbol that indicated "very dangerous."

Another area was more famous: Bugis Street to the east of Singapore's downtown was ordinary by day, *Spartacus* said, but at night "it was full of the most outrageous queens" and transvestites. "Beware of pickpockets (small boys who challenge you to a pencil game or ask for your autograph, etc.), don't carry money or valuables." Bugis, the guide added, was "full of hustlers," but the dangers on the street gave "an added piquancy" to any visit.

There really was only one redeeming aspect to Singapore, *Spartacus* said: "If you want to do shopping on the way to another place, certainly it is worthwhile."[20]

Such was the Singapore where S2 was to grow up. It hardly seemed the place to find someone who fit his list of desires: "good company, good food, good books, good films, beauty and creativity."[21]

For the British, Singapore had never posed the issues of velvet-handed semi-colonization that Siam had. The colonizers did not have to gently tutor in Singapore; they could directly impose their own ideas about civilization and their own laws. As a result, a legal bias against homosexuality had been imported, and even when the colonizers left, the laws remained in place, like cargo that had been intended for transshipment but had gotten stuck in one of Singapore's warehouses.

A trinity of criminal laws closely regulated sexuality between males.

The fiercest was the sodomy law that had emerged from a Victorian imagination focused on theories of degeneracy. In British India, Section 377 of the penal code said: "Whoever voluntarily has carnal intercourse against the order of nature with any man, woman, or animal, shall be punished with imprisonment for life, or with imprisonment which may extend to ten years." British Singapore adopted the exact words and the same numbering, Section 377. The only change added by the money-minded British in Singapore was: "and shall also be liable to fine."[22]

As a legal term, "sodomy" meant any kind of penetration of the mouth or the anus by a man's penis, so Section 377 turned both oral and anal sex into crimes. It also did not matter whether the two people involved were both men or were one man and one woman. Using any part of the body other than a vagina was "against the order of nature," because it might not lead to reproduction. One irony: Lesbianism did not seem to be covered, since sex between women seemed to involve only vaginas.

It never really mattered whether the state enforced the sodomy law. Indeed, most acts of sodomy occurred in private between adults and so could never be detected by the police. Instead, the law mostly enforced what could and could not be talked about publicly: "good" heterosexuals did not advertise the oral and anal sex they had; they openly referred in advertising, movies, and other types of public speech only to reproductive sex, if they mentioned sex at all. For men who engaged in sex with men, all open speech about their desires became stigmatized and chilled, since discussion of it in any positive way meant they were promoting a crime. Sodomy laws were restraints on speech as much as, perhaps more than, they were on actions.

What the sodomy law itself did not forbid about male-male sexual behavior, other criminal laws regulated. The sodomy law, for example, said nothing about the caressing and hugging or dancing together that two male lovers might enjoy, just as two heterosexual lovers would. But a section added to the colony's penal code much later did, Section 377A. Such acts of affection among men were "gross indecencies" to be punished wherever they might occur – in public or private. A man – and Section 377A applied only to men – could be sentenced to two years in prison for kissing or caressing another man. Whereas Section 377 had been imposed in Singapore in the nineteenth century at the height of British colonialism, Section 377A had been added only in 1938, that pivotal year in which the then declining colonial powers were being confronted by the rise of the new Nazi concept of manhood. Walter Spies was about to be prosecuted in Bali, while at the other end of the arc of Southeast Asia, Phibun was starting to promote his own stricter notions of body and gender in Siam.

What was a "gross indecency" was left vague. The courts termed it as whatever a "right-thinking person" might consider to be "gross indecency." As late as 1995, a Singapore appeals court defined it in this circular way: "What amounts to a grossly indecent act must depend on whether in the circumstances and the customs and morals of our time it would be considered grossly indecent by any right-thinking member of the public."[23] Section 377A was a law based on what others considered offensive, not what kinds of behavior might actually harm others.

A final Singaporean law completed the trinity. Section 354 of the penal code outlawed any "outrage of modesty" of another person accomplished through "criminal force." As with the "gross indecency" law, outraging someone's modesty could be punished by two years in prison. Also, as with the sodomy law, a fine could be levied. But, different from the other two, Section 354 also permitted the old British punishment of strapping the man to a metal frame, exposing his buttocks, and then caning him with a piece of rattan.

While the law's wording about "criminal force" seemed to suggest that physical coercion had to be involved for anyone's modesty to be outraged, in fact, as the law came to be interpreted, one man merely suggesting an interest in another – perhaps through a question or a light touch – could result in a Section 354 charge.

It was, in other words, a perfect method for entrapment by the Singaporean police.

Despite those criminal laws, the Singapore of the 1970s still had its subcultures of sex. One Singaporean historian noted that the British heritage may have created religious and legal attitudes toward what was acceptable and what deviant, but the economy and the society that the Chinese, Malay and Indian citizens themselves developed blurred those categories.[24] Add the merchant marine crews who passed through, and the actual sexual history of Singapore was a lot less monochromatic than the trinity of criminal laws suggested.

Two factors had converged to produce what is often remembered as the initial public "queer space" on the island. The first factor was the colony's role as a hub of sex trafficking and prostitution. The second rose from native peoples on the Malay Peninsula and in the nearby Dutch East Indies, many of whom had traditionally believed in a more complex mosaic of gender than the British did. Those two elements helped produce the spectacle of Bugis Street, the road that the 1979 *Spartacus* guide had suggested was full of pickpockets and hustlers, but where the danger added piquancy.

Bugis was located a short distance east of the original British administrative zone. Although Bugis itself was only about two city blocks long, several other smaller roads and alleys intersected it. Both Japanese and Chinese brothels operated in the area, and even after the legal brothels were abolished in 1927, the area continued to offer restaurants and hotels where prostitution occurred on the sly.[25]

One extensive study of early female sex trafficking and prostitution gives at least a hint of the forms of male-male sex that might have existed around Bugis before World War II. Referring to the male children of prostitutes who often ran errands for the brothels, researcher James Francis Warren noted that such a boy often went "from the womb to the street to support himself and back to the brothel in a constant cycle. He was frequently sent out into the five-foot way [the covered pedestrian walkways that bordered the rows of shop houses] at the age of five or six, when there was no longer room in the brothel and his mother needed his income . . . Young boys were efficiently taught the finer points of hustling and were trained by secret societies to support themselves by stealing."[26]

The pickpockets and hustlers *Spartacus* was still warning about in 1979 were the heirs of that tradition.

The street's name itself, Bugis, reflected the diverse traditions of gender in the region prior to the arrival of the European colonizers. An ethnic Malay group, the Bugis, had been well known as seagoing nomads and pirates. Coming from bases in south Sulawesi, they had often sailed their boats into Singapore and perhaps even into a canal close to where Bugis Street was eventually built. Some were apparently fierce and warlike as men, but they also recognized many more types of gender than the British did, probably as many as five instead of just the usual "masculine" and "feminine." The Bugis recognized "male-men" (*orane*) and "female-women" (*makunrai*) that corresponded to British ideas of masculine and feminine behaviors. But they also appreciated the *calalai*, biological women who assumed the roles and dress of men; the *calabai*, biological men who took on the roles and dress of women; and a meta-gender role that blended male and female, the *bissu*.

These *bissus* had drawn the notice of European travelers in the region as early as 1545.[27] Anatomically, they could be either male or female. They dressed androgynously, mixing both men's and women's clothing. In the origin myths of the Bugis, the *bissu* held special roles, helping the gods to start life on earth or assisting male-men and female-women to find and marry one another. Their social role was to conduct rituals for the Bugis nobles, but they were not effeminized males in the way Europeans understood and eventually used the word "effeminate." To become recognized as a *bissu* could require passing harsh tests, such as floating on a bamboo raft for three days without eating or drinking. That was a way to learn how to enter trances. In one of their most famous and fierce rituals – which would find echoes in trance dances on Bali – *bissus* showed their spiritual strength by stabbing themselves with ceremonial knifes. If the *bissu* were truly possessed by gods, the knives did no harm.[28]

After World War II, as Singapore became one of the few places in Southeast Asia that accepted peaceful recolonization, Bugis Street quickly became a recreation zone for all the European militaries moving through the Straits of Malacca to regain old colonies. By then, whatever had been the traditional appearances of *bissus* and *calabai* had instead become parades of cross-dressing men and hordes of sailors looking for pleasure with "women," the regional traditions fusing into whatever the British could tolerate.

A public toilet with a flat roof provided an impromptu stage for drag shows. There, one Singaporean remembered, androgynously dressed men "would tease, cajole and sit on visitors' laps or pose for photographs for a fee. Others would sashay up and down the street looking to hook half-drunk sailors, American GIs and other foreigners on R&R, for an hour of profitable intimacy." In a ritualistic "Dance of the Flamers" on top of the public restroom, the cross-dressing men would perform while those wearing customary male clothing would chant.[29]

By the mid-1970s, the post-World War II battle over nationalism settled, the local attitude changed. Instead, sailors began to be arrested. While Stuart was still studying at Nanyang, police enforcement against the shows at Bugis increased.[30]

Bugis would leave a dual heritage. Local doctors became intrigued enough by cross-dressing male behaviors that they began to introduce male-to-female sex reassignment surgery in 1971, and later they would add female-to-male surgery. Despite its restrictive sex laws, Singapore would become one of the world leaders in sex-change surgery.[31]

The other heritage was that of the dance. Bugis offered the excitement and the memory of a male-male dance that, for a few years at least, had been tolerated as a public ritual — so long as the rules of "civilized" gender, if not of body, were followed — and some males costumed like men and others dressed like women.

When the time came for Stuart's graduation from Nanyang Primary School, the news was good. He had scored high enough to be admitted to Singapore's most prestigious high school, the all-boys Raffles Institution, the same high school that Prime Minister Lee Kuan Yew and Kwa Geok Choo had attended.

The school still used a modified version of the Raffles family shield for its own coat of arms. Atop the symbol, a mythical gryphon sat on a crown, symbolizing — according to the school — stability and success. Two medallions incorporated on the shield were replicas of those that a Muslim prince had given to Raffles, one of them bearing Arabic lettering pledging loyalty. Two eagles looked in opposite directions, one toward the past and the other toward the future.

Below this imperial fusion of Anglo and Islamic images was a Latin motto: *Auspicium Melioris Aevi*. The school translated the meaning as: "The Hope for a Better Age." The school anthem celebrated its students as that hope. The "sons of Singapore," the song promised, would "reign supreme in ev'ry sphere."[32]

White was the school color: white shirts worn with either white shorts or trousers. Shoes had to be at least seventy percent white with no flashy designs or colors. For a long time, white socks were never supposed to be cut below the ankles.[33]

That Raffles and its traditions were important for the entire island had been made clear in 1966 in a speech that Lee Kuan Yew had given to school principals only a year after Singapore had become fully independent. He had talked about the role that education would have in shaping the new Singapore, and he had cast it in gendered terms. After a century and a half of British domination, the new country, he worried, would be in danger of being "a passive society . . . meek, self-deprecating, self-effacing";[34] in other words, its men subject to a feminine role due to its long imperial oversight by British men. Lee Kuan Yew's observations seemed almost an echo of the comments made about the silent Southeast Asian boys who had served the Dutch their gin at the De Vereeniging Club where Walter Spies had played decades earlier, or of Walter's own observations about "delicate, lotus-eyed boys."[35]

Singapore, Lee Kuan Yew had argued, needed a new man. He then told the principals to shape their model of masculinity from that of the man who had been in charge of his own schooling at Raffles.

"There was a principal at R.I. who was a disciplinarian," Lee Kuan Yew told Singapore's first fully independent educators. "But he cared . . . He cared for the pupils. He caned them. He took a personal interest . . . This was his school and he was going to mold the character of this school and he did it."[36]

That man, D.W. McLeod, had written Raffle's 1937 Syllabus of Instruction. Among other things, it had required readings of Shakespearean plays and texts of British military adventurism in the Orient and had constantly referred to "masters" and "schoolboys." McLeod had warned teachers against letting "local schoolboys" read the Shakespearean plays aloud at first, lest they "murder Shakespeare's lines" with their own accents. McLeod insisted on managing precise details: The boys were not to be allowed to write in past tense that "Brutus stabbed Caesar" in the Shakespeare play, but, rather, "Brutus stabs Caesar," since plays, strictly speaking, did not happen in the past tense but only in the present when they were enacted. To his credit, McLeod also emphasized that the Raffles boys should be allowed to form their own opinions about literature, although he seemed to limit the speech to the intellectual elite: "Unorthodox opinions from *bright* boys should not be discouraged," he wrote.[37]

In the vision Lee Kuan Yew offered to the principals, gender and nationalism, a boy's high school, and an emerging nation were fused. Singapore's success would depend on the careful McLeodian/Raffles-style disciplining of a possibly passive society that had little sense of itself as a nation-state and that had, after all, seen its three main groups of Malays, southern Indians, and Chinese bound together only by the exterior British cords that Raffles itself represented.

For Singaporeans, then, Raffles was more than just another school. It was a symbol of the leaders that Singapore needed.

Years later, S2 would remember his years at Raffles:

> Raffles was probably the epitome of snot. It was almost clinging to the walls. But not in the same way that Nanyang was. You basically had to graduate from grade school in the top 1% or 2% of the country in order to make it into RI. The boys in there thought they were god's gift . . . [38]

There was another side to the performances of masculinity at Raffles, something slipperier than the hegemonic layer of imperial rituals.

S2 added in his online blog:

> I happen to like the time I spent there . . . My RI days were when I awoke to my gaiety. I was one happy person. And there were lots of happy people around me . . .
>
> Fortunately, there was almost no stigma attached to being gay. We were basically allowed to have crushes on one another . . . [and] many of my friends had their first experiences with drag at our annual "Drama Fest" with our teachers quite gladly applying the Revlon to those faces which were starting to sprout their first signs of downy mustache.[39]

At Raffles, Stuart would go public with his first romantic love for another schoolboy. The adults may have simply rationalized it as a boyish crush, but Stuart was serious enough that at a Raffles talent show, he sang "Crazy For You" and dedicated the song to his "sweety, one year my senior."

"I didn't win for singing," S2 later wrote, "though I certainly should have for spectacle."

By 1988, S2 had graduated from Raffles, and he had struck a deal with his family, agreeing, like a good elder son, to study his father's trade in pharmacy so that he could assume a role in the family business.

But only if he could escape Singapore.

The center of his world was not moving toward chaos, as Walter's had been, but rather toward too much order for S2 to tolerate. Years later in his blog, S2 would retranslate the Raffles Institution motto:

"For those too lazy to google it," he wrote, "'Auspicium Melioris Aevi' pretty much means 'Looking for a good time?'"[40]

14

Men of the Feast: Babylon

By 1979, the nationalist contests in Southeast Asia that had come to such a climax with the French and then the American war in Vietnam had settled, and the international gay guide *Spartacus*, published in Amsterdam, recognized that Thailand had become exactly what Darrell Berrigan had described in the 1950s as the national goal: a tourist paradise where airline passengers disembarked rather than continuing to Hong Kong or India. "With all those magnificent palaces, temples, and colorful markets," the *Spartacus* editors wrote, Thailand "offers the finest sightseeing in Asia."

Most importantly for the guide's audience, *Spartacus* added that "with such warm, friendly, happy people and such handsome young men, it is a mecca for gays." It was a sharply different description from the one *Spartacus* had printed about Singapore that same year.

The *Spartacus* writers were especially struck by what seemed to be the Thai freedom from restrictive Western thoughts about the male body and its sexual desires and behaviors — despite the changes to Siamese gender that had been urged in the name of *siwilai* and despite the negative comments made in the 1960s about *kathoeys* and the new breed of gay male *nosferatus* like Darrell Berrigan.

Fluidity still ruled, *Spartacus* contended. "Thais do not use the artificial Western way of putting us all into classifications like 'gay' or 'straight.' The most heterosexual young man may readily make love with you if he likes you."

At least according to the guide's editors, the triple supremacy and, for that matter, the triple taboo had not prevailed. Bangkok was an erotic paradise where the male body could be an instrument of play and sensuality and where monumental solidifications into categories were not needed. Even outside Bangkok, the guidebook said, "Anywhere and everywhere in small provincial places you can find willing partners."[1]

How true the observations were is debatable. But as a European media representation, the image of Bangkok as a dissenter — and now a refuge — from the commands of a singular, solidly defined manhood had been maintained.

Spartacus listed fourteen gay bars in Bangkok, more than in any other Southeast Asian city. Most were in the district known as Patpong, lying next to Lumphini

Park, which Vajiravudh, in one of his final efforts, had designed as the grounds for an international European-style exposition that never happened. The most famous statue of the king gazed from the park toward Patpong.[2]

The *Spartacus* editors were more cautious when it came to describing the actual geography in which that expansive image of childlike male play was most likely to be found. It was as if two oppositional narratives existed. The guidebook warned against patronizing five of the fourteen gay bars, for example.[3]

The Tom Boy, the editors wrote, offered "near-naked go-go boys," but in the upstairs rooms over the bar where other sorts of go-go could be had, "the management is said to have spy-holes in the walls."

At the Twilight Bar, supposedly, young men could be rented as "off boys," meaning that the bar owner paid their wages and the customer then paid the owner a fee to "subcontract" the men's time somewhere away from the bar. What then happened between the men became a private matter, neatly sidetracking any questions about the bar owner being involved in illegal prostitution. Recognizing that the system encouraged very poor male migrants from the rural countryside to turn to sex simply for money, *Spartacus* condemned the off-boy approach as "almost a form of slavery and not recommended."

As for other bars – the New Flora, the Stockholm, and the Black – they were "clip-joints" that earned a rating of AYOR – "at your own risk – dangerous places with risk of personal attack or police activity."

For massage, the guide noted that Bangkok offered several hundred parlors for heterosexuals "with females who are invariably riddled with syphilis." The gay scene was a little better, but the guide found only two massage parlors to recommend for gay men, one of which, it said, "was basically hetero, but has some male masseurs."

It also warned readers: "Since many American servicemen from the Vietnam war came to Bangkok, a serious form of syphilis known as 'Saigon Rose' has been widespread. Most clinics did not know how to properly treat it." *Spartacus* referred men to the only one it believed could.

As for cruising outdoors, *Spartacus* noted that Lumphini Park was popular "early evenings and around the King's statue." But it was "very AYOR."[4]

Opposite the downtown Grand Palace several miles away from Patpong, male cruising was also popular in the evenings – in Saranrom Park, the old gardens of Vajiravudh's palace where the crown prince had held his nighttime games with his courtiers and pages.

AYOR.[5]

According to *Spartacus*, then, Bangkok was an erotic mecca filled with friendly and fluid men who subverted Western rules about body and desire and gender. The capital of the Chakri kings was a place of male *sanuk* and male *mai pen rai* – Thai for "fun" and "don't worry about it." Yet, *Spartacus* had also posted a warning sign on one-third of the supposedly gay-friendly geography and had warned of high risk in most actual pursuits.

It was sometime during the year that *Spartacus* published its guide that a twenty-seven-year-old man named Toc was taken by a friend to Patpong for the first time.[6] Like most Thai males, Toc was known by a simple one-syllable nickname, an echo of the days when Vajiravudh had tried to change the Siamese custom of not having last names. Toc had a family name, of course; that had been required since the days of Phibun, but he seldom went by it as a courtesy to those who did not want to utter the usual, long polysyllabic names that Thais used more formally. Born in 1952, Toc was part of the first post-World War II generation in Southeast Asia. He had entered adolescence the year that Darrell Berrigan had been murdered. By then, he had already been sent away from Thailand. Toc's parents had accumulated wealth through banking and mining, and in the 1960s, looking for a good education for him, they had sent him to Hong Kong for primary school rather than keeping him in Bangkok. He was partly Chinese, thanks to a grandparent's blood. In Hong Kong, his parents thought, he could perfect his English more easily than in Bangkok. It was also safely distant from that continuation of the Indochinese war between Americans and Vietnamese. Communist insurgencies in rural Thailand were even more worrisome.[7]

So the young Toc had left to study in a more British setting.

A few years later, he had been moved to the United States for high school, this time at the elite Pennington School for Boys a short distance away from Princeton University. Methodists had founded Pennington as a male seminary during the period of the great evangelical revival that had preceded the American Civil War. Although Pennington had joined the first wave of late-nineteenth-century feminism by admitting women, by 1910 it had returned to its all male-mission, staying that way through Toc's enrollment there. Fewer than 500 young men were allowed to attend, and Pennington turned away five times as many students as applied. Due to the crusades of Methodist missionaries throughout the colonial world, the school had become known as a spot where bright young males from South America and Asia could get their first introductions to America.[8]

As a boy and even a young teen, Toc was a slender Asian male full of lines and triangles but not elliptical muscles. He weighed so little that his classmates at Pennington would tease him into being the first onto the frozen ponds so he could test the ice for skating. His friends say that Toc was also a disciplined overachiever, studying until 1:00 or 2:00 a.m. every night.[9]

His father had encouraged him to study the more practical aspects of life, so Toc eventually ended up studying for a business degree in London. But as had happened with Vajiravudh, the center of the British Empire had simply brought him closer to his real loves: art, architecture, the interior designs of palaces and grand homes, and the expansive yet minutely detailed landscapes of European gardens. His summer vacations with his father included tours of Europe, with plenty of opportunities for treating every period of music and art as contemporary inspirations to be absorbed and then resynthesized. Between the formal schooling and the travel, Toc learned to hold his own in conversations about British history with Londoners, about European music with the Viennese, and even about Catholic doctrine with canon law teachers, all of whom would eventually come to his home in Bangkok.

Once, on the European tours, his father asked for formal wear at the evening meal. A photograph shows him wearing instead a light-colored bowtie offset by a double-breasted dark jacket, and wide white bellbottoms. He had also invited his first boyfriend, a young German, to accompany him to the dinner. The boyfriend was an exactly planned fashion contrast, dressed in a dark bowtie, a light-colored jacket, and dark bellbottoms.[10]

Despite being in the United States and London during the heady 1970s of gay liberation, Toc never went to a gay bar. The trip to Patpong with his friend was his introduction.

That night, they went to the Tulip Bar. It was located near the corner of Silom and Convent Roads in Patpong, and *Spartacus* had noted that the Tulip tended to attract a young crowd interested in dancing. The dark bar had a jukebox and looked something like a crowded shop specializing in long strings of hanging lights and disco balls.[11]

Fresh from the grand palaces and landscapes of Europe, the young Toc was unimpressed. Much later, he would tell a visitor:

"Why should we always settle for something like that? Why should we always be second-class?"[12]

He had returned to Thailand to help manage the family banking business. By then he was old enough to be referred to consistently as the more respectful "Khun Toc," *khun* conveying a meaning similar to but somewhat grander than the English "mister." Calling him "Toc" would not bring rebuke; he was too polite. But his friends would rush to correct the gaffe. By the mid-1980s, a buyout of the banking business had left only the family's real estate to be overseen. Among the landholdings was a sand-colored condominium building at the start of a small road, really more a wide alleyway, that was called Soi Nantha. It was about a half-mile south of the statue of Vajiravudh in neighboring Lumphini Park and of the Patpong district where Darrell Berrigan had taken his last meal. There, beside the tiny street, Khun Toc would begin his construction of what he hoped would be a new, first-class paradise for men in Southeast Asia. He remodeled one condo in the building, then as others became available another, and another, and another, until he had poked holes through walls and created a zigzagging maze that rose to the top of the four-story building and to its crown: a rooftop hanging garden with views that extended across the vast cemented Chao Phraya River delta.

It was the rooftop garden that would inspire the name of his new paradise – Babylon – for its hanging gardens. Khun Toc also enjoyed the meanings of the actual word. For Jews, "Babel" had meant a gate of God; for Christians it had evoked promiscuity. For Khun Toc, the two seemed to go together: spirit and sex.[13]

On May 23, 1987, he opened.

By choosing to build a sauna, Khun Toc had selected what was one of the most controversial types of all gay male geographies. Dennis Altman, an Australian scholar, had described why, in a book just five years earlier. Such a space for men to gather, Altman had written, was one of the aspects of gay male life "that most infuriates" heterosexuals because it uses not just an ordinary space for furtive encounters – like a park or a shopping mall – but a deliberately imagined and consciously built environment where not only male-male sex could occur, but where a different type of masculinity could be enacted. "The willingness," Altman had written, "to have sex immediately, promiscuously, with people about whom one knows nothing and from whom one demands only physical contact, can be seen as a sort of Whitmanesque democracy, a desire to know and trust other men in a type of brotherhood far removed from the male bonding of rank, hierarchy and competition that characterizes much of the outside world."[14]

It was an intentional architecture for savoring male companionship without any presumption of romance, or marriage, or heterosexuality.

In contrast to spaces used for prostitution, inside a male sauna men did not pay for sex. "Everyone pays the same admission," Altman wrote, "and this buys not sex itself but an environment in which there is the possibility of finding a partner or partners. It is this possibility that so enrages critics." Altman had added, "The baths undermine conventional morality in that they are predicated neither on the subordination of women to men, nor on the direct exchange of money."[15]

Shortly after Khun Toc opened Babylon, author Neil Miller described its physical interior. Miller was surprised when his local Thai hosts invited him to meet at a men's sauna as casually as they might have asked him to go to a restaurant, but on Soi Nantha he discovered an island that resembled a sophisticated gentlemen's club in London. Khun Toc had designed Babylon's miniature details a bit like the letters on the discarded catsup bottles that Walter Spies had described in the Surabaya jail:

> I was sitting around the downstairs lounge of the gay baths in Bangkok, reading *The Great Gatsby*. The Babylon sauna had a terrific library of books in English: Fitzgerald, Henry Miller, Gore Vidal, Doris Lessing, and Plato . . .
>
> In *The Great Gatsby*, the characters were talking about golf; on the Babylon stereo, Louis Armstrong and Ella Fitzgerald were singing "Gee, Baby, Ain't I Good to You." The lounge walls were decorated with traditional Thai scroll art; the chairs and couches were made of rattan; sculptures of Buddhist mythological figures adorned teak end tables. On the floor-to-ceiling bookcase, next to all those great works of literature, were a television, a VCR (*Road Warrior*, with Mel Gibson, was promised for the evening),

stacks of a Thai magazine called *Hi-Class*, and a pile of issues of *Architectural Digest*.

The Babylon itself looked right out of the pages of those magazines. Occupying four floors of a converted Art Deco town house in the part of Bangkok where the wealthy lived behind high walls covered with bougainvillea, Babylon was the closest thing to a designer bathhouse that I had ever seen . . .

The Babylon was one of the few gay establishments in Bangkok where the commercial sex trade was not in evidence. There was plenty of sex available at the Babylon − in the cubicles and mazes on the third floor and in the dark and crowded steam room (which was named "Gathering Essence"). But the bathhouse was as much a social meeting place as a sexual one and it was suitably elegant for the reception of foreign guests.

The real triumph of the place was the rooftop garden. Filled with potted plants and flowers, it was open to the sky and overlooked the lush grounds of the Austrian embassy. There, you could eat dinner on marble-top tables and drop your crumbs on parquet floors. The food was superb: American-style barbecued chicken, fish from the Bay of Siam, and Thai stir-fry. Moreover, the roof garden offered the only cool breeze I encountered in Bangkok, a city where the temperature climbed daily to ninety-five degrees Fahrenheit and the humidity was suffocating.[16]

Although Khun Toc's selections of details had been influenced by his travels, his idea for Babylon had emerged from the discipline he had set once he returned to Bangkok. To adjust to Thailand and to meet new friends, he had regularly hosted garden parties at his family's home near Bangkok's Thanon Sukhumvit. The ritual of the Thai garden party − with its appetizers, its music, its notions of playful *sanuk,* its courteous folded-hand bows from servants − became the genesis for Babylon. Other gay saunas might fulfill the function of allowing men to have sex with one another. In Babylon, Khun Toc focused on the type of communication between men that was supposed to occur. Asked once what concept had motivated his design of the sauna, Khun Toc answered quickly: "What's important in a sauna," he said, "is what happens after the sex."[17]

By his fifties, Khun Toc had replaced his slender lines with toned muscles, working out every afternoon in Babylon's private gym. He seldom talked or wrote directly about his methods of masterminding his own paradise. Exceptionally private, he always deferred detailed questions to his friends or shrugged and moved on to whatever next subject he preferred, usually a conversation about a book or a particular recipe or about a singer or a movie. His philosophy of sex and manhood instead had to be extracted from the short comments he made, in the signs he posted around Babylon, or from the design of the sauna itself.

One such sign said: "Step through the gates to find heavenly delights and enter a world where life has a magical touch of deep sensation."

A shower curtain in his home had lyrics written on it from a song by the country western singer "Gentleman Jim" Reeves:

> *Welcome to my world,*
> *Won't you come on in?*
> *Miracles I guess still happen.*
> *Step into my heart*
> *Leave your cares behind.*
> *Welcome to my world, built with you in mind.*[18]

One day in a conversation with a visitor while he was buying plants for the Babylon gardens, Khun Toc passed a display of succulents with thorns. He exclaimed firmly: "No cactuses! I want something I can touch and feel – not all spikes and barbs."[19] An American scholar, David Bergman, had written once that the "hallmark of gay interior design is that it transformed a room not into a space for gracious living but into a stage . . . a site of pageantry, of ritualistic display, of sacred acts."[20] That seemed true of Babylon and, after a decade had passed, a gay guidebook called it "the best gay men's complex in the world."[21]

Khun Toc would eventually adopt a slogan to describe his paradise:

"Babylon, where arts, sex and love converge."[22]

It was as if he intended to evoke the image of King Alcinous of Homer's utopian Phaeacia. On his troubled way home from Troy, Odysseus had found in Phaeacia a sensual land of fraternal males, an aesthetic country of feasting, dancing, and music making and an imagined geography that, as one historian wrote, furnished the clearest picture of "the Homeric hero, that many-sided free man, when he is liberated from the exigencies of warfare."[23]

A gay man from Singapore described Khun Toc's Babylon in 1997. Writing online, as many gay Singaporeans were beginning to do by then, he used the pseudonym Newman (New Man):

> It's April Fool's Day, and the warm air swathes over the half-naked bodies of men on the balcony, waiting, anticipating, expecting something to happen. They sit at their tables . . . hoping the empty chair next to them will soon be occupied by the man of their dreams or just occupied, period . . . I return to my table and find a fat Thai man sitting there. I return to my notepad and resume writing. I don't like the silence and ask him his name . . . It's difficult, my Thai isn't so good but we manage. Am I writing a report on this place? No, just a letter. I shouldn't write in the dark, no good for the eyes. Don't I get a headache? No, I don't. I ask him if he comes here often. This is only his second time here, he says. The first time was on St. Valentine's Day. He sits a while longer and then makes a move.

The old white man standing at the wall all this while approaches and asks if the seat is taken. I say no.

"I'll just sit down and enjoy the music," he says. I smile sympathetically. He asks me if I'm writing in Thai and I explain where I'm from. He's a semi-retired History teacher. Where? In London. At a high school or university? University. LSE [London School of Economics]? No, it's a secret. I tell him I've always wanted to study at LSE but it's just too costly. Where else has he been? China, Hong Kong. He likes Oriental men, do I? I think about it for a while and then say, "No particular preference." I look back at my notepad and he says, "Well, the music has changed, I'll go off now. All the best." I don't understand, all the best for what, for tonight? But I thank him anyway. . .

If you're looking for a man, this is the place to be. Oriental, white, young, geriatrics tottering into their final years, gorgeous faces with tight pecs, abs and biceps, paunchy businessmen whose fortune is anything but their faces. Macho to the bone or queens right down to manicured fingernails – the variety is there; all you have to do is choose. Or you can simply window shop, sample the goods, no commitments, no strings attached . . .

As you leave the building into the real world, you know you have just left Paradise and long to return. Babylon is the place where there is no discrimination, everybody's a minority, everybody sympathizes, everybody understands. In the few hours you have been there, you have left the world and all its prejudices, and entered another stage of existence where only pleasure and fulfillment await.

For 200 baht, Paradise never came so cheap . . . [24]

In the year 2000, Khun Toc relocated Babylon a short distance west on Soi Nantha to a larger family property of five Thai rai, about two acres. He opened his re-created imagination of paradise on November 23, 2000, and Soi Nantha became so crowded with taxis on Saturday nights that drivers sometimes had to wait single file at the opening of the street, quickly dropping their male passengers, executing tight three-point turns in the middle of the narrow lane and then gently edging past other incoming cabs.[25] They flowed through a canyon of walled compounds. North, a forested park protected the Austrian Embassy and gilded gates opened to the consulate of the Sultanate of Oman, while beyond that the Banyan Tree Hotel rose sixty-one floors above the little *soi*. South, condominium towers completed the canyon edges. You could sometimes hear shouts from a vacant dirt lot that served as soccer field for one of Bangkok's largest slums, Suan Plu Pattana. Young Thai males gathered every day for the game that Vajiravudh had brought them from Britain.

Khun Toc's new site broke into two sections: a two-story building of apartments forming a C-shape around a private garden, and a seven-story building that closed the C and had its own pool as well as its own courtyard. Khun Toc claimed one of the apartment wings as his own home, while the seven-story building became the new Babylon: sauna on the bottom three floors, hotel on the top four.

To the right of the entry, Khun Toc placed a memory: the family home at Sukhumvit where he had lived when he had first explored the Tulip Bar on Silom Road and where he had hosted his friends in garden parties. He had had the house moved. It was a reminder of the older Siam, where steeply peaked roofs on teak houses functionally shed rains but were also so intensely decorated with fascias and ridges that the function of runoff was masked behind an idealized art form.

The same would be true of Babylon: Its function of providing a refuge for a marginalized sort of male imagination would emerge from art.

Behind the old home, Khun Toc composed a square courtyard between it and the seven-story building. Statues of men loomed over the courtyard, looking like Egyptian sphinxes that had risen to hold light beacons pointed upward. They bore hard-edged Winckelmann anatomies: smooth, tight abdominal plateaus, bulging pectoral ellipses, triceps powerful enough to seemingly hold the eaves atop the walls, etched thighs the size of a man's waist. At this entry to Babylon, Khun Toc had drawn a male's desire for another male as a thoroughly masculine urge, and not – as often assumed in Southeast Asian cultures – an indication of being part of a third gender like *kathoeys* or of desiring men who were *kathoey*. To enter the sauna, men tugged on heavy gold door handles shaped into rough dragon-like wings. Then they walked past the portrait of the uniformed king who had most wrestled with reshaping gender expectations in Siam, Vajiravudh, the portrait's heavy wood frame spiked by nails. Khun Toc also built counterpoints from miniature feminine textures: a round, raised circular garden of soft peace lilies, a receptionist who was often a slender *kathoey* issuing entry tickets through long, well-manicured fingernails. Details counted.

"Every morning," a friend of Khun Toc's commented once, "he gets up at 5:30 or 6:00, thinking about menus, thinking about music, thinking about movies. He likes the sexual stimulation – the sounds, smells, even the music, depending on what part of the Babylon you're in."[26]

Originally, the apartment mid-rise that Khun Toc's family owned had been little more than a concrete building of the type that had spread across Bangkok in the 1960s and '70s. One guidebook called such a building "a giant egg carton turned on its side,"[27] and while there was not much that could be done to the outside, in the interior remodeling, Khun Toc had driven the building instead toward a style that had prevailed in Bangkok in the 1920s when Vajiravudh had ruled: a type of Thai Deco that blended masculine elements of restrained industrialism with flourishes and illusions coming from the European Deco period.

He stripped open the ceilings to expose their functions, showing the pipes and conduits that carried water and electricity. He painted the pipes in blacks, rusts and tans, but then added many illusory ones. What at first glance could look like a large black pipe functionally on its way through a room to drain off fluid instead collided with an impenetrable concrete beam. The functioning pipes and conduits were almost indistinguishable from the purely decorative ones, which were reminders of the floral fascias that lined the ridges of the old family home outside.

Khun Toc's expression of manhood within the sauna involved plays of textures too. Two large columns past Vajiravudh's picture appeared to be made of smooth rusted iron, but like the frame they had been studded with rings of nails, creating a pattern of alternating smooth and hard textures that would be echoed throughout the sauna's restaurants, patios, and stairways. For smoothness, Khun Toc composed with metal, glass, or cool black Thai slate. For ruggedness he chose white marble-sized river pebbles and coarse sandstone nuggets. He installed metal grates amid interior walkways, ostensibly looking as if they were for drainage – but no drains. Instead, since most of the men walked around barefoot, the grates produced changes in tactile sensations. Along one staircase with smoothly burnished metal railings, rough holes popped opened for no particular function but for the form of stimulating other sudden changes in the sense of touch.

Whether on the floors being trod by thousands of bare feet or on the walls that the men leaned against – or sometimes felt their way along in dark, minotaur-like mazes – Khun Toc insisted that the flat surfaces turn surprisingly tactile and musical.

When it came to lighting, he adopted principles of shadowing. Bright in one place, shafted in another, totally absent in another. Glass expanses or tiny portholes appeared almost everywhere. so that men could see each other moving through different sections of the buildings or, in certain locations, could peer out of the sauna entirely into Khun Toc's private garden next door.

As an architectural text of the male body and its desires and its performance of gender, then, Khun Toc's phrases would be about the constant fluidity experienced through miniature details.

Two days after Christmas 2002, Khun Toc began his evening in his customary fashion. At 7:00 p.m., the men who had been invited began to arrive for gin tonics in his private home across the courtyard from the sauna. The smaller gatherings would start in Khun Toc's library, where the shelves were solid with art and design and architecture books. Larger gatherings began in a baroque-style European reception room, sometimes spilling out into a smaller side courtyard complete with its own pool of koi fish and stage for entertainment. As is Thai male custom, most of the men dressed in white shirts.

About 7:30, after conversations that ranged across politics, art, and movies, they quickly strolled across Khun Toc's courtyard garden, entering Babylon through a private side door. The men passed by Vajiravudh's photograph, walked along the first floor and then – the only fully clothed men in Babylon besides the staff itself – they settled at a specially set banquet-length black marble table. It curved gently like a boomerang so that Khun Toc, who always sat in the middle, could easily see and address men all the way up and down its length. Guests who sat on the side of the table with Khun Toc looked across a restaurant of men dressed only in towels and thence beyond to the swimming pool. Those on the opposite side looked into the courtyard behind Khun Toc.

It was, as Khun Toc once remarked, "the best fishbowl in the world."[28]

At Khun Toc's Babylon, male banqueting was as important as, if not more important than, male sex. Even the square footage devoted to feasting and socializing – the restaurant, two cafés, two outdoor lounges and their courtyards – were as great as or greater than the various passageways, saunas, steam baths, and private rooms available for actual sexual encounters. Khun Toc regularly brought with him guests that included not only his longtime Thai friends but also American ex-pats, Catholic canonical teachers from Europe, Australian dancers and choreographers, Canadian interior decorators, European symphony conductors, global businessmen – and, often, just the astonished wanderer who suddenly received a note hand-delivered by one of Babylon's staff requesting his presence at the banquet.

A typical dinner went like this:

Champagne came before the sauvignon or pinot gris, which in turn was followed by the shiraz or merlot or malbec with the main course. Khun Toc personally served each guest from the common plates of food delivered to the table. Of all the diners, he usually took the least. "High cholesterol," he explained once with a mischievous smile – while still dishing calamari to everyone else.

By 9:00 p.m., and certainly by 9:30 p.m., Khun Toc followed his self-discipline, returning home for work and sleep before an early rise the next day. His guests remained behind if they wanted to explore the rest of Bangkok's Phaeacia for themselves.

That was the pattern followed on a particular Friday night, December 27, 2002. About 9:30, Khun Toc left his guests to the remnants of the nightly banquet and returned across the courtyard to his home. The crowd at Babylon had peaked, filled with local men celebrating the weekend and travelers on longer Christmas journeys to Thailand.

But at the entry to Soi Nantha, police cars had begun to gather, displacing the taxis. Some had been dispatched from the local police district. Others were arriving from the central government's Interior Ministry.

Babylon was no ordinary gay sauna, and this was no ordinary police raid.

15
The Problem with Home (2)

In 1989, the gay guide *Spartacus* modified its previous advice to gay men about bypassing Singapore unless they wanted to shop. The international travel guide still cautioned against going to the male brothels on Johore Road unless "you are desperate," and it still warned that Singapore's sodomy and gross indecency laws carried severe penalties up to ten years' imprisonment. But now the guide noted seven bars had actually begun catering to gay men rather than simply tolerating them. Foreshadowing an important fashion about to arrive, the editors also wrote that the Clark Hatch chain of Western-style workout clubs had opened a branch in the Marco Polo Hotel. Gay men, they said, had begun to go there to exercise, although it warned that they still had to "be very discreet." Finally, shopping itself had become a key to Singapore's gay geography; the guide now listed shopping malls where gay men had begun to cruise more publicly, noting that those spots changed rapidly, "especially in new shopping plazas as they open."

An area of tropical beach east of Fort Road was even being described and recommended. "Well known by Singaporean gays as 'the gay beach,'" the guide said. "Particularly active on Sundays."[1]

That same year, 1989, Stuart's first stop on his journey outward from Singapore was in Philadelphia to study in a pharmacy program, the son sent to learn his father's profession much as Vajiravudh and Khun Toc had been sent to London to learn theirs. Stuart seemed to quickly realize that a skinny, brainy Chinese teenager used to the orderliness of Singapore was no match for the rules of manhood on the streets of Philadelphia. S2 would later write that he had to learn "how to grow eyes on the back of my head."

"I quickly decided that I didn't want to spend the next six years fearing for my life." So he transferred to the University of Minnesota and learned another lesson: "Brilliant. From one of the most dangerous places to one of the coldest! It appeared I really knew how to pick hospitable places to live in."[2]

He ran for various student government offices in his pharmacy college. His Rimbaud-style, slightly cocky attitude strengthened, at least online: "I ran for numerous offices, won some, made lots of alliances, lots of enemies who hated my guts, and ultimately, made a nuisance of myself on all levels. I was definitely not your prototypical 'international student' who only sat in the first three rows and busted the curve. I never went to class . . . and STILL busted the curve. Ha! I don't think they knew what to think of me. I even went for my Board licensure exams with blond hair, a 3-piece Donna Karan suit . . . and that was while I was student government president!"[3]

A photograph of him in his college years echoes the *Hamid* that Walter Spies had sketched generations earlier – but with dramatic changes to the representation of the young Asian male body. S2 had colored his hair a burnished orange to contrast with his black eyebrows. He stared straight at the camera, rather than gazing away as Walter had drawn Hamid. His eyes hid behind fashionable gold-rimmed sunglasses that widened them. As with Walter's *Hamid*, Stuart was still a set of bony lines and deltas – long arms strapped together with muscles that served their job as ropes but little else. No Winckelmann ellipses or ripples. His head was cocked to the side and his face was a pentagon of a broad smile. He posed for the camera bare-chested, but – as had also been the case in Walter's *Hamid* – his nipples and pectoral muscles were left to the imagination, since he had draped his shoulders with a black and red vest, the Rimbaudian anarchist's colors. If in one photograph his hair was orange, in the next it might be blond. He wrote that he went through "a series of six different hair colors in as many weeks."

S2 later blogged: "A new haircut, new look! If people ever start taking you for granted, change your image!"[4]

His pharmacy studies took him to the Mayo Clinic in Rochester, then to San Francisco General Hospital, and then to China to study *qigong* and traditional Chinese medicine. He was happier with his life off the smart island. "The people I met," he wrote, "the things I did, I just don't think it would have been the same had I stayed in Singapore."[5]

Something else had changed. He had fallen in love with a Caucasian medical student. This time he did more about it than just sing a song about romance at a Raffles talent show. They became boyfriends.

By 1992, when Stuart was almost twenty, he had begun coming out to friends in Minnesota, including one named Christine. "What blew me away," he would later write, "was her staunch support for gays and lesbians everywhere. She broke up with a boyfriend because he made a disparaging remark about lesbians. She told off her sister and relatives when they started making homophobic jokes. When I asked her why she stood up so strongly she said, 'Stuart, you're my friend. And there is absolutely nothing wrong with being gay. We're all people, and any form of prejudice or bigotry simply is unacceptable.'"[6]

He was stunned. Later he would blog:

> We're afraid of being branded gay if we stand up against people
> making homophobic remarks. Well, wake up and smell the coffee,
> we ARE gay. When do we start standing up for ourselves?[7]

In March 1992, an afternoon tabloid in Singapore, *The New Paper*, headlined its front page with a single dominant scream: "AMBUSH ON GAY BEACH." Inside, the articles described an isolated, overgrown piece of land along Singapore's East Coast Parkway at the end of Fort Road. The beach there, the newspaper said, had become "a homosexual haunt."[8]

Not one, but two reporters had been assigned to tell the story of the hidden male geography. "Homosexuals," the reporters wrote, "meet there daily to pick up partners and even have intercourse under the canopy of casuarina trees." The reporters had discovered "makeshift beds – sheets of newspaper laid snugly on the grass beneath trees." They had also deciphered what they considered to be the homosexuals' code for communicating: Men would sling daypacks over their shoulders and carry a bottle of mineral water in their right hands so they could be recognized as cruising for sex. The reporters had found "the area strewn with empty mineral water bottles" – apparently a sure sign not just of littering but also of rampant sex.

An accompanying photograph showed a man wearing a T-shirt, shorts, and sneakers. His face had been darkened so that he could not be recognized. He was carrying the requisite backpack and water bottle.

A second headline read: "I was caressed, says cop." In it, Detective Cpl. Stephen Lim, twenty-four, explained how he had gone to the beach to be a magnet. "His job: To hang around the area until he was approached by homosexuals." The journalists described Lim as "clean-cut" and he was quoted as saying, "I suppose I look the part." Just to make sure, he and three other police officers had worn shorts and had carried backpacks and bottles of mineral water. Lim admitted, "It does feel uncomfortable to be caressed by another man, but I see it as part of the job."

He described how one man, a thirty-nine-year-old army officer, had approached him and the two had walked into the bushes, the young, attractive detective voluntarily placing himself in a situation in which he knew he might be touched. The older man had begun with a stroke and a slight kiss. Lim made no protest. The army officer slid his hand toward Lim's groin. At that point – but only at that point – "I identified myself as a police officer and placed him under arrest." Lim also signaled another police officer, a twenty-two-year-old, who had been watching nearby. Six additional officers waited nearby to take suspects into custody as Lim and his partner continued to work the bushes.

The New Paper accompanied the articles with a photograph of four men who had been arrested – all in the requisite T-shirts and shorts. The men peered downward at their feet, and just as had happened with the young Asian men who decades earlier had been pulled into the *Zedenschandaal,* the newspaper writers did not give them any voice in the articles. They were silent.

The police arrested four more men the next day. Again, *The New Paper* portrayed them as shamed, sitting cross-legged on the ground, looking down, towered over by six detectives. And, again, no voice. The second-day operation involved even more police than the first. Twelve officers plunged into the bushes, while three others provided backup. *The New Paper* also published small mug shots of the four who had been previously arrested and who had already pled guilty. Each had been fined 1,000 Singaporean dollars for violating Section 354 of Singapore's criminal code, "outraging modesty."[9]

Then, as quickly as they had appeared, the stories and the raids stopped. It was not constant enforcement or publicity that made Singapore's criminal prohibitions against male desires scary. It was the randomness.

Then came May 30, 1993.

Singapore had had discos since the late 1970s. Managements occasionally posted signs prohibiting male-male dancing — just to be sure there were no violations of Section 354 — and so in some of the earliest discos, gay men sat talking in one half while heterosexual couples danced together in the other half.[10] But sometimes they used the safety provided by disco music itself to dance together. Disco, after all, did not require heterosexual ballroom couples performing a romantic, monogamous ritual together. No one really had to have a partner to dance, so long as the dance floor was crowded enough. If there was a partner, no one really needed to seem to be dancing with — him. It was easy enough to form lines, circles, or chaotic splotches where everyone seemed to be dancing with everyone, and no one with no one.[11]

It had taken until 1983 for Singapore to have its first gay disco where same-sex dancing was fully accepted, appropriately named "Niche."[12] Others had followed, but they had all faltered, since Singapore did not yet have enough gay men willing to be seen in publicly gay locations every night. In larger nations, men might leave their hometowns and go to another city to come out, but Singapore offered no such escape. It was too small, and so by the end of the 1980s, a different tradition had developed: Sunday gay nights at otherwise mostly heterosexual discos.

In 1993, one of those Sunday gay nights was occurring at the Rascals Disco, located in the Pan Pacific Hotel alongside the beach close to Bugis Street.

On May 30, a lawyer named Wilfred Ong had gone there. Suddenly, Ong wrote the next day, "the music stopped, the lights came on and an unnecessarily aggressive voice barked to tell us to 'Shut up!' as it was a 'police raid.'" Ong did not remember there having been any disorderly behavior, "only people dancing, drinking and generally having a good time." A plainclothes officer wearing a striped polo shirt ordered the dancers "to keep quiet or 'I'll knock your heads,'" Ong wrote. "He was shouting through the mike on the DJ's console."[13]

The police photographed the dance-goers, took their names and addresses, and then detained several who were not carrying their official identification cards. Those men were taken to a police station and then released. But then something remarkable happened — at least for Singapore.

Unlike the men who had been silenced at Fort Road, Ong, joined by twenty-one other men, signed a public letter of protest. In Singapore, there had never been such a protest from men willing to sign their names.

Perhaps equally remarkable, the police replied to the formal protest. A commander denied the Rascals visit was a raid to harass the gay patrons. He called it a "police check" to see whether the licensed capacity of 150 was being exceeded, and he explained that everyone's identity cards had been checked so that a specific headcount could be established.

That hardly seemed to explain the need to take names and addresses. But the commander also apologized for the police officers raising their voices.[14]

For the first time, gay men in Singapore had publicly challenged the police and the police had seemed at least mildly apologetic.

But then they responded with another raid at Fort Road. In September 1993, *The New Paper* warned its readers: "Gays surface again at East Coast Beach."[15]

This time, the police arrested even more men than before − twelve − including a flight steward for Singapore Airlines and a producer from the Singapore Broadcasting Corporation. The police went onto the beach in three waves over two days to "flush out the homosexuals," as *The New Paper* reporter put it, as if the gay men were a type of animal that first "surfaced" and then had to be "flushed out" of hiding. Once again, *The New Paper* reported that water bottles had provided the communication code that the police had followed.[16]

A few weeks later, the fears grew to a comic extent at the National University of Singapore west of downtown. Security guards, alerted to noises occurring inside a men's restroom, smashed in a locked stall door, but all they found inside was a hapless young male student who had been too noisily masturbating. No one else was with him. *The New Paper* quoted a university spokeswoman apologetically conceding that the door-crashing had not resulted in the discovery of another homosexual haunt. Even so, the paper still searched for a gay connection:

Loo door broken − but no gays.[17]

It seemed that, even when gay men in Singapore were not involved, they were guilty − and still to be hunted.

Most of the men arrested in the beach raids had immediately pled guilty to try to reduce the amount of public attention, but soon there would be another surprise for Singapore. One man, Tan Boon Hock, had been entrapped the usual way: eye contact, initial advances, and then he had unzipped a willing police officer's pants. Tan Boon Hock had reached his hand into the pants slightly. Then, he had been immediately arrested for outraging the officer's modesty.

When he appeared in court, Tan Boon Hok admitted the details of the crime. At first he was sentenced to four months in jail and three strokes of the cane. But, then his attorney argued against the sentence itself as being too extreme, urging the obvious: that the police officer could not possibly have had his modesty outraged since he had solicited the attention and had allowed Tan to proceed so far. On appeal, a chief justice of Singapore's High Court agreed. He wrote, "Tan had not forced his attentions on an unsuspecting and vulnerable victim of the fairer sex," implying that the law was meant to mostly regulate heterosexual men. The justice added, "I am somewhat bemused" because it seemed as if there was "little question" that the male police officer had at least partly consented to the other male's advances. The judge reduced the sentence to a fine of 2,000 Singaporean dollars. No jail. No caning.

Stunningly, Section 354's reach had been limited. Tan Boon Hock, although fined, had won.[18]

After the beach raids, what had been private talk began to spread outward through small group meetings when a few Singaporean men started gathering to discuss what it was like to be gay on the island. They met in private homes, at first, and then, in a crossover, they moved to rooms at a local arts center called the Substation. Over their tentative assemblies hung a legal threat.

Singapore's constitution assured citizens they had a "right to freedom of speech and expression," as well as "the right to assemble peaceably." It also guaranteed "the right to form associations." Historically, though, some associations in Singapore had specialized in vice and in violence against other racial groups on the small island, and so Singapore had adopted a strict Societies Act that specified that all groups had to register with and receive approval from the government.

It was one way of maintaining public order and trying to ensure that, if speech became offensive, it could be limited. But the Societies Act's requirements could also chill marginalized voices. The government Registrar of Societies, for example, could deny permission to any group believed "likely to be used for unlawful purposes or for purposes prejudicial to public peace, welfare or good order."[19] If, for example, gay men gathered to meet one another and form friendships that might eventually lead to male-male affection or sex, then that could be interpreted as a group "likely to be used for unlawful purposes." If they gathered to speak more openly about their homosexuality or promote positive, rather than shameful, images, then that could be read as a "purpose prejudicial to public welfare."

The registration forms specified that group organizers not only had to list their names, addresses, national identification numbers, and educational qualifications but also their employers' names and addresses. For those who wanted to associate with one another but not come out to their employers for risk of being fired or to their families for risk of being ostracized, that automatically chilled their speech.

Societies were also banned from reinforcing their identities with non-verbal expressions such as flags, emblems, or other insignia, without prior written approval from the registrar. That gave the government a lock on how group-identity symbols such as banners, uniforms, or colors could be employed. Were a gay society to ever be approved, the registrar could still insist on okaying any use of international gay symbols such as the rainbow flag or the pink triangle, the former a celebration of diversity and the latter a reminder of the holocaust against gay men that Nazi Germany had undertaken in the 1940s. Just how seriously the government took this provision regulating symbolic speech was indicated by the severity of punishment: a 3,000 Singaporean dollar civil fine or imprisonment for a year – or both.[20]

Finally, any group of ten or more people regularly meeting that did not register as a society risked even more severe penalties. Individuals who simply attended such a meeting or invited someone to it could be fined 5,000 Singaporean dollars and jailed for up to three years. Those who permitted such meetings in buildings or houses they owned faced similar punishment. Citizens who published or displayed materials from unregistered societies – or even happened to have such materials in their possession – could be fined 5,000 Singaporean dollars and imprisoned for two years.[21]

As the meetings of gay men at the Substation continued, so did the possibility they might be violating the Societies Act. Each Sunday, about forty to eighty men listened to a speaker discuss a topic such as legal rights or housing or relationships, and then broke into smaller discussion groups where they could share their own personal stories. The format was the typical one used earlier by consciousness-raising groups in the United States and Europe, but it was new for Singaporean gay men. One of the group's organizers later wrote that "many who came to the forum half-expected to be arrested by the end of each Sunday."[22]

The group also boldly started a small, printed monthly newsletter, something that under the Societies Act might have brought fines and imprisonment both for those men producing it and for those who carried or read it. The organizers chose a name, "People Like Us," avoiding any mention of what would have been all-too-obvious Western trigger words like "homosexual," "gay," or "queer." "PLU" provided not only a cover but also a homebred attempt to name their identity with a term not as clinical as "homosexual" or as confrontational as "queer." The word also did not divide "gay men" from "lesbian women," or "homosexual" from "bisexual" or "transsexual," or "closeted" from "out."

In this beginning attempt to gain a more public voice, it was left to individuals to define who were "people like us."

Always there was fear. In one case, the three PLU organizers – Alex Au, Russell Heng, and Joseph Lo – discovered a police officer had been sent to the meetings, although apparently as a joke being played on him by others in his department who suspected he was gay. Although he was not actually there to spy, his presence tipped the organizers that some in the police department certainly knew about the meetings.[23]

Another time, a man who borrowed his mother's car and then secretly attended the forum reported that the mother, who had once worked for the police, had received a call from a friend at the department warning her that a check on her car license was in progress to discover why it was sitting at the PLU meeting place.[24]

As the meetings grew in size, the question was whether the police might move first or whether — eager for another homosexual scandal — *The New Paper* would launch its own raid. In Europe or the United States, gay men at the same stage of organizing had sometimes been able to rely on a sympathetic press. Au and the others in PLU had no such confidence in Singapore's press.[25]

In April 1995 came a tip from a friend at *The New Paper*'s newsroom. A mother had searched her son's room and found a copy of PLU's monthly newsletter and then had complained to the paper. Au expected a reporter and a photographer outside the next meeting. The organizers moved quickly to alert everyone who usually attended, using only word of mouth. When the journalists arrived, only Au and one other organizer were there. Although they talked with the reporter, no story resulted. Two homosexuals apparently did not make a scandal. Nor, apparently, did it make for a photograph.[26]

But it was enough to convince Au and the others that it was time to try for licenses, one for the printed newsletter and one for the society itself. Both requests would be groundbreaking.

The application for the newsletter went in first. It got a swift "no."

The application for the society then required a year of lobbying the PLU's own members to find ten persons willing to publicly list themselves on the application.

A few days after that form was filed in November 1996, plainclothes police officers arrived at Au's house on a Saturday about midnight.[27]

While Alex Au and others were trying to maneuver through the particular colonial laws left behind in Singapore, the old Greek ideal of an *agora* in which citizens could exchange opinions, rail with one another, and maybe find new truths in the freedom of the marketplace, had begun to assume a new global dimension that would supersede their efforts. The transformation had begun as the brainstorm of a male student working at a Finnish university. In 1988, he had invented a software program that allowed computer users to exchange immediate messages with one another: instant person-to-person or person-to-group notes rather than costly phone calls or sluggish e-mails. Scientists and engineers at the university and eventually all over the world could instantly "chat." Soon enough, so could everyone else.

Internet Relay Chat channels offered a new medium simultaneously personal but also mass, public but also potentially anonymous. Gay men no longer had to "come out" to what few public spaces existed in Singapore. They could "come home" to their computers, even if their families might be sleeping in the next room. A small survey of gay Internet users in Singapore at the end of the 1990s would confirm the quick change. Almost ninety percent said the chat enabled them to meet more gay friends; more than sixty percent said that instant chat had increased their ability to find out about gay social activities.[28]

Very importantly, the "threads" of their new online conversations as a group did not disappear into air like the spoken talk at the bars or even the lectures at the PLU forums. The new "threads" of gay conversations in Singapore, as well as across the world, could now be archived and cross-referenced, becoming in the process not just oral talk but stored knowledge. The channel names themselves looked like early cross-indexed library card catalogs. "Soc.culture.asean" produced "soc.culture.Singapore." And eventually ".gay" could be added to any other cross-reference. Gay Singaporean men living abroad and enjoying the greater freedom to speak in London or New York or – iike S2 in Minnesota – could talk directly to those back home, engaging not only in debates but also, as one user put it, "name-calling and swearing and nearly all shades in between."[29] Opinions that seldom found their way into Singapore's controlled print and broadcast media could begin to be voiced. Consciousness-raising, of the sort that had been practiced in small gay and lesbian groups in the United States and Europe in the early 1970s, now reached globally.

It was at that point that a gay Singaporean man named Tan Chong Kee hit upon a strategy that would eventually influence Stuart Koe, who was still in college. Born in 1960, Tan Chong Kee was younger than PLU organizers like Au – who was from Lee Hsien Loong's generation – but slightly older than Stuart. He had earned a degree in math and computer science at Cambridge University and then in graduate school in Taiwan had switched to a personal passion: studying the history of Chinese literature. He also pursued another passion: his first boyfriend, a medical doctor.[30] Eventually he left Taiwan to earn a second graduate degree in Asian languages and literature from Stanford University. By 1993, Tan Chong Kee was poised for an epiphany: Binary codes plus literature – his two interests –might equal a voice for a different kind of Singaporean citizen. That same year in February, a graphics-friendly software called Mosaic was released for free to anyone who wanted to use it. Tan Chong Kee walked to a store near Stanford, bought a book on Hypertext, tied into an online tutorial offered by Stanford's computing center, and within a day knew how to create pages for the World Wide Web.

Back in Singapore, the "IT2000" report, and its press release describing the futuristic Singaporean family, had just been released a few months earlier. If Tay Leng Meng was the fictional son in the press release who knew how to find his way home by tapping into public computer terminals, Tan Chong Kee would be one real son who was finding a way to forge a new home online.[31]

The police who appeared at Alex Au's door that Saturday night in November 1996 told him he had to go to the police station the following Monday morning to explain his request for government approval of People Like Us. It felt, Au would later write, like a criminal investigation. Why were the PLU organizers doing what they were doing? How long had they been meeting? What were the names of the people attending?

The application languished. Six months passed before the answer from the Registrar of Societies came. As with the newsletter, the answer was "no."

There was no explanation.

When Au and others with PLU wrote back asking for a reason, the agency responded: "The Registrar is not required to provide any reason for the refusal of any application to register a society as there is no section under the Societies Act requiring the Registrar to do so."[32]

Au and the others then appealed to the Minister for Home Affairs, striking a polite tone of deference, but also showing more willingness to adopt civil rights rhetoric as well as now refer to themselves as "gay and lesbian":

> This appeal may risk being dismissed out of hand as coming from undesirable elements detrimental to the nation's moral fabric. But we hope it will not be, because it is being lodged in the firm belief that Singapore has a government which gives aggrieved citizens a fair hearing.
>
> In the event that you still feel compelled to say no [to the license], then we hope you would oblige us by letting us know your reasons. Asking to know the reasons should not be taken as a challenge to your prerogative but is instead a sincere attempt to understand better the State's objection to the gay and lesbian community . . . Our starting point is that in any civilized society where there is rule of law – and we consider Singapore to be such a society – there must always provisions for citizens to meet each other to discuss issues of mutual interest to them.[33]

Still no response. A follow-up letter tried the tactic of organizing the plea into "the moral arguments," "the family arguments," "the practical arguments," and "other justifications."

Still, no license and no explanation.

In July 1997, the PLU organizers tried one final appeal. This one went to the man who had succeeded Lee Kuan Yew as prime minister years earlier, Goh Chok Tong. Goh in a speech a few weeks earlier had emphasized that Singapore needed to attract more talented and creative individuals from overseas. So Au and the others tried a different rhetoric this time, geared to the demands of the corporate and academic worlds:

> Some top talent happens to be gay or lesbian. Increasingly, senior level decision-makers in multinational corporations, in universities and even governments, are open about their sexual orientation and Singapore will not be an attractive environment if it is perceived to be homophobic. Even gay and lesbian Singaporeans now studying abroad consider favorably the idea of never returning. Such loss of indigenous talent, year in year

out, generation after generation, is something Singapore can ill afford.[34]

The answer was still "no."

"I thought of it," Tan Chong Kee would write later, "as a project to write the history of the common man."[35] He wanted to create a new sort of history of Chinese literature, one written by a widespread net of people. In October 1994, he launched the Singapore Internet Community, Sintercom, and he and the others involved declared a sweeping vision: "To build and maintain an Internet home where all Singaporeans, whatever their concerns are, can meet and feel at home."[36]

Sintercom quickly became an online cultural center, publishing everything from Singaporean jokes to recipes to political commentary to a dictionary of "Singlish," the fusion of local dialect and English. Among the most important rooms was one called "NOT the Straits Times Forum," a reference to the dominant *Straits Times* newspaper owned by Singapore Press Holdings, also the owners of *The New Paper* and its gay-scandal coverage. In the "Not" room, Tan Chong Kee starting publishing the full text of letters that had been sent to the editors of the licensed media and that had either been rejected or severely edited.

Singaporean censors could not control the medium itself without blocking the very computer access they were trying to promote through "IT2000." Nor could they stop the content, because at first Sintercom's messages sat on computer servers located at one of the most prestigious universities in the United States – hardly a site that an island promoting itself as a smart paradise would want to block even if it could. Sintercom, in effect, was an old communication tactic updated, one that the United States and the Western European nations had practiced during the Cold War in order to reach into the Communist empire. Broadcast into the center from the periphery. Back then, it had been called Radio Free Europe. Now, it was Internet Free Everywhere.

As Alex Au and other PLU organizers waited for the outcome of their appeals under Singapore's traditional communication licensing system, they also decided in March 1997 to begin using Internet Relay Channels and imitating Tan Chong Kee's Sintercom by moving those discussions online in a new forum targeted specifically at gay men and women on the island. They called it SiGNeL, short for the "Singapore Gay News List" and, of course, reflective of the kinds of coded "signals" that gay men always had to use to try to identify one another or to speak in public. It was a private Internet e-mail list that did not seem to fall under the control of the Societies Act. It included strict content guidelines so as to avoid censorship problems: no personal ads, no attachments with photographs, no descriptions or "stats" of the sender that might suggest an attempt to encourage sexual interest, no instant chat function.[37]

But it was a new space for thinking and talking collectively.

By 1995, Stuart had graduated from the University of Minnesota. He did not want to lose the lover he had known for two years; he wrote, "It was heartbreaking to leave." But filial obedience to his parents trumped, much as it had with both Vajiravudh and Khun Toc. Stuart had constrained his own rebellion within careful limits. He would not be a Walter Spies trying to imagine a new homeland among people elsewhere; he would take his new status as an outsider back to Singapore and try to create a homeland there. He wrote: "I felt that it was important not to lose my Singapore citizenship, that I owed that much to my parents who had financed my education."[38]

He had turned twenty-three by then, and at first, he simply resumed the life expected of all young Singaporean men. He enlisted for the mandatory two and a half years in the military. Because of his pharmacy background, he became a medical research assistant, had his own office, and, rather than stay in barracks, went home every day after 5:00 p.m. He also did what many other gay Singaporeans in their twenties were then doing: He went on the Net. At Yahoo's Geocities, he set up his first webpage. He also started writing entries for SiGNeL By 1997, S2 had begun to post photographs and diary entries not only about gay life in Singapore but also about his own evolving attitude toward his gay male body.

The skinny boy with colored hair in Minnesota had disappeared, partly thanks to the army. The black hair had returned, and Stuart now wore a shelf of pectoral muscles, an abdominal delta, and a range of more noticeable quadriceps. Ellipses.

Online, he began chatting with other gay men from all over the world. They left encouraging comments:

> stuart...u r so cute!!! . . . your page is so cool . . . so different . . . just like u . . .

> Hi babe . . . nice homepage . . . love the design. (oh, and you're very much my type too!)

> My friends told me that I simply had to see your Homepage. What a stunner, such exquisite beauty! Your page is nice too :)

> What a delightfully arrogant young prick! . . . Without doubt the most elegant website I've come across in Singapore with just the right dash of languid decadence[39]

It was the kind of emotional support gay men in Singapore were not used to hearing. For those isolated on the smart island, online relationships could be better – much better – than the closeted interpersonal encounters that demanded they hide and meet others' expectations.

Walter Spies had had to physically leave Germany to "buy a feeling" of homeland, as he had written. The new lights and sounds and rhythms of this time- and space-compressed magical reality called the Internet began to suggest that a gay man might be able to find that homeland wherever he was.

In May 1997, Stuart attended a play by a Singaporean company called Theaterworks. The actors had combined a reenactment of an old Chinese tale called "Flowers in the Mirror" with one of Singapore's most impressive – and gaudiest – shopping mall attractions: the Fountain of Wealth at the Suntec City Mall. The fountain resembled a huge ring held in the palm of a hand. The ring itself had a circumference of more than 200 feet and reached forty feet into the air.[40] It was a symbol of retaining wealth. Within it hundreds of people could gather.

The play itself focused on a woman who decides to confront her society's injustices by leading other women to a paradise where they perform miracles. Men suddenly conceive children. Children become unrestricted by gender. But opponents defame the women as a cult, capture and lobotomize them so they cannot imagine anymore, and eventually launch a full-scale genocide against them.

In his blog, S2 would write: "I was 'inside' Asia's largest fountain yesterday. What a sublime experience. This is a fountain about the size of a quarter of a football field, with huge jets of water shooting up about 10 stories, and a huge ring of water raining down in a circle from a height of about 6 stories up . . . Amazing . . . what a change of perspective."

S2 speculated that Singapore's licensor for the arts, the Ministry of Information and the Arts, had been unable to read the coded message in the juxtaposition of the play's theme and its presentation at the Fountain of Wealth.

> The plot was powerful (and very sad), but the imagery was even more so. Butoh-inspired white linen costumes billowing in the wind, shaven-heads, spastic movements, fluid dances amongst the jets of water. Perspex, metal sculptures, grey PVC tubes, men with computers who answered your questions. It was chaotic . . . it was interactive, it was everywhere and nowhere.
>
> These talented people CREATED something here. Good on them. They slapped the establishment in Singapore in the face, and no one's noticed. They got away with it, with good press and publicity. But no one's talked about the subtext . . . Many people probably went home either puzzled, or quietly nodding to themselves in agreement.
>
> Perhaps this is but one step towards more vocal demonstrations of our displeasure.
>
> An allegory of our frustrations.[41]

A not-yet-fully formed idea was beginning. The use of the fountain would remain in his mind as a way to transform perspective and to hold oppositional narratives in tension together: a dominant narrative within which a marginalized narrative was also enacted, creating magical-reality.

On September 15, 1997, S2 wrote what would become his own personal manifesto for action. He posted it not only on his own personal webpage but also on the new SiGNeL:

> I am fuming mad! I basically got told by another gay man that by maintaining this webpage which does nothing short of declare that I am an out and proud gay man, I am in fact jeopardizing the entire gay movement in Singapore. His rationale was that Singapore was in no way ready for people to be out, and that each person who "flaunts" his sexuality is giving the authorities more fodder to clamp down on us, discriminate, and carry out other forms of unspeakable acts.
>
> "Ridiculous," I thought. This man has rationalized that . . . by staying in his unhealthy and musky closet that he is helping everyone around him because it wouldn't be "rocking the boat" . . .
>
> We in Singapore need to foster change . . . I am not talking about loud demonstrations, about Pride marches, nor about political upheaval. This change has to come from within. It's all about building a community based on understanding and love and compassion. It's about personal PRIDE . . . about being sure of who you are, and NOT BEING ASHAMED. It's about standing up for yourself whenever you hear someone utter something homophobic. It's about not tolerating another moment of abuse (physical or psychological or otherwise) no matter where you are, because of who you are . . .
>
> Singapore won't change until there is a critical mass of self-respecting, proud gay men and women. No matter how loud the few shout. No matter how many gay plays are written and staged. No matter if the entire government were to change tomorrow. The greatest revolution is within.
>
> It's time to stand up for yourselves, brothers and sisters.[42]

16

A New Man for Thailand

Thaksin Shinawatra was fond of slogans. As a child in the northern Thai city of Chiang Mai, he had attended a Catholic school that promoted *Labor Omnia Vincit,* "Work Conquers All." Later, he adopted a motto he learned at the Thai Police Academy: "Better to die than live like a loser." He would keep a variation posted in his office, a sign that said: "Winners-Losers." He grouped those he knew into the two categories. "A loser," he said, "sees problems at every opportunity, but a winner sees an opportunity in every problem."[1]

His family's accumulation of wealth had followed such a plot. His Chinese great-grandfather had emigrated in the nineteenth century, and when Siam's monarchy wanted taxes from the opium and liquor that Chinese immigrants consumed, it turned to men who could negotiate the tight-knit communities and auctioned to them the right to collect the taxes. Thaksin's ancestor became a "tax farmer," legally pocketing the difference between his bid and the full amount of taxes paid.

The monarchy's problem had become a Chinese entrepreneur's opportunity.

By the 1950s, the Shinawatras had become one of the leading families in Chiang Mai, so much so that when a 1980 book celebrated the area's pioneers, one-fifth of it was devoted to family members.[2] Their original Chinese name had been changed to the Thai word meaning "does good routinely."

Thaksin was born in 1949. Throughout his youth, military officers and civilian prime ministers ruled Thailand, exchanging power in one coup or election after another. After finishing his Catholic school education, Thaksin entered a military cadet academy. Later, in an autobiography called *Eyes on the Stars, Feet on the Ground,* he wrote about how his ideas of masculinity had been shaped:

> The career that every Thai boy wanted to follow was in the armed forces or police. Apart from the glamour of the uniform and external appearance which I myself fell in love with, there was admiration for the men who were patriotic, self-sacrificing, strong, and full of fighting spirit. Also, the fact that the big people with power and influence in the society were all people in uniform made this ideal career for Thai youth.

> The most impressive thing was that everyone had to respect
> those in command, and listen to those with seniority, without
> exception.[3]

Males who were winners were *phuyai* or big persons; males who were not were *phunoi*, little persons.

Thaksin opted for the Police Academy rather than the military, graduating at the top of his class in 1973. Then he earned a doctorate in criminal justice at Sam Houston State University in Texas, choosing for his dissertation the question of why police officers and judges who were supposed to enforce the law instead sometimes broke it. He wondered whether exposure to criminal justice education really made any difference in preventing abuse or corruption. His findings were disturbing. First, he reported that, of the students enrolling at Sam Houston, those studying criminal justice seemed to have the least respect for the rule of law. Then, he discovered that the study of criminal justice seemed to make very little difference in their attitude.[4]

That could be a problem — or an opportunity.

He returned to Thailand at the end of the 1970s, the same time Khun Toc was coming back from London. At first, Thaksin worked in a police planning office. On the side, he launched businesses in silk and real estate — and failed. Then he leased IBM computers to government agencies. That failed too. But by 1986, he realized how to make the overlapping system of Thai government and commerce work. As a police planner, he designed a program to install new computers in the police data center. He followed up with his own bid on the contract. Not surprisingly, he won. Shortly afterward, he helped an American company secure a government contract to offer wireless paging services. He had discovered two things. First, as his great-grandfather had realized, opportunities for large profit lay within government contracts rather than within retail sales. Second, in the information economy emerging in the 1980s, controlling the service was the key to such profits, not selling the computer hardware.

In 1987, as Khun Toc prepared to open his new paradise of Babylon on Soi Nantha, Thaksin Shinawatra quit his job at the police department. Then he set off on his own quest to become a bigger man, a *phuyai*.

Physical designs of cities can promote belonging or enforce exile, and the same may be true of places sought by those who are not treated as equal citizens — paradises like Khun Toc's Babylon. A philosopher of architecture, Christian Norberg-Schulz, once wrote that it all depends on the experience of traveling through different types of communication, a journey seeded by the built environment.[5]

First comes a sense of *arriving*. Norberg-Schulz explained that, in the case of cities, that could be the first view of a set of spires or of skyscrapers breaking through a flat horizon. It is the threshold of saying, "I am here." For Khun Toc's island on Soi Nantha, the threshold came at the small courtyard surrounded by Winckelmann-style sculptures, the dragon-winged door handles, and Vajiravudh's portrait. Along with all those signals that men were crossing into a new magical reality, Khun Toc had posted a more explicit sign: *You are about to enter the Babylon twilight zone. Check reality and prepare to explore your fantasy.*

Beyond the threshold begins the entry into what Norberg-Schulz termed places that communicate *collective agreement*. It is a group answer to the question: "What are we all doing here?" Certain buildings become symbols that turn the invisible common values into visible stone and glass: temples representing common religious values, government buildings signifying political agreement about how the city was run, or theaters for creating a shared culture of stories.[6] Typically, vertical thrusts are emphasized – perhaps through spires or domes or arches. Those architectural elements seem to pull individuals toward a larger mission. Plazas are popular too, a geography where citizens can stop to socialize, often in the presence of those public buildings.

At Babylon, Khun Toc would design areas that might be labeled places of "collective agreement" so that they occupied about two-thirds of the total physical space – unusual in a gay sauna where, typically, more square footage would be given to areas for private sex. The old Babylon had its rooftop skyward-looking garden toward which all paths led; the new Babylon, its swimming pool "plaza" set amid a tropical garden of tall palm trees. The new Babylon would also offer a separate courtyard with a stage for performances and bistro-style tables for drinking. In between those two plazas a two-story restaurant with a high atrium and floor-to-ceiling glass offered vertically framed sightlines in both directions, becoming its own third plaza as well as its own tug upward. A circular staircase wound from restaurant to lockers and another sitting area, completing the verticality. Babylon also had a gym equipped with exercise machines, free weights, and Thai trainers dressed in white shorts and muscle-shirts. Phallic sphinxes, much like those in the entry courtyard, rose above the men in the gym. Finally, Babylon had rooms for Thai as well as Western-style massage, non-sexual massage, as a sign that said "no hand-jobs" reminded everyone about what type of touch could be safely agreed upon.[7]

But if there was a "collective agreement" being communicated, what was it? There were no etched sayings carved in stone porticos. But one detail did suggest a possibility. The restaurant chairs came equipped with white and black coverings depicting iconic Hollywood female stars and a single phrase that seemed designed both to provoke a smile and to raise a question about "what we are all doing here."

It simply, fluidly, asked: "Whatever becomes a legend most?"

Khun Toc had chosen to emphasize the idea of code-switching among the rhythms of manhood being demanded in Southeast Asia. Traditional Bodhisattvas mingled with industrial metallic birds of flight soaring over restaurant tables. Modernistic "found art" composed of everyday objects materialized out of dark shadows, such as in one shower passageway where dozens of hospital intravenous bottles with hanging plastic tubes formed a chandelier. Lucian Freud-style paintings of grotesquely bulbous naked men dominated the restaurant, providing a twist to the Winckelmann-inspired statues rising a few meters away in the gym and the entry courtyard.

Music varied with sounds from "An American in Paris" fading into Tchaikovsky's "Swan Lake" or, on Friday and Saturday nights, during courtyard stage productions, American disco beats. Sunday nights brought black female jazz singers with torch songs.

Whatever had become a legend – culturally, artistically, religiously.

A second statement in Khun Toc's "collective agreement" about manhood seemed to be that the male body – of any physique – was to be savored. Asked once which representations of the Asian male body he preferred – those that showed them as lotus-eyed and smooth boys, those that presented them as gorgeous *kathoeys*, or those that portrayed them fresh from the Winckelmann *gymnasia* with lean swimmers' bodies, Khun Toc answered simply: "I like them all. I don't like an attempt to push out one or the other."[8] Much as the gay Singaporean "New Man" had suggested years earlier, Babylon seemed to both attract "Oriental, white, young, geriatrics tottering into their final years, gorgeous faces with tight pecs, abs and biceps, paunchy businessmen whose fortune is anything but their faces. Macho to the bone or queens right down to manicured fingernails – the variety is there; all you have to do is choose."[9]

Beyond the architecture communicating "collective agreement," Norberg-Schulz also suggested that built environments needed to create a sense of the "bazaar" – the winding raucousness of the marketplace. He named the experience one of *meeting*, that sense of amazement of encountering a vibrant bazaar where every crooked street, he wrote, "becomes a manifestation of the process of discovery." Without discovery, collective agreement on monumental categories could become stifling.

In such places of meeting, Norberg-Schulz argued, encounters were immediate, anonymous, and brief[10] – "light" relationships rather than heavily weighted ones. Mazes were best for creating those experiences, he wrote. Movement proceeded horizontally and pointed in no particular direction. Mazes "do not necessarily lead to a particular goal," he wrote. "They often start and end without precise definition and are characterized by what happens along them."[11] A maze was like music, a composition in architecture that unfolded through fleeting time.

At the new Babylon, Khun Toc had masterminded at least six overlapping mazes where men wearing only towels could *meet* one another – immediately, anonymously, and briefly. "New Man" from Singapore had described one steam bath maze this way: "Sit down on the bench and let the billowing clouds swarm you . . . Go further in and you can't see a damn thing, it's pitch dark . . . It's that chamber in Babylon where you experience maximum pleasure with minimum vulnerability, where looks or personality don't matter."[12]

Two other walking mazes offered "resting cubicles," each differently shaped to ensure that the brief encounters that occurred were still happening in unique zones, not just the uniformly sized cubicles present in many saunas. A fifth maze was positioned into a room the size of a plaza, where a totally darkened labyrinth had been built from cold, smooth, metal walls that Khun Toc's workers regularly rearranged into dead ends.

The sixth maze was a more nuanced way of communicating a sense of moving through time as well as through space. Most gay saunas opened all their spaces at all times, but at Babylon different sections unlocked at particular times of the day or night. At certain moments, metal gates or doors swung open or closed, making areas approachable or not, and turning the entire complex into a maze of time variations.

Such darkened mazes for immediate, brief, and anonymous encounters between men were the most controversial aspect of any gay sauna. It was there that the dissent from the triple supremacy was at its strongest and most sexually explicit.

In 1991, *Rolling Stone* magazine wrote about Thailand very unflatteringly – as unflatteringly as anything that had ever been written in the nineteenth century by Anna Leonowens or by the British and American visitors who had mocked the Siamese.

"Why," the *Rolling Stone* writer asked, "is Thailand the whorehouse of the world?"[13]

The story offered Bangkok as evidence: "The police estimate that there are at least 500,000 sex workers – female and male prostitutes – in Bangkok, a city of six million people." Bangkok, according to an unnamed scholar, had "119 massage parlors, 119 combination barbershop/massage parlor/teahouses, 97 nightclubs, 248 disguised whorehouses and 394 disco-restaurants."

Why nightclubs and restaurants deserved to be grouped with brothels was not explained, nor was any distinction made between "massage parlors" offering clothed, non-sexual massage and what were sometimes called "steam and cream" parlors. Nor was it clear how, in a city that rambled uncontrollably over the vast Chao Phraya River delta, the scholar had managed a precise count.

That did not matter to the new Anna Leonowens though. "The land of smiles is famously *compliant*," the *Rolling Stone* author continued, using terms of sexual dominance and submissiveness. Thailand was a "crossroads country that has survived and kept its independence by accommodating itself to the vagaries of power." He quoted a Western sociologist who claimed Thais did not expect power to be moral. Power was "aggressive and masculine." Goodness, by contrast, lay in "powerlessness" and in being "feminine."[14]

Bangkok was a marginal place – "halfway around the revolving blue globe, thirty hours and three bad in-flight movies from home, as exotic a place as any in the world" – and it had supposedly put one of every twelve of its citizens into

204 Imagining Gay Paradise

commercial sex work, a half-million prostitutes in a city of six million, all trading sex for some semblance of cash and power.

Time magazine followed in 1993, with a cover photo of a Thai bar girl and an estimate that the entire country sported 2 million prostitutes. The same year, Longman's *Dictionary of English Language and Culture* defined Bangkok as "a capital city with many prostitutes."[15]

The fingers pointed in the direction they always had. Foreign sex tourists were unsavory opportunists, but the real problem was the Thai male and his supposedly prodigious sexual appetite. "Thai men," the *Rolling Stone* writer claimed, "consider whoring healthy and manly."[16]

Foundational to the wave of these late-twentieth-century images, coming a century after similar imperial criticism, had been an adjustment to Thai law made during the 1960s. At the time, the Thai military had been cooperating with the Americans to defeat the Viet Cong. The 1966 Entertainment Places Act ostensibly aimed at controlling entertainment venues that affected "public order and morals." Instead, it had created a legal category of special service worker whom bars, nightclubs, and massage parlors could employ to provide entertainment, birthing an "off-girl" and "off-boy" system. Pay the owner of the entertainment place a small fee to "borrow" such a worker, thus compensating for lost work time, and then you could have whatever private "entertainment" both parties wanted, either away or on-site.

Direct fees for sex were never discussed in advance as in Europe or the United States. Whatever money was offered at the end of the private entertainment was incorporated into an English phrase that off-girls and off-boys quickly learned: "Up to you." That made it seem like less of a prostitution business deal and more a gift to a newly made friend who had taken a few hours off of work. A year after the law was in place, the US military announced that soldiers in Vietnam would no longer have to fly all the way to Australia or other distant sites for their rest and recreation. They could now go to nearby Thailand.[17]

Within a decade, the war had ended but the off-system had become entrenched, with the male desire for promiscuous sex seen as the problem, the providers of that sex seen as the victims regardless of whether they were female or male, and the government seen as a willing accomplice. By 1996, three decades after the Entertainment Places Act had been enacted, cartoonists in some newspapers began to satirize the image of Thai masculinity. In the 1920s, the critics had demonized Vajiravudh's sexuality by linking it with political corruption;[18] now they hung that image on what one academic called "the old man of Thai politics – the greedy, oversexed military dictator."[19] In 1996, an election cartoon in the English-language *Bangkok Post* summed the heightened conflict over the old symbols of Thai manhood: In a direct echo of the 1920s, a cartoonist drew the general who was pursuing the prime minister's post as bloated and lascivious. He grasped at a premiership that was depicted as a young woman trying to escape. To counter the image, political parties began looking for male candidates who could seem more like rational, fatherly defenders of women and children.[20]

Within that political problem, Thaksin would find opportunity. Throughout the late 1980s and early 1990s, he had been setting up new wireless contracts via government agencies and capitalizing on the need for new mobile phones in a country with an overloaded demand for landlines. By June 2001, *Forbes* magazine was listing Thaksin as one of the world's richest people, with an estimated worth of US$1.2 billion – despite a crash in Asian economies in 1997.[21]

Using his own money, Thaksin created a new political party, Thai Rak Thai – "Thai Loves Thai."

He admired how Singaporean politics operated: with a single dominant political party legitimized by opposition but not seriously threatened by it. Eventually he would promise Thais that, out of the country's history of small fractious political parties, he would create a two-party system in which Thai Rak Thai, based in the Shinawatra stronghold in the north, would forever dominate a smaller Democratic Party based in the south. Bangkok would be pinched in between.[22]

His website noted his governing philosophy and his ideal of manhood, rolling together his militaristic, academic, and business background: "From Pol. Lt. Col. Dr. Thaksin's point of view, stewardship of the country requires the same foresight as it takes to run a group of companies. In this sense, the country is like a company that is underperforming."[23] He sounded a bit like Vajiravudh had eighty years earlier, when the king had compared Siam to a ship that needed to be run by a captain, all others following his orders.

In a later speech, Thaksin would argue that "democracy is a good and beautiful thing, but it's not the ultimate goal as far as administering the country is concerned . . . Democracy is just a tool, not our goal."[24]

The ideal Thai man was no longer the dharma-based merit-maker nor the Phibunesque warrior derived from nationalist fervor. Thaksin's codification would locate itself in his apparent mastery of that new global arena of multinational corporations and international finance. In his autobiography, Thaksin drew himself as "the son of a coffee-shop owner," who had "started out managing a company of seven people" and now employed thousands with revenue of billions. He was "someone born in the countryside," "who was once a bad debtor," who now wanted the country to "have a modern bureaucracy which serves the people and gives them access to data and information."[25]

Economically, he promised programs that appealed to Thailand's masses, especially a three-year moratorium on debt for farmers and a thirty-baht health-care system assuring free medical care for those with low incomes. Socially, he joined the long-standing concern about the "moral order" – the expression of *siwilai*. In January 2001, he and his new Thai Rak Thai party would win the popular vote overwhelmingly. The line seemed to run straight across the heart of the Chao Phraya delta and split the country in two.

The Friday morning of December 27, 2002 had actually begun with extremely good news for gay men and women in Thailand. At Babylon's breakfast room, it was possible to read the headline in one of the city's leading English-language newspapers, the *Nation*:

Government Endorsement: Homosexuality "not a disease"[26]

In Europe and the United States, religion had condemned male desire for sex with another man as a sin, laws had criminalized behaviors arising from that desire, and psychiatry had completed the trinity by declaring the desire a mental illness.

Thailand had never gone that far. Buddhism had been more concerned with infidelity between committed partners than with same-sex relations, and while it was true that Chulalongkorn had adopted a sodomy law at the beginning of the twentieth century to keep the British happy – as part of *siwilai* – the law had never been enforced and then had been dropped in 1956.[27] Vajiravudh had promoted the cultural ideal of romantic heterosexual monogamy in his plays, but he himself had not demonized same-sex behaviors into a triple taboo. Even polygyny did not bar same-sex desires; the tradition simply insisted that, to be complete, a man also needed sex with women so as to produce children.[28]

The medical history was more complicated. Thais had been slow in adopting the Western psychiatric idea that male desires for one another might be a mental disorder, but the wartime alliance with the Americans prompted new concepts. During the war, the US military had begun questioning soldiers to determine whether they were heterosexual or homosexual. Afterward, as Thai students gained access to medical training in the United States, they brought the labels home, though tentatively at first. In the United States, both McCarthyism and Alfred Kinsey's reports pushed homosexuality into public discourse by the early 1950s, especially for political scandals. But in Thailand, it was not until 1960 that a powerful monk named Phimontham, who argued that communists should be allowed to meditate in Buddhist temples, was falsely accused of homosexual behavior, jailed, and then forcibly disrobed.[29]

Not until 1961 did notable medical studies begin, when two Thai medical students trained in the United States, Dr Sood Saengwichien, an expert in anatomy, and Dr Aroon Parksuwan, trained in mental health, examined several *kathoey* and questioned them about their feelings. Although the word *kathoey* was ancient, the phenomenon of previously unisex-clothed Thai males dressing in Western women's fashion was newer – something made possible only with the Western dress reforms promoted by Chulalongkorn, Vajiravudh, and Phibun. The two doctors wanted to learn whether such men were, in Western terms, hermaphrodites with either ambivalent or dual sex organs. Instead, Sood, the anatomist, would report that most *kathoeys* were men with no ambivalent sex organs whatsoever. He called them *lag-ga-phates*, rather than *kathoeys*, using the first term for the gender performance tied to cross-dressing and trying to reserve the second term for anatomy: androgynous bodies that reflected both male and female sex organs. Both he and Aroon concluded that the gender desire to cross-dress made the men – in Western terminology – transvestites.

Then he made the connection to mental illness. "Therefore, " Sood wrote, "their anomalous manners result from mental disorder, not physical illness."[30]

That particular distinction had set the stage for the *Thai Rath* newspaper, four years later, during its coverage of Darrell Berrigan's murder, to sensationally "discover" there was yet another mental disorder, a *nosferatu*, intruding into Thai society: masculine "gay" men who desired sex with other men.

The Journal of the Psychiatric Association of Thailand had then published four significant articles in 1973, each seeming to adopt Freud's environmental explanation for the cause of transvestitism and homosexuality, but each also arguing that individual men should be medicated and rehabilitated rather than changing negative attitudes about male-male desire. One author noted, "The society nowadays considers that [homosexuality] is becoming a major social problem, which might cause a decline in morality and a legal problem leading to sexual crime. The [medical community], particularly psychiatry, should be readily interested in this matter to research its cause, medication and protection."[31]

As psychiatrists in the West were beginning in the early 1970s to delist homosexuality as a mental disorder, Thailand had actually moved in the opposite direction.

The news in December, then, had been long awaited. The pronouncement had come in an almost offhand way. Anjaree, a group of Thai lesbians, had written asking for clarification about what the government mental health policy was. In *The Nation* story that December 27 morning, one of the directors of the Thai Department of Mental Health conceded that the decision that homosexuality was no longer a mental disorder lagged behind academic and psychological consensus by almost thirty years.[32]

The Nation editorial was upbeat, saying that the official move "toward more sensitivity, compassion and understanding about homosexuality should not be too difficult given the fact that Thailand is already one of the few cultures that displays much less homophobia than the great majority."[33] *Thai Rath*'s earlier calls for criminalizing homosexual acts as imports by outsiders had been forgotten.

That Friday night, Khun Toc joined his friends as usual for their 7:00 p.m. conversations at his home across the courtyard from the Babylon sauna. Then, as always, they walked past the photograph of Vajiravudh and sat to eat at the boomerang-style table in the dining room. Khun Toc left the feast at his usual time, between 9:00 and 9:30 p.m.

By then, the controversial mazes for meetings between men wandering the sections of Babylon set aside for the experience of the bazaar were busy. Shortly after Khun Toc left the dinner, the police cars dispatched by Thaksin's Interior Ministry began to arrive.

17
Men of the Net

Stuart Koe had posted his online manifesto in September 1997. "No matter how loud the few shout," S2 had argued, "the greatest revolution is within."[1] A year later, his service in Singapore's army finished, he fled the island a second time, heading to London. He intended to never return, his status as a kind of *nosferatu* temporarily confirmed. He had chosen to sail into the wrong village at the wrong time. S2 would later write, "I hopped on the first available flight to London knowing I would try my utmost not to come back to Singapore."[2]

He wanted to find a job and live with a man he had met. Ultimately, both pursuits would be futile. After six months, he still had no job in London, and he had broken up with the boyfriend. "My life was absolutely shattered," S2 wrote.[3]

The only part that seemed to go right was working out at the Soho Athletic Club, along with "the only other day-members: students and prostitutes," he would joke in his blog. He had been skinny in college, his Asian male body seemingly factory-assembled from indistinguishably flat planes and screwed-on limbs. That had begun to change in the army. Now he continued the physical transformation. Pecs. Biceps. Triceps. Abs. Quads. He would later start referring to himself as a "gym-rat himbo," substituting the label "him" for the usual female "bim." The photographs he posted online changed. For one picture, he removed his shirt, cocked his arms behind his head, stared straight at the camera, and threw his torso into a sinewy snake curve, accenting an Asian male body that had now become a series of Winckelmann-style ellipses plunging downward from his chin along the wrap of his chest toward the final V-shape of his abdominals.

If Johann Winckelmann had helped set ideals of male beauty for Europe – the ones being enacted at the Soho Club as well as at the new athletic clubs opening in Singapore – a similar role for Chinese males like Stuart had once fallen to Confucius, although with much different results, ones that Stuart now seemed engaged in fusing. Traditional Confucian manhood had promoted a balance of *wen* and *wu*.[4] *Wen* emphasizes male achievement in cultural, literary, and intellectual pursuits and provided the grounding in Confucianism for putting teachers, writers, and scholars at the top of the male hierarchy. It was *wen* that drove the *kiasu*, or competitiveness, of intellectual men – even gay men like Tan Chong Kee and Stuart Koe – and it was pride in male *wen* that led parents to push especially their older sons to earn spots in schools like Nanyang Primary School or the Raffles Institution.

The other element of ideal manhood, *wu*, emphasizes physical attainment through strict discipline, especially in *wushu* or martial arts.

To truly perform masculinity well, a Confucian male had to excel in at least one or the other, although it was the *wen* sage who was typically honored more than the *wu* master. Ideally, manhood meant fusing both.

If Confucius represented the ideal of a *wen* sage, another legend, Guan Yu, wore the *wu* mantle. A military leader who lived at the end of the Han Dynasty in about 220 CE, he had become mythologized as a god of war and inevitably pictured with a fierce red face. Kam Louie, a Chinese scholar, notes that it is difficult to find any male figure similar to Guan Yu in Western ideals, unless one combines the banditry of Robin Hood with the frontier exploits of Daniel Boone, the dragon-slaying of St. George with the spirituality of St. Peter, and the gallantry of a popular cowboy like John Wayne with the brute, muscled body of an Arnold Schwarzenegger.[5]

On the surface, the *wen-wu* dyad appeared to be the same distinction in masculinity that Europeans had long made between their male teachers and their own male warriors. Similarly, Confucianism also emphasized the connection between "manhood" and the "public" or "outer realms" of life, compared to the more feminine occupation of the "private" or inner realms of the domestic household.[6]

But there were important differences.

In the Confucian tradition, Louie argues, the scholar had been recognized as equally masculine as the martial artist – something not typically so when the Western teacher was compared to the Western warrior. The discourses about sex and sainthood or scholarship were kept more separate. In Western narratives, the studious male seldom won the girl solely on the basis of his intellect. It was the Western man able to demonstrate physical prowess who tended to get his pick of sex. The Greek gymnasium had won out over the library, particularly in the Winckelmann imagery of the ideal male body.

But in Confucian literature, Louie argued, it was the *wen* man who was both an active subject able to pursue his own sexual desire and who then became the object of another's sexual desire. It was the *wen* man who had sex and, in the case of heterosexual behavior, created the all-important family.[7]

By contrast, in the literary tradition about Guan Yu, the *wu* warrior formed ties of close and intimate brotherhood with his fellow warriors. He was the one who ultimately suppressed his heterosexual desires as relentlessly as any Western saint – even to the extent of viciously slaying women so he would not be tempted. According to Louie, in the stories written for elite audiences, Guan Yu vanquished any homosexual desires he might have had for his fellow warriors. But in the folk stories, the homosexual desires inherent in *wu* fraternal love were often more explicit. In those stories, the most important love and physical contact was between *wu* males.[8]

China under Mao had dramatically reversed some of these Confucian traditions. The *wu* of the peasant, the worker, and the soldier had been elevated above the *wen* of the teacher, especially during the Cultural Revolution from 1966 to 1976, when students and teachers were beaten and sent to the fields and factories to learn from peasants, rather than the peasants and laborers being herded to schools.

By the 1980s, a global capitalist market making inroads even into the mainland, it was time for another reversal. Confucius himself had actually condemned pursuits of business as an inferior form of masculinity, contrasting the *wen* of the *junzi* — the exemplary gentleman who understood morality — with that of the *xiaoren*, who the sage said understood only profits. But in 1984, just as Stuart was finishing at Nanyang Primary School and preparing for the exams that would take him to Raffles, Lee Kuan Yew was named an honorary director of the new International Confucian Association being created in Beijing.[9] He was not a *wu* sage who had risen from the ranks of the *wushu* or from the peasants or military. His Raffles and Cambridge background gave him claim on the *wen* title — but neither was he a traditional *wen* sage.

He was, as a *Newsweek* reporter had once put it, the man who had "transformed Singapore from a mosquito-ridden backwater into an economic paradigm."[10] Through commerce, he had created the smart paradise. The scholar Louie called it "a revolution the implications of which are truly cataclysmic."

"Far from being a moral and political force, the *wen* icon now embraces an economic component as well . . . Successful *wen* masculinity can now be measured by the acquisition and flaunting of trappings such as the size and power of mobile phones and laptop computers. The Chinese male ideal is moving closer to the image of young executives found in in-flight magazines read by the international jet set."[11]

For Stuart, it was now *wen*, *wu*, Winckelmann — and gay resistance. All different narratives about manhood that had to be held together.

Besides the workouts at the Soho gym, another part of London life more *wen* in nature claimed Stuart's attention — much as the male clubs and theaters had once claimed Vajiravudh's. Every day S2 went online to write to two friends, one in Hong Kong he had met only once and one in San Francisco he had never met. Their return messages propped him up through his depressed exile. The two chat pals finally convinced him of a truth he needed to pursue: He had to reimagine the smart island as his own actual homeland.

"Quite a turning point in my life," S2 later blogged.[12]

At first, he worked for Singapore's Economic Development Board, the agency charged with the most important prong of the government's contract with its citizens: to deliver a better life built on commerce. One of his tasks was to help draft a report promoting new technologies in biological and genetic research. S2 wrote in his online blog that his profession now was: "Ex-drug dealer (i.e. pharmacist), now reformed and abetting other drug dealers (i.e. developing the pharmaceutical industry) in Singapore." In June 1999, he added: "On my first day at work, I had lunch with all my colleagues, and my first impression was 'I'm working with Charlie's Angels!' . . . the women here dress sharp, talk sharp, and shoot from the hip. Not to be messed with."[13]

But the job was wrong for him. "Every day I was there, I was asking myself, what am I doing as a civil servant? I felt muzzled. You do what your superiors say. You never really have your own personal voice."[14]

Gradually the idea occurred to him that he could offer some sort of business or financial services to other gay men – commerce – something for which he had no experience but which he began to pull together from his personal and Internet friendships. He found supporters, among the most important a man two decades older than him: Robert Yeoh, who had trained as a lawyer in Britain and had established a career in investment banking. Yeoh's background included a stint as Asian head of the Chase Manhattan Bank in Malaysia and development work in creating resorts on Indonesia's Bintan Island, a popular destination for Singaporeans. Gradually S2's idea evolved into the creation of not just financial services but a new medium with a variety of content, something that looked more like Sintercom. News briefs. A calendar. A date book of gay happenings around Southeast Asia, Hong Kong, and Taiwan. A section for personals ads. Advice columns. Directories. The latest on celebrities that gay men considered iconic: Madonna, Cher, Kylie Minogue.

Fortunately for S2, at the time people thought it would be easy to make money from Internet-based businesses. Yeoh would become chief executive officer of the new company, helping raise the equivalent of a US$1.5 million from investors, primarily in Hong Kong.[15]

Stuart thought he would call the website "My Man Friday," based on Robinson Crusoe's famous male servant. "The indispensable servant, the gay man Friday," Stuart explained later. The practical difficulty was that Stuart could not legally trademark a word that also referred to a day of the week. A friend suggested he spell "Friday" like an ice cream "sundae" instead. Stuart liked the idea, a play on the weekday Friday – "the end of the week when you let your hair down" – and ice cream – "something you enjoy."[16]

By March 2001, he was ready to launch his magical online island helper. Fridae. com would emerge as a new piece of Singapore's economic future – in the only public space where such a gay medium could emerge in Singapore, as People Like Us had already discovered with its ill-fated permit request for a newsletter. Cyberspace, not print.

Stuart's timing was ironic, if not simply bad. Tan Chong Kee's Sintercom had by then relocated to Singapore from the Stanford servers, becoming a content-provider for a Singaporean multimedia company.[17] That summer of 2001, the Singapore Broadcasting Authority had demanded that Tan Chong Kee's Sintercom site register and that its editors personally assume all responsibility for any messages posted. Faced with the demand that he either self-censor what he saw as a people's grassroots literature or take all legal responsibility for whatever any individual said in what was supposed to be an open *agora*, Tan Chong Kee closed Sintercom, just as Fridae was being born.[18]

The same year Stuart launched Fridae, the Singaporean government issued a sex education packet to be used in all the island's secondary schools. The Ministry of Education emphasized that the packet tried to respect all the island's different ethnic and religious groups, but respecting the island's different sexual and gender groups was left unmentioned.[19]

For Lesson 9, "Homosexuality," the packet defined the learning outcome for students this way: "Pupils will be able to understand that homosexual acts are against the law in Singapore." Teachers were to devote forty minutes to the lesson. One suggested activity was to give students a handout entitled "homosexuals and the society" which consisted of learning the penal code sections "regarding unnatural sex." Teachers would tell the students to tick the "correct" or "incorrect" column that represented their views. Their choices:

1. Homosexual acts are against the law in Singapore.
2. The penal code states that the act of unnatural sex is an offence.
3. Whoever voluntarily has carnal intercourse against the order of nature with any man, woman or animal, shall be punished with imprisonment for life, or with imprisonment for a term which may extend to 10 years.[20]

The statements continued through the definition of "gross indecency." The final statement, with which the students were either to agree or disagree, said: "It is possible to exercise self-control regardless of homosexual orientation." The guide was laced with references to overcoming temptations and not confusing attractions to the same sex with homosexuality. Even blind and deaf Helen Keller was pressed into service with her famous quotation that, although "the world is full of suffering, it is also full of the overcoming of it" − in effect urging homosexuals to overcome their sexual desires. "People's sexual behavior can be changed," the resource guide asserted. "Homosexuality does not offer a complete, natural life experience." The final sentence said, "Destiny is not a matter of chance, it is a matter of choice."[21]

The packet did not explain any of the obvious: That gay men might indeed have a complete life, including relationships and a family. That homosexuals might have a history just as ethnic or religious groups did. That heterosexuality could not be fully explained by science either. That there were other voices to be heard among the different peoples on the island. That supremacist attitudes about heterosexuality had caused violence or discrimination. That the Singaporean laws might be wrong.

As a source for news about gays and lesbians, and perhaps even as a type of organizational base for alternative ideas of sexuality, Stuart's new Fridae walked an edge. From the start, Stuart decided to position it and talk about it solely as commerce, the "Man Fridae" that was part of Singapore's new cyber-mission and that could attract the "pink dollar" of gay tourists to the city. That fitted it into the new *wen* ideal of commerce. Certain features could be accessed online for free, but unlike the free-for-all grassroots Sintercom or SiGNeL, Fridae would sell advertising and charge a membership fee for full access to all of its features. It was to be more like an online magazine than like an open forum.

Whatever personal views he had proclaimed in his 1997 blog, when it came to Fridae, Stuart adamantly disclaimed any intent of open gay activism. Fridae, he argued, was about business, not about starting an *agora*.

Still, there would be no avoiding one fact. While he did not necessarily set out to create a laboratory where Asian gay men could experiment with the types of manhood they wanted to project online, Fridae would enable that − most especially when it began to include personal ads. Stuart had once told a visitor: "A lot of the media portrayals of a gay Asian have been that of a rather fey, rather weak counterpart to a white boyfriend" − the old colonial discourse built on taboos about same-sex desire as well as cross-race and cross-age desire. The group of Southeast Asian men he said he wanted Fridae to appeal to would be "the first large adult cohort of gay men in Asia," gay Asian men who would finally speak in large numbers and write their own story.

Stuart respected the impact of the health clubs, like the Soho club where he had trained in London, and the early Clark Hatch gyms in Singapore that had eventually been replaced by chains that promised that "California Fitness" could be attained, along downtown's Orchard Road. "With the gyms," Stuart said, "gay men were able to take care of themselves. They no longer feel so subjugated."[22]

By the time Stuart started Fridae in 2001, the government's reaction to more public representations of Asian masculinity addressing male sexual attractions had already begun to bear the trappings of a cat-and-mouse game when it came to freedoms of expression and association. Full censorship of dissident cultural voices was difficult in the face of a new Internet medium that Singapore wanted to adopt, so targeted censorship had to suffice. Singapore would try to have it both ways: to shed its image as politically repressive while making the fewest adjustments.

In 1998, Lee Kuan Yew seemed to relax the smart island's surveillance of homosexuality. He told a television interviewer that homosexuality and its visibility "is not a matter which I can decide or any government can decide. It's a question of what a society considers acceptable. But what we are doing as a government is to leave people to live their own lives so long as they don't impinge on other people. I mean we don't harass anybody."[23]

Gay writers in the city celebrated that statement as a virtual proclamation that homosexuals would no longer be pursued and arrested for sodomy as long as the matter remained private and consensual.[24] But in November 2000, Lee Kuan Yew's son Lee Hsien Loong, at the time still a deputy prime minister, seemed to temper his father's words. A BBC reporter noted that, although gays and lesbians in Singapore were not being arrested for sodomy, there was "this fear in the background." Lee Hsien Loong had responded that while "homosexual people are not harassed or intimidated or squeezed in Singapore . . . neither do we encourage homosexual lifestyles to be publicly flaunted or legitimized or presented as being part of a mainstream way of life." He added, "Our judgment is that this is a fairly conservative society and it is not ready to make a qualitative change."[25]

Fridae's news magazine look immediately set it apart from the Internet gay dating sites that had long since sprung up in Europe and America. It was not just a front-page portal to personal ads, nor did it offer live chat. Instead, Stuart first moved to hire editors and writers to make the point, he said later, that there actually was gay *news* in Southeast Asia – a lot of it, not only in Singapore but in Malaysia, Indonesia, Thailand and even, sometimes, in Laos, Cambodia, and Vietnam. By 2004, Fridae's editors were delivering news and feature stories free to about 150,000 members who had signed up for listings. Overwhelmingly, those were men, although women posted profiles too. About a quarter of a million people would be viewing Fridae's pages each month.

The social – and sexual – networking aspects of the Web were the ones that Stuart pondered at first. Would any gay man in Singapore actually post a photograph of himself online like so many thousands were doing already in Europe and America on sites like Gay.com and Gaydar? Singapore was the city where any published photographs of gay men still seemed to show them looking down at the ground with police standing behind them, as had happened in *The New Paper* reports of the police raids at Fort Road.

Yet when Fridae offered the chance, thousands of photographs started arriving and, as was happening elsewhere, gay men began to tick off the pieces of male identity that they wanted to project. If Walter had created his canvases of images of the Asian male body, so now would Fridae. Importantly, Stuart had learned from Sintercom. He housed himself in Singapore, but he kept Fridae on servers outside the city, allowing the canvas to be open. Gay men in Southeast Asia, one at a time, could construct a new collective picture of themselves.

By the end of 2004, what the men of Fridae had built in the first three years looked like this:[26]

The men had created almost 70,000 profiles. About 46,000 were willing to identify as gay men, another 6,400 as bisexual men, and 2,500 as "curious males." Sixty-five percent lived in Asia, mostly in Southeast Asia. An astonishing 21,000

Singaporean males had signed up. Stuart had not only confirmed the existence of a large number of "alternate sexualities" but had instantly created the largest network of local gay men Singapore had ever seen.

Among ethnic and racial groups, Chinese dominated – forty percent of the men. Neighboring nationalities – Malaysian, Thai, Vietnamese, Japanese, Indian, and others – drove the Asian total to about eighty-five percent. Unlike other gay Internet sites originating in Europe or the United States, Caucasians were not the majority; they totaled only about thirteen percent of Fridae's users.

Most of the men of Fridae were young. More than half listed their age as eighteen to twenty-nine; another third said they were between thirty and thirty-nine. Social class and literacy was high: All had access to computers and could read and write at least a little English, the one trade language spoken across Southeast Asia.

On Fridae, "gender" and "sexual orientation" would be complex performances of miniature choices indicated by quilting different labels together, writing a personal narrative and then posting photographs that emphasized whatever aspect of body or gender – or sometimes desire – the man wanted to create.

The beginning point of the performance online was always biology – the male flesh itself. On Fridae, the Asian body's size and structure could be turned into a text about what was, and was not, masculine. Western science had suggested three types of body: the mesomorphs, who were muscular; the ectomorphs, who were elongated; the endomorphs, who were rounded or fat. Colonial depictions of Asian men had typically contrasted Caucasian mesomorphs with Asian ectomorphs – the mountainous Winckelmann ellipses versus the long Asian lines and flat planes of skin such as Walter had drawn. On Fridae, S2 would allow men to choose from nine less scientific but more descriptive identities: "large/solid" and "muscular" covered the typical mesomorphs; "lean/toned" and "slim" seemed to take care of the ectomorphs; "chubby," "curvy," "overweight," and "voluptuous" handled the endomorphs. The description of "average" provided a safe, indistinct final category.

Within the collective canvas that was Fridae, the largest single group of men, forty percent, would opt for that safe "average." The next biggest group would chose categories that seemed to symbolize male virility. Added together, "large/ solid," "lean/toned," and "muscular" represented the same forty percent as "average" did. Significantly, it was a group indistinguishable by race or ethnicity. The same percentage of Asian men chose it, as did Caucasians, collectively rejecting the stereotypes about how an Asian or a Caucasian male body differed.

Biology also played a role in the way a male body literally felt: what its hair and skin texture was, and, with that, the perception of whether the male body was smooth or coarse. It had always been a short orientalist leap from the sense of touch to metaphoric ideas about the "feminine," porcelain-like skin of Asian men or the more pebbled and "rugged" textures of Caucasians. S2 again left it to each of

Fridae's individual males to decide whether he was "smooth" or had "some" or "lots" of hair and whether the hair occurred on his "chest" or "butt" or whether it had been "shaved." For this piece of the representation, Fridae's men chose to maintain the old orientalist brush: More than sixty percent of the Chinese males on the site who made a choice selected "smooth" as their description, while only seventeen percent of Caucasians did.

Finally, biology also provided another way to turn a man's body into a story about his masculinity. The size of his penis could become a symbol, a "phallus" that alluded to the power of male fertility either in the capacity to penetrate or, more metaphorically, in a man's ability to form goals and execute passions. Applied to Asian males, the reference to the penis and its size and visibility had always been crucial in orientalist portrayals. The Asian penis, and thus phallus, had often been described as smaller.[27] On Fridae, Stuart gave gay Asian men the chance to describe their "shoe size." Most did not respond, but those who did rejected the label "small," choosing "average" instead − in almost equal numbers to the Caucasians. It was another gay Asian rejection of the colonial image.

The most important assertions about gender arose from cultural expectations rather than biology. Mannerisms and physical movements also established masculinity − the way a man walked and talked and dressed. The Europeans had insisted on distinctions, the British in Siam pressing both Chulalongkorn and Vajiravudh to promote more gender difference in clothing and behaviors. On Fridae, S2 would collapse the performance of mannerisms into a simple choice: Men were asked whether they identified as "masculine," "femme," or "neither." They also had the option of silence. Overwhelmingly, in defiance of presumptions that male homosexuality equaled being feminine, the men on Fridae opted either for the label of "masculine" or − in equal numbers − for the choice of "neither," which was perhaps the most interesting answer. Since no one was forced to choose a label, actively selecting "neither" amounted to a declaration that many of the men on Fridae did not want to be forced into the other two more traditional categories.

They wanted their mannerisms to be seen as something else − as "neither" − a reminder of one of the very things about the Siamese that the Europeans and Americans had been most perplexed by.

Eventually, S2 would add to Fridae the capacity to let men blog. At that point the writings of gender fusing the old *wen* and *wu* lines with Winckelmann imagery became clearer. The overwhelming tendency of all of the men who started to write was to focus on individual emotions and the angst of personal relationships. Few wrote about the politics of gay life or adopted the popular European and American narratives of the "coming out" story about how they had told parents or friends they were not the men they were expected to be.

Instead, in the Fridae blogs, three male voices dominated.[28]

First, "scholar/poets" continued that *wen* activity of groups of Confucian-influenced men gathering to share poetry with one another, either self-written or read from others. Young men on Fridae loaded their blogs with quotations both from poetry and from the lyrics of popular songs. Second, "fathers" and "big brothers" offered relationship advice about how to find lovers or deal with insults. And, finally, large numbers of what might be termed "lonely romantic lost boys" wrote about trying to find their self-confidence, usually searching for a lover who would also take on the role of mentor.

The men posted photographs that sometimes emphasized the same theme as the words. Often, though, the photographs became a place to offer a contrast or a fusion – to demonstrate, for example, a gym-influenced body fused with a romantic boy's yearning or a scholar/poet's reflections.

Another part of manhood being collectively written on Fridae focused on what desire a man should enact in sex. Did he want the erotic energy of penetrating someone as a "top" or an "active," as it was sometimes called, or did he want to be penetrated as a "bottom" or a "passive?" Western discourses about sex had suggested it was "masculine" to penetrate and "feminine" to be penetrated. In Southeast Asia, orientalist and even nationalist traditions seemed to suggest that gay men, especially Asian ones, were to be defined by their desire to be penetrated and that that desire was to be defined as feminine. That had been one of the sources of the newspaper confusion in Thailand when Darrell Berrigan had been murdered: He had been a man who seemed so masculine – a war correspondent, the "father" taking care of "adopted sons" – but he had then been discovered as having sexual desires that could fit only a feminine *kathoey*.

On Fridae, S2 included three choices so men could label their sexual desires: top, bottom, and versatile, the latter to indicate that a man flexibly enjoyed both. Most of the men of Fridae remained silent on the question, leaving that point of intimacy to be discovered in private communications. But those who made a public choice tended to reject the customary "bottom" label assumed for Asian homosexuals. But they also rejected the label of "top." Instead, they overwhelmingly chose "versatile."

They would not limit themselves to being "like" a heterosexual male who only penetrated or to the old definitions of homosexuals wanting to be penetrated. Defying colonial stereotypes that assumed Caucasian males were "tops" and Asian males were "bottoms," race had no bearing on their answers. Asians and Caucasians answered the same way in equal numbers.

The men of S2's Fridae were confirming what *Thai Rath* had confusedly discovered and then had denounced decades earlier after the murder of Darrell Berrigan: A new public voice of gay manhood was taking root in Southeast Asia. And now it was assisted by a new magical social reality that collapsed spaces and times and allowed oppositional narratives to be lived simultaneously.

Instant metamorphoses of identities were easily possible on the Internet. All it took was a click to change a label or a photograph. As Franz Roh had suggested so many decades earlier, the metamorphoses could be done via forms of representation that were so miniaturized and so individually specific as to evoke a "most prolific and *tactile feeling*"[29] – much as Walter had once painted countless tiny glistening leaves.

18

A Pivotal Day

For Babylon's previous fifteen years of existence, from 1987 through 2002, Khun Toc's architectural paradise on Soi Nantha had never experienced any particular conflict with the Thai police, much less the government's Interior Ministry.

It is not clear whether that was due to the supposed Thai tolerance for playful *sanuk,* or because of deference to the social class of the family from which Khun Toc came. It also may have been that the metaphor of a "periphery" for sexual dissent versus a "center" of sexual acceptability had not solidified in the Thai imagination the way it seemed to have done in Western representations.[1]

But, as had happened in the Dutch East Indies more than a half-century earlier, tolerance could be easily manipulated whenever the link between nationalist politics and gender politics demanded it.

After Thaksin moved into power in 2001, the first rumblings of what was to emerge as the *rabiap sangkhom* began. *Rabiap* refers most specifically to the kinds of rules followed by bureaucracies, which meant that laws that were on the books but had never been enforced were to be applied — like closing times. More broadly, though, the word carries a moral sense of maintaining orderliness and "a proper arrangement of things."[2] The English translation is "the social and moral order campaign," a determined effort to cleanse Thailand's image and, very much like the cellmate Walter Spies had found oddly obsessed, put "a proper arrangement of things" into effect.

The man Thaksin initially charged with the social order campaign was Purachai Piumsombun, whom he had met as a cadet at the Thai Police Academy. Like Thaksin, he had studied criminal justice in the United States, working with the Thai police upon returning, but then teaching and writing. Among his articles was one that described the way in which Thai police routinely collected protection fees and then distributed them throughout the hierarchy as a way of supplementing low police salaries and budgets. Purachai was one of the founding members of Thai Rak Thai, becoming its secretary general before being named interior minister in Thaksin's first cabinet.[3]

He promised to clean up Thailand — which mostly meant cleaning up Thai manhood. "It is my mission," Purachai told the press. News stories noted that he had named his three children after Buddhist precepts, in contrast to Thaksin, who had used Thai words meaning gold and wealth to name his.[4]

The campaign began in an oddly positive way for gay Thais. Purachai charged that heterosexual polygamy was still so widespread that politicians were hiding their bank accounts among several sex partners. The existing anti-corruption law required politicians to declare their assets, but it covered only legal wives and families, not the money tucked away in the bank accounts of minor or "hired" wives or their children. Purachai suggested that those mistresses and their offspring seemed to be playing the role of Swiss bankers for some politicians. Purachai thought even same-sex relationships should be registered or treated as marriages and so he proposed such, albeit to get at any money also stashed with favorite boyfriends rather than out of any notion of civil rights equality. It was an echo of the complaints that had been laid against Vajiravudh – except that now it was politicians who were being accused of favoring male associates with government money.[5]

Purachai's proposal went nowhere.[6]

Throughout the spring of 2001, the Bangkok newspapers carried government reports from the Interior Ministry about youths using drugs in discos, about university students selling sex to earn tuition or buy clothes from Bangkok's trendy shopping malls, or about the need to impose the death penalty on drug dealers. Purachai floated plans to strengthen entertainment zoning, issuing new licenses only to entertainment places in certain restricted areas of major cities like Bangkok. The head of the government-run Tourism Authority of Thailand (TAT) promised to promote the country as a family destination, by encouraging female visitors – ignoring the fact that women tourists, as well as gay men, were filling the shows at the male host bars and "borrowing" the often straight off-boys. The TAT head also promised to launch campaigns to deter anyone from visiting Thailand for sex.[7]

A few weeks later, reporters from iTV – owned by Thaksin's Shin Corporation – smuggled cameras into gay host bars in Patpong and broadcast five reports. Competition had forced such bars in the small niche known as Surawong Boys Town to develop elaborate light, sound, and dance shows with choreographies that at times appeared to be deliberately exaggerated satires of the ongoing remodeling of bodies, desires, and genders that had started in Mongkut's time and had accelerated through Vajiravudh's and Phibun's. On the stages, what Franz Roh had said back in the 1920s about the possible traps of both the monumental and the miniature in art seemed to have come true in the gender liminality of Patpong: Monumental categories that piled up shapes into large classifications – such as "heterosexual" or "homosexual" – could easily slip into caricatures of themselves because of their "emphatic presentation" and their "statuesque turgidity." Meanwhile, unbridled tiny details plunged "into tedious minutia that scatter and confuse our attention."[8]

Some of the men performing their fusions of body and desire and gender offered "emphatic presentations" as macho Western cowboys or motorcycle riders. They paired with sheik lady boys in thin gowns who just as emphatically presented the opposite pole. Other men costumed in nothing more than underwear or groin-tight shorts to contrast with the Thai *jong-barens* that had been banned by Phibun. Some bars specialized in slim, smooth men, the old orientalist stereotype combined with the image of the Thai *phunoi* compliant man; others staged muscle shows enacting gym-created *phuyai*. The shows in the host bars often inevitably ground toward a display of the male body's sexual arousal and even simulated climax, perhaps a lovemaking scene with two or more nude men in a specially installed shower cubicle, or a "big cock" show displaying several male bodies with deliberately tightened cords around their penises and testicles to engorge them, or, most spectacular of all, an act on gymnastic bars featuring male bodies flying into the air while having anal intercourse – an almost exact Thai enactment of the artistic image of Balinese men that Walter's friend Lempad had produced in the 1930s when the discourse about male desires for one another had moved into the public realm on that island.[9] Foreign tourists, including women, poured in each night to gaze at the Thai male body fully phallic and on display as a spectacle, reinforcing the representation of Thai males as promiscuous and fluid, especially since many of the male performers were known to be "heterosexual" and have girlfriends.[10]

The climax to the iTV news coverage came with a report about the aerial anal sex performed by male entertainers on trapezes.

Not long afterward, on a Monday night, July 23, 2001, two plainclothes police officers arrived at the Dream Boy Bar. After a few conversations, Dream Boy cancelled its two shows that included any nudity or sex. By the first week of August, most of the other male host bars in Patpong had closed – even though there had been no actual police raids. The few that remained open had followed Dream Boy's lead and eliminated nude displays of male bodies. Some tried to adjust their audiences to seeing the off-boys now simply sitting in their clothes, a practice more customarily followed in the outlying neighborhoods.[11]

The following week, in the first publicly visible step of Purachai and Thaksin's social order campaign, all bars in Patpong – gay and straight – were ordered to start closing by 2:00 a.m. That was the legal time, but it had so long been ignored that entire night markets had grown up not only in Patpong but also throughout the entertainment areas scattered around the city. The closing times had been disregarded for so long that no one really seemed sure when bars were supposed to impose a "last drink served" policy and when they were to actually shut their doors. Estimates ranged from midnight to 1:00 a.m. to 1:30 a.m., partly because under the old 1966 Entertainment Places Act there were four categories of licenses, each with different opening and closing times.[12]

Purachai also warned the nightspots not to grant entry to any customers under age twenty, although in the odd world of Thai laws, owners could still hire workers for the nightspots if they were eighteen.[13]

On August 10, the public police inspections and raids began. Purachai and the Bangkok police chief, accompanied by thirty police officers, visited nightspots across the city. Two quickly shut down: one a Patpong bar catering to heterosexuals, and the other the city's best-known disco for gay men, DJ Station, also in Patpong. Then began a series of public raids, mostly aimed at enforcing closing hours or checking for underage patrons. In an unusual move that would become commonplace, the police also forced everyone in the bar, restaurant, or disco to take urine tests. The tests supposedly determined whether they had used any drugs — illegal or prescription — whether in the bar or anywhere in previous days. The campaign against drugs became a dragnet, not a targeted operation based on undercover arrests of specific individuals exchanging or using drugs. Purachai accompanied many of the raids, and newspapers and TV stations began showing lines of hundreds of customers detained in bars across the city, waiting for strips of paper to change color and then being taken to police stations for further questioning if the results were positive.

On August 18, police raided a large, gay sauna called the Obelisk, whose owner then shut it down permanently. By October 2001, they moved against one named Farose, following an unusually public dispute between the sauna and its neighbors that had included a *Bangkok Post* reporter taking a tour.[14] The male sex that Thais themselves usually did not talk about was being firmly implanted into public discourse in a way that was not simply aimed at repressing it — no one thought the raids would stop gay sex or gay saunas — but rather at spreading a certain kind of knowledge about it: that men who went to such saunas were carriers of a decadent manhood.[15]

By December 2001, the *Bangkok Post* reported that in this version of a Thai *Zedenschandaal* almost 60,000 people had been "caught" as "suspects" in the first three months of "the social order crusade against gambling, drugs, the flesh trade and nightspots."[16]

Relentlessly, Purachai and the Thaksin administration pushed the campaign, even as Thaksin himself began to publicly comment that perhaps Purachai should temper his zeal for nightlife regulation. In 2002, Thaksin shifted Purachai to a less visible post but continued pieces of the campaign, promising to eradicate drugs from Thailand and setting off a wave of killings that would eventually draw international human rights condemnations. He added a new Ministry of Social Development, telling it to encourage Thai men and women to marry earlier to put an end to the notion that Thai men liked to "whore" around, as *Rolling Stone* had put it — Thaksin's way of enforcing the triple supremacy of romance, monogamy, and heterosexuality.

Efforts were also made to roll closing times for nightspots back to midnight, to set a 10:00 p.m. curfew for teenagers unless they went out with their parents, and to enforce a section of the old Entertainment Places Act that said any woman entering a bar or restaurant had to be accompanied by a man. A new Ministry of Culture was launched to take control of promoting art and promoting a master plan to nurture the "Thai language, Thai manners, Thai food, and Thai dress." An advertisement sponsored by the ministry criticized any youth who failed to follow an old Thai custom of stooping low whenever around anyone older. Just as Phibun had tried to instruct Thais how to dress and reorganize their names and speech to be more masculine or feminine, the Ministry of Culture would eventually organize "language clinics" to help people who pronounced Thai wrong or who used too many English words.

Ironically, given Thaksin's source of wealth, it had been the rapid spread of cell phones with their short message texting that had become the newest major source of introducing English words among Thais.[17]

Eventually, the *New York Times* would describe the impact of the social order campaign:

> Imagine a city where bars, nightclubs and even movie theaters shut down early, where young people are off the streets by curfew, where universities stage surprise drug tests and where a woman cannot enter a restaurant without a male escort.
>
> That wouldn't be the racy, all-night Bangkok that people like to call "fun city."
>
> But it is Bangkok – and the rest of Thailand – as imagined by powerful government reformers who have already begun to put a crimp in the fun.[18]

One of Khun Toc's American friends, Rick Werwie, had joined the banquet that Friday night, December 27, and was still sitting and talking at the table inside Babylon when the police cars began to arrive. Using his cell phone, he called Khun Toc at his home across the courtyard. Because of all the publicity about the other saunas and bars being raided, Khun Toc seemed unsurprised, Werwie recalled. He responded calmly, telling Werwie to have the Babylon staff offer the police some soft drinks and desserts, since the dining room and café were still open. He also suggested they rearrange the tables in the courtyard however the police wanted, so as to make whatever they proposed to do move along a little easier and faster.

In response to a question from Werwie, he said no, he did not think he would return to Babylon to see the esteemed if uninvited visitor, the deputy minister of the Interior Department, Pracha Maleenont, whose family controlled a concert, record, film, and television conglomerate in Bangkok and who had decided to accompany the police. Nor did he want to talk to the reporters the deputy minister had invited.[19]

The police began to test every man's urine for drugs, mixing it with another chemical. If it turned what the Thais called *she-muang* – slang for "piss-purple" – the result was positive and a ride to the police station guaranteed. The testing went on, Werwie said, until about 3:30 a.m. He remembered there being about 400 men at Babylon when the police arrived, although later news accounts said about 200.[20]

Of those, twenty tested positive, although it does not appear to have been clear for what. Werwie would later recall: "They never told you what you were being tested for. They didn't even know what drug people were being accused of taking if it turned purple. Several older *farang's* urine turned purple and they clearly were not taking drugs illegally. They were taking prescription drugs – heart medicine, high blood pressure medicine. They were all herded down to the police station."

Werwie thought the Thai police from the local district were not at all interested in the raid. "They were not game for what was going on." Werwie later asked one of the *farang* men taken to the police station what had happened. "He said, 'We got down there and then they told us to leave. And they apologized. They apologized to all the foreigners and let them go.'" The Thai men were also released.[21]

By early Saturday morning, the raid had ended and Pracha Maleenont and the police had left. That day, the videos and pictures of the raid appeared on television and in the newspapers.

Stories and comments defending Babylon quickly appeared on the Internet, one particularly heated exchange occurring on the forum board of a gay-oriented magazine distributed throughout Patpong, *Thai Guys*. The comments documented what some men thought of Babylon's importance, of Thailand as a gay paradise, of the compliance of Thai *phunoi* in the face of Thaksin's assertion of a morally cleansed *phuyai* manhood, and of the idea of whether male desires for another man should be part of a legally protected "center" or forced to remain on an ever-threatened periphery.[22]

A man listed as "visitor" wrote: "The whole problem about these raids is that thai people just accept what the government wants."

One named "Thonglor" added: "The Thais are not worried about this because they know the best thing is to shut up and let it blow over."

From "thailover": "There are obviously higher ups who are in this game, and as for the court system, it is a joke."

From "anon bkk": "The old system was to have crackdowns which usually lasted some days just as a matter of tea-price influence. The new system is that a few individuals are imposing their morality on the rest."

From "James," comments that actually supported the crackdown, but not the press coverage of it, which he felt had been done in an un-Thai-like fashion: "I saw the report on Thai TV last night and was a bit shocked that TV cameras were allowed free access to the sauna. I felt so sorry for all the guys, mainly Thai whose faces appeared on the news. Many Thai habitués of Babylon are closeted types, many are married and I am sure that they do not want their wives, families, colleagues, etc., seeing them clad in a towel and branded as a homosexual! Pracha and his troops are well within their rights to raid wherever they want, whenever they want but I think it should be done with a bit more subtlety and compassion."

From "bkkjunky": "It's just luck I wasn't at Babylon on Fri.nite . . . I can understand raids on go-go bars with the underage/drug problems. But why respectable places like Babylon? . . . And why carry out these raids over the Xmas holidays when these places are packed with overseas visitors . . . Reluctantly I am coming to the conclusion that this program is anti-gay with the ultimate objective of forcing Babylon . . . to close. Also this practice of allowing the press along to photograph on these raids is terribly unjust and just reinforces my belief that gays have no rights in Thailand. And it will stay this way as no one will fight."

Not long afterwards, the editors at *Thai Guy* closed the forum to comments. They explained: "Unfortunately there are too many slandering remarks in the forum which were harming too many people and figures. This situation isn't appropriate to the best sides of Thai traditional morality . . . For the time being all contributions to the forum are suspended."[23]

The night after the raid, Khun Toc's friends once again joined him promptly at 7:00 p.m. Werwie remembered that Khun Toc seemed unshaken as well as undeterred by the raid.[24] If anything, the mastermind of Babylon seemed bemused by the attempt Thaksin was making to reshape the way ideal Thai males should behave – which apparently meant being home by curfew, tending to jobs in global corporations, accepting a government run as if by a CEO, and adhering to ideals of romantic, heterosexual monogamy.

Friends recalled that, with something of a smile, Khun Toc played a song by one of his favorite blues and jazz performers, Dinah Washington. The lyrics, like Vajiravudh's plays decades earlier, promoted romantic, monogamous heterosexuality. But the lyrics playing in Khun Toc's study in his male island of Babylon suggested a different understanding of body, desire, and gender. The song was titled, "What a Difference a Day Made."[25]

> *What a difference a day made*
> *Twenty-four little hours . . .*
>
> *My yesterday was blue, dear*
> *Today I'm a part of you, dear . . .*
>
> *It's heaven when you find romance on your menu*
> *What a difference a day made*
> *And the difference is you*[26]

Khun Toc would shortly have a notice posted on Babylon's website. It was polite and shorter than Walter's musings about the oddities of men who wanted to enforce their notions of order. But it was also defiant and echoed the feeling he had had years earlier after visiting the Tulip in Patpong:

The police did not find any wrong doing . . . The Babylon remains open for business (pleasure) as usual. This unfortunate event at the Babylon, we are afraid, was nothing more than an annual publicity campaign to promote the Thai government's "new social order" movement at our expense.

Our only endeavor is to provide a tasteful and respectable Gay meeting place on par with those abundantly available to straight people.[27]

At the paradise on Soi Nantha, conversations in the library would still be followed by the walk past Vajiravudh's portrait. The male feast would continue to unfold at the boomerang-shaped banquet table in the "best fishbowl in the world."

19

Dancing under the Merlion

A few months after Babylon was raided, a *Time* magazine writer reviewed the difficult choices Singapore faced because of what the magazine termed an "unprecedented economic downturn" and the desires of many of the island's intellectual elite "to head for greener pastures."

"The wealthy city-state still thrums with technocratic efficiency," the article noted. "But beneath the gloss of its modern skyline, an unprecedented economic downturn has produced the worst identity crisis since the traumatic 1960s, when the island gained independence from Britain." Fully one-fifth of the country's population had indicated in a survey that they were thinking about leaving. Coincidentally, a book by Richard Florida called *The Rise of the Creative Class* had become popular reading. It argued that the cities that did best in attracting new talent were those that showed the most encouragement of openness and diversity – including of gay men and women.[1]

Singapore, *Time* said, had begun to try to foster more creativity in its citizens, even to the point of indulging certain bohemian zones and more nightlife. "The city now boasts seven saunas catering almost exclusively to gay clients, for example, something unthinkable even a few years ago." It noted the city had "a sprinkling of gay bars, and many dance clubs set aside one night each week for gay customers." Then, the *Time* writer mentioned a change few on the island seemed to have been aware of, one that had been initiated by Lee Kuan Yew's successor as prime minister in 1990, Goh Chok Tong:

> Prime Minister Goh says his government now allows gay employees into its ranks, even in sensitive positions. The change in policy, inspired at least in part by the desire not to exclude talented foreigners who are gay, is being implemented without fanfare, Goh says, to avoid raising the hackles of more conservative Singaporeans. "So let it evolve, and in time the population will understand that some people are born that way," Goh says. "We are born this way and they are born that way, but they are like you and me."[2]

The action and the quotation thundered like a sudden storm. Goh confirmed his statement for *The Singapore Straits Times* on July 4. "In the past, if we knew you were gay," he told the newspaper, "we would not employ you. But we just changed this quietly."[3] In other nations, such as the United States, acceptance of openly gay men and women into the government civil service had been an important civil rights line that had to be crossed so that invisibility in other arenas of life could begin to end.[4] Goh had also clearly stated that he did not believe homosexuality was a choice but rather determined from birth.

Letters rained on Singapore's newspapers. Columnists began to debate the pragmatic value of what was called the "pink dollar." It was a term that included not only the dollars to be spent by the gay tourists who would now find Singapore a much more comfortable place to visit than had once been described by *Spartacus* but also the dollars to be generated by gay entrepreneurs and by the gay creative talent to be tapped for the country's newfound interest in information technology and bio-genetic research.

Within the week, a *Straits Times* reporter was on the telephone to Stuart Koe. As CEO of a high-tech startup like Fridae, who better to be a spokesman for the new, suddenly valuable national asset?

S2 surprisingly demurred.

"I told them, we're trying to position ourselves as a business. I never call myself an activist. So I don't want to dilute that message by suddenly talking about what it was like growing up as a gay child."

But he had a suggestion.

"Why don't you talk to my boyfriend?"[5]

So it was that his boyfriend at the time, Jim Chow, who was working as Fridae's marketing director, soon appeared on the front page of *The Straits Times*. Possibly, it was the first time that a gay man in Singapore actually had his face pictured in the local media in something other than an arrest at Fort Road.

"Ma, I'm Gay," the headline said. Echoing and seemingly validating Prime Minister Goh's stance, another headline added: "'Mum asked if I could change' . . . but how to change something as basic as being gay?"[6]

As portrayed in *The Straits Times*, Jim Chow was exactly the type of gay male body and gender that Prime Minister Goh seemed to be willing to allow as a valuable cog in Singapore's economic engine. He had a young, Winckelmann-style body, muscular, not overly slender or effeminate, suitably *wu*. For the new commerce-oriented *wen*, he was deemed a thirty-two-year-old "marketing executive" by the newspaper, although Fridae was never named. The article called him "an articulate man who loves to read and exercise" – a merger of the two chief characteristics of traditional Confucian masculinity: *wen* and *wu*.

As described in the story, his male desires were limited to those for a familial relationship with his mother. He did not discuss his romantic or sexual relationships with men. His boyfriend, Stuart, was described as an "information technology professional" – *wen* – was never named, and only lightly mentioned. Jim was presented as safely monogamous.

The story's opening paragraphs focused on the fact that as early as primary school, Jim had begun to wonder why he was attracted to images of male movie stars, as if *The Straits Times* was trying to assure its readers that Jim was one of those who had "been born that way," even though the prime minister's words were not directly included. In the sixth paragraph, the reporter quoted Jim saying that he had never felt discriminated against in Singapore – an implicit affirmation of the government stance that homosexuals were not harassed. The article moved immediately into telling the story of Jim's relationship with his divorced mother, who, the reporter wrote, now invited Jim's partner – the still unnamed Stuart – home for Chinese New Year and treated him "as part of the family."

For a few months, there seemed to be hope that the government would go even further in allowing homosexuals more visibility. In early January, Fridae optimistically titled a story about a speech that Lee Hsien Loong had given to the Harvard Club this way: "S'pore may allow gay activist groups: Singapore's oldest – however unofficial – gay activist group, People Like Us, may soon be officially recognized as Deputy PM Lee Hsien Loong promises to loosen the apron strings on political freedom."[7]

Lee's actual quotation in the story made the title look overly optimistic. The son of Lee Kuan Yew had simply said: "There will be other groups formed, I'm quite sure, to campaign for specific issues – gay rights, for example, and that is a sensitive one." He had not really indicated what the government would do if confronted with such a group wanting a public presence in any of the customary citizen discourses about "collective agreements" in political rights, or educational programs in schools or museums, or representation in health care.[8]

Within six months, the government was signaling that any new acceptance of a fluid concept of male bodies and their desires – and of the creative images of manhood that might offer – would still be a game of cat-and-mouse. Jim Chow as an entrepreneur or civil servant could be tolerated as the talent needed by the smart island. But S2 and his new business, Fridae, as cyber-voices for an openly sexual, gay Asian manhood, were problematic – as much a nuisance as *Java-Bode* had considered some other Asian "boys" to be decades earlier.

Hints of the government's limits came quickly, not against Fridae or S2 but against a print magazine called *Manazine*, which had begun to publish images of Asian masculinity that fused an eroticized expression of *wen* and *wu* in combination with the growing athletic club fascination with Winckelmann.

Manazine had begun the previous October and was being distributed every other month both free and by subscription. It targeted a young, urban, hip male audience rather than an explicitly gay one and included articles about men's health, fitness, and fashion. *Manazine* promoted itself as a metrosexual publication – or, as its subtitle said, "men's lifestyle redefined." In one column, the editor, a youthful Dutch ex-pat named Arjan Nijen Twilhaar, said the 100-page publication was about "personal growth, a balanced lifestyle and approaching life with an open mind and without judgment" – something he noted could be "quite tough if you live in Singapore."[9]

Each issue promoted a theme about manhood. The first issue, "Reflection," encouraged men to recognize and accept their differences. The second examined "Paradox."[10] In the photographs, both Asian and Caucasian men decorated the pages, most modeling in slacks, underwear, or swimsuits. None showed full frontal nudity. *Manazine* was no racier than something like *Men's Health* or *Men's Fitness* magazines that also had their appeal among gay men. Significantly, though, *Manazine* usually showed its males either alone or in fraternal groups with each other; it was largely devoid of the pairings with female models that kept other male publications at least nominally heterosexual.

In February 2004, eight months after Goh's statement appeared in *Time,* the Media Development Authority (MDA), which licensed publications in Singapore, summoned Twilhaar to a meeting. The imagery in *Manazine*, it complained, seemed too gay.[11] Of particular concern was "Reflection," the premier edition in October 2003. It had begun with a full-page cover promoting male friendship rather than male contest: "Liquid Reflex: A couple of good friends, a sunny afternoon at the beach. Signal to the world that you are there, waiting . . . accessible."[12]

The photographs offer a barely disguised takeoff on the previous Fort Road arrests, except that now the fear of the *nosferatus* in their haunts – gay men waiting for and signaling each other, carrying backpacks, and being sexually accessible – was recast as a positive liberation. Three Asian males in their twenties dressed in sleeveless muscle shirts and shorts, just as the police entrappers had. At first they stood apart on an isolated stretch of beach, signaling with mirrors held in their left hands. In another photo, two playfully tossed a red daypack to each other, one wrapped only in a towel and precariously holding it as he leaped in the air. "Liquid Reflex" spread over eight pages, and on its final page, the three Asian male friends were shown close up as headless Greek-like torsos, their elliptical pectoral muscles and marbled abs oiled to create a sheen for the camera. They crowded, like fraternal dominos ready to fall atop one another. Whatever isolation as men they had felt at the beginning of the photo spread had clearly been resolved in favor of a very homoerotic *wu*-based friendship.[13]

Another photograph the MDA found objectionable had occurred in the second issue, "Paradox," in a fitness article designed for the Asian male who was trying to project a more Winckelmann-influenced image. "Yes," the article had warned, "there are many fine male specimens out there whose upper body is a work of art to rival Michelangelo's *David*. But go further down their body and what do we find? Whoa – chicken legs!" A photograph showed a man sitting on his knees and stretching backward. He was nude, his head thrown backward in a pose more often used for females, his body lean and trim but not fully etched, a visual representation of what the new male body was, potentially penetrative but also versatile and vulnerably receptive. A well-trimmed triangle of pubic hair was visible. The model was Caucasian, but in a fusion of Western and Asian imagery, brown tanned rather than white, smooth and soft-skinned rather than marbled or haired.[14]

By American advertising standards the pictures were tame; by European ones, positively puritanical. Still, *The Singapore Straits* reported that a representative of the MDA told Twilhaar "that the current state of the magazine, which features nudity and homosexual content, is unacceptable."[15]

By the time of the MDA complaint, the third issue of *Manazine* had already been partly distributed – with its now untimely theme of "Lust and Love." Twilhaar ordered the distribution stopped. In a news release, he tried to rhetorically fit the magazine's purpose within the Singapore government's own interest in commerce and in building a smart paradise. The magazine, he argued, "is in strong synergy with Singapore's goal towards a vibrant global media city as well as stimulating a creative economy and connected society."[16]

In the next issue of *Manazine*, called "Essence," Twilhaar protested in words and photos. In his column he wrote, "I hear so many people say: 'You don't understand Chinese tradition,' but all these people are wrong . . . The norms and values of Singapore have been influenced by Victorian Western culture. All the norms and values held with high regard these days are not foreign to me at all. It is like being thrown back to my small hometown about 22 years ago, with its closed minds and conservative thinking. Gone are the days of the true Chinese values, where innovation and progress are upheld."

"Oops," he finished. "Maybe we are causing a stir again . . . "[17]

"Essence" pointedly opened with the story of Zeus's overthrow of his "aged father," Kronos. Twilhaar wrote that "family should be a shelter against the harshness of the world, but what if that nest is infested with stubbornness, non-acceptance or even lack of love? Should we still see family as being the ESSENCE of our society?"

The opening and closing photographs were also protests. Twilhaar dressed a *wu*-like, goateed, muscular and bare-chested Asian man identified only as "Sam" in a pleated Greek tunic and leather wristbands. He juxtaposed "Sam," looking quite stern, in front of the Corinthian columns of Singapore's Supreme Court. A quotation on the closing photograph of this image of fused Asian manhood defiantly read: "Ultimate freedom comes when you let go of your personal history."[18]

Confucius, it seemed, had met Corinth and had birthed a new Guan Yu. For *Manazine*, young Asian male bodies were not delicate, lotus-eyed boys. They were Winckelmann bodies ready for a new role within a classic Greek family struggle.

Even before he started Fridae, Stuart had helped choreograph dances in Singapore, including fundraisers for the city's fledgling Action For AIDS. After the cyber side of Fridae had been launched, he immediately set about creating a second canvas for explorations: a dance open to everyone but primarily announced online through Fridae to its growing circle of Asian gay men. He would call it Nation I, scheduling it on August 8, Singapore's National Day. He urged those attending to wear Singapore's national colors, red and white. Fliers announcing the event wrapped it into all the other celebratory rhetoric common that day: "You're proud," the fliers said. "Of your country. Of your community. Of who you are."[19]

Much as Walter had carefully selected the kind of dance he would include in his construction of a paradise in Bali — both as a Scriabinesque media representation and as an actual ongoing performance in real life — Stuart carefully scripted the elements of his. The context would be Singapore's Sentosa Island, an offshore amusement park with a high-tech outdoor musical fountain capable of splaying flames and lasers into a nighttime sky. Above the fountain rose a 122-foot-high Merlion, the fanciful half-lion, half-fish that Singapore's government had adopted as the island's symbol. While visitors might see the Merlion as just tourist branding, it was also a legally protected national symbol — rather like a national flag. It had been given special protection from any form of derogatory speech against it or any kind of trademark infringement. Souvenirs or posters portraying the Merlion had to be in good taste, reproduced only in full, and never have any other wording, graphics, or objects superimposed over it. Any person using the Merlion symbol without permission from the Singapore Tourist Board could be fined up to 2,000 Singaporean dollars and imprisoned for up to six months.[20]

Stuart pointedly declined media interviews from those curious about what Agence France-Presse would call the country's "coming out" party."[21] Whatever statement was to be communicated would come as two oppositional narratives held in tension in the same space beside the Merlion, much as had been the case with the insertion of the *kecak* into the *Island of Demons* headed to Germany, or the case four years earlier when Stuart had stood inside the fountain at the Suntec City Mall watching "Flowers in the Mirror" with its offering of a new paradise where men would be transformed.

Fridae cautiously reported: "Nation is just a party. It has no political agenda, no statement to make, no underlying subversive message."[22]

Over the years, though, S2's dance would steadily grow.

For Nation III, commerce-oriented market surveyors came to find out who the foreigners were who were attending and — most importantly — what they were spending. "After they collected the data," Stuart said, "they called me and asked, 'Are you sure this is correct?' I said, I don't know. I didn't do the study. Why? They said, the numbers are really good. They were spending about four or five times the average tourist."[23]

Stuart saw it as a hopeful opening, the possibility that the "pink dollar" would lead to wider acceptance of gay men in Singapore.[24]

On August 8, 2004, just a few months after *Manazine* was reprimanded by the Singapore licensors, Nation IV would draw about 8,000 people, several thousand of them foreign tourists. By then, S2 was staging three nights of dances: a kickoff at the Singapore International Convention and Exhibition Center, a closing at the Zouk Club, a well-known bar, and, in between, the Nation IV party itself at the fountain in front of the Merlion.

Photographs of the event showed that, under the Merlion that night of Nation IV, thousands of men danced. Flames and lightning-like lasers fired. Male fingers splayed in the air. Costumes confused notions of gender. Hypnotic dance music drummed. Chants rose and fell. Even *The Wall Street Journal* took note of the display of Asian male flesh in trancelike ecstasy beneath the illuminated statue, a *Journal* reporter writing: "Laser lights played across the bodies of revelers, many shirtless and some stripped down to their Speedos, as they danced through the humid tropical night."[25]

It was the new *kecak*.

Five days during the summer of 2004, shortly before Nation IV, *Lianhe Wanbao*, a Chinese-language tabloid owned by the same company that published *The Straits Times*, began printing front-page headlines quite in contrast with those about Jim Chow only one summer earlier.

The series' first article, titled "Secrets of the Gay Circle," appeared on July 9.[26] It described a gay sauna, quoted an anonymous patron about what happened inside, and then interviewed a psychologist who warned that men at such saunas might face psychological trauma. The following day, the newspaper described another sauna where nude male parties occurred every full moon and where male bodies, the newspaper said, would *hu gao* – engage in sex indiscriminately. Yet another sauna was featured in the third article, which also quoted a female lawyer urging complaints to the police.

In the fourth article, reporters ventured into Singapore's gay bars. Headlined "Gay Bar Gets More Decadent With the Night," the story quoted one server code-named Peter, who claimed to be straight and complained that customers touched him.

"Our reporters further enquired, 'Which part of your body do they touch?'

"'They would draw out their hands and touch my buttocks,' Peter lamented."

What did the server do then, they asked?

"'All we can do is push their hands gently, lightly and in a polite manner. This is our job and we absolutely have no choice about it,' Peter answered despondently."

The majority of the servers, the article assured readers, have "normal sexual inclinations" – in contrast, presumably, to the gay men in the bar who wanted to touch one another.

The reporters continued exploring the bar, discovering "a group of handsome 20–30 year old young gays" whose "actions seemed to be very daring and open." "Some of them actually kissed and stroked each other in the presence of others. Although their public displays of affection lasted only a few seconds, it was extremely 'R-rated.' Their acts of intimacy, decadent and daring behavior was absolutely unbelievable and definitely an eye-opener to the non-homosexual customers."

For a man to touch a man in any form was clearly outside the bounds of legitimate male desire as far as *Lianhe Wanbao* was concerned.

The article closed by quoting "a local famous pastor" who first offered a view of the causes of homosexuality as well as his own lesson on what constituted manhood and its performance of gender. Supposedly, he said, gay men had seen their mothers abused by their fathers. Then, by choosing anal sex as a role, they were somehow enjoying sex with men on behalf of their mother. The pastor advised religious counseling.[27]

On August 12, four days after the Nation IV party, Lee Kuan Yew's son Lee Hsien Loong, who had attended Nanyang Primary School as S2 had, was sworn in as Singapore's third prime minister. In his inauguration speech, Lee Hsien Loong said that "ours must be an open and inclusive Singapore . . . People should feel free to express diverse views, pursue unconventional ideas or simply be different." The BBC news reported "one of Lee Hsien Loong's most urgent challenges will be to act on the increasing calls for liberalization."[28]

The day before the swearing-in, on August 11, representatives of the MDA again called Arjan Twilhaar to a meeting. *Manazine* had just published an interview with the winner of the "UK Idol" talent show, a gay man named Will Young. In the interview, Young mentioned he wanted to find a boyfriend. Such a comment, the MDA suggested, promoted homosexuality and, as such, was against the nation's laws.[29]

As summer 2004 ended, then, anti-gay articles such as those in *Lianhe Wanbao* could be published in Singapore at will, but statements about a young male desiring a boyfriend could violate the law.

That autumn, S2 introduced a new monthly columnist on Fridae. Alvin Tan was to write a campy, creative, tongue-in-cheek column about sex and relationships. On November 5, he wrote frankly about men forming ongoing fraternal friendships with other males where sex was a focus. "Chances are," Tan wrote, "that there will be a point (or many points) in your life that you would have had the pleasure of having a fuck buddy (or many fuck buddies)."

"Fuck buddies are to gay men as mistresses and prostitutes are to heterosexual men – except that they do not demand payment and are nowhere as demanding."

He offered some lighthearted rules for maintaining a healthy relationship between such men: Stay silent about it, do not spend too much time together, and do not turn it into a romance.[30]

In other words, avoid the triple supremacy.

Just a few days later, Dr Balaji Sadasivan, Singapore's minister of health, was scheduled to deliver a routine dinner speech at one of the city's most important hospitals, Tan Tock Seng. Balaji had studied neurology at the Royal College of Surgeons and at Harvard University; he also represented the same political district, Ang Mo Kio, as Lee Kuan Yew's son Lee Hsien Loong. In addition to being minister of health, he oversaw the Ministry of Information, Communication and the Arts – the agency that controlled Singapore's media and culture industry.

Balaji had often been called on to address Singapore's response to AIDS, the topic scheduled at Tan Tock Seng. Unlike Europe or the United States, where the disease had hit the gay community hardest, Singapore's statistics looked more like those of Africa. By the end of 2002, more than seventy-five percent of Singapore's AIDS cases were among heterosexuals, while gay-identified men represented only about thirteen percent of the cases. Many of those heterosexuals were blue-collar workers between the ages of thirty and forty-nine, and among them were those who sought pleasure at the nearby Indonesian island of Batam, a forty-five minute ferry ride away to what one island website in 2004 referred to as "a new, fresh, raw and vibrant frontier." The website had noted: "Local girls often do not insist on the use of condoms and the temptation to go 'bareback' is very great on Batam." Rather than warn against such behavior, the website had instead reassured men that "there is still a VERY low incidence of HIV/AIDS in Batam and the risk to men from uncovered vaginal or oral sex is low."[31]

Overwhelmingly, the men going to Batam from Singapore were Chinese. *The Straits Times* had interviewed ten earlier that year. Four did not know how AIDS was transmitted; two others did not even know what the disease was.[32]

Yet, at Tan Tock Seng, Balaji surprisingly targeted a different group.

"The gays," he declared, "are the bigger concern."

Seventy-seven had been diagnosed with AIDS during 2004, Balaji said, more than a forty percent jump from the same period the year before. He called it an "explosion of cases" and blamed "the promiscuous and unsafe lifestyle advocated and practiced by some gays."[33] He said nothing about Batam or heterosexual promiscuity.

Then he made the blame more specific. He told the doctors that he had been reading a website – Fridae.

"I was shocked by what I read."

"A 'sexpert' called Alvin Tan," he fumed, "was advocating a promiscuous and reckless lifestyle."[34]

It was the first time a government official had commented so publicly – and so negatively – about S2's new male cyber-paradise. Tan's column, along with the Nation dances, would finally propel S2 onto a collision course with the new government of his fellow alumnus from Nanyang Primary School.

The Nation had not been the only dance Stuart was organizing. He had also launched a second, smaller dance at Christmastime. Snowball, he had called it, although there was never snow in Singapore. Instead, the first time, he had substituted thousands of Styrofoam beads falling from the ceiling – not just for a few moments but long enough to pile knee high.[35]

Jungle Media, a Fridae subsidiary S2 had created, had applied for entertainment licenses for Snowball.04, scheduled for Christmas Day 2004, as well as for a follow-up Meltdown Party on Boxing Day, December 26. An old cavernous warehouse along the Singapore River had been rented. Stuart was planning to transform it into what he said would be a "dazzling palace" of lasers.

He had never encountered any significant problems securing the license, an indication that Singapore under Goh had become more comfortable accepting the idea of gay men being part of the nighttime entertainment discourse in the city. But on December 8, only a few weeks after Balaji's speech and only a few weeks before the dance, that changed.

The Singapore police refused to okay Snowball.

Normally, as had been the case with the People Like Us requests that Alex Au had filed, such rejections came with little explanation. This time the police wrote a lengthy press release. It opened by denying any assumption of a freedom of association for gay men. The "assessment is that the event is likely to be organized as a gay party which is contrary to public interest in general," the release said, noting that the promotion materials for the dance had been "widely advertised on fridae.com, a known gay portal."

For evidence that the upcoming Snowball might prove offensive to some in Singapore and therefore deserved the prior restraint represented by a license denial, the police cited the kickoff dance that had preceded the Nation IV events:

> Observations during the Indoor Opening Ball at Suntec showed the patrons of the same gender openly kissing and intimately touching each other. Some of the revelers were cross-dressed, for example, males wearing skirts. Patrons were also seen using the toilets of the opposite sex. The behaviour of these patrons suggested that most of them were probably gays/lesbians and this was thus an event almost exclusively for gays/lesbians . . .
>
> [In addition] a number of couples of the same sex were seen hugging and kissing in public [and] several letters of complaint were received from some patrons about the openly gay acts at the Ball.[36]

In a not-so-veiled warning about the prospects for Nation V, the release added, "Future applications for events of similar nature will be closely scrutinized."

Stuart immediately appealed to the Ministry of Home Affairs. In just five days, he had his answer from another government press release:

> Singapore is indeed opening up. But we are still, by and large, a conservative society. The blatant public display involving intimate behavior of people of the same sex exhibited at the previous events organized by Jungle Media/Fridae.com would be an affront and unacceptable to the large majority of Singaporeans.[37]

The government response did not halt there.

A few days later, when reporters asked Lee Hsien Loong what he thought of the decision, the prime minister replied it was a correct approach that showed "balance and judgment."

"It's a question of where to draw the line," he added. "We made it quite clear that the party should not be targeted at gays alone."

"There are certain norms and limits which we have to observe," he added. "This was beyond what we are prepared to accept."[38]

Despite or perhaps because of the controversy, the number of profiles posted on Fridae rose, from about 85,000 in December 2004, when Snowball was rejected, to about 95,000 within the following two months. Two thousand new profiles came from Singapore alone.

Even with the setback, S2 announced that the planning for the Nation V dance below the Merlion would continue as usual.

Early on December 26, 2004, the morning the Snowball party would have ended had it been held on Christmas evening as planned, an earthquake with a magnitude between 9.1 and 9.3, one of the largest ever recorded, struck just west of the tip of Sumatra.

It was centered a few kilometers north of Nias Island, not far from where the *Van Imhoff* had sunk six decades earlier, drowning Walter Spies. The unexpected tsunami it forced moved silently and treacherously fast.

20
A New Nation

Once Singapore refused to license Stuart's Snowball dance, the government moved swiftly to set other limits, illustrating its dual approach of seeking to be at the forefront of cyber-technology while controlling what could be said.

On March 5, Dr Balaji Sadasivan, in his role as minister for Information, Culture and the Arts, spoke at a meeting organized by the Singapore Computer Society. He reported that Singapore's information infrastructure was expanding. International data capacity had jumped twenty-five percent; cell phone penetration stood at ninety-two percent; broadband had almost doubled; and more than 600 wireless points had been set up in cafés and fast-food outlets. Balaji urged the technologists to help attract "the brightest talents of the info-com industry."[1]

Four days later, reporting to Parliament on the spread of AIDS as minister of Health, Balaji attacked one of those very talents in info-com. "We do not know the reasons for the sharp increase of HIV in the gay community," he admitted. But he pointed at Stuart. "An epidemiologist," he continued, not identifying the alleged expert, "has suggested that this [the increase] may be linked to the annual predominantly gay party in Sentosa – the Nation party." S2's dance, he claimed, had "allowed gays from high-prevalence societies to fraternize with local gay men, seeding the infection in the local community." It was the threat of the gay male *nosferatu* bringing plague to the center of the village.[2]

The next day, the front page of *The Straits Times* headlined the unsubstantiated attack: "Gay parties may have led to sharp rise in Aids cases."

The story's lead: "There was a sharp rise in new Aids cases last year and it could be linked to a popular annual 'gay party' on Sentosa, Dr. Balaji Sadasivan said yesterday, quoting an unnamed expert."[3] The story buried a further comment by Balaji that the "unnamed expert" had offered the opinion solely as a hypothesis.

Three days later, *The Sunday Straits Times* added another megaphone. Under the headline "What happened at Sentosa gay parties," the newspaper seemed to discover that gay men were not just asexual civil servants or marketing directors. "They come to party," the lead said, "but many end up pairing off and going to hotel rooms." The taint of sodomy loomed. It warned that "these goings-on at the annual Nation parties" were evidence enough for what Balaji had suggested: "that the Nation parties might be the reason for the spike in Aids cases last year."

The paper described a "pairing off" between a thirty-eight-year-old Singaporean and a man from Hong Kong. The two had "sneaked off" and gone to a hotel room. The Singaporean told the newspaper the two men had used condoms during sex; still, *The Straits Times* insisted, "his behaviour is cause for concern."[4]

Four days later, the tabloid *The New Paper* joined in, using a tone recalling its previous coverage of the Fort Road beach entrapments. Under the headline "Dangerous Liaisons," the paper's reporter suggested the Nation party was not "just a bash" or a chance "to drink, make merry and meet people" – as heterosexual parties presumably were – but rather was "best known as a gay event" that provided an "opportunity to hook up with strings of sexual partners, say insiders."[5] Even the attribution to unnamed "insiders" made the Nation dance sound like a nefarious, closed event. Journalists had been issued media passes and could easily talk to any of the several thousand men attending, quoting some by name if they had chosen.

If "gay" equaled "promiscuous," *The New Paper* added another prong of the triple taboo: an interracial insult. Again quoting one of the unnamed "insiders," local gay Asian men at the parties were compared to "sarong party girls," who the reporter explained were "local women who hang on to Caucasian men."

When the story eventually turned to Balaji's accusation, it included none of even the slight qualifications the minister had used. *The New Paper* instead reported that Balaji had "said the sharp rise in new HIV and AIDS cases last year could be linked to these Nation parties." The anonymous epidemiologist had disappeared as the source. He had now been replaced authoritatively by a government minister. Balaji's own hedges about not knowing the real cause had vanished from the story.

The associations worsened as *The New Paper* continued. No one had seen open sex at the dances, but, the reporter speculated, "in the toilets or once they leave the party, it could be a different story." *The New Paper* acknowledged that S2's dances did include AIDS education and condoms but insisted that the parties were "associated with promiscuity," a part of the gay culture the reporter claimed had "carried over" from parties in Sydney attended by the gay "jet-setting crowd."[6]

Nosferatus.

After those articles, other attacks continued.

At the end of March, a gay-friendly Christian group called Safehaven was swept into the controversy. It had been planning to hold a fundraising concert to assist Singapore's non-profit Action for AIDS, featuring two gay Christian singers, Jason and deMarco. The government MDA, operating under Balaji's Ministry of Information, Culture and the Arts, refused the license, saying the two used "their musical performances and their own example of being a couple to celebrate and promote a gay lifestyle."

The MDA declared, "Performances that promote alternative lifestyles are against the public interest."[7]

Early that summer, *The New Paper* would hit again, with a series about Singaporean gay teenagers and AIDS. "They're bold, immature and completely out of their depth when it comes to sex," the paper wrote in June. Throwing in the taboo against cross-age sexual desire, it added that older men were using the teens to practice sex without condoms. Yet the one anecdote the story related described an older gay male helping a younger male teen be tested for sexually transmitted diseases. Statistics supporting the series were weak: Only seven teens in Singapore had been infected with AIDS since 2000, and three of those had been heterosexuals. *The New Paper* series did address a few actual problems – gay teens not having enough information about AIDS, or enough condoms available, or family who supported them – but it did so by smearing the gay teens as well as older gay men, while leaving the other half of the statistic – the infected heterosexual teens – unsmirched.[8]

A few days after Balaji's Parliamentary attack on the Nation dance, Khun Toc hosted a special dinner at the Babylon in Bangkok.

It followed the usual pattern: 7:00 p.m. conversations at his home library, the quick walk to the restaurant, the settling at the banquet table. Five Thai friends had joined, along with one Caucasian friend and his Thai partner now living on an island near Seattle. An additional special out-of-town guest had come too. Much younger at thirty than the others, he had a sculpted Winckelmann-style body. He joked to the group that he had once been skinny but then had joined a workout club in Singapore.

Stuart had put Gary Siow in charge of Jungle Media, the Fridae subsidiary that organized dances. Officially, Siow would tell his banquet mates at Babylon that planning for the Nation dance was still proceeding as it had in past years. The fountain under the Merlion had already been reserved, and the park authorities there "were fine with it," as they had been for the previous four years. But he also told them his task was to prepare a backup plan, possibly bringing the dance to Bangkok.

By no means was it certain that Bangkok itself could provide a refuge. The Thaksin government's social crackdowns and sporadic raids had dampened the image of Thailand as a land of *sanuk*. Gay discos in Patpong now closed at night far earlier than they had in the past, and neighborhood gay bars were either closing earlier or maintaining very discrete after-hour entries through side doors. The police raids for drug checks seemed to have passed. Purachai had long since been removed as Interior Minister, and Pracha Maleenont, who had led the raid on Babylon, had been assigned to another ministry. But no one was naïve enough to believe the raids could not occur again if they seemed likely to produce good publicity for a Thaksin minister.

In a morning walk in his garden on the day of the dinner, Khun Toc told a visitor that the way Balaji's anti-gay attacks had turned to linking homosexuality to AIDS was a "big worry."[9]

In one moment at the dinner, the two men's approaches about how to argue for more dignity for gay men in Southeast Asia seemed to briefly surface. Pragmatically, Siow remarked, some of the "pink dollars" Singapore would lose could now be shifted to Bangkok, perhaps even to Babylon, if the city hosted a relocated Nation party.

Khun Toc smiled politely at the suggestion that dollars might be a motivator for Babylon. "Oh, I don't do things just for money," he said, waving his hand around at the paintings and sculptures, the gardens, and the restaurant with its chairs posing their question about identity: "Whatever becomes a legend most?"

He added, "These are little things I like to do."[10]

The discussion moved quickly. Phuket, not Bangkok, was the place to go, those around the table advised. The tsunami generated by the earthquake on December 26 had crushed the island, killing hundreds of Thais as well as foreigners. Tourist businesses there were in disarray. Phuket was a paradise that needed help. The pink dollar – or, as it was called in Thailand, the "purple baht" – might indeed be attractive. But more importantly, Thaksin's ideal of a social and moral crusade to establish a new Thai man had never enamored the Thais in Phuket. In elections, Phuket had voted solidly Democratic rather than for the Thai Rak Thai party.[11]

In May, to no one's surprise, Lee Hsien Loong's government denied the license for Nation V. This time, the Singapore licensors did not bother with lengthy announcements or justifications. They simply faxed Stuart a denial, and then a spokesperson reiterated the same explanation that had been given for Snowball: "The event is likely to be organized as a gay party which is contrary to public interest in general."[12]

A few months later, Lee Hsien Loong would add more explanation. The Singapore Foreign Correspondents Association listened as he once again sounded the themes of his inaugural National Day speech, urging a Singapore where all would feel included. At the question-answer session, a reporter then pointedly asked him why inclusivity did not seem to include homosexuals. "The reason for asking," the reporter explained, "is that sometimes your administration manages to give every impression of being somewhat homophobic."

Lee made it clear that his guideline for determining what kind of speech and assembly to allow gay men in the city turned not on the standard of whether it posed or ignited any actual harm but whether it had a tendency to create any offense:

> I don't think we are homophobic. I agree with Minister Goh Chok
> Tong that homosexuals are people like you and me, but there
> is some segment of Singaporeans who vehemently disagree with
> that . . . Our job as a government is to create an environment
> and manage an environment in which there is maximum space
> for each person – each view – for each person to live his own

life without impinging on other people . . . If you say I am gay and therefore I am entitled to get married, well that's a very contentious subject. Or even, I'm entitled to have a parade and flaunt my gayness – gay pride. You can do that in Sydney and London and San Francisco but I'm not sure that I want to do that in Singapore because I think it will be offensive to a large number of Singaporeans and it will be very divisive. From the government's point of view, therefore, it is not a wise thing to do. So when it comes to the Nation party and things like that, those are the considerations that we have to bear in mind.

Lee Hsien Loong then became animated, lifting his voice and stretching out both hands.

How do we provide the maximum space without it becoming intrusive and oppressive on the rest of the population and without causing a backlash that will lead to polarization and animosity. That's our responsibility and challenge.

It's very hard to do. You cannot find – there's no easy balancing point . . . It's a dynamic balance and one we'll have to manage very delicately.[13]

As part of that "dynamic balance," S2's Nation had been officially expelled. In August 2005, when the dance would normally have been staged at Sentosa, gay men in Singapore instead launched a series of events running under the pointed name of "IndigNation." They took advantage of the fact that Singapore had promised at least one loosening of the rein on public assemblies: Indoor educational talks no longer had to secure government licenses so long as only *words* were to be exchanged, not anything that might be considered visual art or displays of actual bodies in motion. Some portrayed IndigNation as not being resistance to the government at all but rather as an assertion against Stuart: Gay events, they argued, should be "intellectual and aesthetic" rather than a "frenzied carnival atmosphere."[14]

More obviously masculine *wen*, in other words, rather than the exposed *wu* and Winckelmann male flesh at the dances.

Sintercom's Tan Chong Hee gave the opening talk, a review of "Same-Sex Love in Classical Chinese Literature." As if to emphasize its academic and Chinese nature, he delivered the talk in Mandarin, not English. Similar forums followed: a history of same-sex love in classical Indian literature, a history of gay life in Singapore, conversations about how gay Christians should live, interpretations of scriptural comments about homosexuality. At the end of the month, Alex Au organized the final event, carefully constructed as "not a forum about being gay" in Singapore but a "forum about being Singaporean and what gays and lesbians have to say about nationhood in matters important to both straight and gay people."

"It is about building a place we can call home," the description of Au's event said.[15]

November 1, 2005 marked the start of the first tourist season after the great tsunami caused by the Boxing Day earthquake that had struck Southeast Asia. The wave, sometimes thirty meters tall, had left confusion about how paradise could be so astonishing. One moment, the tropical sea had seemed orderly and predictable. The next, it had been wildly free.

To kick-start the post-tsunami tourist season, 1,000 Thai masseurs and masseuses had gathered at Patong Beach on Phuket Island. Patong lies at the mid-point of the Thai beaches along which 5,000 people had died, half of them tourists, many from Germany, Scandinavia, and Britain. This particular day, November 1, the Thais planned to form a chain of hands to knead and relax whatever shoulders could be found — at no charge. Close by, musicians and food vendors were preparing to transform the seafront road where the wave had struck. Instead of a strip of death, the road would become a mall of rock bands and papaya salads.

It rained — a bad start. Planes landing at Phuket's small international airport flew through crazed angles of lighting while clouds shaped a crazy quilt of space. A Thai guide sent to fetch visitors with a van apologized for the damp. He said Pui was his name, and he was in his 30s, square-headed, and extremely earnest.

"We are very happy you still come," he told a visitor. "We still need your help."

After the tsunami had hit, *Time* magazine had reminded its readers that Phuket was one of the best known of the many scattered tropical paradises that had come to characterize Southeast Asia.

The van that Pui accompanied moved quickly past Phuket's Patong Beach and over the headlands to the next beach, Karon. Pui assured the visitors that Karon had not been as hard hit by the tsunami as Patong. Only a single hotel had been destroyed by the wave, he said, one named "On the Beach." Unfortunately, it had actually been located there.

As the van rolled into the driveway of the Crowne Plaza Resort at Karon and headed toward the hotel's acres of cottages and swimming pools, two uniformed Chubb Security guards suddenly stepped out to stop it. They flashed mirrors on long sticks underneath the chassis.

"Trouble in Indonesia," Pui explained. He apologized again. Over the decades, the rhetoric about "paradises" in Southeast Asia had become not only serious but also deadly serious. Increasingly afoot was another idea, one quite at odds with the aesthetic paradise of Bali, the erotic *sanuk* of Bangkok, and the computer-Eden in Singapore. A mostly male jihadist movement was beckoning another imagination.

Immediately after the September 11, 2001 attacks on the World Trade Center in New York City, Singapore had discovered a jihadist cell burrowing silently on the smart island itself. Then had come the 2002 terrorist attack on the aesthetic island, when bombs loaded into a van and backpack had killed more than 200 people in Bali's bars – mostly youths who had been seen as using their bodies incorrectly by drinking and dressing in ways not approved of by the jihadists. Bombs had hit again in Bali only a few days before Pui's van rolled into the Crowne Plaza, this time in beachside restaurants where Balinese rather than foreigners enjoyed tropical sunsets. At the northern end of the Chao Phraya delta cemented over by Bangkok, a man known as Hambali had been arrested in Ayutthaya, the pre-Chakri royal capital of Siam. Somewhere in Southeast Asia, he was being held in a secret prison, accused of being the force behind the bombings in Bali as well as mentor of the jihadist cell in Singapore. Hambali, it was said, had been planning more attacks so as to catalyze the creation of a new Islamist paradise arching from southern Thailand through Malaysia and then stretching across Bali to the southern Philippines – effectively isolating Singapore.

Although Pui wanted his visitors to think that the tension was centered in the old Dutch East Indies, conflicts had also been inflamed in Thailand's three Muslim-dominated provinces located just south of Phuket. The incorporation of those provinces into Buddhist Siam by Chulalongkorn at the turn of the century did not go smoothly.[16] Thaksin had ratcheted up the violence by responding to Muslim protestors who would not follow his orders with a military crackdown; in turn, separatists had taken to beheading Buddhist monks and schoolteachers.

A well-placed bomb at the start of the new tourist season was not something Pui wanted to contemplate. The Crowne Plaza would soon be locked down, and burly black-suited security guards in dark glasses, looking very much like a Hollywood movie cast, were being imported from Bangkok to augment the hotel's own police.

Paradise in Southeast Asia was beginning to seem not so much like dance and music to be savored, or sex and art to be enjoyed, or even computers to be touched. Instead, it was a battle to be won.

Satisfied that Pui's van carried no bombs beneath its frame, the Crowne Plaza security guards waved it in.

That afternoon, beside one of the Crowne Plaza's swimming pools, Stuart appeared. He paced quickly, trailed by Jim Chow and seven others on his staff, all walking a sweep around the pool to decide first where to put the colored balloons, and second where to put the black-suited guards who had been hired to defend one narrative about male bodies and desires and gender against another.

Jim carried a thick blue binder titled "Security Meetings." That morning, Stuart had agreed to move one event from a nearby stadium back to the Crowne Plaza. The Thai police worried about how easily jihadists could attack the stadium.

Stuart had reserved the entire Crowne Plaza – every room in a tower that overlooked the blue Andaman Sea, every ground-level cottage with its own small soaking pool, every ballroom, the entire morning breakfast room, each of the several bars, the two pools, and the new fitness club that workers were rushing to ready.

For the weekend, the global resort would be Stuart's own new island — except that it was so fully booked that he and his own staff from Fridae had had to stay at a neighboring hotel. In a paradise trying to rebuild, Stuart intended to help. He had trucked in a sound system, strobe lights, and thousands of glow-in-the-dark light sticks that looked like candy canes. He had hired disc jockeys from Taiwan, America, and Australia — as well as the black-suited security guards from Bangkok. The Merlion, of course, was missing.

Stuart's cell phone kept ringing.

Reporters.

Why, they wanted to know, had Singapore exiled, of all things, a dance?

A reporter from *The Sydney Morning Herald* in Australia had just interviewed him. Stuart had countered Lee Hsien Loong's remarks about managing a "delicate balance."

"I told them it's just homophobic."

The Herald had headlined the article, "Thailand wins as Singapore's brief gay fling grinds to a halt." Stuart urged the reporter to write about action that just been taken by Warwick University in Britain. The university had spurned Singapore's encouragement to build a branch campus on the smart island, saying it feared for academic freedom, given the government's restrictions on speech.[17]

Stuart set aside his cell phone long enough to stand quietly at one of the railed balconies. He looked out toward the Andaman Sea. The waves had returned to normalcy. The sea was back to its orderly self. But there did seem to be a special glistening of unusual light left by the rain clouds.

S2 smiled and told a visitor:

"Now we're the news."[18]

About 1,500 men as well as a much smaller group of women registered for Nation V, fewer than had previously attended when it was close at hand below the Merlion, but enough to fill the Crowne Plaza as well as rooms scattered around Karon and Patong Beaches. Nation was assuming a new canvas, the first time apparently in Southeast Asia than an entire hotel had been taken over mostly by gay men.

"I may lose money," S2 admitted. All the sound equipment, the DJs, the security guards, and countless other kinds of logistical support had to be imported to the island from Bangkok or Singapore.[19]

After inspecting the pool and the ballroom, and deciding where security guards would be posted, Stuart and Jim Chow moved into a meeting room converted into ground zero for operations. A dry erase board had been marked with sleeping times: "Gary Siow, 5:00 a.m.–noon; Jim Chow, 6:00 a.m.–noon." Stuart's name was there, too, but no rest time had been scheduled. Jim slumped in a chair and closed his eyes. "Should I send another letter of thanks to the governor?"

Stuart: "I don't think you have to."

Jim: "I've already sent one to the mayor. I think I'll send another to the governor."[20]

Local Thai officials were already proving more welcoming than Singapore's. Phuket's governor, Udomsak Uswarangkura, had even written a short welcome message, calling the party an "annual celebration of diversity." The governor had also explicitly rejected Singapore's reasons for banning the party, telling news reporters that, so long as "they don't break any laws," the gay men were welcome. The local director of the government's Tourism Authority of Thailand had also endorsed the Nation. In contrast to Balaji's attack on the Nation party as a place where AIDS was being spread, a Phuket hospital official pointed out that infections stemmed from behavioral problems of all kinds of people, not just gay men.[21]

As men registered for the party, Thai volunteers asked their countries of origin, their education, whether they were aware of their HIV status, and whether they used condoms. The data were projected on-screen in a steady stream of graphs. S2 explained: "It's useful for people to be aware of their HIV status and their use of condoms."[22] A Dutch epidemiologist from Bangkok who had helped set up the display noted that eighty-six percent of those registering said they had university education, and forty-four percent had had a test for the HIV virus in the last three months – indicating a much higher degree of awareness than in the general population. S2 was also paying for an on-site testing center in one of the hotel rooms. "They don't have to be doing this," the epidemiologist noted. "They could just take their money and run."[23]

Stuart finally got a short sleep time listed on the operations board: six hours from 7:30 a.m. until 1:30 p.m.

By Friday afternoon, Eric Smutney, the marketing communication manager for the Crowne Plaza, had begun to handle last-minute problems. He and his wife, married in the other paradise of Bali, lived in one of the villas on the Crowne Plaza grounds. By Friday afternoon, the hotel had filled, and Smutney explained that although the decision to host Nation V had been relayed to the regional corporate headquarters – in Singapore – the ultimate choice had been left to the hotel manager in Phuket.

"There was never a question about it," he said. As a global corporation, the Crowne Plaza had adopted a non-discrimination policy both for employees and for its rentals, and that extended to groups like Fridae. But, he added, security would be tight, not only within and at the perimeters of the compound but along the road separating the hotel wall from the beach. Referring to the bombings that had killed global partygoers as well as locals in Bali, he said, "We don't want any black vans pulling up and parking."[24]

When the time came for the main event on the Saturday night of Nation V, men streamed down the Crowne Plaza's corridors, joking, laughing, pulling at the gleaming "bling-blings" they had collected from Singapore's priciest department stores and at Bangkok's Sunday market. Inside the ballroom, which could hold 1,200, circles formed. Single bodies appeared from within the circles, then vanished back into them. As the music played, male bodies heaved, sank, pressed rhythms into the holes formed by the circles of multiple heads. Some men danced with their eyes closed. A wail of lyrics broke the steady bass chants. On stands surrounding the center, men swayed their bodies, stood in lines and then shot their arms into the air, fingers piercing the lasers above and twining the air between. The music grew in accelerandos with sudden stops and fresh bursts. Light played on the men's splayed fingers like sparks. They mouthed wails from Madonna and Kylie, their sounds growing hoarse as the night wore on toward early morning and sunrise.

What Walter Spies and Beryl de Zoete had written of the male *kecak* still seemed true decades later and hundreds of miles away from Bali. "To seek a consecutive theme in the wandering voices, the cracked strings and wailing cries," they had said, "is a vain quest . . . like trying to find a meaning for the intricacy of melody, harmony and rhythm in a musical symphony."[25]

As Walter had written of the very first *kecak* he had seen in Bali: "They were bewitched, spellbound, and I would have liked to have screamed and danced with them!"[26]

For much of the night, the choreographer of it all, S2, sat quietly outside on a couch near the bar. Occasionally he peeked inside, but mostly he chatted with friends and sometimes with Phuket's police officers. At one point, he took the chief of police inside. "Parties change attitudes about gay stereotypes," S2 said later. "The chief looked around at the crowd very seriously and then he asked me, 'Are all these gay men?'"

S2 laughed.

"I told him some were lesbians."[27]

After Nation V ended, Bangkok's *Nation* newspaper published a long column about its effects. Unlike the Singapore press's characterization of the dance as dangerous, the Thai columnist described the Nation as "an annual social gathering . . . to enjoy music, making friends, and activities like swimming, volleyball, surfing, diving, and sunbathing." He argued that "for the many participants who still live 'in the closet' because of legal or traditional discrimination in their societies, the event offers a chance for them to be themselves." He also included the global economic argument: "Around the world, gays and lesbians are a newly discovered and lucrative target for the tourism industry. Yet many countries, including Thailand, have yet to fully explore this segment of the tourist market."

The dance had brought to Phuket "a whopping 30 million baht," about US$750,000, he noted; "not much compared to the huge economic losses caused by the tsunami" but of potentially great impact if "crowds like this" continued to visit Phuket and other parts of Thailand. He closed with a swipe at Singapore:

> The present government of Prime Minister Lee Hsien Loong, while claiming to continue the non-discriminatory stance famously initiated under the previous administration, appears to have jumped to the conclusion that having gay activities is contrary to the "public interest." In other words, it means gays have the right to live and pay taxes in Singapore, but not be seen as promoting their lifestyle in public. Worse, a government agency also employed an old stereotype, in stating that gay parties have helped contribute to the recent rise of HIV transmission rates in the country.[28]

Bloomberg News quoted an enthusiastic response from the regional director of Thailand's tourist authority, who said she hoped the Nation party would become bigger and bigger each year. "It's a good start," she said.[29]

Perhaps more important than the news reports aired when Nation V was occurring were the male voices on Fridae itself. The silence and isolation of Walter's "delicate, lotus-eyed boys" had been abandoned. The comments were quickly written, at times with all the simplified spellings and grammar that had become online custom, the kind of passionate online people's literature that Tan Chong Hee had promoted on Sintercom.

A man who called himself "Togs" wrote: "Fridae has educated me . . . I now understand how isolated and scared so many gay & lesbians are in Singapore. Thanks to Fridae they can communicate to others in a virtual queer world. I hope that this progresses into real physical interaction in the non-virtual world so that we who are invisible to the heartlands, the aunties and uncles eventually know we exist . . . come to know us and accept us."[30]

From "Iep:" "Fridae have help me open up my circle of friends. I'm more open now compare to yrs ago. Meet many wonderful friends."[31]

Much simpler, from "klwl": "After almost four decades of existence, I finally met – through Fridae – the love of my life, who is romantically interested in me, and who loves me for who I am."[32]

A month after Nation V, a man who pointedly chose the name "Hurts" posted a comment that seemed to capture the dream of a different manhood lived, not only imaginatively but also in reality:

> Most non-gay people treat us as "Abnormal"/ "Freaks"/"Crazy"
> cos' simply we're different from them . . . I just hope that, one day,

> i can tell the world that i'm who i am . . . Tell anyone who ask
> me, that i like the same gender as i am . . . Without having them
> to lecture/avoid me . . .
>   That's what i truly hope.[33]

More than a year later, on a Saturday in April 2007, Lee Kuan Yew was driven near Sentosa Island, the old site of S2's Nation dances. His son Lee Hsien Loong had begun promoting the conversion of parts of the island for a gambling casino so as to polish Singapore's tourist image as a smart paradise where it was also possible to have fun. Lee Kuan Yew had an appointment with his political party's youth branch, the teens who would eventually hold political power in Singapore. The site that had been chosen, the St. James Power Station, symbolized both Singapore's past as well as its hoped-for future. It had been built as the island's first coal-fired power plant in 1927 – the same year Walter Spies had moved to Bali. A makeover had now turned it into an entertainment cathedral embracing several lounges and dance floors.[34]

Lee Kuan Yew dressed casually in a white shirt without a tie and sat on the stage taking questions in front of a Yamaha synthesizer. One young woman, a playwright, asked: "Where is censorship headed for the next two decades?" She explained that the government had permitted her play about a Singaporean female pornography star to be staged, but only after she had agreed to remove a sentence that had reversed the Christian Gospel's assertion that "In the beginning was the Word . . . and the Word became Flesh."

She had instead written: "In the beginning was the Body."[35]

Lee Kuan Yew turned the question into one about tolerating sexual differences. "You take this business of homosexuality," he answered. "It raises tempers all over the world."

> If in fact it is true . . . that you are genetically born a homosexual
> because that's the nature of the genetic random transmission of
> genes, you can't help it. So why should we criminalize it? But
> there's such a strong inhibition in all societies – Christianity,
> Islam, even the Hindu, Chinese societies. And we are now
> confronted with a persisting aberration. But is it an aberration?[36]

He altered his wording from "aberration":

> It's a genetic variation. So what do we do? I think we pragmatically
> adjust, carry our people . . . don't upset them and suddenly upset
> their sense of propriety and right and wrong, but at the same
> time let's not go around like this moral police do . . . barging into
> people's rooms . . . That's not our business. You have to take a
> practical, pragmatic approach to what I see is an inevitable force
> of time and circumstance.[37]

He seemed to be suggesting that an "inevitable force of time and circumstance" would lead to queer differences becoming less isolated and more acceptable.

That night and the next day, his comments appeared in news stories not only in Singapore but also across the world. Had he meant that the smart paradise should finally drop its British-inspired criminal sodomy law that prohibited homosexual acts? On the Tuesday following Lee's appearance at St. James, a Reuters news service reporter questioned him further.

S2 would place the transcript of that interview in Fridae's online archive. In it, Lee Kuan Yew seemed to struggle with the tension of homosexuals coming in from the periphery and making a home in the center:

> Q: Did we read this correctly you saying that we should decriminalize it eventually?
>
> Mr. Lee: Eventually. I would say that if this is the way the world is going and Singapore is part of that interconnected world and I think it is, then I see no option for Singapore but to be a part of it . . . They tell me, and anyway it is probably half-true, that homosexuals are creative writers, dancers, etcetera. And there is some Biblical evidence of that and if we want creative people, then we've got to put up with their idiosyncrasies.
>
> So long as they don't infect the heartland.[38]

Postscript

The pursuit of a homeland can extend across generations, especially if the homeland is to become one that no longer has to feel like a paradise created from magical realities but part of the ordinary landscape and ordinary imagination. By October 23, 2010, a century had passed since Vajiravudh's accession to the throne.

In the *Spartacus* gay international guide, the editors had started tempering their description of Vajiravudh's former Siam as early as 2005. They now referred to gay life in Thailand only as "*relatively* unrestricted" and complained that nightlife had become "strictly controlled."[1] Thaksin had ultimately been ousted in a coup in September 2006 while attending a United Nations meeting in New York. His attempt to turn Thailand toward a Singaporean model of manhood and political control had run afoul of corruption charges, especially when he and his family had decided to sell their telecommunications company, Shin Corporation, to the government investment arm of Singapore, the Temasek Corporation. Estimates were that the Thai prime minister and his family members netted almost US$2 billion, but they had avoided paying taxes. His opponents were outraged, both by the tax techniques and the takeover of a significant piece of Thailand's communication network by outsiders. Nearly 1,000 demonstrators burned photographs of Lee Hsien Loong and his wife, Ho Ching, who headed Temasek. The protestors then cut a picture of Thaksin's head into a photograph of the Merlion and burned it too.[2]

Critics before and after the coup argued that the Thais already had an ideal male — Bhumibol and his *dharmic* kingship — and Thaksin seemed to be trying to usurp that role with his own ideas about how to be a *phuyai*. Thaksin, one scholar commented to *The Nation*, wanted to be a "magical person."[3] The military and royalty aligned against him, Thaksin escaped into a rich man's exile, his Thai Rak Thai party banned. His supporters remained a force, however, and once the Thai military returned control to political parties, power shifted back and forth, anti-Thaksin crowds wearing yellow shirts, the king's color, and pro-Thaksin crowds red shirts. Yellow shirts seized control of that all-important symbol of globalization that Darrell Berrigan had once written about — the airport — its tourists determining Thailand's future by either passing through or staying. Red shirts later blockaded an equally important symbol of globalization, the gleaming shopping malls that had been built east of the university that Vajiravudh had named after his father, Chulalongkorn. The red shirts camped in Lumphini Park, sporadically launching grenades past Vajiravudh's statue into the streets along the red light district of Patpong. When the Thai Army finally dispersed the red shirts, one of the largest malls of the new commercial Thailand that Thaksin had wanted to build, Central World, was torched. Within another few months, Thaksin supporters would give a new party headed by his younger sister the majority control of the parliament. Yingluck Shinawatra would become the nation's first female prime minister. Thailand's "new man," it seemed, might be a woman.

Khun Toc's refuge for a different manhood along Soi Nantha had escaped any dramatic harm from Thaksin's social order campaign, other than the raid. Khun Toc continued to mastermind his paradise, adding computer stations for men in towels to use and turning the traditional Thai home he had moved to Babylon's entryway into a newly named "Botticelli House." It meshed the fretwork Thai exterior with interior Florentine reliefs and sculptures. Babylon also added its own channel on YouTube, opening the once private world of the gay Asian sauna to cyber-view − complete with videos of its shirtless males dancing in light-streaked foam-party *kecaks* as well as a tour of its art and gardens backed by lyrics from "I'm Mad About the Boy."[4] During the red shirt protests in summer 2010, Khun Toc could see the smoke from hundreds of tires set aflame just a few blocks away, near Vajiravudh's statue, and he could hear the explosions of grenades. He sent a friend a text message: "Despite violence all is well at BB. Do try to come in fall."[5]

That same year of 2010, at Surabaya where Walter had been jailed, activists from across Southeast Asia attempted to hold a meeting of the International Lesbian, Gay, Bisexual, Transgender and Intersex Association. They rented rooms at the Mercure Surabaya, owned by the international Mercure chain, a fashionably globalized space with 126 rooms, two restaurants that served Indonesian and Chinese cuisine, an American-style coffee lounge, a pool bar, and the usual fitness center and spa.[6] But hard-line Islamic groups had protested, forcing the conference to be cancelled.[7]

In Bali, the Kerobokan jail, where Walter had first been imprisoned for a short time, held the young jihadist men who had gone there in fall 2002 to send a message from one concept of male paradise to another. Three brothers had overseen the actual deployment of the first bombs in Bali. Two had worked at Malaysian construction camps and would sometimes tell the third the abhorrence they felt about the paradise Bali represented.[8] It was said that Hambali, the jihadist arrested near Bangkok, had designed the attack. The necessary male network had stretched from Hambali's headquarters down through Singapore and on to Denpasar.

National borders did not matter when it came to deploying manhood or paradise.

Walter's most famous legacy, the *kecak*, still was being performed every week in Ubud, mostly for tourists. It had also taken on a life as a soundtrack in Western films, in which its multilayered incantation remained unfamiliar enough to audiences to evoke the strange aspects of manhood and of the battle of good and evil.[9] Its most famous performer, Walter's original dancer Limbak, had lived to see his old Bali bombed by the Islamists — to the age, some said, of 106, dying in September 2003. Of course, no one could really be sure how old Limbak was, since — as both Margaret Mead and Gregory Bateson had argued during Walter's trial — the Balinese simply did not keep track of their ages.[10]

Walter's life itself had drawn the attention of novelists. He became a character in at least three fictional works, usually depicted as a dilettante and a seducer of both the wealthy and of Balinese boys. His guilt in molesting underage Asian "boys" was often simply assumed, the context of the *Zedenschandaal* having been largely forgotten. One novelist described him as "having a face that looked to have been modeled in a confectioner's shop" and characterized him "as a saboteur capable of demoralizing an entire class."[11] Another may have come closer to the truth by observing that the paradise Walter had helped create had not been about Bali at all but about himself as a homosexual male living in the 1930s, when the empires were descending into chaos. "The myth that he purveyed," Nigel Barley wrote in a book titled after the von Plessen film *Island of Demons* "was the myth of himself, as a man who had found that contentment we all seek, who always sat in golden sunshine, who lived a life without the oppression of wage-slavery or anxiety, a Parsifalian Peter Pan for whom every day brought joy and the pleasure of beauty, what he, himself, might have called a *Lebenskünstler*, an artist *at* living."[12]

Walter probably would have considered himself more a *gesamtkunstwerk*, a holistic work of art and life of the type that had been sought by the Brücke artists who had influenced him in Dresden as well as, of course, the type of fusion promoted by his early idol, Scriabin.

In Singapore by autumn 2010, the nineteenth-century British Section 377 had been dropped from the penal code, ending the criminal sanctions against consensual adult oral and anal sex, but, as it turned out, only for heterosexual acts. After an impassioned Parliamentary debate, the government had retained Section 377A, the colonial law that had been adopted in 1938, when the faltering empires of Britain and the Netherlands had been trying to defend "European values" and manhood against the attacks of Nazi sympathizers — when Walter had been arrested in Bali. Section 377A still criminalized all "outrages on decency" between males, maintaining the possibility of two-year prison sentences for a wide range of male-male affections.

Lee Hsien Loong promised his government would not enforce the old law that had helped solidify part of the triple taboo on the use of male bodies and their desires, but the rhetorical condemnation in it would remain. "It's better to accept the legal untidiness and the ambiguity," he said. "It works; don't disturb it."[13]

Just a few weeks before the century since Vajiravudh had become king was to close, Dr Balaji Sadasivan died of colon cancer. He had served as the Singapore government's most outspoken critic of Fridae and of S2's Nation dances. Yet in the years since, he and Stuart had traveled together to Sydney to study that city's efforts to control AIDS among gay men and then had worked to begin similar efforts in Singapore. In 2007, as senior minister for Media, Information, Communication and the Arts, he had become the first minister in Singapore to attend a predominantly gay event: the rescheduled staging of the concert by the gay Christian singers Jason and deMarco, which had been banned in 2005 after the Snowball dance was prohibited. At an apparently critical moment, when the government seemed poised to prohibit the singers a second time, Balaji had told the concert organizers to inform the licensors that he would be attending as a guest of honor. At the time of his death, S2 praised him as "a friend to Singapore's gay community," although, in keeping with the new open *agora* S2 had created for queer male voices in Singapore, it was a tribute that other gay Asian men hotly contested in their postings.[14]

As had happened with Walter, S2 also began to find his life becoming a blend of reality and fiction. A novel published in 2009 focused on the Singapore gay activism of the late 1990s and early 2000s and presented him as the boyfriend of an aging writer worried about losing his Winckelmann-style muscle tone. A review in Fridae noted that the boyfriend was a "party-going, gym-obsessed CEO of a local gay website, Adonis.com." It added that the character was "obviously modeled after Fridae.com's Stuart Koe, but not in a flattering way."[15]

By then, S2 had decided he no longer needed to continue to organize the Nation dances. "I've never stopped evolving," he commented, "so it all depends on when you decide to draw the line and stop documenting." He would later add that by autumn 2010, he had come to a "critical juncture." The time was arriving for a new S2.[16] Fridae's slogan, which in its early years was "Asia's Gay and Lesbian Network," had become the firmer "Empowering Gay Asia."[17] By summer 2011, Fridae and S2 were parted.

The last Nation, number VI, occurred in autumn 2006. As with number V, it was held in tsunami-torn Phuket, although by then the coastal resorts had been scrubbed and repaired and the ocean's wild transformation was now hidden again if not forgotten. The dance was at the Hilton Arcadia Resort, a hotel so large that Nation-goers did not fill it entirely. They instead mingled in pools and restaurants with those who themselves seemed to represent the discourse of the triple supremacy: heterosexual families of men and women and their children.

Some might have read the move to Phuket and the end of the dance as a surrender in the face of the Singapore government's opposition. S2 had instead pointed out that, in both a real and a magical sense, the center and the periphery now overlapped. That was the news. The border between the representatives of the triple supremacy and the representations of the triple taboo was no longer as fixed. This time there were no men in dark glasses and no guards at the hotel gates checking the underbellies of cars.[18]

In the final program for the dance, S2 wrote: "Enjoy the party. We do this for the love of it, to be a part of the love, and to share the love. And really, that is all that matters."[19]

Two oppositional narratives had tensed together.

To accommodate more Thai men at the last Nation VI party, S2 had scheduled it on a long national holiday weekend in late October 2006, so that more Thais could travel from Bangkok.

Strangely, realistically, magically, the final Nation party had occurred on the holiday that each year marked Vajiravudh's accession to the throne.

Once again, queer men went streaming down the corridors of a globalized hotel. Beneath the laser lights, their voices rose and fell and their circles heaved. Within the throbbing bass sounds, the music grew in nuances of accelerandos with sudden stops and fresh bursts.

The final *kecak* of S2's Nation filled those early morning hours of October 23, when so many decades earlier Chulalongkorn had passed and Vajiravudh had been summoned from his homeland at Saranrom Palace.

Ironically, the holiday did not actually honor Vajiravudh, the prince in paradox. It was instead known as *Wan Piya Maharat,* the day for honoring the king who had died, the one who had maintained the greatest Inner City known to Southeast Asia.

Chulalongkorn.

Notes

Prelude

1. Walter Spies to Jane Belo, July 6, 1939, Walter Spies Archive, Oriental Collections, University of Leiden, 1.
2. Reproductions of Walter Spies' art can be accessed at various websites. Among the most comprehensive is a site that at the time of the research for this book was maintained by Geff Green, a principal lecturer in Communication at Sheffield Hallam University in the United Kingdom, http://homepages.shu.ac.uk/~scsgcg/spies/
3. Walter Spies to his mother, Cardiff, August 23, 1923, Walter Spies Archives at the Oriental Collections section of the University of Leiden, Netherlands; also in Hans Rhodius, *Schönheit und Reichtum Des Lebens: Walter Spies (Maler und Musiker auf Bali 1895-1942* (The Hague: L.J.C. Boucher, 1965), 134. Translation by Malcolm Carr.
4. Walter Spies to Jane Belo, July 6, 1939, Walter Spies Archive, Oriental Collections, University of Leiden, 1.
5. ——, July 6, 1939, 2-3.
6. ——, July 6, 1939, 4-5.
7. ——, July 6, 1939, 5.
8. ——, July 6, 1939, 6.
9. ——, July 6, 1939, 6.

Chapter 1

1. Background information from Walter Vella, *Chaiyo! King Vajiravudh and the Development of Thai Nationalism* (Honolulu: University of Hawaii Press, 1978), 1.
2. Tamara Loos, "Sex in the Inner City: The Fidelity between Sex and Politics in Siam," *The Journal of Asian Studies;* November 2005, 64:4, 883.
3. ——, *Subject Siam: Family, Law, and Colonial Modernity in Thailand* (Bangkok, Silkworm Books, 2002), 113.
4. ——, 2002, 115.
5. Vella, 1978, 8.
6. Loos, 2005, 883.
7. Vella, 4; Loos, 2002, 116.

8. Stephen Greene, *Absolute Dreams: Thai Government under Rama VI, 1910-1925* (Bangkok: White Lotus, 1999), 2.
9. *Vanity Fair* article quoted in Greene, iv.
10. Knowlton Mixer, "Rama Prepared Siam For Democratic Rule," *New York Times*, December 6, 1925, 26.
11. For a recent English edition, see Richard von Krafft-Ebing, *Psychopathia Sexualis* (New York: Arcade Publishing, 1998, trans. 12th German ed.).
12. For an English edition, see Max Nordau, *Degeneration* (New York: D. Appleton & Company, 1895), vii–viii. For a discussion of how widely Nordau's theory became distributed during the Wilde trial, see Peter Boag, *Same-Sex Affairs: Constructing and Controlling Homosexuality in the Pacific Northwest* (Berkeley: University of California Press, 2003), 128–33.
13. I was unable to find any specific English-language references that Vajiravudh might have noticed the Wilde trial. However, there might be some references in his Siamese letters or essays. This could be an area of future historical work.
14. Attributed to Sir Henry Norman, *Peoples and Politics of the Far East* (London: T. Fisher Unwin, 1895, 434, republished by Elibron Classics Series, Adamant Media Corporation, 2005) in "Chowfa Maha Vajiravudh, the New King of Siam," *New York Times*, Nov. 6, 1910, C3.
15. "Chowfa Maha Vajiravudh, the New King of Siam," C3.
16. Loos, 2005, 4.
17. John Girling, *Thailand: Society and Politics* (Ithaca: Cornell University Press, 1981), 22.
18. See, for example, the translation in Joe Cummings, Sandra Bao, Steven Martin, and China Williams, *Lonely Planet: Thailand* (Melbourne: August 2003, 10th ed.), 141.
19. Loos, 2002, 2.
20. For an overview of the Chakri situation, see Loos, 2002, 1–28; and Peter Jackson, "Performative Genders, Perverse Desires: A Bio-History of Thailand's Same Sex and Transgender Cultures," *Intersections: Gender, History and Culture in the Asian Context*, Issue 9, August 2003, 8–10, published online at: http://wwwsshe.murdoch.edu.au/intersections/issue9/jackson.html.
21. Winichakul Thongchai, "The Quest for 'Siwilai': A Geographical Discourse of Civilization Thinking in Late Nineteenth and Twentieth Century Siam," *Journal of Asian Studies*, 59(3): 528–49. Also Rachel Harrison and Peter Jackson, eds., *The Ambiguous Allure of the West: Traces of the Colonial in Thailand* (Hong Kong: Hong Kong University Press, 2010), 17.
22. Harrison and Jackson, 26. Originally quoted in Benjamin Batson, *The End of Absolute Monarchy in Siam* (Singapore: Oxford University Press, 1984), 14.
23. Edmund Roberts, *Embassy to the Eastern Courts of Cochin-China, Siam and Muscat in the U.S. Sloop-of-War Peacock, David Geisingger, Commander, During the Years 1832-34* (Wilmington, DE: Scholarly Resources, Inc [1837, Harper and Bros., New York], 1972), 248, quoted in Jackson, 12.
24. Anna Leonowens, *The English Governess at the Siamese Court: Being Recollections of Six Years in the Royal Palace at Bangkok* (Singapore: Oxford University Press, [1870], 1989), 94, quoted in Jackson, 12. For details of Anna's identity invention, see Susan Morgan, *Bombay Anna: The Real Story and Remarkable Adventures of the "King and I" Governess* (Berkeley: University of California Press, 2008), esp. Ch. 6.

25. Accounts quoted in Jackson, 19.
26. From Count C. deForbin, *Memoires* (Amsterdam: Girardi, 1729) quoted in Jackson, 10.
27. George Bacon, *Siam, The Land of the White Elephant as It Is and Was* (New York: Charles Scribner's & Sons, [1881], 1892), 239–40, quoted in Jackson, 9–10.
28. Jackson, 21.
29. Quoted in Franck Proschan, "Eunuch Mandarins, *Soldats Mamzells*, Effeminate *Boys*, and Graceless Women: French Colonial Constructions of Vietnamese Genders," *GLQ: A Journal of Gay and Lesbian Studies*, 8:4, 2002, 439–40.
30. Ann Laura Stoler, *Carnal Knowledge and Imperial Power: Race and the Intimate in Colonial Rule* (Berkeley: University of California Press, 2002), 46. Stoler adds, "Who bedded and wedded whom in the colonies of France, England, Holland, and Iberia was never left to chance." (47)
31. I have adopted the term "polygyny" here, following the practice of historian Tamara Loos (2002). She explains that the better-known word "polygamy" refers to a system in which either a man or a woman could have two or more spouses, whereas "polygyny" is limited solely to men having more than one wife, a system that more accurately describes the practice in Siam.
32. Craig Reynolds, "A Nineteenth-Century Buddhist Defense of Polygamy and Some Remarks on the Social History of Women in Thailand," paper prepared for the Seventh Conference of the International Association of Historians of Asia, Bangkok, August 22–26, 1977, 16, quoted in Leslie Ann Jeffrey, *Sex and Borders: Gender, National Identity and Prostitution Policy in Thailand* (Honolulu: University of Hawaii Press, 2002), 6–7.
33. Abbot Low Moffat, *Mongkut, King of Siam* (Ithaca: Cornell University Press, 1961), 135, cited in Jeffrey, 7.
34. Ronald Spector, "The American Image of Southeast Asia, 1790–1865," *Journal of Southeast Asia Studies*, (3:2, September 1972, 301, cited in Jeffrey, 7.
35. Loos, 2005, 883.
36. Quoted in Jeffrey, 6–7.
37. Jackson, 21–2 . See also Harrison and Jackson, 18.
38. Tanaprasitpatana Suwadee, "Thai Society's Expectations of Women, 1851–1935," Ph.D. dissertation, Sydney University, 1989, cited in Scot Barmé, *Woman, Man, Bangkok: Love, Sex and Popular Culture in Thailand* (Bangkok: Silkworm Books, 2002), 22.
39. Jeffrey, 6–8.
40. For an overview of the history of romance, see, for example, Jamake Highwater, *Myth and Sexuality*, (New York: Penguin Books, 1991), 127–48.
41. For a review of the development of the word "heterosexual" and the character creation in mass media, see, for example, Jonathan Katz, *The Invention of Heterosexuality* (New York: Penguin Books, 1995), especially 19–32 and 83–112.
42. See, for example, the discussion of colonialism and race in Ann Stoler, *Race and the Education of Desire,* (Durham, NC: Duke University Press, 1995), Chapter 2, especially, p. 32, for a discussion of degeneracy.
43. Loos, Chapter 4 especially.
44. Vella, 10.

45. Source of the painting uncertain, reprinted in Greene, iii. For a discussion of the use of "shoe size" to indicate male phallic size, see Chapter 17.
46. Photographs of Vajiravudh and Chulalongkorn during the tour, as well as during other periods of their life, can be accessed at the Wikimedia Commons website. See "Chulalongkorn and Princes," http://commons.wikimedia.org/wiki/File:Chulalongkorn_and_Princes.jpg
47. For a summary of Chulalongkorn's and Vajiravudh's focus on *siwilai* and the accompanying royal challenges, see, for example, Harrison and Jackson, 66–7, 194–7, 200–1.

Chapter 2

1. Peter Gay, *Weimar Culture: The Outsider as Insider* (New York: W.W. Norton & Company, 1968), 153–4.
2. Walter Spies to Frau Jaenichen-Woermann, Berlin, July 1923. Walter Spies's original letters are available in the Walter Spies Archives at the Oriental Collections section of the University of Leiden, Netherlands. Most are also published in Hans Rhodius, *Schönheit und Reichtum Des Lebens: Walter Spies (Maler und Musiker auf Bali 1895–1942)* (The Hague: L.J.C. Boucher, 1965), 127–31. Trans. M. Carr.
3. ——; also in Rhodius, 127–31. Trans. M. Carr.
4. Daisy Spies, "Memories," in Rhodius, 54. Trans. J. Dorion.
5. Leo Spies, "My Brother Walja," in Rhodius, 57. Trans. J. Dorion.
6. Walter Spies to Frau Jaenichen-Woermann. Also in Rhodius, 127–31. Trans. M. Carr.
7. Walter Spies to his mother, Cardiff, September 1923. Also in Rhodius, 136–7. Trans. M. Carr.
8. ——, August 23, 1923. Also in Rhodius, 134. Trans. M. Carr.
9. ——, Hamburg, August 23, 1923. Also in Rhodius, 134–5. Trans. M. Carr.
10. ——, Cardiff, September 1923. Also in Rhodius, 1965, 136–7. Trans. M. Carr.
11. Heinrich Hauser to Daisy Spies, Cheribon, October 28, 1923. In Rhodius, 1965, 139. Original trans. M. Carr.
12. Walter Spies to Heinrich Hauser, Bandung, October 1923. Also in Rhodius, 145. Original trans. M. Carr.
13. ——, 145.
14. ——, 145.
15. Walter Spies to his mother, Bandung, November 1, 1923. Also in Rhodius, 147. Original trans. M. Carr.
16. Reproductions of Walter Spies's art can be accessed at various websites. Among the most comprehensive is a site that at the time of research is maintained by Geff Green, a principal lecturer in Communication at Sheffield Hallam University in the United Kingdom, http://homepages.shu.ac.uk/~scsgcg/spies/
17. Ira Spies, "Memories," trans. from Hans Rhodius, *Walter Spies: Schönheit und Reichtum Des Lebens (The Beauty and Wealth of Life)*. (The Hague: L.J.C. Boucher, 1965), 51. Original trans. J. Dorian.
18. Daisy Spies, "Memories," trans. from Rhodius, 52–4.
19. Harold Schonberg, *The Lives of the Great Composers* (New York: W.W. Norton & Company, 1970), 497–8.

20. Quoted in Faubian Bowers, *Scriabin: A Biography* (Toronto: Dover Publications, Inc., 1996), 319.

21. M.D. Calvocoressi and Gerald Abraham, *Masters of Russian Music* (New York: Tudor Publishing Company, 1944), 453. The story is also told in Bowers, 114.

22. Schonberg, 500.

23. ——, 500.

24. Simone Wesner, Michael Hitchcock, and I Nyoman Darma Putra, "Walter Spies and Dresden: The Early Formative Years of Bali's Renowned Artist, Author and Tourism Icon," *Indonesia and the Malay World*, 35:102, July 2007, 216.

25. Schonberg, 504.

26. ——, 509.

27. ——, 500.

28. Leo Spies. In Rhodius, 57. Trans. J. Dorian.

29. Hans Rhodius and John Darling, *Walter Spies and Balinese Art*. Edited by John Stowell (Amsterdam: Tropical Museum, 1980), 11.

30. Leo Spies. Trans. from Rhodius, 1965, 57. Original trans. J. Dorian.

31. Wesner, Hitchcock, and Putra, 218.

32. George L. Mosse, *The Image of Man: The Creation of Modern Masculinity* (New York: Oxford University Press, 1996), 3–16.

33. Rictor Norton, "Johann Joachim Winckelmann," *The Great Queens of History*, December 30, 2000. http://www.infopt.demon.co.uk/winckelm.htm. On Winckelmann generally, see Denis M. Sweet, "The Personal, the Political and the Aesthetic: Johann Joachim Winckelmann's German Enlightenment Life," in Kent Gerard, Gert Hekman, eds., *The Pursuit of Sodomy: Male Homosexuality in Renaissance and Enlightenment Europe* (New York: Harrington Park Press, 1989), 147–62.

34. For an extensive historical discussion of Winckelmann, see Mosse, 1996, especially Chapter 2. This quotation is from page 29. An extended analysis of Winckelmann's importance in the aesthetic theory can be found in Whitney Davis, *Queer Beauty: Sexuality and Aesthetics from Winckelmann to Freud and Beyond* (New York: Columbia University Press, 2010), especially the Introduction and Chapter 1.

35. Mosse, 34.

36. ——, 44.

37. Josef Chytry, *The Aesthetic State: A Quest in Modern German Thought* (Berkeley: University of California Press, 1989), 17.

38. Mosse, 34.

39. For an overview, see Rhodius and Darling. Letters from Leon Spies to the American counsel in Moscow, pleading for intervention and help, can be found in the Walter Spies Archives, Oriental Collections, Leiden University, Microfilm A1080. Historical background on the Spies family – with the assertion that the family might be considered Russian rather than German – can be found in blog postings by Mikhail Tsyganov, "Walter Spies: A Russian or A 'Russian-Born,'" http://mikejkt.livejournal.com/10095.html

40. Daisy Spies, "Memories," trans. from Rhodius, 52–4. Original trans. J. Dorian.

41. Walter Spies to his father, Sterlitamak, April 2, 1916, Walter Spies Archives. Also Rhodius, 65–6. Original trans. J. Dorian.

42. Walter Spies to his mother, Sterlitamak, July 10, 1916 ; also in Rhodius, 67. Original trans. J. Dorian.

43. ——, April 23, 1917. Also in Rhodius, 71. Original trans. J. Dorian.

44. ——, September 2, 1917. Also in Rhodius, 72. Original trans. J. Dorian.

45. Zverev's homosexuality is referenced in Schonberg, 497–8. An overview of gay culture in late imperial Russia can be had from Daniel D. Healey, "Russia," and Douglas B. Turnbaugh, "Vaslav Nijinsky," *Encyclopedia of Gay, Lesbian, Bisexual, Transgender and Queer Culture,* http://www.glbtq.com/

46. Rhodius and Darling, 11.

47. For a reference to the belief that Spies first practiced his homosexuality during his internment, see note from Jane Belo, May 5, 1958, referenced in materials held in the Walter Spies Archives, Microfilm A1019. Originals in Margaret Mead Papers, Library of Congress.

48. Quoted in Rhodius, 33.

49. Rhodius and Darling, 13.

50. Walter Spies to his father, Dresden, May 5, 1919. Also in Rhodius, 81. Author's translation.

51. ——, 81.

52. ——, 81.

53. Rhodius and Darling, 21.

54. Walter Spies to "Everybody," December 18, 1923. Also in Rhodius, 165–9. Trans. M. Carr.

55. ——, 165–9.

56. ——, 165–9.

57. ——, 165–9.

58. Walter Spies to Hans Jürgen von der Wense, Walter Spies Archives. Also in Rhodius, 184–6. Trans. M. Carr.

59. Quoted in Rhodius and Darling, 21.

60. Walter Spies to his mother, Bandung, November 1, 1923. Also in Rhodius, 147. Original trans. M. Carr.

61. Mosse, 32.

Chapter 3

1. "Siamese Prince's visit," *New York Times,* September 28, 1902, 4.

2. The detail about the ship choice comes from "Visit of the Crown Prince of Siam," *New York Times,* October 10, 1902, 1. Information about the ship comes from *The Ship's List,* http://www.theshipslist.com/ships/descriptions/ShipsF.html

3. "Visit of the Crown Prince of Siam."

4. ——.

5. "Siamese Prince at Cramps," *New York Times,* October 19, 1902, 1.

6. Walter Vella, *Chaiyo! King Vajiravudh and the Development of Thai Nationalism* (Honolulu: University of Hawaii Press, 1978), 8.

7. Malcolm Smith, *A Physician at the Court of Siam* (London: Country Life Limited, 1946), 111–2.

8. Tamara Loos, "Sex in the Inner City: The Fidelity between Sex and Politics in Siam," *The Journal of Asian Studies;* November 2005, 64:4, 895–6.

9.   ——, 895. Loos also notes, "In other words, licit and illicit forms of sex and sexuality in Siam were not mapped isomorphically onto heterosexual and homosexual practices. This stands in contrast to most contemporaneous Western sex and gender regimes that defined categorically same-sex erotic practice as immoral crimes." 882–3.

10. For a brief history and architectural photographs of Saranrom today, see the Thailand Ministry of Foreign Affairs site, http://www.mfa.go.th/web/2215.php

11. For background on Henry Alabaster, see, for example, an article written by Derick Garnier, "Henry Alabaster," accessible at http://www.anglicanthai.org/alabaster. htm ; The Alabaster Society site, http://www.alabaster.org.uk/index.htm. Basic information about Saranrom Park is available at the Thailand Department of Environment Public Parks site on Saranrom, http://203.155.220.217/office/ppdd/publicpark/english/mainpark/E_Saranrom.html

12. The list of organizations Vajiravudh joined comes from Stephen Greene, *Absolute Dreams: Thai Government under Rama VI, 1910–1925* (Bangkok: White Lotus, 1999), 3. Further information on the clubs themselves comes from a "List of London's Gentlemen's Clubs" assembled on Wikipedia, http://en.wikipedia.org/wiki/List_of_London's_gentlemen's_clubs. For another introduction to London's male clubs, see http://www.bluffton.edu/~sullivanm/england/london/clubsintro/intro.html

13. Greene, 4–6.

14. Scot Barmé, *Woman, Man, Bangkok: Love, Sex and Popular Culture in Thailand* (Bangkok: Silkworm Books, 2002), 112–3.

15. Greene, 4–6, and Vella, 6.

16. Greene, 6.

17. George Mosse, *The Image of Man* (New York: Oxford University Press, 1996), 46.

18. Greene, 18.

19. ——, 76.

20. From British Foreign Office archives, quoted in Greene, 78.

21. Greene, 77. Greene spells Rarn Rakkhop's name with two "K's."

22. ——, 87.

23. Vella, 161.

24. Quoted in Vella, 163. A slightly different translation of the royal policy for the Royal Pages College can be found at the Vajiravudh College site on Wikipedia, http://en.wikipedia.org/wiki/Vajiravudh_College

25. Loos, 902.

26. ——, 900–1.

27. See, for example, a history of "Siam, Cambodia and Laos, 1800–1950," posted at the time of research for this book by Sanderson Beck, http://www.san.beck.org/20-9-Siam,Laos,Cambodia1800-1950.html. A similar entry at a website for those working in global economies, EconomicExpert.com, speculated about a connection between Vajiravudh's enjoyment of late night work with "good looking young men," http://www.economicexpert.com/a/Vajiravudh.html

28. Loos, 900.

29. Marcus Virginius and Carlton H. Terris (pseudo.), "Lord Vermont V.C.," in *Three More Early Plays: King Vajiravudh's Centennial Series: Plays in English, Vol. II* (Bangkok: Thai Watana Panich Press Co., Ltd., 1979), unpaginated.

30. ———.
31. ———.
32. Dilton Marsh (pseudo.) "A Turn of Fortune's Wheel," in *Three Early Plays: King Vajiravudh's Centennial Series: Plays in English, Vol. I* (Bangkok: Thai Watana Panich Press Co., Ltd, 1979), unpaginated.
33. ———.
34. R.W. Connell, "Globalization, Imperialism, and Masculinities," in Michael Kimmel, Jeff Hearn, and R.W. Connell, eds., *Handbook of Studies on Men & Masculinities* (Thousand Oaks, CA: Sage Publications, 2005), 79.
35. Barmé, 52.

Chapter 4

1. All quotations from Journal of Hans Jürgen von der Wense, excerpted in Hans Rhodius, *Schönheit und Reichtum Des Lebens: Walter Spies (Maler und Musiker auf Bali 1895–1942)* (The Hague: L.J.C. Boucher, 1965), 85–90. Original trans. M. Carr.
2. See reference to comments by Hansheinz Stückenschmidt in 1922, in the notes to Steffan Schleiermacher, *Hommage à Walter Spies* (Musikproduktion Dabringhaus und Grimm MDG 613 1171–2, 2003), 6.
3. For more information on Hellerau, see Simone Wesner, Michael Hitchcock, and I Nyoman Darma Putra, "Walter Spies and Dresden: The Early Formative Years of Bali's Renowned Artist, Author and Tourism Icon," *Indonesia and the Malay World*, 35:102, July 2007, 218–20, 224–7.
4. Hans Rhodius and John Darling, *Walter Spies and Balinese Art*. Edited by John Stowell (Amsterdam: Tropical Museum, 1980), 15.
5. Journal of Hans Jürgen von der Wense, June 20, 1919, 86.
6. For an overview of artistic imagery and the Weimar Republic, see Peter Gay, *Weimar Culture: The Outsider as Insider* (New York: W.W. Norton & Company, 1968, 2001.), vi.
7. Journal of Hans Jürgen von der Wense, June 20, 1919, 86.
8. ———, July 1, 1919, 87.
9. ———, July 2, 1919, 87.
10. ———, July 4 and July 7, 1919, 87.
11. ———, October 1–3, 1919, 88.
12. ———, October 3, 1919, 88.
13. ———, October 3, 1919, 88.
14. ———, October 3, 1919, 88.
15. ———, October 5, 1919, 88.
16. ———, October 9, 1919, 88.
17. ———, October 13, 1919, 88.
18. ———, October 14, 1919, 88.
19. Reproductions of Walter Spies's art can be accessed at various websites. Among the most comprehensive is a site that at the time of research is maintained by Geff Green, a principal lecturer in Communication at Sheffield Hallam University in the United Kingdom, http://homepages.shu.ac.uk/~scsgcg/spies/

20. Rhodius and Darling, 17.
21. Rhodius, 85. Original trans. M. Carr.
22. ——, 85.
23. Wesner, Hitchcock, and Putra, 220–4.
24. Gay, 103–5.
25. Gay, 105. For the scores that accompanied the movie, see Julie Hubbert, "Modernism at the Movies: The Cabinet of Dr. Caligari and a Film Score Revisited," *The Musical Quarterly*, Spring 2005 88:1, 63–94. Also Robert Wiene, director, *The Cabinet of Dr. Caligari*. Original: Germany, 1920. Chatsworth, CA: Image Entertainment, DVD.
26. Richard Oswald and Magnus Hirschfeld, *Different from the Others*. Original: Germany, 1919. New York: Kino International Corp., 2004, DVD. For a brief summary of *Different from the Others*, see Craig Kaczorowski, "European Film," Encyclopedia of Gay, Lesbian, Bisexual, Transgender and Queer Culture, http://www.glbtq.com/arts/eur_film,9.html. For a discussion of the Reich Moving Picture Law, under which the film was banned except for viewing by clinicians, see Laura Bezerra, "Peculiarities of the Reich Moving Picture Law," Deutsches Filminstitut, *Censorship Regulations in the Republic of Weimar*, at the time of research at http://www.deutsches-filminstitut.de/collate/collate_sp/se/se_03a03.html. Also see excerpt from Helga Belach and Wolfang Jacobsen, "Anders Als Die Andern (1919): Dokumente zu einer Kontroverse: *Cinegraph*, at the time of research at http://www.cinegraph.de/cgbuch/b2/b2_03.html
27. For biographical information on Murnau, see, for example, Lotte Eisner, *Murnau* (Paris: Le Terrain Vague, 1964; English translation: Berkeley: University of California Press, 1973), especially 13–27.
28. For a brief review of Spies's relationship with Murnau, see Rhodius and Darling, 15–9.
29. The similarity caused legal problems with Stoker's estate. A version of the film, using Stoker's names (Count Dracula) rather than Murnau's names (Count Orlock) can be accessed at the Internet Archive, http://www.archive.org/details/nosferatu
30. Thomas Elsaesser, "Six Degrees of Nosferatu," *Sight and Sound*, February 2001, http://www.bfi.org.uk/sightandsound/feature/92.
31. ——.
32. See, for example, http://homepages.shu.ac.uk/~scsgcg/spies/
33. Gay, 153.
34. Georgette Schoonderbeek-Vreedenberg, "Memoir," in Rhodius, 120–2. Trans. M. Carr.
35. ——, 122.
36. Rhodius and Darling, 17.
37. Schoonderbeek-Vreedenberg, 123.
38. Walter Spies to Mrs. Jaenichen-Woermann, July 1923, Walter Spies Archives, Oriental Collections, Leiden University. In Rhodius, 127–31. Trans. M. Carr.
39. Rhodius and Darling, 19.
40. Schoonderbeek-Vreedenberg, 122.
41. Walter Spies to his mother, Cardiff, September 1923. Walter Spies Archives. Also in Rhodius, 136. Original trans. M. Carr.

Chapter 5

1. Photographs of Chulalongkorn and Vajiravudh can be accessed via the Wikimedia Commons website. See especially "King Chulalongkorn of Siam," http://commons.wikimedia.org/wiki/File:King_Chulalongkorn_of_Siam. jpg and "King Vajiravudh portrait," http://commons.wikimedia.org/wiki/ File:King_Vajiravudh_portrait_photograph.jpg and "Chulalongkorn with Queen Saovabha and Crown Prince Vajiravudh," http://commons.wikimedia.org/wiki/ Chulalongkorn

2. Quoted in Scot Barmé, *Luang Witchit Wathakan and the Creation of a Thai Identity* (Singapore: Institute of Southeast Asian Studies, 1993), n. 35–6.

3. For a discussion of two different theories of hybridity and their application in the Siamese/Thai context, see Rachel Harrison and Peter Jackson, eds., *The Ambiguous Allure of the West: Traces of the Colonial in Thailand* (Hong Kong University Press, 2010), 189–205.

4. "Nationalism" is a problematic word. For a good review of "official" nationalism as practiced by Chulalongkorn and Vajiravudh versus "popular" nationalism, see Barmé, 5–8.

5. Tamara Loos notes, "'Homosexuality,' whether associated with the monarch or *caocom* [referring in Thai to a woman or women], reflects an understanding of sexual desire based on a heterosexual-homosexual binary that does not encapsulate Siam's historical organization of sexual desire. The gender and sexual system dominant in nineteenth-century Siam regulated sexual behavior on the basis of social status *and* gender rather than categorically on sexual object choice. The social status (rather than the gender or sex) of the parties involved was crucial in determining whether sexual intercourse was illicit or licit." Tamara Loos, "Sex in the Inner City: The Fidelity between Sex and Politics in Siam," *The Journal of Asian Studies*, November 2005, 64:4, 906.

6. Quoted in Barmé, 21.

7. Barmé, 22.

8. Quoted in Barmé, 29.

9. Quoted in Walter Vella, *Chaiyo! King Vajiravudh and the Development of Thai Nationalism* (Honolulu: University of Hawaii, 1978), 159.

10. For a review of the various ways Vajiravudh attempted to follow Western models, see Vella, Chapter 6.

11. Vella, 129–33.

12. "Visit of the Crown Prince of Siam," *New York Times*, October 10, 1902, 1.

13. George Mosse, *The Image of Man* (New York: Oxford University Press, 1996), 46.

14. Vella, 144–51.

15. Norman C. McLeod, "Sports and Scout Work Making Siam New Nation," *New York Times*, February 17, 1924, XX18.

16. Vella, 140.

17. ——, 143.

18. For a fuller discussion, see Loos, 900.

19. Scot Barmé, *Woman, Man, Bangkok: Love, Sex and Popular Culture in Thailand* (Bangkok: Silkworm Books, 2002), 160.

20. ——, 160.

21. ——, 160.
22. Vella, 156.
23. Loos, 903.
24. Great Britain, Foreign Office, Dispatches from Siam, F.). 371/2462, March 6, 1912, quoted in Barmé, 1993, 36.
25. British Foreign Office archive, from Stephen Greene, *Absolute Dreams: Thai Government under Rama VI, 1910–1925* (Bangkok: White Lotus, 1999), 78, 163.
26. Barmé, 2002, 112–7. Also see Harrison and Jackson, 200–1.
27. Barmé, 2002, 116.
28. Stephen Greene examines Dusit Thani's role as a possible model for administrative reform but does not examine it as an activity intended to promote male social relationships among the king's friends. Greene, 120–3.
29. ——, 123.
30. ——, 123.
31. Vella, 154.
32. Greene, 132.
33. *Bangkok Times,* March 21, 1925, quoted in Greene, 132.
34. Vella, 157–8.
35. *Bangkok Times,* August 22, 1922, quoted in Greene, 133.
36. For descriptions, see Usnisa Sukhsvasti, "A royal love story," *The Bangkok Post,* June 6, 2005, 1; and Carol Lutfy, "The Country Homes of Thai Kings," *The New York Times,* January 28, 1996, XX, 16.
37. His Majesty King Vajiravudh, "P'ra Ruang: drama in verse," trans. H.H. Prince Purachatra (Bangkok: Pigkanes Press, 1979), Act I, Scene I, 1.
38. Story told in Sukhsvasti, 1. Attributed to Thanpuying Putrie Viravaidya, deputy principal private secretary to His Majesty the King.
39. "Siamese Simplicity," *The Harvard Crimson,* November 9, 1925. Accessed at http://www.thecrimson.com/article/1925/11/9/siamese-simplicity-psiam-whose-king-translates/
40. Sukhsvasti, 1.
41. Barmé, 1993, 36.
42. ——, 2002, 117–8.
43. British Foreign Office archive, quoted in Greene, 133.
44. The white uniform in the portrait, and the pose of the king, is similar to that which can be found at the Wikimedia Commons website, "King Vajiravudh portrait," http://commons.wikimedia.org/wiki/File:King_Vajiravudh_portrait_photograph.jpg
45. Author's interview with Khun Toc, August 2007.

Chapter 6

1. Walter Spies to "a friend," from Kintamani, April 16, 1925, Walter Spies Archives, Oriental Collections, University of Leiden. Also in Hans Rhodius, *Schönheit und Reichtum Des Lebens: Walter Spies (Maler und Musiker auf Bali 1895–1942)* (The Hague: L.J.C. Boucher, 1965), 205. Trans. author.
2. Walter Spies and Beryl de Zoete, *Dance and Drama in Bali* (London: Faber and Faber, 1938), 70.

3. *Leyaks* are discussed in several places in the book that Spies and de Zoete would eventually author, especially 55 (note) and 87-9.
4. Walter Spies to "a friend," 205-8.
5. ———, 205-8.
6. ———, 205-8.
7. Walter Spies's letter from Yogyakarta, dated end of April 1925, Walter Spies Archives. Also in Rhodius, 209.
8. Franz Roh's original book is *Nach Expressionismus, Magischer Realismus: Probleme der neuesten Europäischen Malerei* (Berlin: Leipzig, Klinkhardt and Biermann, 1925). A translation, "Magical Realism: Post-Expressionism" is available in Lois Parkinson Zamora and Wendy B. Faris, *Magical Realism: Theory, History, Community* (Durham, NC: Duke University Press, 1995), 15-31. Quotations from 15, 17, 19, 27. See in the same volume, Irene Guenther, "Magic Realism, New Objectivity, and the Arts during the Weimar Republic," 34-73.
9. From the translation of Roh, 29.
10. ———, 28.
11. For the evolution of the term "magical realism," see Christopher Warnes, "Magical Idealism and the Legacy of German Idealism," *Modern Language Review,* April 2006, 101:2, 488-98.
12. Walter Spies to Franz Roh, September 1922, Walter Spies Archives. Also in Rhodius, 108. Trans. author.
13. Spies to Roh, June, 1926, 219. Trans. author.
14. For racial degeneracy fears, especially in the Dutch East Indies, see Ann Stoler, *Carnal Knowledge and Imperial Power: Race and the Intimate in Colonial Rule* (Berkeley: University of California Press, 2002), 66-7, 70-8.
15. Spies to Roh, September 22, 1936, 222. Trans. author.
16. See Stephen Slemon's discussion in "Magical Realism as Postcolonial Discourse," in Zamora and Faris, 407-26, especially 411.
17. Slemon. In Zamora and Faris, 409
18. Zamora and Faris, "Introduction: Daiquiri Birds and Flabertian Parrot(ies)." In Zamora and Faris, 6.
19. Spies to Roh, September 22, 1936, 222. Trans. author.
20. For "amok" in the Balinese context, see Adrian Vickers, *Bali: A Paradise Created* (Australia: Penguin Books, 1989), 15-8.
21. For early European views of Bali, see Vickers, 11-36.
23. Hugh Mabbett, revised edition, and English translation of Gregor Krause, *Bali 1912* (Singapore: Pepper Publication, revised edition 2001), 10.
24. ———, 57.
25. ———, see especially photographs on 31, 40, 49, 53, 60, 61, 67, 76.
26. ———, 10.
27. Vickers, 93.
28. See accounts quoted in Peter Jackson, "Performative Genders, Perverse Desires: A Bio-History of Thailand's Same Sex and Transgender Cultures," *Intersections: Gender,_History and Culture in the Asian Context,* Issue 9, August 2003, 9-10, online at the time of research at http://wwwsshe.murdoch.edu.au/intersections/issue9/jackson.html.

29. Adolf Hitler's speech at the 1927 Nuremburg Rally, accessed at http://www.calvin. edu/academic/cas/gpa/rpt27c.htm, originally from Alfred Rosenberg and Wilhelm Weiß, Reichsparteitag der NSDAP Nürnberg 19./21. August 1927 (Munich: Verlag Frz. Eher, 1927), 38–45.
30. Spies to his mother, September 1927, Walter Spies Archives. Also in Rhodius, 250–1. Trans. by author.
31. Aldrich, Robert, *Colonialism and Homosexuality*, (London: Routledge, 2003), 164.
32. Reproductions of Walter Spies's art can be accessed at various websites. Among the most comprehensive is a site that at the time of research is maintained by Geff Green, a principal lecturer in Communication at Sheffield Hallam University in the United Kingdom, http://homepages.shu.ac.uk/~scsgcg/spies/
33. In 2001, Christie's auctioned the sketch for almost US$50,000. Price from www. artprice.com/
34. For descriptions of the cockfights, see Magnus Hirschfeld, *Men and Women: The World Journey of a Sexologist* (New York: G.P. Putnam's Sons, 1935). 116. Also Clifford Geertz, "Deep Play: Notes on the Balinese Cockfight," Chapter 15, *The Interpretation of Cultures* (New York: Basic Books, 1973), 412–54.
35. For the role of duels in establishing European masculinity, see George Mosse, *The Image of Man* (New York: Oxford University Press, 1996), 17–23.
36. Quotations taken from Sotheby's Newsletter, September 5, 2001. Sotheby's sold the painting in 2001 for more than US$750,000.
37. See, for example, http://homepages.shu.ac.uk/~scsgcg/spies/

Chapter 7

1. Hans Rhodius and John Darling, *Walter Spies and Balinese Art*. Edited by John Stowell (Amsterdam: Tropen Museum, 1980), 35.
2. André Roosevelt, director, *Goona Goona*, original, 1932. Baker City, OR: Nostalgia Family Video, 1996, videocassette.
3. For information about *leyaks* see, for example, Walter Spies and Beryl de Zoete, *Dance and Drama in Bali* (London: Faber and Faber, 1938), especially 55 (note), and 87–9.
4. Walter Spies to "a friend," from Kintamani, April 16, 1925, Walter Spies Archives, Oriental Collections, University of Leiden. Also in Hans Rhodius, *Schönheit und Reichtum Des Lebens: Walter Spies (Maler und Musiker auf Bali 1895–1942)* (The Hague: L.J.C. Boucher, 1965), 205–8. Trans. author.
5. Spies and de Zoete, 80.
6. ——, 80.
7. This calculation of Limbak's age is based on news accounts at the time of his death in 2003, which placed his age at 106. See I Wayan Juniartha, "Bali mourns 'Kecak' maestro," *Jakarta Post*, September 7, 2003. However, a newspaper interview just a year earlier said that Limbak was 90, which would have made him about 18 at the time he began dancing the *kecak*. See Tantri Yuliandini, "Limbak, Rena: Two generations of 'kecak' dancers," *Jakarta Post*, May 18, 2002. Such confusion about Balinese ages was later to play a significant role in Spies's trial.
8. On this point, Walter was deferential. Spies and de Zoete, 83.

9. Spies and de Zoete, 80–5.

10. ——, 80–1.

11. ——, 81.

12. ——, 85.

13. ——, 85.

14. Michael Bakan, "The Abduction of the Signifying Monkey Chant: Schizophonic Transmogrifications of Balinese *Kecak* in Fellini's *Satyricon* and the Coen Brothers' *Blood Simple*," *Ethnomusicology Forum*, 18:1, June 2009, 91.

15. Claire Holt, "Walter Spies," in Rhodius, 312.

16. Adrian Vickers, *Bali: A Paradise Created* (Australia: Penguin Books, 1989), 109

17. Holt. In Rhodius, 312.

18. Rose Covarrubias, "Memory: Walter Spies," in Rhodius, 278–81.

19. Lotte H. Eisner, *Murnau* (Paris: Le Terrain Vague, 1964; English trans. Berkeley: University of California Press, 1973), 221–2.

20. Walter Spies to his mother, March 26,1931, Walter Spies Archives. Also in Rhodius, 297. Trans. author.

21. Josef Chytry, *The Aesthetic State: A Quest in Modern German Thought* (Berkeley: University of California Press, 1989), 449.

22. ——, 449, 454–5. See Chapter 12 in general for Chytry's entire argument about Spies.

23. Roelof Goris and Walter Spies, *The Island of Bali: Its Religion and Ceremonies* (Batavia: Koninklijk Paketvaart Maatschapij, 1931).

24. Walter Spies to Claire Holt, April 22, 1931, microfilm A1020.

25. Conrad Spies to Willem Stutterheim, October 26, 1931, microfilm A1020.

26. Conrad Spies to Jane Belo, January 7, 1932, microfilm A1020.

27. ——, microfilm A1019.

28. Walter Spies to Rudolf Spies, March 8, 1932, from Rhodius, 302. Trans. author.

29. ——, March 8, 1932, 300.

30. ——, March 8, 1932, 300.

31. Walter Spies to Jane Belo, March 26, 1932, microfilm A1019.

32. Walter Spies to Willem Stutterheim, March 29, 1932, microfilm A1020.

33. Willem Stutterheim to Walter Spies, April 4, 1932, microfilm A1020. Trans. M. Carr.

34. Peter Gay, *Weimar Culture: The Outsider as Insider* (New York: W.W. Norton & Company, 1968), 160.

35. Magnus Hirschfeld, *Men and Women: The World Journey of a Sexologist* (New York: G.P. Putnam's Sons, 1935), 95.

36. C.L.M. Penders, *The West New Guinea Debacle* (Honolulu: University of Hawaii Press, 2002), 57.

37. One protagonist argued: "If Java, Sumatra, etc., should be severed from the Netherlands within the foreseeable future – which God forbid! – then that does not need to be the case for New Guinea . . . Neither the Javanese, the Acehnese, nor the inhabitants of Palembang have any right to this 'empty' country. The Dutch were the first to occupy it, and have the right to use it for the population surplus of the Netherlands." From P.E. Winkler, *Nederlandsch Nieuw Guinea: een nieuw stamland voor oons volk* (Amsterdam: 1936), quoted in Penders, 57–8.

38. Pieter Koenders, *Tussen Christelijk Reveil En Seksuele Revolutie: Bestrijding van zedeloosheid in Nederland, met nadruk op de repressie van homoseksualiteit* (Amsterdam: International Institute of Social Studies, 1996), 309. Koenders's discussion of the "morals scandal" expands upon a details from Gosse Kerkhof, "Het Indische Zedenschandaal, een koloniaal incident" (Doctoral thesis, University of Amsterdam, 1982), which can be found at the International Gay/Lesbian Information Center and Archive (formerly Homodok) in Amsterdam. Koenders's and Kerkhof's work has been partially summarized in English in Robert Aldrich, *Colonialism and Homosexuality* (New York: Routledge, 2003).

Chapter 8

1. Adrian Vickers, *Bali: A Paradise Created* (Australia: Penguin Books, 1989), 86–8.
2. Interview with A.A.M. Djelantik by Dennis Raymond, December, 2003. Djelantik helped establish the Walter Spies Foundation in Bali. A memorial to him written by Horst Jordt of the German Walter Spies Society, is at the time of research at http://news.ubud.com/2007/09/in-memoriam-dr-aa-mad-djelantik.html
3. Magnus Hirschfeld, *Men and Women: The World Journey of a Sexologist* (New York: G.P. Putnam's Sons, 1935), 115–9.
4. Vickers, 145.
5. An overview of the Augustinian and tragic romance ideas can be found in Jamake Highwater, *Myth and Sexuality* (New York: Penguin Books, 1991), Chapters 5 and 6.
6. On Java, a Dutch psychiatrist noted what had happened when two teenage males unskilled in sexual exploration, Ali and Hassan, had fallen in love. Importantly, the fact that they were two males in an erotic friendship seemed to make no difference whatsoever to their village.

> They live together, sleep together on a baleh-baleh, share each other's lives. Ali is focused on Hassan with all his being, but Hassan . . . is [also] in love with a young widow from a neighboring *desa* [village] and wants to marry her. They talk about this together and among all three, and it seems that Ali can resign himself to this. But one night, as Hassan lies sleeping next to Ali, the jealousy flares up and in a sort of wild rage he cuts Hassan's penis off at the root with a piso blati [a sharp knife] and does the same to himself immediately after . . .
>
> The deed was regarded as a crime of passion, and the fact this had occurred between men played no role in the commentary. Justice was satisfied, since the perpetrator had carried out the retribution on himself. Ali's reaction was labeled with the term *imata gelap,* a frenzied state that had erupted into violence.

From Dr. P.M. van Wulfften Palthe, "Zedenlicten in het Oosten," *Psychiatrisch Juridisch Gezelschap,* May 19, 1951, quoted in Gosse Kerkhof, *Het Indische Zedenschandaal: Een Kolonial Incident* (Ph.D. thesis, University of Amsterdam, 1982), 23. Trans. M. Carr.

7. Gregory Bateson, "Bali: The Value System of a Steady State," original in 1949, reprinted in *Steps to an Ecology of the Mind* (Chicago: University of Chicago Press, 2000), 113.

8. Hirschfeld, 115–9.
9. Walter Spies and Beryl de Zoete, *Dance and Drama in Bali* (London: Faber and Faber, 1938), 33.
10. Noted in a description of a late-nineteenth-century Balinese painting, Vickers, illustration 7.
11. On the management of racial intimacy as a matter of state politics, see Ann Stoler, *Carnal Knowledge and Imperial Power: Race and the Intimate in Colonial Rule* (Berkeley: University of California Press, 2002), especially Chapter 3, "Carnal Knowledge and Imperial Power: Gender and Morality in the Making of Race."
12. Timothy Lindsey, *The Romance of K'Tut Tantri and Indonesia: Text and Scripts, History and Identity* (Kuala Lumpur: Oxford University Press, 1997), 32.
13. Vickers, 144, image no. 25, 148–9. Vickers includes a note that Margaret Mead believed Lempad's explicit drawings of male-male sex reflected his own fantasies rather than European tastes. In her field notes, she commented that none of his drawings made "the kind of point the special European pervert would think up to suggest." From Mead-Bateson field notes, Ubud, Feb. 8, 1938, Bangli, Feb. 21, 1938, Library of Congress.
14. H.T. Damste, "Balische Splinters – Zending," *Koloniaal Tijdschrift* 13 (1924): 538, cited in Geoffrey Robinson, *The Dark Side of Paradise: Political Violence in Bali*, (Ithaca: Cornell University Press, 1995), 41.
15. Robinson, 41.
16. Han Rhodius and John Darling, *Walter Spies and Balinese Art.* Edited by John Stowell (Amsterdam: Tropen Museum, 1980), 39.
17. Reproductions of Walter Spies's art can be accessed at various websites. Among the most comprehensive is a site that at the time of research is maintained by Geff Green, a principal lecturer in Communication at Sheffield Hallam University in the UK, http://homepages.shu.ac.uk/~scsgcg/spies/
18. Rhodius and Darling, 43.
19. The summary of the Ries affair and the subsequent *Zedenschaandal* in the Dutch East Indies relies on translations from Pieter Koenders, *Tussen Christelijk Reveil En Seksuele Revolutie: Bestrijding van zedeloosheid in Nederland, met nadruk op de repressie van homoseksualiteit* (Amsterdam: International Institute of Social Studies, 1996), Chapter 4, in particular, 227–323; and Gosse Kerkhof, "Het Indische Zedenschandaal, een koloniaal incident" (Ph.D. thesis, University of Amsterdam, 1982), 32–8, which can be found at the International Gay/Lesbian Information Center and Archive (formerly Homodok) in Amsterdam. Koenders's and Kerkhof's work has been partially summarized in English in Robert Aldrich, *Colonialism and Homosexuality* (New York: Routledge, 2003), 198–200.
20. For the Ries affair, see Koenders, 295–302. Also, Paul Snijders, "Ries, Leopold Abraham," in Robert Aldrich and Gary Wotherspoon, eds., *Who's Who in Gay and Lesbian History, from Antiquity to WWII* (Routledge, London, 2001), 371–2.
21. Koenders, 307–8.
22. Miguel Covarrubias, *Island of Bali* (New York: Alfred A. Knopf, 1937), xxii.
23. Walter Spies to Miguel and Rose Covarrubias, April 1938. In Hans Rhodius, *Schönheit und Reichtum Des Lebens: Walter Spies (Maler und Musiker auf Bali 1895–1942)* (The Hague: L.J.C. Boucher, 1965), 371.

24. Vicki Baum, *A Tale From Bali* (Singapore: Periplus Editions (HK) Ltd. Paperback edition 1999; original 1937), 7–8, 10.
25. Walter Spies to his mother, May 1938, the Walter Spies Archives, Oriental Collections at the University of Leiden. Also in Rhodius, 372–3.
26. Walter Spies to Willem Stutterheim, June 10, 1938, microfilm A1020, Walter Spies Archives, Oriental Collections, Leiden University. The English translation is contained on the microfilm but the translator is not indicated.
27. Willem Stutterheim to Walter Spies, June 15, 1938, microfilm A1020, Walter Spies Archives, Oriental Collections, Leiden University. The English translation is contained on the microfilm but the translator is not indicated.
28. Walter Spies to his mother, July 28, 1938. Also in Rhodius, 373–5. Trans. J. Dorion.
29. Walter Spies to Willem Stutterheim, August 12, 1938, microfilm A1020, Walter Spies Archives, Oriental Collections, Leiden University. The English translation is contained on the microfilm but the translator is not indicated.
30. Walter Spies to his mother, October, 1938. Also in Rhodius, 377–8. Trans. J. Dorion.

Chapter 9

1. C.L.M. Penders, *The West New Guinea Debacle* (Honolulu: University of Hawaii Press, 2002), 57.
2. "The Morals Scandal: Again, New Arrests Made," *Java-Bode*, December 27, 1938, 1.
3. ———, 1.
4. ———, 1.
5. ———, 1.
6. ———, 1.
7. This summary relies on translations from Pieter Koenders, *Tussen Christelijk Reveil En Seksuele Revolutie: Bestrijding van zedeloosheid in Nederland, met nadruk op de repressie van homoseksualiteit* (Amsterdam: International Institute of Social Studies, 1996), 306–9; and Gosse Kerkhof, "Het Indische Zedenschandaal, een koloniaal incident" (Ph.D. thesis, University of Amsterdam, 1982), 32–8, which can be found at the International Gay/Lesbian Information Center and Archive (formerly Homodok) in Amsterdam. Koenders's and Kerkhof's work has been partially summarized in English in Robert Aldrich, *Colonialism and Homosexuality* (New York: Routledge, 2003), 198–200.
8. Unknown author, "Mary Pos," *Het Damescompartiment Online*, at the time of research at http://www.damescompartiment.nl/biomp.htm
9. Many of Covarrubias's paintings are reproduced in Adriana Williams and Yu-Chee Chong, *Covarrubias in Bali* (Singapore: Editions Didier Millet, 2005). See especially frontispiece and 37–8.
10. Quoted in Kerkhof, 1–3. Trans. M. Carr.
11. Colin McPhee, *A House in Bali* (London: Victor Gollanez Ltd., 1947 original edition; Singapore: Periplus Ltd., 2000 paperback edition), 201–10.
12. ———, 201–10.
13. "The Vice Scandal: Still More Arrests Made," *Java-Bode*, December 30, 1938, 1. Trans. M. Carr.
14. Henk Schulte Nordholt, *Bali: Colonial Conceptions and Political Change, 1700–1940* (Rotterdam: Erasmus University, 1986), 47.

15. McPhee, 202–3.
16. "The Vice Scandal: Development of the Investigation," *Java-Bode*, December 31, 1938, 1.
17. Anecdote mentioned in Timothy Lindsey, *The Romance of K'Tut Tantri and Indonesia* (Kuala Lumpur: Oxford University Press, 1997) n. 86, p. 97.
18. Lindsey, 92.
19. Attributed to personal communication from Spies biographer John Stowell in Lindsey, n. 86, p. 97.
20. "The Vice Scandal," January 3, 1939, 1. Trans. M. Carr.
21. Walter Spies to his mother, Denpasar, December 31, 1938, Walter Spies Archives at the Oriental Collections section of the University of Leiden, Netherlands. Also in Hans Rhodius, *Schönheit und Reichtum Des Lebens: Walter Spies (Maler und Musiker auf Bali 1895–1942)* (The Hague: L.J.C. Boucher, 1965), 378–80. Trans. J. Dorion.
22. H.J.E. Moll, Resident of Bali and Lombok, March 2, 1939, Colonial Ministry Secret Archive, Box 562, National Archive, The Hague. Trans. M. Carr.
23. ⸻.
24. A search of the Dutch colonial archives produced no transcripts or reports detailing any actual evidence. Research was conducted at the Dutch National Archive in The Hague in May 2003. Although the records include information on arrests and trials of minor officials, I found none on the major figures arrested in Bali. Other scholars have advised that any locally stored records were likely destroyed during the subsequent Japanese invasion, although thorough searches of Indonesian archives might eventually prove otherwise. Moll's lengthy report appears to be the most detailed description of the Balinese arrests available.
25. Maarten Salden, "The Dutch Penal Law and Homosexual Conduct," 155–79. In A.X. van Naerssen, ed., *Gay Life in Dutch Society* (New York: Harrington Park Press, 1987), 172. Also in *Journal of Homosexuality*, 13:2–3, Winter 1986–Spring 1987, 155–79.

Chapter 10

1. See, for example, this story told, but not sourced, in Hans Rhodius and John Darling, *Walter Spies and Balinese Art*. Edited by John Stowell (Amsterdam: Tropen Museum, 1980), 45.
2. H.C. Zentgraff, *Java-Bode*, January 5, 1939, 1.
3. ⸻, 1.
4. Walter Spies to Jane Belo, January 18, 1939, the Walter Spies Archives, Oriental Collections, University of Leiden.
5. ⸻, January 19, 1939.
6. ⸻, February 4, 1939.
7. ⸻, February 5, 1939.
8. ⸻, February 5, 1939.
9. H.C. Zentgraff, "Scandal," *Java-Bode*, January 17, 1939, 1. Trans. M. Carr.
10. Walter Spies to his mother, February 6, 1939, the Walter Spies Archive. This letter was not published in the collection of Spies's letters contained in Hans Rhodius,

Schönheit und Reichtum Des Lebens: Walter Spies (Maler und Musiker auf Bali 1895-1942) (The Hague: L.J.C. Boucher, 1965). Trans. M. Carr.

11. Jane Belo interview with Seken, about February 14, 1939, the Walter Spies Archives, microfilm A019.
12. Jane Belo to her Johnny [no last name included], February 10, 1939, microfilm A1019.
13. Gregory Bateson to Witsen Elias, February 28, 1939, microfilm A1019.
14. ——, February 28, 1939, microfilm A1019.
15. ——, March 4, 1939, microfilm A1019.
16. ——, February 28, 1939, microfilm A1019.
17. ——, March 4, 1939, microfilm A1019.
18. ——, March 4, 1939, microfilm A1019.
19. Margaret Mead to Witsen Elias, March 2, 1939, microfilm A1019.
20. Walter Spies to his mother, March 28, 1939. This letter was not published in the collection of Spies's letters contained in Rhodius. Trans. M. Carr.
21. Jane Belo to Willem Stutterheim, March 9, 1939, microfilm A1019.
22. Quoted in Rhodius and Darling, 45.
23. See, for example, short notices on the front pages of the April 18, 1939 and April 28, 1939 editions of *Java-Bode*. The first reported that Balinese officials were deciding whether to expel from the island "undesirable elements" who had been involved in the sex scandals, once their punishment was completed. The second said Europeans would be sent back to Europe, while those born in the Indies would be allowed to stay.
24. Two novels with unsavory portraits of Spies, for example, are Jim Shepard, *Nosferatu* (New York: Alfred A. Knopf, 1998) and Jamie James, *Andrew and Joey* (New York: Kensington Books, 2002).
25. G. Witsen Elias to Margaret Mead and Gregory Bateson, July 10, 1939, microfilm A1019.
26. Walter Spies to Jane Belo, April 13, 1939.
27. ——, April 13, 1939.
28. Margaret Mead to Walter Spies, June 18, 1939, originals at Margaret Mead Collection, Library of Congress. Accessed at Walter Spies Archives, Oriental Collections, University of Leiden, microfilm A1019.
29. Walter Spies to Daisy Spies, July 2, 1939, Walter Spies Archives. This letter was not published in the collection of Spies's letters contained in Rhodius. Trans. M. Carr.
30. Walter Spies to his mother, July 1939, Walter Spies Archives. This letter was not published in the collection of Spies's letters contained in Rhodius. Trans. M. Carr.
31. Reproductions of Walter Spies's art can be accessed at various websites. Among the most comprehensive is a site that at the time of research is maintained by Geff Green, a principal lecturer in Communication at Sheffield Hallam University in the United Kingdom, http://homepages.shu.ac.uk/~scsgcg/spies/
32. Quoted in Rhodius and Darling, 49.
33. Walter Spies to Kasper Niehaus, July 19, 1939. In Rhodius, 386. Trans. J. Dorion.
34. Rhodius and Darling, 45. In 1995, Christie's auction house sold *The Landscape and Its Children* for US$628,000; seven years later, it sold for more than US$1 million. (Prices from http://www.artprice.com/ and http://www.christies.com/)

35. Walter Spies to Jane Belo, April 17, 1939, Walter Spies Archives.
36. See, for example, http://homepages.shu.ac.uk/~scsgcg/spies/
37. Memoir of Edward and Irene Erdmann, quoted in Rhodius, 117–8. Trans. author.
38. Walter Spies to his mother, July 1939, Walter Spies Archives. This letter was not published in the collection of Spies's letters contained in Rhodius. Trans. M. Carr.
39. Walter Spies to Jane Belo, May 23, 1939, Walter Spies Archives.
40. Walter Spies to Kasper Niehaus, July 19, 1939. In Rhodius, 389. Trans. J. Dorion.
41. Walter Spies to Leopold Stokowski, quoted in Rhodius and Darling, 49.

Chapter 11

1. Walter Spies to Leo Spies, September 17, 1939, Walter Spies Archives, Oriental Collections, University of Leiden. Also in Hans Rhodius and John Darling, *Walter Spies and Balinese Art*. Edited by John Stowell (Amsterdam: Tropenmuseum, 1980), 392. Trans. J. Dorion.
2. Margaret Mead to Walter Spies, August 17, 1940, Walter Spies Archives, microfilm A1019.
3. Marianne van Wessem, "Memory, "in Hans Rhodius, *Schönheit und Reichtum Des Lebens: Walter Spies (Maler und Musiker auf Bali 1895–1942)* (The Hague: L.J.C. Boucher, 1965), 405.
4. Walter Spies to Hen van Wulfften Palthe-Moinat, May 29, 1940. Walter Spies Archives. Also in Rhodius, 438. Trans. author.
5. ——, August 9, 1940, 441. Trans. author.
6. ——, October 29, 1940. Walter Spies Archives. Also in Rhodius, 442. Trans. author.
7. Cornelius Conyn, "In the Internment Camps," in Rhodius, 433–6. Trans. J. Dorion.
8. F.W. Block to Leo Spies, October 13, 1944. In Rhodius, 436. Trans. J. Dorion. Block was the nephew of the German artist Josef Block.
9. Walter Spies to Hen van Wulfften Palthe-Moinat, April 22, 1941. Walter Spies Archives. Also in Rhodius, 444. Trans. author.
10. ——, July 15, 1941. Walter Spies Archives. Also in Rhodius, 446. Trans. author.
11. ——, September 19 and 30, 1941. Also in Rhodius, 447–8. Trans. author.
12. F.W. Block to Leo Spies, October 13, 1944. In Rhodius, 436. Trans. J. Dorion.
13. Marianne van Wessem, "Memory, "in Rhodius, 1965, 405.
14. Ezekiel 37:14, New International Version.
15. Ezekiel 1:4–28, New International Version.
16. See reference to the painting in Rhodius and Darling, 51.
17. Ezekiel 24:16, New International Version
18. Walter Spies to "Pieter," December 9, 1941. Walter Spies Archives. Also in Rhodius, 449. Trans. author.
19. Cornelius Conyn, "In the Internment Camps," in Rhodius, 436. Trans. J. Dorion.
20. Oral history recollection from source identified only as Brother Aloysius, Warring States Sinology Project, University of Massachusetts, at time of research at http://www.umass.edu/wsp/sinology/persons/zach2.html
21. ——.
22. ——.

23. Details from the Mercantile Marine website, a project collecting stories about the merchant marine in wartime, at time of research at http://sites.google.com/a/ mercantilemarine.org/mercantile-marine/War-time-Stories/kom-ships. A recollection of the disaster is available from http://www.umass.edu/wsp/sinology/persons/zach2. html

Chapter 12

1. From "The Press: Old Orient Hand," *Time*, July 21, 1958. Accessed at http://www.time.com/time/magazine/article/0,9171,868668-1,00.html
2. Leslie Ann Jeffrey, *Sex and Borders: Gender, National Identity and Prostitution Policy in Thailand* (Honolulu: University of Hawaii Press, 2002), 56.
3. For Phibun's impact on gender in Thailand, see Peter Jackson, "Performative Genders, Perverse Desires: A Bio-History of Thailand's Same Sex and Transgender Cultures," *Intersections: Gender, History and Culture in the Asian Context*, Issue 9, August 2003, 24, at the time of research online at: http://wwwsshe.murdoch.edu.au/intersections/issue9/jackson.html.
4. Jackson, 24, published online at: http://wwwsshe.murdoch.edu.au/intersections/issue9/jackson.html.
5. ——, 25–6.
6. Ironically, today a tourist guide like *Lonely Planet* warns Europeans who have now become accustomed to public nudity in their own countries that "bathing nude at beaches in Thailand is illegal." Joe Cummings, Sandra Bao, Steven Martin, and China Williams, *Thailand*, (Melbourne: Lonely Planet Publications, 2003), 46.
7. Jeffrey, 96.
8. ——, 96.
9. "The Press: Hors de Correspondence," *Time*, January 19, 1942, accessed at http://www.time.com/time/magazine/article/0,9171,766338,00.html Also "The Press: Old Orient Hand," *Time*, July 21, 1958, accessed at http://www.time.com/time/magazine/article/0,9171,868668-1,00.html
10. Darrell Berrigan, "Weary British Retreat in Burma, Knowing That They Face Disaster," *New York Times*, April 29, 1942, 4.
11. Quoted in Dickson Hartwell, "The Mighty Jeep," *American Heritage*, December 1960, 12:1, accessed at http://www.americanheritage.com/articles/magazine/ah/1960/1/1960_1_38.shtml
12. William Warren, *Jim Thompson: The Unsolved Mystery* (Singapore: Archipelago Press, 1970, 1998), 41–4.
13. Cable from Acting Secretary of State Dean Acheson to the US Ambassador in London, Dec. 13, 1945, published in Wimon Wiriyawit, *Free Thai: Personal Recollections and Official Documents* (Bangkok: White Lotus Press, 1997), 287–93, quotation from 290–1.
14. Donald F. Cooper, *Thailand: Dictatorship or Democracy?* (London: Minerva, 1995), 32, referenced in Peter Jackson, "An American Death in Bangkok: The Murder of Darrell Berrigan and the Hybrid Origins of Gay Identity in 1960s Thailand," *GLQ: A Journal of Lesbian and Gay Studies*, 5:3 (1999) 372. See also articles in the *New York Times*: "Thailand Concerned About Reparations," October 10, 1945, 3; "British

Deny Charge of Victimizing Siam," December 21, 1945, 3; "Peace Comes to Siam," January 3, 1946, 17; "Accord with Siam Sealed by Britain," 9.

15. Jackson, 1999, 373–4.

16. One of Thompson's biographies by William Warren seems to deny his homosexuality while noting his artistic interests. Another, by journalist Alexander MacDonald, who worked with Thompson and started the English-language *Bangkok Post*, calls him "foppish" and says "he wore dancing pumps most of the time." It was Thompson's interest in ballet and costumes that led to his interest in Thai silk, which in turn he contributed to stage productions about Thailand, such as *The King and I*. Alexander MacDonald, *My Footloose Newspaper Life* (Bangkok: Post Publishing, 1990), 98 quoted in Jackson, 1999, 369.

17. Darrell Berrigan, "Thais' Economy in Modern Phase," *New York Times*, January 12, 1960, 57.

18. ——, "Thailand's Opulent Sights Viewable in Luxury," *New York Times*, March 6, 1960, X39.

19. ——, X39.

20. ——, X39.

21. "The Press: Old Orient Hand," *Time*, July 21, 1958. Accessed at http://www.time.com/time/magazine/article/0,9171,868668-1,00.html

22. ——.

23. Darrell Berrigan, "This Wonderful World," *Bangkok World*, October 1, 1965, 10.

24. ——, 10.

25. "World Editor Found Slain," *Bangkok World*, October 4, 1965, 1.

26. This shift is documented in Jackson, 1999, 361–411. I have drawn upon Jackson's Thai translations and analysis in this section, while adding materials from other English-language sources.

27. ——, 375–6.

28. ——, 380.

29. "Berrigan killer to re-enact crime," *Bangkok Post*, October 14, 1965, 1.

30. A fuller discussion of the word *jikko* can be found at Jackson, 1999, 380. Jackson also quotes an analysis from Andrew Harris, *Bangkok after Dark* (New York: MacFadden-Bartell, 1968), 82.

31. Jackson, 1999, 379–80.

32. ——, 1999, 379–80.

33. *Thai Rath*, October 4, 1965, 16, translated in Jackson, 1999, 375.

34. "Kathoey phoey chiwit 'lakkaphet' Berrigan – wa liang dek-num thana sami," *Thai Rath*, October 9, 1965, 1, 16. From Jackson, 1999, 378.

35. ——, 1, 16; Jackson, 1999, 376.

36. Jackson, 1999, 382–8.

37. "Thai Rath phop laeng 'phu-chai kai tua' – mi samachik ruam 200, rai-dai sung," *Thai Rath*, October 11, 1965, 1, 2, 16, trans. from Jackson, 1999, 388–9.

38. For a discussion of the importance of *farang* as a category in the Siamese and Thai cultural imagination, see Pattana Kitiarsa, "An Ambiguous Intimacy: Farang as Siamese Occidentalism," in Rachel Harrison and Peter Jackson, eds., *The Ambiguous Allure of the West: Traces of the Colonial in Thailand* (Hong Kong University Press, 2010), 57–74.

39. "Thai Rath phop laeng 'phu-chai kai tua' – mi samachik ruam 200, rai-dai sung," *Thai Rath,* October 11, 1965, 1, 2, 16, trans. from Jackson, 1999, 388–9.
40. ——, 1, 2, 16, trans. from Jackson, 1999, 388–9. Jackson studied the language used in the Berrigan case. He argues that not only did these new *gay* men violate the traditional rules of gender and sexual desire but also the rules of class. They were not lower-class, karmic-bound *kathoey* who had to struggle to achieve femininity. They freely capitalized on their masculinity and on their undenied desires for sex with other men.
41. "Arayachon nai mum meut," *Thai Rath,* October 16, 1965, 3. From Jackson, 1999, 391.
42. Jackson, 1999, 391.

Chapter 13

1. See population statistics for Singapore, http://www.populstat.info/Asia/singapoc.htm
2. For a history of prostitution in Singapore, see James Francis Warren, *Ah Ku and Karayuki-san: Prostitution in Singapore, 1870–1940* (Singapore: Singapore University Press, 2003).
3. Warren. Children of prostitutes are discussed on 80–1, 231–4.
4. For information on Nanyang Primary School, see the school website: http://www.nyps.moe.edu.sg/homepage.aspx.
5. ——.
6. ——.
7. ——. Further information is also available at http://www.answers.com/topic/nanyang-primary-school. A sometimes caustic reminiscence available at the time of research is http://gssq.entori.net/detritus/nyps.htm. For information about dress codes and propriety, see reminisces and photographs from the online Nanyang History Book, http://www.nanyang.org.sg/HistoryBook/
8. Information on and photographs of the early Telok Kurau School are available from the school's current website, http://www.telokkuraupri.moe.edu.sg/
9. Biographical information on Lee Kuan Yew and Lee Hsien Loong is available from a number of books such as Alex Josey, *Lee Kuan Yew* (Singapore: Donald Moore Press Ltd, 1968), as well as from the Singapore government's official website: http://www.cabinet.gov.sg/. See also "Kwa Geok Choo, wife of Singapore's first prime minister and mother of current premier, dies at 89," *Los Angeles Times,* October 2, 2010, http://latimesblogs.latimes.com/afterword/ .
10. Lee Hsien Loong, National Day Rally 2004 speech, August 22, 2004. Posted at time of research at http://stars.nhb.gov.sg/stars/public/.
11. Stuart Koe, "Biography," at the time of research at http://www.geocities.com/WestHollywood/8869/BIO.HTM.
12. ——. Also reposted at http://www.stuartkoe.com/
13. ——.
14. ——.
15. ——.

16. Chun Wei Choo, "IT2000: Singapore's Vision of an Intelligent Island," from Peter Droege, *Intelligent Environments* (North-Holland, 1997). Online at the time of research at http://choo.fis.utoronto.ca/FIS/ResPub/IT2000.html. Also see Singapore Media Development Authority Report, "Media 21: Transforming Singapore into a Global Media Center" (August, 2003). Online at www.mda.gov.sg/wms.ftp/media21. pdf

17. The Tay family was described in a press release that accompanied the release of the National Computer Board report, "A Vision of an Intelligent Island: The IT2000 Report," April 1992. The fictional family is described in Sandy Sandfort, "The Intelligent Island," *Wired Magazine*, September/October 1993, http://www.wired. com/wired/archive/1.04/sandfort_pr.html.

18. Sandfort.

19. *Spartacus International Gay Guide.* 9th Edition (Amsterdam: Spartacus, 1979), 405–6.

20. ——.

21. Koe.

22. For a review of the adoption of Section 377 in British colonies, see Douglas Sanders, "377 and the Unnatural Afterlife of British Colonialism." Paper presented at the Fifth Asian Law Institute Conference, National University of Singapore, May 22– 23, 2008. Posted at http://www.iglhrc.org/files/iglhrc/program_docs/Doug%20 Sanders%20377.pdf. Accessed June 2008.

23. *Ng Huat v. Public Prosecutor* (1995) 2 SLR 783. Section 377A reads: "Any male person who, in public or private, commits, or abets the commission of, or procures or attempt to procure the commission by any male person of any act of gross indecency with another male person, is punishable by law."

24. Warren, 20.

25. ——. See map at front of book.

26. Warren, 234.

27. Tom Boellstorff, *The Gay Archipelago: Sexuality and Nation in Indonesia* (Princeton: Princeton University Press, 2005), 38–40. Also, Sharyn Graham, "Sex, Gender, and Priests in South Sulawesi, Indonesia," *International Institute for Asian Studies Newsletter*, 29 (November 2002), 27. For hundreds of years, the *bissus* existed peacefully with the Islamic faith that was imported into Sulawesi, but by the 1960s, an Islamic fundamentalist movement, Kahar Muzakar, drove them underground. The sacred regalia was tossed into the ocean or burned, their rituals forbidden, and the *bissus* were given the choice of either dressing like "normal" men and leaving behind their traditional professions, or dying. As a warning, the leading *bissu* of one region was beheaded, and his head then publicly displayed.

28. Boellstorff, 38–40, and Graham, 27.

29. An account given on Wikipedia, "Bugis Street," at the time of research at http:// en.wikipedia.org/wiki/Bugis_Street See also Russell Heng, "Where Queens Ruled! A History of Gay Venues in Singapore." Public lecture, August 16, 2005, at the time of research at http://www.yawningbread.org/guest_2005/guw-101.htm. Also, Russell Heng, "Tiptoe Out of the Closet: The Before and After of the Increasingly Visible Gay Community in Singapore." In Gerald Sullivan and Peter Jackson, eds., *Gay and Lesbian Asia: Culture, Identity, Community* (New York: The Harrington Park Press, 2001), 81–97.

30. Heng, 2005, at the time of research at http://www.yawningbread.org/guest_2005/ guw-101.htm. By1985, the bulldozers of urban redevelopment rolled in, and Bugis would become a modern shopping mall. See Heng in Sullivan and Jackson, eds., 81–97.
31. For an account, see "Singapore Gay History," Wikipedia, http://en.wikipedia.org/ wiki/Singapore_gay_history.
32. Raffles Institution website: http://www.ri.sch.edu.sg/.
33. —— and at the time of research at http://www.answers.com/topic/raffles-institution.
34. Lee Kuan Yew, "Transcript of a Speech by the Prime Minister at a Meeting with Principals of Schools at Victoria Theater on 29 August 1966," Singapore: Ministry of Education, n.d. Quoted in Philip Holden, "The Significant of Uselessness: Resisting Colonial Masculinity in Philip Jeyaretnam's *Abraham's Promise*," at the time of research at http://social.chass.ncsu.edu/jouvert/v2i1/Holden.htm
35. Hans Rhodius and John Darling, *Walter Spies and Balinese Art*. Edited by John Stowell (Amsterdam: Tropical Museum, 1980), 21.
36. Lee Kuan Yew, Holden, at the time of research at http://social.chass.ncsu.edu/ jouvert/v2i1/Holden.htm
37. D.W. McLeod, "Syllabus of Instruction, Raffles Institution, 1937." Posted by Philip Holden, National University of Singapore, at the time of research at http://courses. nus.edu.sg/course/ellhpj/resources/mcleod.HTM
38. Koe. Also reposted at http://www.stuartkoe.com/
39. ——.
40. Accessed at http://www.fridae.com/personals/?S2, January 2007.

Chapter 14

1. *Spartacus International Gay Guide*. 9th Edition (Amsterdam: Spartacus, 1979), 461
2. Stephen Greene, *Absolute Dreams: Thai Government under Rama VI, 1910–1925* (Bangkok: White Lotus, 1999), 164–5, 168–9. For a description of the statue, designed by Italian architect Corrado Feroci and placed in 1942, see, for example, http://www.bangkok.com/monuments-and-statues/index.html.
3. *Spartacus*, 461.
4. ——, 463.
5. ——, 463.
6. Information about Khun Toc comes from the author's many conversations with him between 2004 and 2007 and with Richard Werwie, an American to whom he referred specific questions about his life and about Babylon, in particular an extensive interview with Werwie conducted on April 24, 2004.
7. Author's interview with Richard Werwie, April 24, 2004. Werwie commented: "His parents were very much in the upper class and they believed in education. They believed at that time that the only proper, quality education was not in Thailand but outside of Thailand."
8. The Pennington School website, http://www.pennington.org/
9. Author's interview with Richard Werwie, April 24, 2004.
10. Author's conversation with Khun Toc, April 2006, and observation of family photographs.

11. *Spartacus,* 462. The Tulip is also mentioned in Eric G. Allyn, *The Men of Thailand.* 6th Edition (Bangkok: Floating Lotus, 1997), 128. An update of the Allyn section on the web available in 2005 included an early picture of the Tulip, but the Floating Lotus site was no longer available by time of publication.

12. Author's interview with Richard Werwie, April 24, 2004. Quotation from the author's conversation with Khun Toc, April 19, 2004.

13. Author's interview with Richard Werwie, April 24, 2004.

14. Dennis Altman, *The Homosexualization of America* (Boston: Beacon Press, 1982), 79–80.

15. ——, 81.

16. Neil Miller, *Out in the World: Gay and Lesbian Life from Buenos Aires to Bangkok* (New York: Random House, 1992), 108–9.

17. Author's conversation with Khun Toc, April 19, 2004.

18. Jim Reeves, "Welcome to My World," EMI Music Publishing, Sony/ATV Music Publishing LLC, Warner/Chappell Music, Inc., Original: 1964.

19. Author's observation with Khun Toc.

20. David Bergman, *The Violet Hour: The Violet Quill and the Making of Gay Culture* (New York: Columbia University, 2004), 233.

21. Allyn, 177.

22. From Babylon website at the time of research, http://www.babylonbangkok.com/

23. For a detailed review of the contributions of *The Iliad* and *The Odyssey* to the Greek and European idea of the aesthetic state, as well as an examination of the evolution of that idea through Winckelmann and later Germans, see Josef Chytry, *The Aesthetic State: A Quest in Modern German Thought* (Berkeley: University of California Press, 1989). The review of *The Iliad,* in particular, occurs on xxxvi–xxxix. The review of Winckelmann comes in Chapter One, 11–37.

24. Author identified only as Newman, "Stepping into Paradise, umm, Babylon," an article written in 1995 and archived in 1998 on *Yawning Bread,* http://www.yawningbread.org/guest_1998/guw-025.htm

25. A video view of the new Babylon was available on YouTube starting in 2008. Appropriately, it was set to one of Khun Toc's favorite songs, "Mad About the Boy" sung by Dinah Washington. http://www.youtube.com/watch?v=a-h7T-hUG0Q&feature=channel

26. Author's interview with Richard Werwie, April 24, 2004.

27. Joe Cummings, et al., *Thailand* (London: Lonely Planet Publications, 2003), 37.

28. Author's conversation with Khun Toc, April 2004.

Chapter 15

1. *Spartacus International Gay Guide.* 18th Edition (Berlin: Spartacus, 1989), 693–5.

2. Stuart Koe, "Biography," at the time of research at http://www.geocities.com/WestHollywood/8869/BIO.HTM. Also reposted at http://www.stuartkoe.com/

3. ——.

4. ——.

5. ——. In 2010, Koe would be a "featured leader" in an article posted at the Center for Leading Healthcare Change website sponsored by the University of Minnesota's

College of Pharmacy. See "Stuart Koe: Challenging the Status Quo," June 25, 2010, http://www.pharmacy.umn.edu/clhc/featuredleaders/koe/home.html

6. Stuart Koe, "Journal," April 25, 1997, at time of research at http://www.geocities.com/WestHollywood/8869/. Also reposted at http://www.stuartkoe.com/

7. ——.

8. Yaw Yan Chong and Dave Ang, "Four nabbed in police ambush at Gay beach," and Yaw Yan Chong, "I was caressed, says cop," *The New Paper*, March 9, 1992.

9. —— and Ang, "Four nabbed in police ambush at Gay beach"; Chong, "I was caressed, says cop"; Chong, "Gay Beach: 4 more arrested," *The New Paper*, March 10, 1992. Gay cruising in Singapore in the early 1990s is described in detail in an undergraduate thesis written for the Department of Sociology at the National University of Singapore, Low Kee Hong, "Recognizing Strangers: Gay Cruising in the City,"1994/95.

10. Russell Heng, "Tiptoe Out of the Closet: The Before and After of the Increasingly Visible Gay Community in Singapore." In Gerald Sullivan and Peter Jackson, *Gay and_Lesbian Asia: Culture, Identity, Community* (New York: Haworth Press, 2001), 82.

11. For a discussion of the impact of music on gender, see, for example, Susan J. Douglas, *Where the Girls Are: Growing Up Female with the Mass Media* (New York: Random House, 1994), especially Chapter 4, "Why the Shirelles Mattered," 83–98.

12. For an account, see "Singapore Gay History," Wikipedia, http://en.wikipedia.org/wiki/Singapore_gay_history

13. Wilfred Ong, Letter of protest to the Singapore police, written May 31, 1993. Accessed at http://www.yawningbread.org/apdx_2004/imp-149.htm

14. Yap Sze Hon, Letter of reply to Wilfred Ong, June 29, 1993. Accessed at http://www.yawningbread.org/apdx_2004/imp-149.htm

15. Chong, "Gays surface again at East Coast beach," *The New Paper*, September 24, 1993.

16. ——.

17. Jennifer Tan, "Loo door broken – but no gays," *The New Paper*, October 20, 1993.

18. *Tan Boon Hock v. Public Prosecutor (1994) 2 SLR 150*. At the time of research at http://www.yawningbread.org/apdx_2005/imp-182.htm

19. Singapore Statutes, Chapter 311 (Singapore Societies Act) Section 4(b).

20. ——, Section 13.

21. ——, Chapter 311 (Singapore Societies Act) Section 14(3), 15(1), 16(1). and 18.

22. "History of People Like Us," http://www.plu.sg/society/

23. ——.

24. ——.

25. See, for example, my discussion of a similar organization in Seattle in the 1960s, the Dorian Society, and its relationship with media publicity: Gary L. Atkins, *Gay Seattle: Stories of Exile and Belonging* (Seattle: University of Washington Press, 2003), 111–5.

26. See "History of People Like Us," http://www.plu.sg/society/

27. ——.

28. From Ng King Kang, *The Rainbow Connection: The Internet and the Singapore Gay Community* (Singapore: KangCuBine Publishing Pte. Ltd, 1999), 14–6, 78–9. See

also Christopher Low, "Self-Discovery, Coming Out and Morality." In Joseph Lo and Huang Guoqin, *People Like Us: Sexual Minorities in Singapore* (Singapore: Select Books, 2003), 41.

29. Quoted in Cherian George, *Contentious Journalism and the Internet: Towards Democratic Discourse in Malaysia and Singapore* (Singapore: Singapore University Press, 2006), 101.

30. See various articles about or by Dr Tan Chong Kee in Fridae.com, including "My Boyfriend Died of AIDS," *Fridae,* August 7, 2006. http://www.fridae.com/newsfeatures/2006/08/07/1684.my-boyfriend-died-of-aids?n=sea&nm=tan+chong+kee and Sylvia Tan, "Tan Chong Kee," *Fridae,* August 1, 2005, http://www.fridae.com/newsfeatures/2005/08/01/1464.tan-chong-kee?n=sea&nm=tan+chong+kee.

31. The Tay family was described in a press release that accompanied the release of the National Computer Board report, "A Vision of an Intelligent Island: The IT2000 Report," April 1992. The fictional family is described in Sandy Sandfort, "The Intelligent Island," *Wired Magazine,* September/October 1993, at the time of research at http://www.wired.com/wired/archive/1.04/sandfort_pr.html.

32. The various exchanges may be found at http://www.yawningbread.org/

33. The PLU letters may be found at http://www.yawningbread.org/

34. ——.

35. Quoted in George, 101.

36. ——, 102.

37. Content guidelines for SiGNeL at the time of research at http://www.plu.sg/main/signel_02.htm

38. Stuart Koe, "Biography," at the time of research at http://www.geocities.com/WestHollywood/8869/

39. Koe, "Guestbook," May–June 1997, at the time of research at http://www.geocities.com/WestHollywood/8869/

40. From the Suntec City website, at the time of research at http://www.sunteccity.com.sg/fountain/index.htm

41. Koe, "Journal," May 10, 1997, at the time of research at http://www.geocities.com/WestHollywood/8869/ Also reposted at http://www.stuartkoe.com/

42. Koe, "Journal," September 15, 1997.

Chapter 16

1. At the time of research at the website for Monfort College in Chiang Mai, http://www.montfort.ac.th/english/vision.html; "Thaksin Shinawatra – a biography," *Bangkok Post,* August, 2001, http://www.bangkokpost.net/election2001/thaksinprofile.html: and website Thaksin.net, http://www.thaksin.net/

2. Pasuk Phongaichit and Chris Baker, *Thaksin: The Business of Politics in Thailand,* (Bangkok: Silkworm Books, 2004), 26–34.

3. Thaksin Shinawatra, *Ta du dao that tit din (Eyes on the Stars, Feet on the Ground)* (Bangkok: Matichon, 1999), 55. Trans. and quoted in Phongaichit and Baker, 36–7.

4. Phongaichit and Baker, 40.

5. Christian Norberg-Schulz, *The Concept of Dwelling: On the Way to Figurative Architecture* (New York: Rizzoli International Publications, Inc., 1985).

6. ——, 13, 71.
7. Author's observations of the sauna.
8. Author's interview with Khun Toc.
9. Author identified only as Newman, "Stepping into Paradise, umm, Babylon," an article written in 1995 and archived in 1998 on *Yawning Bread*, at the time of research at http://www.yawningbread.org/guest_1998/guw-025.htm
10. Norberg-Schulz, 56.
11. ——, 59.
12. Newman.
13. Richard Rhodes, "Death in the Candy Store," *Rolling Stone*, November 28, 1991, 62–71.
14. ——, 62–71.
15. Scot Barmé, *Woman, Man, Bangkok: Love, Sex and Popular Culture in Thailand* (Bangkok: Silkworm Books, 2002), 5. See also "Thais ban dictionary over 'city of prostitutes' slur," *The Independent*, July 6, 1993, http://www.independent.co.uk/news/world/thais-ban-dictionary-over-city-of-prostitutes-slur-1483226.html
16. Rhodes.
17. Leslie Ann Jeffrey, *Sex and Borders: Gender, National Identity and Prostitution Policy in Thailand* (Honolulu: University of Hawaii Press, 2002), 38–9.
18. Barmé, 112–5.
19. Jeffrey, 107
20. ——, 107.
21. For details of Thaksin's rise via the telecommunications industry, see Phongaichit and Baker, 41–51, 57–9.
22. Duncan McCargo and Ukrist Pathmanand, *The Thaksinization of Thailand* (Copenhagen: NIAS Press, 2005), 84.
23. At the time of research at http://www.thaksin.net/life.html
24. Quoted in Phongaichit and Baker, 171.
25. From a press advertisement that ran a month before the election. Trans. L. A. Jeffrey, 84–8.
26. "Govt Endorsement: Homosexuality 'not a disease,'" *The Nation*, December 27, 2002. http://www.nationmultimedia.com/search/read.php?newsid=71491&keyword=homosexuality+2002
27. Peter Jackson, "Performative Genders, Perverse Desires: A Bio-History of Thailand's Same Sex and Transgender Cultures," *Intersections: Gender, History and Culture in the Asian Context*, Issue 9 (August 2003), 3, at the time of research at http://wwwsshe.murdoch.edu.au/intersections/issue9/jackson.html
28. Tamara Loos, *Subject Siam: Family, Law and Colonial Modernity in Thailand* (Bangkok, Silkworm Books, 2002), 114.
29. Peter Jackson, *Buddhism: Legitimation and Conflict: The Political Functions of Urban Thai Buddhism* (Singapore: Institute of Southeast Asian Studies, 1990), 94–112.
30. I am grateful to historian Terdsak Romjampa for this account and the translations. See Terdsak Romjampa, "The Construction of Male Homosexuality in the Journal of Psychiatric Association of Thailand," unpublished paper presented at AsiaPacifiQueer 3 Conference, Singapore, August 13–19, 2003, 2. Romjampa quotes

Sood Saengvichien, "Anatomy and Hormones of Lag-ga-Phates," *Thailand Medical Society Bulletin* (July 1961), 44:7, 442.

31. Trans. and quoted in Terdsak Romjampa, 3. From Sompotch Sukavatana, "The Treatment of Homosexuality," *Journal of the Psychiatric Association of Thailand* (April 1973),18:2, 119.

32. "Government endorsement: Homosexuality 'not a disease,'" *The Nation*, December 27, 2002, http://www.nationmultimedia.com/page.arcview.php3?clid=2&tid=71491&usrsess=1

33. "Healthy attitudes to homosexuals," *The Nation*, December 27, 2002. http://www.nationmultimedia.com/search/read.php?newsid=71476&keyword=homosexual

Chapter 17

1. Stuart Koe, "Journal," September 15, 1997, at the time of research at http://www.geocities.com/WestHollywood/8869/ Reposted at http://www.stuartkoe.com/

2. ——, "Biography," June 28, 1999, at the time of research at http://www.geocities.com/WestHollywood/8869/BIO.HTM. Reposted at http://www.stuartkoe.com/

3. ——.

4. See Kam Louie, *Theorising Chinese Masculinity* (Cambridge: Cambridge University Press, 2002) for an extensive discussion of these concepts of Confucian manhood, from which this section is summarized.

5. ——, 24.

6. Futoshi Tage, "East Asian Masculinities." In Michael Kimmel, Jeff Hearn, and R.W. Connell, eds., *Handbook of Studies on Men & Masculinities* (Thousand Oaks, CA: Sage Publications, 2005), 130.

7. ——, 19.

8. ——, Chapter 2 in particular.

9. ——, 54.

10. Michael Hirsch, "Rethinking Confucius: Lee Kuan Yew Recants," *Newsweek*, web exclusive story, January 28, 2001, at the time of research at http://www.singapore-window/org/sw01/010128nw.htm

11. Louie, Chapters 1–3 in particular; quotation from p. 43.

12. Koe, "Biography," June 28, 1999. The "gym-rat himbo" comment comes from one of his online profile postings on Fridae.com.

13. ——, June 28, 1999.

14. Author's interview with Stuart Koe, May 5, 2004.

15. Robert Yeoh died in July 2007. For more information, including tributes to him, see Sylvia Tan, "Fridae Co-Founder Robert Yeoh Passes On," *Fridae*, July 11, 2007, http://www.fridae.com/newsfeatures/article.php?articleid=1973&viewarticle=1

16. Author's interview with Stuart Koe, May 5, 2004.

17. Cherian George, *Contentious Journalism and the Internet: Towards Democratic Discourse in Malaysia and Singapore* (Singapore: Singapore University Press, 2006), 106.

18. On the closure of Sintercom, see George, 114–66.

19. The section on homosexuality in the Singapore Ministry of Education sex education packet at time of research is archived at http://www.yawningbread.org/apdx_2001/

imp-081.htm In May 2009, the Ministry of Education issued a press release stating that it did "not promote alternative lifestyles to our students. MOE's framework for sexuality education reflects the mainstream views and values of Singapore society, where the social norm consists of the married heterosexual family unit." The ministry announced it was discontinuing a vendor-provided educational supplement that seemed to "convey messages which could promote homosexuality." At the time of research at http://www.moe.gov.sg/media/press/2009/05/moes-statement-on-sexuality-ed.php. See also http://www.moe.gov.sg/education/programmes/social-emotional-learning/sexuality-education/

20. The section on homosexuality in the Singapore Ministry of Education sex education packet at the time of research is at http://www.yawningbread.org/apdx_2001/imp-081.htm

21. ——.

22. Author's interview with Stuart Koe, May 5, 2004.

23. Quoted in Amy Tan, "Singapore Gays Find Tacit Acceptance but Some Seek More," *Reuters,* circulated July 2001, at the time of research archived at http://www.yawningbread.org/apdx_2001/imp-082.htm

24. The government, though, did continue to occasionally prosecute heterosexuals, such as a bizarre case in which an adult son caught his 56-year-old mother giving oral sex to his 65-year-old great uncle. He reported her and the police arrested the uncle for sodomy. A report on this case can be found at Alex Au, "Don't Turn the Doorknob," *Yawning Bread,* http://www.yawningbread.org/index2.htm (January 2004).

25. Christopher Gunness, "Out in Asia," *British Broadcasting Corporation,* Nov. 13, 2000. Transcript posted in *Yawning Bread,* "Radio Journalists Ask the Gay Question," at the time of research at http://www.yawningbread.org/arch_2000/yax-216.htm

26. All statistics are based on a study of Fridae undertaken during the final two weeks of December 2004 using Fridae's own search engine to find different "types" of men. During this study period, Fridae added about 3,000 profiles; the percentages cited in the text were always checked against the most current total number of profiles. Random checks of percentages calculated at the beginning of the period were made with percentages calculated at the end of the period, to see whether significant changes had occurred in particular categories. There were only slight fluctuations, usually of less than half a percent. A fuller description of the results can be found in Gary Atkins, "My Man Fridae: Re-producing Asian Masculinity," *Seattle Journal for Social Justice,* 4:1 (Fall/Winter 2005), 67–100.

27. See, for example, Richard Fung, "Looking for my Penis: The Eroticized Asian in Gay Video Porn." In *How Do I Look: Queer Film and Video.* Edited by Bad Object-Choices (1991). Although Fung's article was written two decades ago and it is now possible to find many examples of the Asian male penis on display in Internet pornography, many of his points are well taken.

28. The results from the blogs on Fridae are summarized from an unpublished paper presented by the author, Gary Atkins, "Wen, Wu and Winckelmann: The Poetics and Politics of Gay Manhood in a New Asian 'Nation,'" presented at the 9th Asia Oceania Congress of Sexology, Bangkok, Thailand, November 2006.

29. Franz Roh's original book is *Nach Expressionismus, Magischer Realismus: Probleme der neuesten Europäischen Malerei* (Berlin: Leipzig, Klinkhardt and Biermann, 1925). A translation, "Magical Realism: Post-Expressionism," is available in Lois Parkinson Zamora and Wendy B. Faris, *Magical Realism: Theory, History, Community* (Durham, NC: Duke University Press, 1995), 19.

Chapter 18

1.   For a discussion of the spatial concepts of "center" and "periphery" and how they might be recast in the case of Thailand, see Sant Suwatcharapinum, "The Centre of Periphery: The Case of Contemporary Bankgok's Gay Spaces," paper presented at the conference on Queer Space: Centers and Peripheries, University of Technology, Sydney, Australia, February, 2007. Suwatcharapinum asks, for example, "Do Thai gays need to identify themselves as repressed, oppressed, and positioned in the site of the *imaginary Western periphery*, while in fact the place of the *real-Thai centre* has never been fully recognized?" At the time of research at http://www.dab.uts.edu.au/conferences/queer_space/proceedings/cities_suwatcharapinun.pdf

2.   Pasuk Phongaichit and Chris Baker, Thaksin: *The Business of Politics in Thailand*, (Bangkok: Silkworm Books, 2004), 168.

3.   ——, 68.

4.   Denis Gray, "Thailand's 'Mr. Clean Aims To Sweep Out Sleaze," Associated Press report, *Los Angeles Times*, July 7, 2002, at the time of research at http://articles.latimes.com/2002/jul/07/news/adfg-moral7. See also Douglas Sanders, "'Colorful Shows' and 'Social Order': Gay bars and moral campaigns in Bangkok," March 24, 2004, 7, a revision of a paper presented at the International Convention of Asia Scholars, Singapore, August 2003.

5.   Scot Barmé, *Woman, Man, Bangkok: Love, Sex and Popular Culture in Thailand* (Bangkok: Silkworm Books, 2002), 115–9.

6.   Yuwadee Tunyasiri, "Law change urged to get at mistresses," Bangkok Post, April 4, 2001; and "Purachai has lost his way," Bangkok Post, April 13, 2001.

7.   Mukdawan Sakboon, "In-flight warnings proposed," The Nation, July 2, 2001, 6A. Quoted in Sanders, 7, a revision of a paper presented at the International Convention of Asia Scholars, Singapore, August 2003.

8.   From the translation of Franz Roh's Nach *Expressionismus, Magischer Realismus: Probleme der neuesten Europäischen Malerei* (Berlin: Leipzig, Klinkhardt and Biermann, 1925). In "Magical Realism: Post-Expressionism," Lois Parkinson Zamora and Wendy B. Faris, *Magical Realism: Theory, History, Community* (Durham, NC: Duke University Press, 1995), 28.

9.   See discussion in Chapter 8 and in Adrian Vickers, *Bali: A Paradise Created* (Australia: Penguin Books, 1989), 144. Image no. 25 between pages 148 and 149.

10. Descriptions in this paragraph are based on the author's observations at various times, 2001–07.

11. Sanders, 4.

12. Pona Antaseeda, "Killjoy clampdown sends nightlife reeling," *Bangkok Post*, August 26, 2001.

13. Sanders, 4.
14. Manop Thip-osod, "Locals in lather over gay sauna," *Bangkok Post*, October 7, 2001.
15. The notion that condemnatory discourse about sex is not so much a way of repressing it as expanding it comes, of course, from Michel Foucault's famous chapter on "The Incitement to Discourse." In *The History of Sexuality* (New York: Random House, 1978), 15–35.
16. "Thousands arrested in crackdown," *Bangkok Post*, December 4, 2001.
17. Phongaichit and Baker, 168–9.
18. Seth Mydans, "Bangkok Journal: At 10 p.m., Thais better know where their children are," *New York Times*, February 27, 2004.
19. Author's interview with Richard Werwie, April 24, 2004.
20. "Bangkok police raid famous gay sauna," *Fridae.com*, December 30, 2002, http://www.fridae.com/newsfeatures/2002/12/30/482.bangkok-police-raid-famous-gay-sauna?n=sea&nm=babylon+
21. Author's interview with Richard Werwie, April 24, 2004.
22. All comments taken from *Thai Guys* forum site and published online between December 25 and 29, 2002. Oddly, on the forum site, some comments about the raid were dated prior to it actually taking place. The forum at the time of research at http://www.thaiguys.org is no longer accessible.
23. From *Thai Guys* forum site, December 25–29, 2002.
24. Communication from Richard Werwie, June 27, 2005.
25. ——.
26. "What a Difference a Day Made," original lyrics by Maria Grever, 1934; English by Stanley Adams, 1934; single with Dinah Washington released in 1959 on Mercury Records. A version can be heard on YouTube, http://www.youtube.com/watch?v=OmBxVfQTuvI
27. At the time of research from the Babylon website, http://www.babylonbangkok.com, January 18, 2003.

Chapter 19

1. Simon Elegant, "The Lion in Winter," *Time Asia* , July 7, 2003, http://www.time.com/time/asia/covers/501030707/sea_singapore.html. The reference is to Richard Florida, *The Rise of the Creative Class* (New York: Basic Books, 2002).
2. Elegant.
3. M. Nirmala, "Government more open to employing gays now," *Singapore Straits Times*, July 4, 2003. The article as well as a commentary about the change by Alex Au, one of the founders of People Like Us, can be found at "Gay civil servants, and what next?" *Yawning Bread*, July 2003, at the time of research at http://www.yawningbread.org/arch_2003/yax-319.htm
4. Pressure to keep homosexuals out of the US Civil Service peaked in the 1950s because of fears about national security. Federal courts gradually dismantled the link by ruling that the government had to prove, not simply assume, a connection between homosexuality and dangers to government service. The US Civil Service Commission institutionalized a policy change in 1975.
5. Author's interview with Stuart Koe, May 5, 2004.

6. Theresa Tan, "Ma, I'm Gay," *Singapore Straits Times,* July 13, 2003, 1, 4. At the time of research at http://www.yawningbread.org/apdx_2003/imp-106.htm

7. "S'pore may allow gay activist groups" *Fridae,* January 8, 2004, http://www.fridae.com/en20040108_1_1.php

8. See the previous discussion of Christian Norberg-Schulz's idea of architectural representations of "collective agreements" in Chapter 16.

9. Arjan Nijen Twilhaar, Untitled editor's column *Manazine,* April 2004, 6.

10. ——, "Philosophy: Life is about Balance" *Manazine,* Winter 2004.

11. Gregory Leow, "Magazine gets a warning," *Streats,* February 27, 2004, at the time of research at http://www.yawningbread.org/arch_2004/yax-362.htm . For a later MDA complaint in 2005, see Leow, "Ministry warns gay magazine," *The New Paper,* March 19, 2005, at the time of research at http://www.yawningbread.org/apdx_2005/imp-195.htm

12. "Liquid Reflex," *Manazine,* October 2003.

13. ——.

14. Wendy Cho, "Shake a Leg," *Manazine,* December 2003.

15. Leow, February 24, 2004. At the time of research at http://www.yawningbread.org/arch_2004/yax-362.htm

16. Twilhaar, Untitled press release, *Manazine,* March 4, 2004.

17. ——, Untitled editor's column, *Manazine,* April 2004.

18. "Essence," introduction, *Manazine,* April 2004.

19. "Gay and Lesbian Community parties into Singapore's National Day," *Agence France-Press,* August 6, 2001, reprinted in *Frida,* August 8, 2001, http://www.fridae.com/aboutus/inthenews010806.php

20. For the legal restrictions, see the website of the Singapore Tourism Board, "Use of the Merlion symbol," at the time of research at http://app-stg.stb.gov.sg/asp/form/form01.asp Penalties are detailed in the Singapore Tourism Board Act, Ch. 305B:24.

21. "Gay and Lesbian Community parties into Singapore's National Day."

22. Glenn Chua, "Nation and the Nature of Pride," *Fridae,* August 9, 2001, http://www.fridae.com/magazine/en20010809_1_1.php

23. Author's interview with Stuart Koe, May 5, 2004.

24. ——.

25. Gordon Fairclough, "For Its Own Reasons, Singapore is Getting Rather Gay-Friendly," *Wall Street Journal,* Oct. 26, 2004.

26. The *Lianhe Wanbao* articles were translated into English and archived at the time of research at http://www.yawningbread.org/arch_2004/yax-389.htm. See also "Outrage over gay exposés in S'pore tabloid," *Fridae,* July 14, 2004, http://www.fridae.com/newsfeatures/article.php?articleid=1281 Also see a website set up to protest the tabloid coverage, at the time of research at http://www.antiwanbao.cjb.net/ .

27. "Outrage over gay exposés in S'pore tabloid."

28. "Profile: Lee Hsien Loong," *BBC News,* August 11, 2004.

29. "S'pore gay magazine for subscribers only," *Fridae,* September 19, 2004, http://www.fridae.com/newsfeatures/article.php?articleid+1303; Twilhaar, "Manazine[RA] – Not for the conservative mainstream," October 5, 2004 press release from Xung Asia, at the time of research at http://www.emanazine.com/pressrel11-print.htm;

June Lee and Gary Kitching, "A contradiction in terms," *I-S Magazine*, September 17, 2004, reprinted in *Fridae*, September 19, 2004, http://www.fridae.com/newsfeatures/article.php?articleid=1314

30. Alvin Tan, "Fuck buddies," *Fridae*, November 5, 2004, http://www.fridae.com/news/features/article.php?articleid=1341
31. At the time of research from http://www.batamlnfo.com
32. As quoted in "Singapore's AIDS prevention programs to undergo revamp," *Agence France-Press*, May 24, 2004, at the time of research at http://www.aegis.com/news/afp/2004/AF0405A7.html
33. Balaji Sadasivan, "The AIDS Epidemic in Singapore," November 10, 2004, at the time of research at http://app.sprinter.gov.sg/data/pr/2004111090.htm
34. ——.
35. Author's interview with Stuart Koe, May 5, 2004.
36. Singapore Police, "Press Statement on the Rejection of Snowball.04 Application," December 8, 2004, at the time of research at http://www.yawningbread.org/arch_2004/yaw-396.htm
37. Quoted in "Press statement regarding unsuccessful appeal," *Fridae*, December 14, 2004, http://www.fridae.com/news/features/article.php?articleid=1364
38. "Party should not be targeted at gays alone: PM Lee," *Fridae*, December 20, 2004, http://www.fridae.com/news/features/article.php?articleid=1367

Chapter 20

1. Dr Balaji Sadasivan, "Be Ready to Seize Opportunities," speech to the Singapore Computer Society, March 5, 2005; at the time of research at http://stars.nhb.gov.sg/stars/public/
2. The text of the speech was archived at the time of research at http://www.yawningbread.org/apdx_2005/imp-183.htm and at the Singapore Ministry of Health website, http://www.moh.gov.sg/mohcorp/speeches.aspx?id=1930
3. Leslie Koh, "Gay parties may have led to sharp rise in new Aids cases," *The Straits Times*, March 10, 2005, p. 1.
4. "What happened at Sentosa gay parties," *The Sunday Straits Times*, March 13, 2005, accessible at http://www.yawningbread.org/apdx_2005/imp-187.htm
5. Steo Nu-Wen, "Dangerous Liaisons," *The New Paper*, March 14, 2005, at the time of research at http://newpaper.asia1.com.sg/printfriendly/0,4139,84480.00.html
6. ——.
7. "Singapore Authorities Refuse Permit for AIDS Fundraising Concert," *Fridae*, March 23, 2005; http://www.fridae.com/newsfeatures/article.php?articleid=1413&viewarticle=1&searchtype=all
8. "No Fears, No Tears," *The New Paper*, June 6, 2005, at the time of research at http://newpaper.asia1.com.sg/printfriendly/0,4139,89439,00.html
9. Author's observation, March 13, 2005.
10. ——.
11. See an analysis of Thai election results in Pasuk Phongaichit and Chris Baker, *Thaksin: The Business of Politics in Thailand*, (Bangkok: Silkworm Books, 2004), 90, 194.

12. See, for example, "Annual Singapore Gay Party Moves to Phuket After Police Ban," *Agence France-Presse,* June 7, 2005, at the time of research at http://www.aegis.com/news/afp/2005/AF050611.html

13. A video of Lee Hsien Loong's remarks at the Foreign Press Association's meeting at the time of research on YouTube.com at http://www.youtube.com/watch?v=Y1h3KiD1GLE

14. For example, the opening of a description of IndigNation carried on Wikipedia in 2006 and 2007 emphasized this non-contentious approach: "From the germ of its conception, IndigNation was intended to be a series of LGBT-themed events that would be relatively more sedate in nature, intellectual and aesthetic if possible, to render itself in stark contrast with the frenzied carnival atmosphere of the largely gay Nation parties which were held for 4 consecutive years prior to and suddenly banned in 2005 (see the article Singapore public gay parties). These sides of the gay and lesbian community had not had much attention since the success of Nation, and with the government demonising gay parties of late, there was a risk of rising homophobia. The LGBT community needed a morale-booster which at the same time could also be an opportunity to correct skewed impressions that Singapore's mainstream society may have had of the LGBT community as one only interested in partying." At the time of research at http://en.wikipedia.org/wiki/IndigNation

15. For reports on IndigNation 2005, see Sylvia Tan, "Singapore to celebrate pride month in August," Fridae.com, July 26, 2005, http://www.fridae.com/newsfeatures/article.php?articleid=1487; Sylvia Tan, "Tan Chong Kee," Fridae.com, August 1, 2005; http://www.fridae.com/newsfeatures/article.php?articleid=1492; "Russell Heng," Fridae.com, August 16, 2005, http://www.fridae.com/newsfeatures/article.php?articleid=1501; Alex Au, "Singapore's Indignation," Fridae.com, August 25, 2005, http://www.fridae.com/newsfeatures/article.php?articleid=1506

16. For a discussion of the Siam colonial policies pursued by Chulalongkorn and Vajiravudh, see Tamara Loos, *Subject Siam: Family, Law and Colonial Modernity in Thailand* (Bangkok: Silkworm Books, 2002), especially 80–99.

17. Connie Levett, "Thailand wins as Singapore's brief gay fling grinds to a halt," *Sydney Morning Herald*, November 4, 2005, at the time of research at http://www.smh.com.au/news/world/thailand-wins-as-singapores-brief-gay-fling-grinds-to-a-halt/2005/11/03/1130823343452.html

18. Author's observations and interview with Stuart Koe, November 1, 2005.

19. Author's interview with Stuart Koe, November 3, 2005.

20. Author's observation, November 4, 2005.

21. "Phuket to host gay festival rejected by Singapore," *Phuket Gazette*, June 13, 2005. Also, *Nation V Program*, 2.

22. Author's observation, November 4, 2005.

23. Author's interview; source requested anonymity, November 4, 2005.

24. Author's interview with Eric Smutney, Crowne Plaza marketing communication manager, November 4, 2005.

25. Walter Spies and Beryl de Zoete, *Dance and Drama in Bali* (London: Faber and Faber, 1938), 85.

26. Walter Spies to "a friend," from Kintamani, April 16, 1925, Walter Spies Archive, Oriental Collections, University of Leiden. Also in Hans Rhodius, *Schönheit und*

Reichtum Des Lebens: Walter Spies (Maler und Musiker auf Bali 1895-1942) (The Hague: L.J.C. Boucher, 1965), 205-8. Trans. author.

27. Author's interview with Stuart Koe, November 5, 2005.

28. Vitaya Saeng-Aroon, "Thailand's chance to tap into lucrative market for gay visitors," *The Nation*, November 10, 2005, available at http://www.fridae.com/aboutus/news051110_1.php

29. "Tsunami-hit Phuket Resorts Woo Gay Dollars Shunned by Singapore," *Bloomberg News*, November 15, 2005, at the time of research at http://www.bloomberg.com/apps/news?pid=10000080&tsid=aitTiPiHWuCs

30. "Togs" November 24, 2005, originally posted at http://www.fridae.com/forums/index.php?showtopic=7997

31. "Iep," November 23, 2005, originally posted at http://www.fridae.com/forums/index.php?showtopic=7997

32. "Klwl," October 12, 2005, originally posted at http://www.fridae.com/forums/index.php?showtopic=7997

33. "Hurts," December 2, 2005, originally posted at http://www.fridae.com/forums/index.php?showtopic=7997

34. At the time of research, background on the conversion is available at the St. James Power station website, http://www.stjamespowerstation.com/

35. See transcript at Fridae.com, http://www.fridae.com/newsfeatures/article.php?articleid=1907&viewarticle=1&searchtype=all

36. ——. At the time of research a portion of Lee Kuan Yew's statement is also posted on YouTube at http://www.youtube.com/watch?v=u25ssjfmiRg

37. ——.

38. Geert DeClerq and Sara Webb, "Singapore considers legalizing homosexuality: Lee," *Reuters*, April 24, 2007; at the time of research at http://www.reuters.com/article/reutersEdge/idUSSP5349120070424 and http://www.fridae.com/newsfeatures/article.php?articleid=1907&viewarticle=1&searchtype=all

Postscript

1. See, for example, *Spartacus International Gay Guide*. 34th Edition (Berlin: Spartacus, 2005/2006), 973

2. For an explanation of the deal, see, for example, "Deal of the Century," *The Nation*, January 26, 2006, http://www.nationmultimedia.com/specials/shincorp/shin22.html. For the demonstration, see "Protestors burn images of Lee, wife," *Bangkok Post*, March 18, 2006. At the time of research at AsiaMedia Archives, University of California Los Angeles, http://www.asiamedia.ucla.edu/article.asp?parentid=41204

3. For a sample of the criticism of Thaksin's construction of manhood, see "Why Thaksin did not have the moral legitimacy to lead," *The Nation*, September 10, 2009, http://www.nationmultimedia.com/2009/09/10/opinion/opinion_30111886.php . In the article, an American professor, Stephen Young, son of a former US ambassador to Thailand, comments: "He's not really a Thai Thai. He has other ideas in his head . . . He does not think about merit and sin. He thinks about how he can be a powerful man. He wants to be the leader of everybody, the big boss of everybody. This kind of thinking to me reflects not Thai Buddhism, but Chinese

imperial thinking . . . This idea was that, above the earth is heaven, or tian, and there's one man – and underneath is everybody else. And when Thaksin wants to control the government, police, army, judges, businesses, TV, newspapers – that's bringing everything under him. No Thai leader in history has ever tried to do this.

4. See http://www.youtube.com/BabylonBangkok

5. Personal communication from Khun Toc to the author, May 15, 2010.

6. Details come from the Mercure Surabaya website at the time of research, http://www.mercure.com/gb/hotel-6155-mercure-surabaya/index.shtml

7. Sylvia Tan, "Islamic protestors force evacuation of ILGA conference participants in Surabaya," *Fridae.com*, March 26, 2010, http://www.fridae.com/newsfeatures/2010/03/26/9786.islamic-protestors-force%20-evacuation-of-ilga-conference-participants-in-surabaya%3E

8. For an account of the bombing details, see Jeremy Allan, *Bali Blues*, (Denpasar, Bali: Media Makara, 2005), Chapter 26. Also various news articles, such as Matthew Moore, "How We Did It: Bali Bomber Takes the Stage," *Sydney Morning Herald*, February 12, 2003, http://www.smh.com.au/articles/2003/02/11/1044927599789.html; "The Bali Bombing Plot, *BBC News*, January 25, 2007, http://news.bbc.co.uk/2/hi/asia-pacific/3157478.stm

9. Michael Bakan, "The Abduction of the Signifying Monkey Chant: Schizophonic Transmogrifications of Balinese *Kecak* in Fellini's *Satyricon* and the Coen Brothers' *Blood Simple*," *Ethnomusicology Forum*, 18:1 (June 2009), 83–106.

10. For Limbak's obituary, see "Wayan Limbak, Balinese Dancer, Is Dead at 106," *New York Times*, September 14, 2003, http://www.nytimes.com/2003/09/14/obituaries/14LIMB.html Also see an earlier interview with Limbak by Tantri Yuliandini, "Limbak, Rina: Two generations of 'kecak' dancers," *The Jakarta Post*, May 18, 2002, http://www.thejakartapost.com/news/2002/05/18/limbak-rina-two-generations-039kecak039-dancers.html

11. Jim Shepard, *Nosferatu: A Novel* (New York: Alfred A. Knopf, 1998), 20.

12. Nigel Barley, *Island of Demons* (Singapore: Monsoon Books, 2009), 388. A third novel that draws upon Walter Spies's life is Jamie James, *Andrew and Joey* (New York: Kensington Books, 2002).

13. For Fridae's report, see Sylvia Tan, "Allow space for gays, but gay sex ban to stay: Singapore PM," October 24, 2007, http://www.fridae.com/newsfeatures/2007/10/24/1970

14. ——, "Dr. Balaji Sadasivan, 'a friend to Singapore's gay community,' has passed away at 55," *Fridae.com*, September 27, 2010. For a description of Dr Balaji's role with the Jason and DeMarco concert, see the comments by C.Z. Zhou. http://www.fridae.com/newsfeatures/2010/09/27/10324.dr-balaji-sadasivan-a-friend-to-singapores-gay-community-has-passed-away-at-55

15. Ng Yi-Sheng, "Quiet Time: Singapore's best gay novel ever," *Fridae.com*, January 5, 2009, http://www.fridae.com/newsfeatures/2009/01/05/2185.quiet-time-singapores-best-gay-novel-ever

16. Personal communication with the author, July 11, 2010 and February 22, 2011.

17. See "Nation VI to be the grande finale, fridae to focus on web and advocacy," *Fridae.com*, October 13, 2006, http://www.fridae.com/newsfeatures/article.php?articleid=1776&viewarticle=1 . An article reflecting on the Fridae motto drew lengthy

commentary from readers about what it might mean to be "empowered." See Shinen Wong, "Empowering Gay Asia," *Fridae.com*, January 16, 2009, http://www.fridae.com/newsfeatures/2009/01/16/2199.

18. Author's interview with Stuart Koe, October 20, 2006. See also Alvin Tan, "Nation Retrospective 2004/2005 and 2006 Preview," *Fridae.com*, October 19, 2006, http://www.fridae.com/newsfeatures/2006/10/19/1725.nation-retrospective-2004-05-2006-preview?n=sea&nm=nation+VI Also, Victor Chau, "Nation VI: danse royale," *Fridae.com*, October 22, 2006, http://www.fridae.com/newsfeatures/2006/10/22/1728.nationvi-danse-royale

19. From Stuart Koe's introduction to the Final Program for the Nation VI party, October 2006.

Select Bibliography

Aaron, Michele, ed. *New Queer Cinema: A Critical Reader* (New Brunswick, NJ: Rutgers University Press, 2004).

Aldrich, Robert. *Colonialism and Homosexuality* (London: Routledge, 2003).

Allan, Jeremy. *Bali Blues* (Denpasar, Bali: Media Makara, 2005).

Allyn, E.G. *The Men of Thailand* (Bangkok: Floating Lotus, 6th edition, 1997).

Altman, Dennis. *The Homosexualization of America* (Boston: Beacon Press, 1982).

Bakan, Michael. "The Abduction of the Signifying Monkey Chant: Schizophonic Transmogrifications of Balinese *Kecak* in Fellini's *Satyricon* and the Coen Brothers' *Blood Simple.*" *Ethnomusicology Forum,*18:1 (June 2009), 83–106.

Barmé, Scot. *Luang Witchit Wathakan and the Creation of a Thai Identity* (Singapore: Institute of Southeast Asian Studies, 1993).

———. *Woman, Man, Bangkok: Love, Sex and Popular Culture in Thailand* (Bangkok: Silkworm Books, 2002).

Bergman, David. *The Violet Hour: The Violet Quill and the Making of Gay Culture* (New York: Columbia University, 2004.

Blackstone, William. *Commentaries on the Laws of England, Vol. 4* (Oxford: Clarendon Press, 1769).

Boellstorff, Tom. *The Gay Archipelago: Sexuality and Nation in Indonesia* (Princeton: Princeton University Press, 2005).

Chytry, Josef. *The Aesthetic State: A Quest in Modern German Thought* (Berkeley: University of California Press, 1989).

Connell, R.W. "Globalization, Imperialism, and Masculinities." In Michael Kimmel, Jeff Hearn, and R.W. Connell, eds. *Handbook of Studies on Men & Masculinities* (Thousand Oaks, CA: Sage Publications, 2005), 71–89.

Covarrubias, Miguel. *Island of Bali* (New York: Alfred A. Knopf, 1937).

Davis, Whitney, *Queer Beauty: Sexuality and Aesthetics from Winckelmann to Freud and Beyond* (New York: Columbia University Press, 2010).

DeRoever-Bonnet, H. *Rudolf Bonnet* (Wijk en Aalburg: Picture Publishers, 1991).

Eisner, Lotte. *Murnau* (Paris: Le Terrain Vague, 1964; English translation, Berkeley: University of California Press, 1973).

Elsaesser, Thomas. "Six Degrees of Nosferatu." *Sight and Sound,* February 2001. http://www.bfi.org.uk/sightandsound/feature/92

Eribon, Didier. *Insult and the Making of the Gay Self* (Trans. M. Lacy). (Durham, NC: Duke University Press, 2004).

Gay, Peter. *Weimar Culture: The Outsider as Insider* (New York: W.W. Norton & Company, 1968).

Geertz, Clifford. *Negara: The Theater State in Nineteenth Century Bali* (Princeton, NJ: Princeton University Press, 1980), 20.

George, Cherian. *Contentious Journalism and the Internet: Towards Democratic Discourse in Malaysia and Singapore* (Singapore: Singapore University Press, 2006).

Gerard, Kent and Gert Hekman, eds. *The Pursuit of Sodomy: Male Homosexuality in Renaissance and Enlightenment Europe* (New York: Harrington Park Press, 1989).

Girling, John. *Thailand: Society and Politics* (Ithaca: Cornell University Press, 1981).

Greene, Stephen. *Absolute Dreams: Thai Government under Rama VI, 1910–1925* (Bangkok: White Lotus, 1999).

Hanna, Judith Lynne. *To Dance is Human: A Theory of Nonverbal Communication* (Austin: University of Texas Press, 1979).

Harrison, Rachel and Peter Jackson, eds. *The Ambiguous Allure of the West: Traces of the Colonial in Thailand* (Hong Kong: Hong Kong University Press, 2010).

Highwater, Jamake. *Myth and Sexuality* (New York: Penguin Books, 1991).

Hirschfeld, Magnus. *Men and Women: The World Journey of a Sexologist* (New York: G.P. Putnam's Sons, 1935).

Hitchcock, Michael and Lucy Norris. *Bali: The Imaginary Museum: The Photographs of Walter Spies and Beryl de Zoete* (Kuala Lumpur: Oxford University Press, 1995).

Holden, Philip. "The Significance of Uselessness: Resisting Colonial Masculinity in Philip Jeyaretnam's *Abraham's Promise,*" http://social.chass.ncsu.edu/jouvert/v2i1/Holden.htm

Jackson, Peter. *Buddhism: Legitimation and Conflict: The Political Functions of Urban_Thai Buddhism* (Singapore: Institute of Southeast Asian Studies, 1990).

——. *Dear Uncle Go: Male Homosexuality in Thailand* (Bangkok: Bua Luang Books, 1995).

—— and Nerida M. Cook, eds. *Genders and Sexualities in Modern Thailand_*(Bangkok: Silkworm Books, 1999).

Jackson, Peter. *The Intrinsic Quality of Skin* (Bangkok: Floating Lotus Books, 1994).

——. "Performative Genders, Perverse Desires: A Bio-History of Thailand's Same Sex and Transgender Cultures." *Intersections: Gender, History and Culture in the Asian_Context,* Issue 9 (August 2003). Published online at http://wwwsshe.murdoch.edu.au/intersections/issue9/jackson.html

Jagose, Anamarie. *Queer Theory: An Introduction* (New York: New York University Press, 1996).

Jeffrey, Leslie Ann. *Sex and Borders: Gender, National Identity and Prostitution Policy in Thailand* (Honolulu: University of Hawaii Press, 2002).

Josey, Alex. *Lee Kuan Yew* (Singapore: Donald Moore Press Ltd., 1968).

Katz, Jonathan Ned. *The Invention of Heterosexuality* (New York: Penguin, 1995).

Kerkhof, Gosse. "Het Indische Zedenschandaal: Een Kolonial Incident" (Ph.D. thesis, University of Amsterdam, 1982).

Kimmel, Michael, Jeff Hearn, and R.W. Connell, eds. *Handbook of Studies on Men & Masculinities* (Thousand Oaks, CA: Sage Publications, 2005).

Koenders, Pieter. *Tussen Christelijk Reveil En Seksuele Revolutie: Bestrijding van de Zedeloosheid met de Nadruk op Repressie van Homoseksualiteit* (Amsterdam, 1996).

Kramer, Mark and Wendy Call, eds. *Telling True Stories* (New York: Penguin Books, 2007).

Lindsey, Timothy, *The Romance of K'Tut Tantri and Indonesia: Text and Scripts, History and Identity* (Kuala Lumpur: Oxford University Press, 1997).

Lo, Joseph and Huang Guoqin. *People Like Us: Sexual Minorities in Singapore* (Singapore: Select Books, 2003).

Loos, Tamara. *Subject Siam: Family, Law and Colonial Modernity in Thailand* (Bangkok, Silkworm Books, 2002).

——. "Sex in the Inner City: The Fidelity between Sex and Politics in Siam." *The Journal of Asian Studies* (November 2005), 64:4.

Manderson, Lenore and Margaret Jolly. *Sites of Desire, Economies of Pleasure: Sexualities in Asia and the Pacific* (Chicago: University of Chicago Press, 1997).

McCargo, Duncan and Ukrist Pathmanand. *The Thaksinization of Thailand* (Copenhagen: NIAS Press, 2005).

McClintock, Anne. *Imperial Leather: Race, Gender and Sexuality in the Colonial Contest* (New York: Routledge, 1995).

McLeod, D.W. "Syllabus of Instruction, Raffles Institution, 1937." Posted by Philip Holden, National University of Singapore. Accessed April 2008, http://courses. nus.edu.sg/course/ellhpj/resources/mcleod.HTM

McPhee, Colin. *A House in Bali* (London: Victor Gollanez Ltd., 1947 original edition; Singapore: Periplus Ltd., 2000 paperback edition).

Miller, Neil. *Out in the World: Gay and Lesbian Life from Buenos Aires to Bangkok* (New York: Random House, 1992), 108–9.

Moll, H.J.E. Resident of Bali and Lombok, March 2, 1939. Colonial Ministry Secret Archive, Box 562, National Archive, The Hague.

Morgan, Susan. *Bombay Anna: The Real Story and Remarkable Adventures of the "King and I" Governess* (Berkeley: University of California Press, 2008).

Mosse, George. *The Image of Man* (New York: Oxford University Press, 1996).

——. *Nazi Culture: Intellectual, Cultural and Social Life in the Third Reich* (New York: Grosset & Dunlap, 1966).

Murnau, F.W., director. *Nosferatu: A Symphony of Horror.* Original: Germany, 1922. Chatsworth, CA: Image Entertainment, DVD.

Ng King Kang. *The Rainbow Connection: The Internet and the Singapore Gay Community* (Singapore: KangCuBine Publishing Pte. Ltd., 1999).

Norberg-Schulz, Christian. *The Concept of Dwelling: On the Way to Figurative Architecture* (New York: Rizzoli International Publications, Inc., 1985).

Oswald, Richard and Magnus Hirschfeld. *Different from the Others.* Original: Germany, 1919. New York: Kino International Corp., 2004, DVD.

Phongaichit, Pasuk and Chris Baker. *Thaksin: The Business of Politics in Thailand* (Bangkok: Silkworm Books, 2004).

Pringle, Robert. *A Short History of Bali: Indonesia's Hindu Realm* (Crow's Nest, Australia: Allen & Unwin, 2004).

Rhodes, Richard. "Death in the Candy Store." *Rolling Stone,* November 28, 1991, 62–71.

Rhodius, Hans. *Schönheit und Reichtum Des Lebens: Walter Spies (Maler und Musiker auf Bali 1895–1942)* (The Hague: L.J.C. Boucher, 1965).

—— and John Darling. *Walter Spies and Balinese Art.* Edited by John Stowell (Amsterdam: Tropenmuseum, 1980).

Robson, Stuart, ed. *The Kraton: Selected Essays on Javanese Courts.* Trans. R. Robson-McKillop (Leiden: KITLV Press, 2003).

Robinson, Geoffrey. *The Dark Side of Paradise: Political Violence in Bali* (Ithaca: Cornell University Press, 1995).

Roosevelt, André, director. *Goona Goona.* Original: 1932. Baker City, OR: Nostalgia Family Video, 1996, videocassette.

Sachs, Curt. *World History of the Dance* (London: George Allen and Unwin, 1938).

Said, Edward. *Orientalism* (New York: Random House, 1978).

Sandfort, Sandy. "The Intelligent Island." *Wired Magazine,* September/October 1993. Accessible at http://www.wired.com/wired/archive/1.04/sandfort_pr.html.

Schonberg, Harold C. *The Lives of the Great Composers* (New York: W.W. Norton & Company, Inc., 1970).

Schulte Nordholt, Henk. *Bali: Colonial Conceptions and Political Change, 1700–1940* (Rotterdam: Erasmus University, 1986).

Smith, Malcolm. *A Physician at the Court of Siam* (London: Country Life Limited, 1946), 111–2.

Spies, Walter and Beryl de Zoete. *Dance and Drama in Bali* (London: Faber and Faber, 1938).

Stoler, Ann Laura. *Carnal Knowledge and Imperial Power: Race and the Intimate in Colonial Rule* (Berkeley: University of California Press, 2002).

——. *Race and the Education of Desire* (Durham, NC, Duke University Press, 1995).

Sullivan, Gerald and Peter Jackson. *Gay and Lesbian Asia: Culture, Identity, Community* (New York: Haworth Press, 2001).

Thongchai, Winichakul. "The Quest for 'Siwilai': A Geographical Discourse of Civilization Thinking in Late Nineteenth and Twentieth Century Siam." *Journal of Asian Studies,* 59(3): 528–49.

Van Naerssen, A.X., ed. *Gay Life in Dutch Society* (New York: Harrington Park Press, 1987).

Vella, Walter. *Chaiyo! King Vajiravudh and the Development of Thai Nationalism* (Honolulu: University of Hawaii, 1978).

Vickers, Adrian. *Bali: A Paradise Created* (Australia: Penguin Books, 1989).

Warren, James Francis. *Ah Ku and Karayuki-san: Prostitution in Singapore, 1870–1940* (Singapore: Singapore University Press, 2003).

Warren, William. *Jim Thompson: The Unsolved Mystery* (Singapore: Archipelago Press, 1970, 1998).

Wesner, Simone, Michael Hitchcock, and I Nyoman Darma Putra. "Walter Spies and Dresden: The Early Formative Years of Bali's Renowned Artist, Author and Tourism Icon." *Indonesia and the Malay World,* 35:102 (July 2007), 211–30.

Wiene, Robert, director. *The Cabinet of Dr. Caligari.* Original: Germany, 1920. Chatsworth, CA: Image Entertainment, DVD.

Williams, Adriana and Yu-Chee Chong. *Covarrubias in Bali* (Singapore: Editions Didier Millet, 2005).

Wiriyawit, Wimon. *Free Thai: Personal Recollections and Official Documents* (Bangkok: White Lotus Press, 1997).

Zamora, Lois Parkinson and Wendy B. Faris. *Magical Realism: Theory, History, Community* (Durham, NC: Duke University Press, 1995).

Index

Note: Individuals are indexed according to prevalent cultural custom. Thus, Thais are alphabetized under the personal first names by which they are predominantly known, such as "Toc, Khun" and "Thaksin Shinawatra." Singaporeans are indexed by their family name with the English name written with commas and the Chinese name without commas: "Koe, Stuart" and "Lee Kuan Yew."